EDUCATION FOR ALL AND MULTIGRADE TEACHING

Education for All and Multigrade Teaching

Challenges and Opportunities

Edited by

ANGELA W. LITTLE
Institute of Education,
University of London, U.K.

🐎 Springer

A C.I.P. Catalogue record for this book is available from the Library of Congress.

ISBN-10 1-4020-6647-3 (PB)
ISBN-13 978-1-4020-6647-4 (PB)
ISBN-10 1-4020-4590-5 (HB)
ISBN-13 978-1-4020-4590-5 (HB)
ISBN-10 1-4020-4591-3 (e-books)
ISBN-13 978-1-4020-4591-2 (e-books)

Published by Springer,
P.O. Box 17, 3300 AA Dordrecht, The Netherlands.

www.springer.com

Printed on acid-free paper

ACKNOWLEDGEMENTS

I wish to acknowledge support from the UK Government's Department for International Development (DFID) for the funding of several of the research projects reported in this book and their dissemination through conferences and seminars. I also thank DFID for its support for the establishment and maintenance of the website on Learning and Teaching in Multigrade Settings (LATIMS) that accompanies this book (www.ioe.ac.uk/multigrade).

I thank a number of persons and institutions who have collaborated with us over several years, including Carmen Montero and the Instituto de Estudios Peruanos, Lima; M.Sibli and the National Institute of Education, Colombo; N.H. Chau of the National Institute of Education Sciences, Hanoi; Kate Owen of the British Council, Hanoi; and H. Bhajracharya of the Research Centre for Educational Innovation and Development, Kathmandu. Most of all I thank the many students who welcomed us into their classes and their teachers with whom we spent many hours talking and reflecting on the challenges and opportunities of multigrade teaching. I am also grateful to Brigid Hamilton-Jones for her copy editing of the text and Chris Purday and Abdul Mukith for translating photographs from many sources into a common format. Photo credits are due to the Fundación *Escuela Nueva* Volvamos a la Gente and to the contributors to this book.

Finally, and on behalf of all contribution, I thank our respective institutions for the time to make visible the largely invisible, marginalised and widespread phenomenon of learning and teaching in multigrade settings.

CONTENTS

LIST OF CONTRIBUTORS

Editor and contributor

Angela W. Little is Professor of Education (Developing Countries) at the Institute of Education, University of London and was formerly a Fellow at the Institute of Development Studies at the University of Sussex. Since 1998 she has directed the research programme 'Learning and Teaching in Multigrade Settings' funded by the Department for International Development (DFID), UK. She has researched and written extensively on Education for All (EFA), has a specialised knowledge of Sri Lanka and is a Past President of the British Association of International and Comparative Education. She can be contacted at a.little@ioe.ac.uk

Contributors

Sheila Aikman is Global Education Adviser with OxfamGB and currently co-coordinator of the Beyond Access: Gender, Education and Development project with the Institute of Education, University of London. Prior to working with OxfamGB she taught at the Institute of Education and from 1998 to 2001 was an associate director of the international research programme, 'Learning and Teaching in Multigrade Settings'. Sheila has written and researched extensively on intercultural education and indigenous education in South America and Peru and continues to publish on areas of gender equality in education, multigrade teaching and learning and indigenous rights. She can be contacted at saikman@oxfam.org.uk

Albert K. Akyeampong is a Senior Lecturer in International Education at the Centre for International Education (CIE), University of Sussex, and convenor of the International Professional Doctorate in Education at the Sussex School of Education. He has served as an Education Consultant for basic education reforms in Ghana and Rwanda. His current research interests are in teacher motivation and incentive structures in Africa and South Asia, and improving access to primary and post-basic education. He writes on teacher education, science and mathematics education, secondary education, access and quality in basic education, and teacher assessment. He can be contacted at a.akyeampong@sussex.ac.uk

Patricia Ames is Researcher and Lecturer at the Faculty of Education at the Universidad Peruana Cayetano Heredia and member of the Institute of Peruvian Studies. She completed her doctoral research on 'Multigrade schools in context: literacy in the community, the home and the school in the Peruvian Amazon' at the Institute of Education, University of London in 2004. She writes on rural education, including multigrade schooling, socialisation, intercultural and indigenous education, gender equity, literacy and textbook use. She can be contacted at pames@upch.edu.pe

Chris Berry is currently an Education Adviser with the Department for International Development. Formerly a researcher and lecturer at the Institute of Education, University of London, he completed his doctoral research on 'Achievement effects of multigrade and monograde primary schools in the Turks and Caicos Islands' in 2001. He has extensive field experience as a teacher and teacher trainer in West Africa, Indonesia and the Caribbean. He has collaborated with the Commonwealth Secretariat on the development and piloting of multigrade teaching materials and has advised the governments of Belize and Dominica on the implementation of policies to meet the needs of teachers in multigrade and multi-level classrooms. He can be contacted at c-berry@dfid.gov.uk

Alison Croft is a Lecturer in Education at the Sussex School of Education, University of Sussex. Her career in education has included teaching in the UK and Japan, working as a regional special education adviser in Namibia and researching UK government policy on inclusive education. Her current research and teaching interests lie mainly in the field of international education, particularly primary education, teacher education, gender and inclusive education. Her doctoral research focused on the relationship between pedagogy and culture in aid to education in Malawi and other developing countries. She can be contacted at a.m.croft@sussex.ac.uk

Hanan el Haj works with Oxfam GB as urban programme coordinator in Khartoum, Sudan. She focuses on basic education for the internally displaced and urban poor and for pastoralist communities in eastern and western Sudan. Hanan is responsible for programme design and plans that focus on strengthening civil society capacity to advocate improved education especially for girls. Hanan graduated from the University of Gezira, Sudan with a degree in Agricultural Science. She can be contacted at helhaj@oxfam.org.uk

Daniel Escobar-Rodríguez is Senior Analyst at the Social Foundation in Bogotá, Colombia. For three years he was a member of the research team on schooling methods and peaceful social interaction in the School of Economics of Universidad del Rosario. He can be contacted at descoba@claustro.urosario.edu.co

Clemente Forero-Pineda is Professor at the Universidad de los Andes School of Management. With Universidad del Rosario he directed research on schooling methods and peaceful social interaction. He was director of Colciencias, Colombia's National Science Fund and is a Past President of Colombia's National Participatory Planning Council. He writes on economic aspects of education and science in developing countries. He can be contacted at cfp@adm.uniandes.edu.co

Keith M. Lewin is currently Professor of Education at the University of Sussex and Director of the Centre for International Education. He has worked extensively in Asia and Africa on educational planning and finance, EFA and post-basic education strategies, science and technology education policy, and teacher education. His projects include the 'Multi Site Teacher Education Research Project (MUSTER)' in Ghana, Lesotho, Malawi, South Africa, Trinidad and Tobago. He has acted as a special adviser to several Ministries of Education on the development and implementation of national plans at both primary and post-basic levels. He can be contacted at k.m.lewin@sussex.ac.uk

Danielken Molina is Research Assistant at the Inter-American Development Bank in Washington, DC. He has been an educational researcher at Universidad del Rosario in Bogotá, Colombia. He participated in the team that evaluated the expansion of secondary schooling, in the design of an information system for Higher Education, and in the project on schooling methods and peaceful social interaction. He can be contacted at dmrmolin@cable.net.co

Pat Pridmore is a Senior Lecturer in Education, Health Promotion and International Development at the Institute of Education, University of London and has more than 20 years experience of working in education and health in low- and middle-income countries. From 1998 she was associate director of the international research programme, 'Learning and Teaching in Multigrade Settings', becoming co-director in 2004. She has a special interest in curriculum adaptation for multigrade settings and has extended and disseminated her research through work with the World Bank and UNICEF. She can be contacted at p.pridmore@ioe.ac.uk

Takako Suzuki is a Project Formulation Advisor in Education with the Japan International Cooperation Agency. She is currently undertaking research and project planning work on community schools and EFA in Zambia with a special focus on HIV/AIDS orphans and vulnerable children. She completed her doctoral research on 'Multigrade practice in primary schools in Nepal: practice and training' at the Institute of Education, University of London in 2004. She can be contacted at suzuki.takako@jica.go.jp

Manjula Vithanapathirana is a Senior Lecturer at the Faculty of Education, University of Colombo, Sri Lanka, where she specialises in child development and educational psychology. She was formerly a researcher with the Department of Education Research, National Institute of Education, Sri Lanka. She completed her research on 'Improving multigrade teaching: action research with teachers in rural Sri Lanka' at the Institute of Education, University of London in 2005. She is currently researching and developing teacher education materials on multigrade teaching. She can be contacted at manjulananayakkara@yahoo.com

Son Vu is a researcher at Hanoi University of Education, in Vietnam. Her current research is on learner activity, autonomy and creativity. She previously worked as a researcher with the National Institute for Educational Sciences, under the Ministry of Education and Training with a focus on improving the quality of teaching and learning in primary education. Her doctoral research with the Institute of Education, University of London on 'Improving teaching and learning for health in multigrade schools in Vietnam' was completed in 2005. She can be contacted at vuson101@hotmail.com

LIST OF ABBREVIATIONS

APEID	Asia and the Pacific Programme of Educational Innovation for Development
BAGET	Bachelor of General Education and Training
BCE	Before Common Era
BPEP	Basic and Primary Education Project
CE	Common Era
CERID	Research Centre for Educational Innovation and Development
CERT	Centre for Education Research and Training
DANE	Departamento Administrativo Nacional de Estadística
DIJIN	Dirección de Policía Judicial
DEO	District Education Office
DfES	Department for Education and Skills
DFID	Department for International Development
DNP	Departamento Nacional de Planeación
EFA	Education For All
EMIS	Education Management and Information System
FCUBE	Free, Compulsory, Universal Basic Education
FS	Foundation Studies
GDCA	Ghana Danish Communities Association
GDP	Gross Domestic Product
GER	Gross Enrolment Ratio
GES	Ghana Education Service
GMR	Global Monitoring Report
GNP	Gross National Product
HMG	His Majesty's Government of Nepal
HMI	Her Majesty's Inspectorate of Schools
IDS	Institute of Development Studies
INSET	In Service Education and Training

IREDU-CNRS	Institut de Recherche sur l'Education, Centre National de la Recherche Scientifique
LATIMS	Learning and Teaching in Multigrade Settings
LEA	Local Education Authority
LLECE	Latin American Laboratory for the Evaluation of the Quality of Education
MECEP	(Spanish) Special Programme to Improve the Educational Quality of Primary Education
MIITEP	Malawi Integrated In-Service Teacher Education Programme
MOE	Ministry of Education
MOEC	Ministry of Education and Culture
MOECSW	Ministry of Education, Culture and Social Welfare
MOEHE	Ministry of Education and Higher Education
MOET	Ministry of Education and Training
MUSTER	Multi-site Teacher Education Research
NEC	National Education Commission
NEP	(Spanish) New Pedagogical Approach
NER	Net Enrolment Ratio
NGO	Non Governmental Organisation
NIE	National Institute of Education
NIER	National Institute for Educational Research
NIES	National Institute of Educational Sciences
NLS	New Literacy Studies
NUT	National Union of Teachers
PMP	Primary Mathematics Project
PTR	Pupil Teacher Ratio
PTTU	Primary Teachers' Training Unit
QCA	Qualifications and Curriculum Authority
QT	Qualified Teacher
REV	Rural Education Volunteer
SABER	Sistema Nacional de Evaluación de la Calidad de la Educación
SATs	Standardised Assessment Tests
SCF-UK	Save the Children, United Kingdom

SEAMEO INNOTECH	Southeast Asian Ministers of Education Organisation Regional Centre for Educational Innovation and Technology
SFL	School For Life
SLA	Self Learning Activity
SPLM/A Movement/Army	The Sudan Peoples' Liberation
SSA	Sub Saharan Africa
ST	Student Teacher
SWA	South and West Asia
TCI	Turks and Caicos Islands
TDU	Teacher Development Unit
TSO	The Stationery Office
UK	The United Kingdom
UPE	Universal Primary Education
UN	United Nations
UNESCO	United Nations Education, Science and Cultural Organisation
UNICEF	The United Nations Children's Fund
USA	The United States of America
USAID	The United States Agency for International Development
VDC	Village Development Committee
WCEFA	World Conference on Education For All

LIST OF PLATES

1. Colombia: self-learning guides encourage learners to use books from the class library, Escuela Nueva programme

2. Colombia: students learn together using self-learning guides, Escuela Nueva programme

3. England: in the monitorial system in 19th Century England students, grouped by achievement level, were taught by monitors. A single teacher taught and supervised the monitors.

4. Nepal: a student receives personal support from a teacher in a small multigrade school

5. Malawi: students enrolled in Standard 1 (Grade 1) class: same class, same grade but clearly not same age

6. Malawi: where resources are scarce, what you bring from home makes a significant contribution to pupil diversity. Here, students without pencil and paper are encouraged by their teacher to learn to write in the sand.

7. Peru: children learn after school

8. Peru: girls learn together to become literate

9. Sri Lanka: One teacher is responsible for three grade groups, working in a temporary classroom in rural Sri Lanka

10. Sri Lanka: Grade 1 students work together in a multigraded class

11. Turks and Caicos Islands: the teacher divides the blackboard space between two grades: students work individually on individual grade-level work

12. Turks and Caicos Islands: students work collaboratively

13. Vietnam: a grade-group monitor takes charge of her peers while the teacher works with another grade-group

14. Vietnam: A typical multigrade school in the Northern Highlands

15. Sudan: The El Shiekh teacher with his sheep, Darfur

16. Sudan: Large Class of learners in temporary classroom, Darfur

CHAPTER ONE

EDUCATION FOR ALL

Multigrade realities and histories

ANGELA W. LITTLE

MAHESWARI: A MULTIGRADE TEACHER

It is 7.30 and Maheswari, the school principal, unlocks the door to the single-room school in the tea estate where she resides. Schoolchildren have been arriving since 7.15: some alone or in small groups; others in a long snaking line, led by an elderly retired labourer. Maheswari's colleague, Siva, a young untrained teacher, lives 25 miles away and will arrive at the school by bus at around 9.00. But the bus often arrives late, and sometimes not at all.

The school day runs from 7.30 to 1.30, and there are 120 pupils on roll. After a short assembly, Maheswari fills out the attendance registers for each of the classes. Today one-third of the children are absent. Each grade occupies its own space in the open hall, and each is treated as a class. No class has its own walled room, but each class has its own blackboard.

It is now 8.30 and the children await direction from the teacher, quietly and expectantly, their books piled high on their desks. The five classes reflect the graded structure of the national system of education. Officially children enter Grade 1 in the academic year following their fifth birth-day, but many in Maheswari's school start later. Others repeat a year because of low academic achievement, resulting in mixed ages within the same grade. The national syllabus is organised into content and learning objectives for each of the five grades, and textbooks and teaching guides are produced for each.

Maheswari moves from grade to grade, giving instructions, opening text and exercise books and writing exercises on the blackboard for the upper grades. Siva will assume responsibility for Grades 4 to 5 when he arrives. Maheswari tries to keep the children in the upper grades occupied by asking them where yesterday's lesson finished, setting a related exercise, or asking them to read the text of the next lesson. Even though several of the children were absent yesterday, this does not influence the tasks she sets for the

1

A.W. Little (ed.), Education for All and Multigrade Teaching: challenges and opportunities, 1–26.

whole class, because the children are expected to proceed through the textbooks together.

Meanwhile, the children in Grades 1 to 3 still wait, quietly, patiently. Maheswari hands out maths work cards to Grade 3. There is no time for any introduction to the tasks, and she offers them as exercises in practice and reinforcement. She asks the children in Grade 2 to read out loud from their reading books in unison. At last she reaches Grade 1 and begins their lesson on letters and sounds, writing letters on the blackboard, sounding out the letter and asking children for words that start with the same sound.

Siva arrives at 9.30 and relieves Maheswari of the responsibility for the upper grades. Maheswari continues similarly through the rest of the day, trying to work through the teacher's guidebook as best she can, teaching each of the grades in turn. The guidebook is designed for teachers who work in schools where a single teacher is responsible for a single grade. Maheswari tries to reproduce faithfully this graded structure in her two-teacher school.

Later that morning an education official arrives to check the attendance registers and school logbook and to convey information about a forthcoming training course for the teachers and examination dates for pupils. Maheswari attends to his questions and, with the help of two children, offers him a cup of tea.

In the meantime, Grades 1 to 3 are finishing their set work and becoming a little restless. She sends Grade 1 outside with an older child to practise their letters with sticks in the sand. A monitor from an upper grade supervises Grades 2 and 3, darting around quickly, distributing verbal punishment here, physical there. The official leaves and Maheswari continues teaching, stopping briefly only when the children break for half an hour in the late morning heat.

Across the official school year of 190 days, Maheswari is absent for 30 days and Siva for 40. When these days coincide, the school is closed.

Maheswari's experience is similar to that of hundreds of thousands of teachers worldwide. Such multigrade teachers are responsible for the organisation of children's learning in more than one grade, within a national system of education in which the curriculum is prescribed for each separate grade. The schools in which these teachers teach are multigraded through necessity – too few teachers and students to justify the allocation of one teacher per grade.

EDUCATION FOR ALL

Education for All (hereafter EFA) is a worldwide movement that promotes the expansion and quality of learning for all children, young people and adults. Building from many national and local movements over time, the contemporary movement resonates at the global, the regional, the national and the local levels. It has six goals (www.unesco.org/education/efa). These are:

- access to and improvement of early childhood care and education
- access to and completion of free and compulsory primary education of good quality for all, especially girls, children in difficult circumstances and those belonging to ethnic minorities
- appropriate and life-skills programmes for all young people and adults
- improvements in levels of adult literacy
- elimination of gender disparities
- improving all aspects of the quality of education.

In this book we are concerned mainly with the second and the last of these goals.

The EFA Framework for Action identifies primary schools as the institutional means through which these two goals can be achieved. Within primary schools learners are generally divided into grades for teaching purposes. The graded groups are known by different terms in different countries, for example, grade, year, class, standard, but they generally refer to cohorts of children who enter, progress through and graduate from school at the same time and who follow grade-specific curricula. In most primary schools around the world a single teacher is responsible for a class formed of students from a single year grade at any given time in the school day. This is known as monograded teaching. This may be contrasted with settings where a single teacher is responsible for a class formed of children from two or more year grades. This is known as multigraded teaching.

Many of the current shortfalls in achievement of the EFA goals are found among those communities who live at the margins of society and who participate in the margins of the formal education system. At many of these margins, schools either do not exist at all, or where they do, they often involve multigrade teaching.

Learning and teaching in multigrade settings – invisible and persistent

Maheswari is but one agent in the worldwide movement for EFA. Her school may be described as a multigrade school. Maheswari herself is a multigrade teacher, i.e. a teacher who is responsible within the same time period for learners from across two or more year grades. She may be contrasted with a monograde teacher who, within the same time period, is responsible for learners from a single curriculum grade. Monograde schools, monograde teachers and the children who learn in monograded settings form the dominant and visible elements of all national systems of education worldwide. Multigrade schools, multigrade teachers and the children who learn in multigraded settings operate at the margins of these systems and are largely invisible to those who plan, manage and fund education systems. Yet they persist.

The rest of this chapter explores the invisibility and persistence of learning and teaching in multigraded settings in three ways. First, it collates evidence from around the world on its extent. Second, it analyses how monograde classes have come to dominate systems of primary education worldwide during the twentieth century. Third, it outlines the conditions under which multigrade classes arise and persist. The chapter concludes with an overview of the issues that arise from this analysis to be addressed in the rest of the book.

EXTENT AND SIGNIFICANCE OF MULTIGRADE TEACHING

So how prevalent are multigraded classes around the world? How many learners are in these types of class? How many teachers are teaching across two or more grades? How many schools have only one teacher? And why is it important for EFA to focus on the needs of these teachers and learners?

One of the difficulties in answering questions about extent is the absence of comparable, and, in some countries, any, education statistics. While some countries make available information about the number of one-teacher schools, others focus on the number of multigrade classes and still others the number of multigrade teachers. Still others make no information available.

Terms vary from country to country and can obscure similar settings. In our research (www.ioe.ac.uk/multigrade) we have found the following terms used to describe what we would recognise as a multigrade class – combination class, composite class, vertically-grouped class, family-grouped class, un-graded class, non-graded class, mixed-year, mixed-grade class, mixed-age class, multi-aged class, consecutive class, double class, classe multigrade, classe unique.

Although these various terms have been used in a range of settings to indicate what we mean by a multigraded class the reader should not assume that the terms are always synonymous. Similarities in terms can often obscure differences in meaning and hinder communication across cultural and national boundaries. Take the terms mixed-year and mixed-age for example. In England there is a close correspondence between 'year' and 'age'. Children enter school at the same age (within a calendar year) and move through classes with their age peers. The number of children who repeat a year are few indeed. In such an education system the meanings of a mixed-year class and a mixed-age class coincide. But in many developing countries, despite an official age of school-entry, children enter at different ages and many repeat grades. In Malawi, for example, a recently stated government objective is the reduction of the age *range* in a class from 10+ years to 5 years (Croft, this volume Chapter 6). In Tanzania the ages of pupils in Grade 1 primary vary from 7 to 15 and that of entrants to Form 1 secondary from 12 to 17+ years (Lewin, this volume Chapter 12). In such settings it would be erroneous to equate the terms mixed-year with mixed-age.

With this caveat in mind, the following statistics reflect the current extent of the multigrade reality in very different countries, expressed in slightly different ways.

- In Australia in 1988, 40% of schools in the Northern Territories had multigrade classes.
- In Burkina Faso in 2000, 36% of schools and 20% of classes were multigraded; 18% of school children were studying in multigrade classes.
- In England in 2000, 25.4% of all classes in primary education were classified as 'mixed-year' i.e. two or more curriculum grades were being taught by one teacher; 25% of all learners were studying in mixed-year classes.
- In France in 2000, 34% of public schools had 'combined' classes; 4.5% of these were single-teacher schools.
- In India in 1996, 84% of primary schools had 3 teachers or fewer. Since primary schools have five curriculum grades this means that if learners are to be 'on task' for most of the prescribed school day, then some teachers must be responsible for two or more grades for some part of each day.
- In Ireland in 2001/2, 42% of all primary school classes comprised two or more grades. Of these 64% were composed of two consecutive grades and 36% three or more grades.
- In the Peoples' Democratic Republic of Laos in 2003/4 64% of all primary schools had multigrade classes; 24.3% of all classes were multigraded.

- In Mauritania in 2002/3, 39% of all pupils were educated in a multigrade class; 82% of these pupils attended schools in rural areas.
- In Nepal in 1998, the teacher–primary school ratio was 3.8. Primary schools comprised five curriculum grades. If learners are 'on task' for most of the prescribed school day, it follows that most teachers must be responsible for two or more grades for some part of each day.
- In the province of New Brunswick, Canada, in 2003/4, 13.9% of all classes in Elementary schools (K–G8) combined grades.
- In Northern Ireland in 2002/3, 21.6% of all classes (Years 1–7) were 'composite' classes (i.e. two or more grades taught together).
- In Norway, in c. 2000, 35% of all primary schools were small schools using multigrade teaching.
- In Peru in 1998, 78% of all public primary schools were multigrade. Of the multigrade schools 41% had only one teacher; 59% had more than one. In rural areas 89.2% of all public primary schools were multigrade, of which 42% had only one teacher and 58% more than one.
- In Sri Lanka in 1999, 63% of all public schools had 4 or fewer teachers. Some are primary schools with five grades and some are primary and post-primary with up to 11 grades. If learners are 'on task' for most of the prescribed school day, it follows that some teachers must be responsible for classes spanning two or more grades for some part of each day.

(Brunswic and Valérien, 2003; Hargreaves et al., 2001; Kamil et al., 2004; Little, 2004, 2001, 1995; Mulryan, 2004; New Brunswick, 2004; Phommabouth, 2004; Solstad, 2004; Suzuki, 2004; UNESCO/APEID, 1989).

It is clear from the above that learning and teaching in multigrade schools and classes is extensive in a wide range of countries.

These figures are significant for the achievement of EFA and the Millennium Development Goals in two main ways. First, most EFA planning and funding is predicated on the monograded classroom. In many respects learning and teaching in multigraded and monograded classes are similar. Teachers need training and support; students need stimulation, support, learning materials and feedback from assessment. But needs are also different. Teachers in multigraded classrooms need to support learning across grades – for which curricula, teacher education, and assessment need to be planned differently. Conventional norms on school resources and teacher deployment to monograded classes do not necessarily map well onto schools where teachers are responsible for two or more grades. Second, access to primary education for all remains an elusive goal in many countries, and especially in geographically isolated, economically poor and socially disadvantaged settings. These settings are often those that give rise to multigrade, not monograde schooling, a fact that is frequently overlooked by EFA planners. Recent enrolment data place the numerical challenge in perspective. In 2000 it was estimated that 562 million primary age children were enrolled in primary schools in developing countries, 62.3 million in developed countries and 11.1 million in countries in transition. Among these 46.5%, 48.7% and 48.6% respectively were girls. Out-of-school children were estimated at 100.1 million, 1.8 million and 2.1 million in developing, developed and transition countries respectively. The corresponding percentages of out-of-school girls were 57%, 43% and 43% respectively. The majority of out-of-school children in developing countries were female; and in developed and transition countries male (UNESCO, 2003). A conservative estimate of 30% of children currently in multigrade classes in all countries yields a world total of 192.45 million. Add this to, say, 50% of the currently out-of-school children for whom opportunities to learn are most likely to occur in a multigraded class. This generates an additional 52 million children. This totals 244.45 million children worldwide for whom a multi-graded pedagogy is likely to be the one through which they learn in primary school. For the developing countries alone the total estimate is 218.60 million. And this excludes children in monograded classes who are seeking opportunities to learn on days when teachers are absent. These estimates barely scratch the surface of the challenge, for EFA is concerned not only about access but access to good quality, completion of the primary stage and learning achievement.

THE PARADOX OF MULTIGRADE TEACHING

The significance of multigraded schooling for EFA is greater in developing than in industrialised countries. As the figures above indicate, learning and teaching in multigrade settings is widespread in many countries with well-developed education systems and very high rates of participation. Yet the pedagogic challenges appear to be fewer for reasons that will be explored in subsequent chapters. Elsewhere, we have suggested that these challenges represent a *paradox* (Little, 1995, 2001; Pridmore, 2004).

> For children to learn effectively in multigrade environments teachers need to be well-trained, well-resourced and hold positive attitudes to multi-grade

teaching. However, many teachers in multi-grade environments are either
untrained or trained in mono-grade pedagogy; have few if any teaching/
learning resources; and regard the multi-grade classroom as the poor cousin of
the better-resourced mono-grade classroom found in large, urban schools,
staffed by trained teachers.

                                                            (Little, 2001: 477)

In the classrooms studied in the research undertaken for this book many
teachers regarded multigrade teaching as the poor relation. In Peru teachers'
attitudes to multigrade teaching are generally negative (Ames, 2004 and
Chapter 3 this volume). The monograde classroom is perceived as the
'normal' classroom; the multigrade classroom as a 'second-class' option.
The teachers did not choose to work in the multigrade school and felt
unprepared to work in these classes. They felt that children don't 'get the
same' as in monograde classrooms. The isolated and isolating conditions of
work and the poverty of the communities they serve contribute to the
negative attitude. In Sri Lanka attitudes of multigrade teachers to multigrade
teaching are generally negative. This is partly due to unawareness about the
effectiveness of multigrade teaching strategies (Vithanapathirana, 2005). In
Nepal, teachers' attitudes to multigrade teaching were generally negative.
Fifty out of 56 teachers interviewed who were currently engaged in or had
previous experience of multigrade teaching thought that multigrade teaching
is more difficult than monograde teaching (Suzuki, 2004, see Chapter 5 in
this volume). In the Turks and Caicos Islands, teachers reserved their most
negative comments for the planning burden imposed by the multigrade
classroom. One teacher commented that she 'hates multigrade classes' and
'would prefer to teach a monograde class with fifty pupils in it' because in
the former she has to prepare a separate plan for each grade in the class.
Only in our London study did we encounter some teachers with positive
attitudes. While half of the multigrade teachers interviewed expressed a
preference for monograde teaching, the other said they did not mind either
way, expressed a clear preference for multigrade or gave qualified responses
(Chapter 4 this volume).

Subsequent chapters of this book will explore these and other challenges
posed by multigrade settings, and will outline contemporary attempts at
resolving the paradox through planned interventions. Before that however
this chapter steps back in time to explore how and why the monograde class
emerged as the dominant form of school organisation around the world in
the late twentieth and early twenty-first century.

THE EMERGENCE OF MONOGRADE SYSTEMS OF EDUCATION IN THE TWENTIETH CENTURY

The history of the emergence of monograded classes within primary education in different countries is long and complex. Historical texts remind us that many forms of so-called 'traditional education' were transacted in one-teacher schools with pupils of various ages and experience. Casual observations of children learning within families and local communities remind us how much and how effectively children develop certain skills and attitudes within mixed-age groups and how this form of learning is as old as mankind. A particular form of the multigraded school, the 'one-teacher school' has roots that dig deep into the histories of most contemporary education systems. The history of monograded schooling is much shorter.

This chapter constructs an account of the emergence of the monograded system of schooling in Europe during the late Roman, late Medieval, Renaissance and Enlightenment periods. It draws on a variety of secondary historical sources and focuses on secular education for children in their initial stages of formal education beyond the home.

One-teacher schools in the late Roman and medieval periods

Morgan (2001) focuses her account of late Roman education on the arrangements made for literacy learning among young children. Drawing from Latin and Greek texts she explains how

> [t]here were no designated school buildings in the Roman world; teachers taught in private houses, or in public places like gymnasia, wrestling grounds and town lecture halls or simply under a portico or in the street.
>
> (Morgan, 2001: 13)

'Schools' were generally run by an individual teacher, working alone or sometimes with a subordinate teacher. Children seemed to learn on their own with texts provided by the teacher. There appears to have been no notion of a curriculum in the modern sense of a legal framework of knowledge/skills to be addressed or in the sense of a course to be followed by children of similar ages together. At the elementary stage of education children did not appear to be grouped together as a class.

> Children all seem to work on their own, though they talk to each other (and fall out). Except when a teacher dictates grammatical information, there is no sense of the group as a focused 'class' and this impression is reinforced when ... pupils arrive and depart at different times.
>
> (Morgan, 2001: 13)

Unlike in contemporary Western education there was no notion of cohorts of same-age children entering school at the same time in order to learn to read and write. Children entered school at different ages. Learning was assessed by the teacher informally, as the work progressed. There were no entrance, aptitude or achievement tests, a fact that reflects the absence of any legal requirement that children be educated, nor any guidance on the ages at which children should enter or leave school (Morgan, 2001: 15).

The teacher's focus on the individual child rather than the whole class was reinforced by educational theorists of the day. One of the most famous, Quintilian (*c.* 35–90 CE), advocated a child-centred approach to pedagogy in which the teacher

> must attend to the behaviour of the child and watch for his responses; by choosing tasks appropriate to the child's age, and relating the size and difficulty of the task to his attention span and capacity, better results will be achieved.*
>
> (Bowen, 1972: 202)

Although there was no legally prescribed curriculum for any stage of education, Quintilian's text prescribes one that spans the elementary stages of literacy and language and the subsequent stages of grammar and rhetoric. Far from it being a wish list, Bowen maintains that Quintilian's curriculum reflected current Roman and Greek practice.

> Education should begin with reading, progressing from letters through syllables to words and sentences; upon such a foundation the *grammaticus* can build with instruction in grammar – accidence, analysis, declension and conjugation – along with syntax and orthography. Literature too should be taught by the standard method of *praelectio*. To that verbal core Quintilian adds mathematics and music, though not for any intrinsic reasons: geometry's value is in its exemplification of logical reasoning, music is useful as a social grace. Instruction in rhetoric, proceeding from those foundations, is detailed in nine books, following customary practices.
>
> (Bowen, 1972: 201)

More advanced training, especially in rhetoric, appears to have departed from the individualistic approach of teaching and learning at the elementary stage. All pupils were expected to follow the same set of exercises. Teachers interacted with groups of pupils as a whole class, with pupils 'declaiming' to the whole class, and the teacher feeding back corrections for the benefit of everyone and not just the individual. A separate strand of education – athletic training – was also organised in groups divided strictly by age (Morgan, 2001). Over time two strands of the classical curriculum became

---

* I am grateful to Andy Green for drawing my attention to Bowen's volumes on the History of Education and for his comments on an earlier draft of this chapter.

established – the trivium (grammar, logic and rhetoric) and the quadrivium (music, arithmetic, geometry and astronomy).

The course of elementary education in Europe between the end of the Roman period and the Renaissance is difficult to track. For some historians this is the period of the Dark and Middle Ages when classical education and culture were replaced by a cultural vacuum. Lawton and Gordon (2002) present a slightly more positive account of educational developments during the period. Roman traditions endured in some parts of Europe, despite the barbarian invasions. Islamic, monastic and other forms of religious education flourished. In non-monastic schools run by the Christian church a liberal curriculum comprising the classical trivium and the quadrivium was adopted. Also at this time the first Universities were being established.

Ariès provides an account of schooling in Late Medieval France (c. AD 1300–1400). Medieval schools were 'confined to the tonsured, to the clerics and the religious' (Ariès, 1962: 137). Elementary knowledge, he maintained, including reading and writing, was taught at home not at school. Nonetheless, many of the characteristics of the ideal-typical medieval school resonate with Morgan's account of elementary education in the late Roman period. Formal learning was directed by a single private teacher, learners entered his tutelage at varying ages and all studied the same texts and subjects in the same room. There was no notion of a graduated curriculum, no precondition of age for starting or finishing a course of study, and hence, no link between age, class and curriculum level. Learners were differentiated only by the number of times they had repeated or memorised the same (few) books selected by the teacher (Ariès, 1962: 141–50).

Hamilton's description of the medieval school is similar:

> a medieval school was primarily an educational relationship entered into by a private teacher and a group of individual scholars. Like guild masters and their apprentices teachers took students at all levels of competence and, accordingly, organized their teaching largely on an individual basis. Such individualization fed back, in turn, upon the general organization of schooling. First, there was no presumption that every student was 'learning' the same passage. Secondly, there was no pedagogical necessity that all students should remain in the teacher's presence throughout the hours of teaching – they could just as easily study (cf. memorize) their lessons elsewhere. And thirdly, there was no expectation that students would stay at school after their specific educational goals had been reached. Essentially, medieval schooling was a loose-textured organizational form which could easily encompass a large number of students. Its apparent laxity (for example absenteeism, or the fact that enrolments did not match attendance) was not so much a failure (or breakdown) of school organization as a perfectly efficient response to the demands that were placed on it.
>
> (Hamilton, 1989: 38)

*The emergence of classes and classrooms during
the European Renaissance*

The shift from ungraded groups of learners, heterogeneous in achievement and age, to the present-day notion of classes graded by age and achievement was a slow process spanning five centuries. Ariès suggests that in France the shift began during the fifteenth century.

> The heterogeneous body remained in a single room under the common supervision of the masters, but it was broken up into groups according to the extent of the pupil's knowledge, and the masters got into the habit of addressing each of these groups separately. The pedagogic practice was the result of the passage from the simultaneous pedagogy of medieval tradition to the progressive pedagogy which would carry the day.
>
> (Ariès, 1962:173)

The separation of groups based on the level of pupil knowledge was the beginnings of the notion of a 'class'. In France the modern notion of pupils moving from the sixth or fifth class to the first class was established during the second half of the sixteenth century.

From the end of the sixteenth century it was generally accepted in France that every 'class' had its own teacher, but not yet its own class*room*. The idea of a separate room for each class became established during the seventeenth century and seemed to arise from increases in the school population. Each class*room* would comprise pupils separated now by their achievements and the difficulty of the subject matter but not yet by age (Ariès, 1962: 176–82). In England the shift to the teaching of single classes in separate classrooms would be slower. Describing the hesitation of the English grammar schools to increase the numbers of teachers, Ariès (1962: 177) illustrates his case with an example from Eton where, in the mid-sixteenth century, there were still only two teachers – the master and the usher.

The re-emergence of the idea of a graded curriculum

The idea of a 'curriculum' or course of study – implicit in Quintilian's texts on education and in the liberal education of elites in medieval Europe – developed further during the Renaissance period. Bowen (1981) describes how the recovery of classical Greek and Roman texts and their translation into vernaculars by the Renaissance humanists and advances in printing and book production led to the dissemination of learning 'now organised into pedagogical sequences' (Bowen, 1981: 6). In the sixteenth century Erasmus of Rotterdam wrote a treatise, *On the Right Method of Instruction*, in which he argued for

> a graded progression of studies from an elementary grammar through a series of Latin and Greek texts to the study of selected passages of classical and Christian literature, with an emphasis on grammatical, syntactical and textual exegesis.
>
> (Bowen, 1981: 8)

Bowen (1981) maintains that the principle of text grading was transferred to the schools where programmes of instruction were also graded. Joannes Sturmis and the city council of Strasbourg are credited with establishing the systematic organisation of schools by grade, a form that spread throughout Protestant Europe.

> Pupils were grouped in a series of classes according to their fitness, promotions from one class to another were made annually with solemn ceremony, the classes were subdivided into sections of ten under the charge of an older pupil called a decurion.
>
> (Boyd and King, 1975)

Linking the notion of a curriculum with the emergence of separate classes, Ariès notes how, by the beginning of the seventeenth century in France, classes had arisen in order to divide students by capacity and 'the difficulty of subject matter' (Ariès 1962: 182).

Hamilton (1989) traces developments in the notion of curriculum to the practices of the Universities rather than schools. Sixteenth- and seventeenth-century records of the Universities of Leiden and Glasgow indicate that the curriculum referred to an entire course spanning several years of study prescribed for each student. Hamilton explains:

> Any course worthy of its name was to embody both 'disciplina' (a sense of structural coherence), and 'ordo' (a sense of internal sequence). A 'curriculum' should not only be 'followed'; it should also be 'completed'. Whereas the sequence, length and completeness of medieval courses had been relatively open to student negotiation (for example, at Bologna) and/or teacher abuse (for example, in Paris), the emergence of 'curriculum' brought ... a greater sense of control to both teaching and learning.
>
> (Hamilton, 1989: 45)

Although almost all the schools referred to above conducted studies in the classical languages rather than vernaculars, and were attended by only a minority, developments in the way of organising pupils for instruction and the subject matter of what is to be taught would have far-reaching effects on forms of education throughout the modern world.

The expansion of educational opportunity, costs and
the graded school

The gradual expansion of educational opportunity to the poorest (the social group on whom current movements for EFA are most focused) followed different routes in the countries of Europe. In England the processes of industrialisation in the late eighteenth and nineteenth centuries and the migration of populations from rural to urban areas led to changes in attitudes to formal education and the numbers of children who participated in it. Children were widely employed in factories, worked long hours under difficult conditions and lived unhealthily. The social reformers of the Enlightenment led movements for the expansion of education to the poorest groups in society. While there seemed to be general agreement about the need for education among the poorest groups in society – civilising, socialising, moralising and industrialising – there was a lack of consensus over responsibility for its provision. But if there was dispute over who should provide and pay for education for the poorest there was less controversy over the form that it should take. As Lawton and Gordon explain,

> In 1796, Sir Thomas Bernard, one of the founders of the Society for Bettering the Conditions of the Poor, stated that the monitorial system was 'the division of labour applied to intellectual purposes. The principle in schools and manufactories is the same'.
>
> (Lawton and Gordon, 2002: 117)

As we shall see, the monitorial system combined the traditional idea of the single-teacher school with the emerging and progressive idea of separate 'teachers' for each curriculum grade. The monitorial system involved a single master responsible for large numbers of learners in one large room, assisted by a team of monitors. Learners were divided into 'classes' or 'rows', each the responsibility of one monitor. Each higher class tackled subject matter of a higher order of difficulty. Efficient use of pupil time and low teacher costs were central to this system. This was effected through a division of learners into homogeneous groups, differentiated from each other in terms of achievement level, each group working under the strict supervision of a monitor, the monitors working under the strict supervision of the master. The parallel between the division of labour in the factory and in the school was clear.

In England the monitorial system was promoted by two voluntary and rival bodies, their rivalry contributing to the expansion of mass primary education. The 'Institution for Promoting the British System for the

Education of the Labouring and Manufacturing Classes of Society of Every Religious Persuasion' (otherwise known as the British and Foreign Schools society), employed Joseph Lancaster to promote the monitorial system. The 'National Society for the Education of the Poor in the Principles of the Established Church' (otherwise known as the National Society) employed Dr Andrew Bell to do likewise. Bell is credited by some to have 'invented' the method in Madras, India where, as chaplain to five army regiments, he had perfected a method of teaching reading and writing using bright pupils as monitors.

Taylor (1996) provides a detailed account of the monitorial school established by Joseph Lancaster in South London in 1804.

> Each boy ... sat in his place on a long bench shared with the other nine boys in his class. They were all at roughly the same stage of learning and all were under the guidance of one monitor ... some children might only spend a few months at school. Every moment of their time was precious and Joseph endeavoured to see that none of it was wasted.... Every monitor concentrated on instructing his class in one or two carefully designated tasks and doing it thoroughly ... the efficiency of the (Monitorial) Plan depended on the monitor knowing exactly what he had to do. It was essential that he was examined by the teacher before he undertook his duties. Some of the monitors were very young, and Joseph took care that their own education was not neglected. But, in teaching others, they were reinforcing their own learning. Each boy in each class knew the immediate goal at which he was aiming and was spurred on to master it by the enthusiasm of his monitor, by the rivalry of his classmates, and by the knowledge that a small reward would be his, once he had mastered the task. He would then move to a new class and a new goal. Each child was able to progress at his own pace and was not necessarily in the same class for every subject. The slow child spent longer at each stage than his quicker classmate.... The quick child was able to progress by leaps and bounds.
>
> (Taylor, 1996: 4–7)

Monitorial schools were notable for their rigid and hierarchical differentiation or grading of classes and subject matter. Meritorious performance was encouraged through praise and points, the accumulated points leading, in Lancaster's schools, to prizes of bats, balls and kites (Lancaster 1803: 49). Rows were differentiated by the levels of knowledge mastery of the learners rather than their age. The monitorial schools combined elements of what we would term today monograde and multigrade organisation. The monitor was responsible for a single grade at any one time; the single schoolmaster was responsible for organising the teaching and learning of multiple grades of learners.

Monitorial schools for girls were established in urban areas, though in terms of total enrolments boys would outnumber girls. Monitorial schools spread to many other countries. Lancaster promoted the system in the United

States, where he lived for much of his later life. The system was also adopted in eight countries in Africa, ten in Asia, two in North America, eight in South America (including Chile where it was used as the state system), Australia, 13 in Central America and the West Indies and five in Europe (Taylor, 1996: Appendix 2). Lancaster's 1803 booklet was translated to French and widely distributed by the Société pour l'Instruction Elémentaire. By 1820 the association had established 1,500 monitorial schools in France, mainly in industrial areas. The French monitorial system challenged the two main methods in use prior to the French Revolution. These were the simultaneous method (i.e. whole-class teaching) used mainly in the large church schools and the individual method used mainly in the small rural schools (Alexander, 2000: 56). Citing the work of Reboul-Sherrer (1989), Alexander explains:

> whole-class teaching (for this is what the simultaneous method was) had signalled competence as well as the luxury of a school with several teachers, while the individual method was generally associated with incompetence, as the lone teacher struggled to keep the triply disparate members of a large class (mixed age, mixed attainment and mixed motivation) occupied.
>
> (Alexander, 2000: 56)

By the mid-nineteenth century the monitorial system fell out of favour, but its influence on the creation of national mass education systems would be considerable (Little, 1988).

Class division by age

If the concepts of 'class' and 'curriculum' had been adopted by the sixteenth century in much of Europe, their respective links with age were established only in the nineteenth century. This is the period, Ariès (1962: 20, 29) suggests, when the concept of childhood became the 'privileged age'. This age stood in contrast with the privileged age of 'youth' in the seventeenth and 'adolescence' in the twentieth centuries respectively. During the nineteenth century the school removed the child from daily working and mixing with adults and adult society, a separation that would lead to ever finer divisions between children themselves. The correspondence between class, curriculum and age became part and parcel of a gradual regularisation of schooling that involved

> the annual cycle of promotions, the habit of making all the pupils go through the complete series of classes instead of only a few, and the requirements of a new system of teaching adapted to smaller, more homogeneous classes
>
> (Ariès 1962: 230)

Ideas about classifying learners into ages and attainment flowed from country to country, conveyed by travellers, educators and officials. By the mid-nineteenth century the division of classes by age had been firmly established in the urban schools of Prussia. In 1842/3 Horace Mann, Secretary of the Massachusetts Board of Education in the USA, was particularly impressed by his observations of Prussian practice.

> The first element of superiority in a Prussian school ... consists in the proper classification of scholars. In all places where the numbers are sufficiently large to allow it, the children are divided according to ages and attainments, and a single teacher has the charge of only a single class ... there is no obstacle whatever ... to the introduction at once of this mode of dividing and classifying scholars in all our large towns.
>
> (Mann quoted in Pratt, 1986)

By the twentieth century developments in psychology, learning theory and child development would reinforce the notion that classes and curricula be organised hierarchically and that all children should pass through them in order. The age-grading of classes and the curriculum that had appeared during the nineteenth century was further reinforced and legitimised.

TOWARDS CONVERGENCE WORLDWIDE

In the mid-nineteenth century Horace Mann borrowed ideas and practices in education from countries in Europe and adapted them for use in urban America. Elsewhere, ideas and practices were being heavily lent rather than borrowed. European colonialism from the fifteenth century had lent – or more properly, imposed – ideas about the purposes of and arrangements for education in many countries from the Americas to Asia and Africa. In many cases these were superimposed on longstanding traditions and practices, some pre-dating the beginnings of the European story in the Roman period. For example, the history of Buddhist education in Sri Lanka suggests that notions of curriculum, of stages of knowledge and of graded progression through them were established between the third century BCE and the twelfth century CE (Jayasuriya, 1979; Rahula, 1956). The history of Aztec education in Mexico, as depicted in the Codex Mandoza, indicates the strictly age-differentiated curriculum that surrounded the initiation of young people into the economic life of society (Ross, 1978).

From the sixteenth to the twentieth centuries the European colonisers – in the case of Sri Lanka, the Portuguese, the Dutch and the British – imposed new ideas and new arrangements for learning. Never mirror images of practices then current in the domestic system of the colonising country the resemblances were nonetheless strong. By the end of the twentieth century the practice of admitting cohorts of learners to formal education at a prescribed age to following a graded curriculum sequentially and the deployment of teachers for single grades and working in separate classrooms was as recognisable in Sri Lanka as in England. The convergence was more general still – in Mozambique as in Portugal, Indonesia as in Holland, Peru as in Spain, Mauritania as in France and the Philippines as in the United States.

The regularisation and systematisation of schooling by age would come to characterise education systems worldwide in the twentieth century, even in societies where, in the terms of Ariès (1962), childhood and its finer gradations had not yet attained privileged status. The projection of curricular gradation by age became a 'Western cultural theme of great importance, influencing both the conception of education and that of child development' (Serpell, 1999: 117).

Most systems of education worldwide are predicated on the notion that learners enter and exit from graded classes as members of a cohort. In some systems learners progress from graded class to graded class, automatically, at a regular time of the year; in others, progress is determined by an assessment of learning achievement. Those who fail to be promoted become grade repeaters and join a group of learners in the previous graded class. Graded classes correspond closely with the age of the student and usually comprise students who share birthdays within one calendar year. In systems where, for various reasons, the age of entry of learners varies by more than one year, learners move through the system with peers who entered the first graded class within the same calendar year. Large numbers of new entrants may result in the creation of parallel graded classes. Each class is usually taught by a single teacher at any one time. Most systems of education prescribe national curricula for teachers and learners that are 'graded'. If these are not prescribed nationally then they will be prescribed at a sub-national level, e.g. by province or state. Textbooks and other learning materials correspond with grades; so too do formats for the assessment (including examinations) of learning achievement. Most pre-service and in-service teacher training systems prepare teachers to teach in monograded schools.

And yet, as the statistics presented earlier indicate, *very large numbers of learners and teachers worldwide work together in settings where two or more 'official' grades are combined.* These settings are, *de facto*, multigraded, not monograded. They deviate from the national blueprint of how a school should be organised. They fail to fit the monograded system that emerged in response to the needs of large populations in urban areas in industrialising countries. The national curricula, assessment systems and learning materials with which teachers are expected to work today are part and parcel of the blueprint of the monograded, not multigraded, school. These schools and classes pose a major challenge for the achievement of EFA.

CURRENT CONDITIONS GIVING RISE TO MULTIGRADE CLASSES

So, why do multigraded classes persist in the twenty-first century? To date, our research has identified eleven conditions that give rise to multigraded classes. They arise in:

(i)   Schools in areas of low population density where schools are widely scattered and enrolments low. Schools may have only one or two teachers responsible for all grades.

(ii)   Schools that comprise a cluster of classrooms spread across different locations, in which some classes are multigrade for the same reasons as (i), and some are monograde. Some teachers within the same 'school' will spend most of their time with multigrade classes; some with monograde classes.

(iii)   Schools in areas of where the population, students and/or teachers are declining, and where previously there was monograded teaching.

(iv)   Schools in areas of population growth and school expansion, where enrolments in the expanding upper grades remain small and teacher numbers few.

(v)   Schools in areas where parents send their children to more popular schools within reasonable travel distance, leading to a decline in the potential population of students and teachers in the less popular school.

(vi)   Schools in which the number of learners admitted to a class exceed official norms on class size, necessitating the combination of some learners from one graded class with learners from another grade.

(vii)   Schools in which the general structure of classes is monograde but, where, because of fluctuating annual admission numbers, groups of learners need to be combined.

(viii) Mobile schools in which one or more teacher moves with nomadic and pastoralist learners spanning a wide range of ages and grades.

(ix)   Schools in which teacher absenteeism is high and supplementary teacher arrangements are non-effectual or non-existent.

(x)   Schools in which the official number of teachers deployed is
        sufficient to support monograde teaching but where the actual
        number deployed is less (for a variety of reasons).
(xi)   Schools in which learners are organised in multigrade rather than
        monograde groups, for pedagogic reasons, often as part of a more
        general curriculum and pedagogic reform of the education system.

Most of the above conditions suggest that multigrade classes have arisen by
default or necessity, rather than pedagogic or administrative choice. The
final condition (xi) – deliberate pedagogic choice – is of a different order.
Here, teachers, headteachers and/or local authorities either choose to
organise learners in multigraded groups because of its perceived pedagogic
advantages for the learner, or they accept the necessity of multigrade
teaching and plan curriculum and other interventions in order to create a
positive pedagogy.

Necessity

All of the chapters in this book describe conditions where imbalances of
teacher and learners within national systems of 'graded' education give rise
to multigraded classes. From the Turks and Caicos Islands in the Caribbean
(Chapter 2), to the Ucayali Amazon in Peru (Chapter 3), to the Nuwakot and
Kavre districts in Nepal (Chapter 5), to Kegalle district in Sri Lanka
(Chapter 7), to BacGiang province in Vietnam (Chapter 8), to the Gusheigu-
Karaga district of Northern Ghana (Chapter 11) and on to Manizales in
Colombia (Chapter 13), small and sedentary populations of children are
taught by small numbers of teachers. Because there are fewer teachers than
curriculum grades, classes are combined to form multigraded classes. In
London, England, by contrast (Chapter 4) large and sedentary populations of
children can also find themselves in multigraded class because of the annual
pupil intakes, legal limits on class size and restrictions on teacher
deployment. Within the mobile pastoralist communities of the Dafur
region in the Sudan (Chapter 10) single teachers move with respective
communities.

Choice

In England there have been times when multigraded schooling has been
promoted as a pedagogy of choice. The most sustained advocacy for a

multigraded organisation of schooling emerged in the 1970s in the wake of the Plowden Report (Department of Education and Science, 1967) and its promotion of active and individualised learning. The term used to describe the multigrade class was the 'vertically-grouped' class. Schools were encouraged to group together in one classroom learners from two or more grade groups – to slice the age cohorts of children vertically, rather than horizontally. In schools that otherwise would have had age-graded classes, there would be several parallel vertically grouped classes. The underlying philosophy of teaching promoted by the Plowden committee was child-centred. Teachers used a range of methods (telling, listening, stimulating, supporting) and social groups (pairs, small groups, whole class) to promote the individual development of the child. The approach could be used to advantage both within grades (as in monograde teaching) or across grades (as in multigrade teaching) and many schools adopted vertical grouping as the classroom organisation and pedagogy of choice. By the 1980s the child-centred approach was being criticised in England and Wales for the heavy burden placed on teachers and for the logical contradiction of developing general principles of teaching when its starting point is the uniqueness of each individual child (see for example, Simon, 1981). Despite this and other critiques, and the swing back to whole-class teaching methods in the English classroom of the 1990s, the child-centred approach became very influential worldwide.

Transforming necessity into a positive pedagogy

Multigrade teaching that arises through necessity is often considered to be a second-class education. However, in some cases, necessity has been trans-formed into a positive pedagogy. The well-known *Escuela Nueva* programme is a current example of such a transformation. Initiated over twenty years ago in Colombia, the programme has been adapted for use in Brazil, Guatemala, Panama, Chile, El Salvador, Nicaragua, the Dominican Republic, Mexico, Peru, Ecuador, Guyana, Uganda and the Philippines. Escuela Nueva is a comprehensive strategy that involves curriculum development, teacher training, multigraded classes, school–community relations and local management (Colbert *et al.*, 1993). The *Escuela Nueva* programme is notable for its proactive strategy. It has been designed for use mainly in rural areas and, in the case of Colombia, has been sanctioned by the national government as the programme of choice in rural areas. The general approach has also been adopted by secondary schools which are opening up to accommodate the demand for secondary education from among the primary graduates. This stands in contrast to the situation faced by many thousands, if not millions of multigrade teachers around the world, where multigrade is perceived as second-class education and from which teachers seek an escape. Chapter 13 provides an up to date review of the status and impact of the *Escuela Nueva* programme while Chapter 14 will review its curriculum strategy and that of programmes in India and elsewhere that have transformed the necessity of multigrade teaching into positive pedagogy.

Neither multigrade nor monograde

The above discussion has outlined a number of conditions that give rise to multigraded classes within systems that are predominantly monograded. However, in the context of the implementation of EFA on the ground, we must also acknowledge that conditions that call for multigrade teaching guarantee neither that multigrade schools will be open nor that multigrade teaching will occur. Some schools offer neither multigraded nor monograded opportunities for learning. They offer *no* opportunities. In her study of multigrade schools in the Peruvian Amazon Ames (2004) reports that, officially, schools were open for 34 days during the months of June and July. One school was open for 19 days and all three teachers were available only on 12 of those 19 days. Suzuki (2004 and this volume) describes strategies adopted by teachers in multigrade schools in Nepal. In one of the five strategies described, teachers avoided multigraded teaching by shortening the length of each timetabled period, teaching single-graded classes for less than the officially prescribed period and abandoning other grades in the meantime. This absence of responsibility for some groups of learners for some parts of each day may seem an extreme way of coping with the challenge of multigrade teaching. But it may well be a common practice as teachers cope with the multiple challenges of the multigraded school. The abandonment strategy is certainly very common in monograded schools when teachers are absent. In the context of EFA, it is insufficient to know that children have access to school, that the school is open and that children have attended school for all or part of the official school day. One also needs to know how many teachers are present and the nature of the interaction between teachers and children, and between children themselves, during the day.

MAKING THE INVISIBLE VISIBLE

Despite its prevalence in many educational systems, multigrade teaching, multigrade classrooms and multigrade schools remain highly visible to those who teach and learn in them, but invisible to those who work beyond them and yet who plan and manage EFA. This book aims to make the invisible visible. It aims to address the realities faced by teachers like Maheswari. Based on original research on the problems of and prospects for multigrade teaching its focus is on the hundreds of thousands of teachers and millions of children in, mainly, developing countries who, if they are to have any chance of participating in education will do so in multigraded classrooms. In the global effort to achieve Education for All (EFA) in the post-Dakar decade the needs of multigrade teachers, classes and schools must be addressed.

Subsequent chapters extend earlier reviews and reports of research (Little, 1995, 2001) with analyses of field studies of multigrade teaching from England, Colombia, Ghana, Malawi, Nepal, Peru, Turks and Caicos, Sri Lanka, Sudan and Vietnam. The field studies explore the extent of multigrade teaching, the recognition of multigrade teaching within curriculum and teacher education systems, the diversity of multigrade teaching practices and the training and curriculum needs of multi grade teachers. They identify the cognitive and social outcomes of multigraded learning. They identify the potential for teachers to re-construct curricula to meet the needs of the multigraded classroom and identify similarities between the ways that children learn within families and communities and within the multigrade classroom. They identify pupil diversity in all classes, whether multigrade or monograded, and the need for all types of teacher training to address diversity. They also explore the costs and benefits of multigrade teaching and non-government and government programme designs for one-teacher schools.

Maheswari is just one of hundreds of thousands of teachers worldwide who struggle to achieve EFA. The purpose of the book is to raise the awareness of educational policymakers worldwide of the realities in which teachers like Maheswari work, to explore the implications for teacher education and curriculum reform, and to raise the awareness of all teachers, whether multigrade or monograde, of the challenges posed and the opportunities for learning presented by the multigraded setting.

REFERENCES

Aikman, S. and el Haj, H. (2006) 'Mobile multigrade schooling as a pragmatic response to EFA for pastoralist peoples'. In A.W. Little (ed.) *Education For All and Multigrade Teaching: Challenges and opportunities.* Amsterdam: Springer.

Alexander, R. (2000) *Culture and Pedagogy: International comparisons in primary education.* Oxford: Blackwell.

Ames Ramello, P.P. (2004) 'Multigrade schools in context: literacy in the community, the home and the school in the Peruvian Amazon'. Unpublished PhD thesis, Institute of Education, University of London.

Ariès, P. (1962) *Centuries of Childhood.* Trans. R. Baldick. London: Cape.

Berry, C. (2006) 'Teachers in multigrade classrooms in the Turks and Caicos Islands'. In A.W. Little (ed.), *Education For All and Multigrade Teaching: Challenges and opportunities.* Amsterdam: Springer.

Berry, C. and Little, A.W. (2006) 'Multigrade and multi-age teaching in classrooms in London, England'. In A.W. Little (ed.), *Education For All and Multigrade Teaching: Challenges and opportunities.* Amsterdam: Springer.

Bowen, J. (1972) *A History of Western Education,* Vol. 1. London: Methuen.

Bowen, J. (1981) *A History of Western Education,* Vol. 3 London: Methuen.

Boyd, W. and King, E. (1975) *The History of Western Education.* London: Adam and Charles Black.

Brunswic, E. and Valérien, J. (2003) Les classes multigrades: une contribution au développement de la scolarisation en milieu rural africain? *Principes de la planification de l'éducation 76,* Paris: UNESCO, Institut international de planification de l'éducation.

Colbert, V., Chiappe, C. and Arboleda, J. (1993) 'The new school program: more and better primary education for children in rural areas in Colombia'. In H. Levin and M.E. Lockheed (eds), *Effective Schools in Developing Countries.* London: Falmer Press.

Croft, A. (2006) 'Prepared for diversity: teacher education for lower primary classes in Malawi'. In A.W. Little (ed.), *Education For All and Multigrade Teaching: challenges and opportunities.* Amsterdam: Springer.

Department of Education and Science (1967) *Children and their Primary Schools.* London: Her Majesty's Stationery Office.

Hamilton. D. (1989) *Towards a Theory of Schooling.* London: Falmer Press.

Hargreaves, E., Montero, C., Chau, N., Sibli, M. and Thanh, T. (2001) 'Multigrade teaching in Peru, Sri Lanka and Vietnam: an overview'. *International Journal of Educational Development,* 21, 6, 499–520.

Jayasuriya, J.E. (1979) *Educational Policies and Progress.* Colombo: Associated Educational Publishers.

Kamil, H.A.W., Mohamed, L.O.M.A. and Mohamed, V.O.C (2004) Les classes multigrades: l'expérience Mauritanienne. *World Bank Colloquium on Multigrade Teaching and Learning.* Dakar: 24–28 May.

Lancaster, J. (1803) *Improvements in Education.* London: Printed and sold by Darton and Harvey, Grace-Church Street; J. Mathews, Strand; and W. Hatchard, Piccadilly.

Lawton, D. and Gordon, P. (2002) *A History of Western Educational Ideas*. London: Woburn Press.

Lewin, K.M. (2006) 'The costs of multigrade teaching'. In A.W. Little (ed.), *Education For All and Multigrade Teaching: challenges and opportunities*. Amsterdam: Springer.

Little, A.W. (1988) *Learning from Developing Countries*. London: Institute of Education, University of London.

Little, A.W. (1995) *Multigrade Teaching: A review of research and practice*. Education Research, Serial No. 12, London: Overseas Development Administration.

Little, A.W. (2001) 'Multigrade Teaching: towards an international research and policy agenda'. *International Journal of Educational Development*, 21, 6, 481–497.

Little, A.W. (2003) 'Access and achievement in Commonwealth countries: support for learning and teaching in multigrade classrooms'. In S. Matlin (ed.), *Commonwealth Education Partnerships 2004*. London: TSO.

Little, A.W. (2004) 'Learning and teaching in multigrade settings'. Background paper for UNESCO (2004) *EFA Global Monitoring Report 2005. Education for All: The quality imperative*. Online. Available HTTP: http://portal.unesco.org/education/en/ev.php-URL_ID=36184&URL_DO=DO_TOPIC&URL_SECTION=201&URL_PAGINATION=20.html (accessed 18 January 2005). Also available on *www.ioe. ac.uk/multigrade*

Morgan, T. (2001) 'Assessment in Roman education'. *Assessment in Education*, 8, 1, 11–24.

Mulryan, C. (2004) 'The multigrade classroom as a context for effective teaching and learning: insights from research on teaching and the Irish context'. *World Bank Colloquium on Multigrade Teaching and Learning*. Dakar: 24–28 May.

New Brunswick, Canada (2004) *Education Statistics*. New Brunswick, Canada: Policy and Planning Department of Education.

Phommabouth, C. (2004) 'Multi-grade teaching for remote and disadvantaged areas in Lao PDR'. *Second International Multigrade Teaching Conference: Turning biases into benefits*. Armidale: Centre for Research on Education in Context, University of New England.

Pratt, D. (1986) 'On the merits of multiage classrooms'. *Research in Rural Education*, 3, 3, 111–115.

Pridmore, P. (2004) 'Education for All: the paradox of multigrade teaching'. *Second International Multigrade Teaching Conference: Turning biases into benefits*. Armidale: Centre for Research on Education in Context, University of New England.

Rahula, S. (1956) *History of Buddhism*. Colombo: M.D. Gunasena.

Reboul-Scherrer, F. (1989) *Les Premiers Instituteurs, 1833–1882*. Paris: Hachette.

Ross, K. (1978) *Codex Mendoza: Aztec Manuscript*. Fribourg: Productions Liber S.A.

Serpell, R. (1999) 'Local accountability to rural communities: a challenge for educational planning in Africa'. In F.E. Leach and A.W. Little (eds), *Education, Cultures and Economics: Dilemmas for development*. New York and London: Falmer.

Simon, B. (1981) 'Why no pedagogy in England?' In B. Simon and W. Taylor (eds) *Education in the Eighties*. London: Batsford Academic and Educational Limited.

Solstad, K.J. (2004) 'Basic principles for making small schools work'. *World Bank Colloquium on Multigrade Teaching and Learning*. Dakar: 24–28 May.

Suzuki, T. (2004) 'Multigrade teachers and their training in rural Nepal: practice and training'. Unpublished PhD thesis. Institute of Education, University of London.

Suzuki, T. (2006) 'Multigrade teachers and their training in rural Nepal'. In A.W. Little (ed.), *Education For All and Multigrade Teaching: Challenges and opportunities*. Amsterdam: Springer.

Taylor, J (1996) *The Poor Child's Friend: Educating the poor in the early nineteenth century*. Kent: The Campanile Press.

UNESCO (2003) *EFA Global Monitoring Report 2003–04. Gender and Education for All: The leap to equality*. Paris: UNESCO.

UNESCO (2004) *EFA Global Monitoring Report 2005. Education for All: The quality imperative*. Online. Available HTTP: http://portal.unesco.org/education/en/ev.php-URL_ID=35939&URL_DO=DO_TOPIC&URL_SECTION=201.html (accessed 18 January 2005).

UNESCO/IBE (1961) *The One Teacher School*. Geneva: 24th International Conference on Public Education.

UNESCO/APEID (1989) *Multigrade Teaching in Single Teacher Primary Schools*. Bangkok: UNESCO Principal Regional Office for Asia and the Pacific.

Vithanapathirana, M. (2005) 'Improving multigrade teaching: action research with teachers in rural Sri Lanka.' Unpublished PhD thesis. Institute of Education, University of London.

Vu, T.S. and Pridmore, P. (2006) 'Improving the quality of health education in multigrade classes in Vietnam'. In A.W. Little (ed.) *Education For All and Multigrade Teaching: Challenges and opportunities*. Amsterdam: Springer.

CHAPTER TWO

LEARNING OPPORTUNITIES FOR ALL

*Pedagogy in multigrade and monograde classrooms
in the Turks and Caicos Islands*

CHRIS BERRY

INTRODUCTION

This chapter reports the main findings and conclusions of a study that was carried out in the Turks and Caicos Islands, a Dependent Territory of the United Kingdom located in the Caribbean. The aim of the study was to compare teaching in multigrade and monograde classes with a view to finding out whether or not multigrade organisation offers increased or decreased learning opportunities to pupils in comparison to monograde organisation. Learning opportunities is being used in the 'Education for All' sense of giving every pupil access to classroom experiences that meet their cognitive and social needs (World Education Forum, 2000). This requires a diversity of teaching practices and approaches that are sensitive to the range of pupil learning styles and preferences, and to their current level of cognitive and social development.

BACKGROUND

The Turks and Caicos Islands (TCI) are a multi-island archipelago. The territory consists of approximately 30 islands with a surface area of 193 square miles. The islands are located at the southern tip of the Bahamas chain, approximately 550 miles south east of Miami, Florida and about 90 miles north of Haiti and the Dominican Republic. Six of the islands are inhabited. Recent estimates by the TCI ministry of education (MoE) put the total population of the islands at 25,000 (MoE, 1999). The islands are an overseas territory of the United Kingdom, although they exercise a high degree of local political autonomy. The economy of the islands rests mainly on tourism, with some contribution from offshore banking and fisheries. Per capita GDP was almost US$7,000 in 1995 (Caribbean Development Bank, 1997). GNP per capita statistics are unavailable, but TCI is a 'developing

27

A.W. Little (ed.), Education for All and Multigrade Teaching: challenges and opportunities, 27–46.
© *2007 Springer.*

country' in relation to its economy and its level of industrialisation. For this reason, the United Kingdom government provides the country with substantial amounts of aid (Caribbean Development Bank, 1997).

Primary schooling is divided into eight grades, with most pupils entering at the age of 4 years and leaving at the age of 12 years. The first two years of schooling are referred to as kindergarten and have a separate curriculum and materials. Grades 1–6 are covered by a graded curriculum in maths, language, and science that increases in difficulty as pupils get older. There are graded textbooks to support the graded curriculum. There is little repetition and pupils are expected to progress through primary school in their age cohorts. At the end of primary schooling, pupils sit an examination that serves to stream them in the secondary school setting. Primary and secondary school enrolment is virtually universal.

There are a total of ten government primary schools on the islands (see Table 2.1). Of the ten schools, seven are large enough to organise their pupils into single grade classrooms. Pupils in these schools are generally grouped by age into mixed ability classes. The remaining three schools, because of their small pupil numbers, operate with multigrade groupings. The latter schools are located on the islands of Salt Cay, Middle Caicos and North Caicos. They serve communities with small populations whose children cannot travel to a neighbouring larger primary school. Pupils in these classes span up to three grade and age groups.

Table 2.1 Government primary schools by location, type and population

Island	No. of schools	No. of students
Grand Turk	2	513
Salt Cay	1	15
South Caicos	1	133
North Caicos	2	186
Middle Caicos	1	48
Providenciales	3	1223
Total	10	2118

Source: TCI government statistics, 2001/02

Primary school teachers tend to teach using whole-class teaching formats and in general they pay little attention to the lower attaining pupils in their classrooms. As a result, there is substantial under-achievement, with 50% or more of pupils failing to reach the minimum standards required at each grade level (MoE, 1999). Against this background, there is some evidence of better overall achievement of pupils attending multigrade as compared to monograde schools (Miller *et al.*, 1994).

Berry (2001) studied these attainment differences in more depth in a longitudinal study of reading progress (with assessment data collected annually between 1993 and 1996). This study showed significantly better reading progress for low-attaining pupils (especially boys) in multigrade schools when compared to monograde schools. There were no significant differences between the progress of medium attainers, but older high-attaining pupils (mainly girls) made significantly more progress in mono-grade schools than in multigrade schools. This study did not include any robust qualitative data that could offer an explanation for these differences. The present research seeks to explore whether the variations in attainment might be associated with differences in the teaching approaches in multigrade and monograde classrooms.

PREVIOUS LITERATURE

The purpose of this review is to find out whether the existing literature indicates any areas of difference in pedagogy between multigrade and monograde teachers. It should be noted at the outset that the literature base is limited. Very little research has been carried out into multigrade classroom teaching, and even less that compares multigrade and monograde teachers' practice. In addition, almost all of what there is has been carried out in developed country contexts. For the purposes of this review, three main literature sources have been reviewed: first, empirical studies that have sought to compare teaching in multigrade and monograde classrooms; second, empirical studies that have examined how multigrade teachers deal with their classes, but with no comparative element; third, literature based on secondary sources that seeks to conceptualise the dimensions of an effective multigrade teacher. A careful reading of this literature base indicates at least five critical dimensions along which multigrade practice can differ from monograde practice. These are:

- Classroom organisation
- Planning
- Assessment
- Grouping pupils for instruction
- Pupil independence and interdependence.

Classroom organisation

A consistent theme in the literature examining effective multigrade practice is that the multigrade teacher needs to pay special attention to the way her classroom is organised (UNESCO, 2001; Miller, 1999a; Commonwealth Secretariat, 1997; Birch and Lally, 1995; Thomas and Shaw, 1992; Collingwood, 1991). This includes the physical arrangement of the seating, the use of activity centers, the provision of a classroom library, adequate space to move around, two or more chalkboards, and storage space. The reason for this is that effective multigrade teaching should maximise opportunities for both independent work and for collaborative groupwork. The former is facilitated by the provision of learning corners and classroom libraries which can be accessed without help from the teacher. The latter is made easier if classroom seating is configured to promote groupwork.

There is, however, evidence from studies of primary schools in rural areas that multigrade schools are frequently very impoverished. They may lack the most basic amenities, including seats and desks, or a school building itself. Where instructional materials are available, these may be irrelevant as they are often biased towards urban settings and based on a graded model (UNESCO/APEID, 1989; Little, 1995; Carron and Chau, 1996; Aikman and Pridmore, 2001; Hargreaves *et al.*, 2001). It is probable that such impoverished school conditions reduce the learning opportunities available in these settings. Where multigrade teachers have more favourable material conditions, there is evidence that this can lead to an improvement for pupils in cognitive attainment in comparison to other multigrade and monograde school settings (Lungwangwa, 1989; Psacharopoulos *et al.*, 1993; Nielsen *et al.*, 1993; McEwan, 1998; Kotze, 2000).

Planning

Emphasis is placed on lesson planning in the literature because the multigrade teacher needs to think carefully about how she will manage instruction for the different grade level groups in her class. Teacher education materials frequently propose quite complex planning formats that involve the teacher in mapping her movements during the lesson, and deciding whether she will be interacting with the whole class, a small group, or individuals (Thomas and Shaw, 1993; Commonwealth Secretariat, 1997; Miller, 1999b). Miller (1999b) points out that developing a schedule is a very personal process and will differ from context to context. Careful planning ensures that 'dead time' is minimised in the multigrade classroom and meaningful instructional time for different learner needs is maximised.

There is a fairly large body of empirical work, collected through interviews conducted in a range of contexts, which shows that in practice teachers find planning and preparation for multigrade classes more difficult and time consuming than planning and preparation for monograde classes (Knight, 1938; Bennett *et al.*, 1983; Veenman *et al.*, 1985; Pratt and Treacy, 1986; Brown and Martin, 1989; Mason and Burns, 1996; Berry and Little, this edition). This is mainly because the graded structure of school curricula means that multigrade teachers have double, triple, or quadruple the planning task of their monograde counterparts. It is not clear what this planning load means for pupil learning, although a consistent thread running through the empirical literature is that the extra planning demands tend to demoralise the multigrade teacher. This may lead to teacher demotivation and have a negative effect on pupil learning.

Assessment

Multigrade classes do not lend themselves to traditional models of graded assessment, based on summative measures of curriculum coverage and tied to particular grade level content. Because the multigrade class contains more than one grade level of pupil this type of assessment is not only time-consuming for the teacher to administer, but also inappropriate. Hargreaves (2001) has written the most developed theoretical paper on assessment in multigrade classes to date. She suggests that 'assessment for learning' is a more appropriate model of assessment in the multigrade classroom. This is assessment 'whose primary purpose is to improve learning rather than to certify and select pupils or make schools more accountable.' She goes on to describe some of the strategies that encourage assessment for learning. These include giving pupils more responsibility for their own learning, using the children as an assessment resource, and setting learning tasks that have built-in assessment potential. These strategies have equal value in the monograde classroom.

The subject of assessment in the multigrade classroom has attracted little empirical attention, but what there is indicates that multigrade teachers find the task of assessing the level of their pupils a difficult one. In one study of multigrade teaching in England, for example, it was concluded that teachers in monograde classes were better able to pitch instruction to the level of their pupils than multigrade teachers (HMI, 1978). A number of studies have also shown that multigrade teachers find it more difficult to give individual attention to their pupils than monograde pupils because of the press to manage two or three grades (Mason and Burns, 1997). One consequence of this decrease in individual attention may be that opportunities for teacher assessment of pupil progress may be more limited in the multigrade classroom. This may explain why multigrade innovation frequently involves the development of self-study materials, which the teacher periodically corrects before the pupil moves on to the next level (Schiefelbein, 1991; Rishi Valley Education Centre, 2000; Kotze, 2000).

Grouping for instruction

Multigrade classes contain two or more grade-level groups, and consequently delivering a grade-based curriculum is more complicated than it is in a single-grade class. Most of the teacher development literature proposes that the multigrade teachers use a variety of different grouping arrangements in order to maximise instructional opportunities for their pupils. Both cross-grade and within-grade grouping is advocated and three possibilities are usually identified. First, whole-class teaching is suggested for subject content that is relatively undifferentiated, such as music and Physical Education (Collingwood, 1991; Commonwealth Secretariat, 1997; Miller, 1999c). It is also recommended that a whole-class introductory stage should sometimes precede work pitched at each grade level in the class. Second, small groups are recommended, both for setting different work to the various grade levels in the class, and also for introducing cross-grade ability groups in, for example, reading and maths (Birch and Lally, 1995; Miller, 1999c; Commonwealth Secretariat, 1997; Thomas and Shaw, 1992.) Third, pair work is frequently promoted as an effective way of maximising the teacher's time. In particular, peer instruction is proposed, with older or more advanced children tutoring a counterpart (Rowley and Nielsen, 1997; Miller, 1999d; Thomas and Shaw, 1992).

Existing observational research almost invariably reports that multigrade teachers tend to teach grade by grade. They deliver instruction to one grade while the other grade(s) is engaged in seatwork. Then, they switch attention to the other grade when they have finished. This applies in a variety of contexts, including Australia (Pratt and Treacy, 1986), Holland (Veenman *et al.*, 1985; Veenam *et al.*, 1987), USA (Mason and Good, 1996). Veenman (1995: 370) summarises this research as follows:

> Studies ... on the instructional processes in multigrade classes suggest that the most popular method is to teach a lesson to one group while the other grade works on follow-up activities to previous instruction (individual seatwork). The teachers' time is usually divided between two or more groups, instructed separately.

What this also means is that pupils in multigrade classes spend more time working individually than pupils in monograde classes, and are less likely to receive direct instruction from the teacher. Veenman (1995) has hypo-thesised that this heavy reliance on individualised instruction in the multigrade classroom reduces their effectiveness.

Pupil independence and interdependence

Dodendorf (1983) identified pupil independence and interdependence as positive characteristics of the multigrade classroom, based on her ethnographic study conducted in a rural two-room school in America. Independence refers to pupils taking control of their own learning. Pupils in her study had specific timelines and assignments to meet, and passed out corrected notebooks without teacher prompting. Interdependence refers to mutual pupil support. In her study, younger pupils often approached older children for help, and mixing of grades and ages was common. Miller (1991) concludes from a review of this and other literature from the USA that successful multigrade classrooms are characterised by teaching that maximises opportunities for peer instruction and self-directed learning. Both of these features are repeatedly referred to in the wider literature (Veenman, 1995; Rowley and Nielsen, 1997).

Pupils in multigrade classes have to operate more autonomously because they spend much time working without the teacher. What little evidence there is suggests that this does not necessarily lead to a reduction of 'time on task' in the multigrade classroom (Veenman *et al.*, 1985; Veenman *et al.*, 1987). In terms of interdependence, Mason and Good (1996) found that pupils in multigrade classes in the USA engaged in less co-operative work than pupils in monograde classes. They hypothesise that this is because of the 'press (in multigrade classes) to provide two presentations, to monitor two groups, and to adapt instruction to meet individual needs'. In the context of Belize, Central America, Nielsen *et al.* (1993) found that more effective multigrade teachers made use of peer instruction and collaborative groupwork. The limited use of co-operative groupwork in some multigrade classrooms has also been put forward as a reason why multigrade pupils do not perform better on tests of cognitive ability (Veenman, 1995).

Summary

The picture that emerges from the theoretical literature is a conceptualisation of the multigrade classroom as a potential site for innovative instruction. This includes the use of a wider variety of grouping patterns compared to the traditional monograde classroom, and a greater emphasis on the learning needs of individual pupils. In particular, the positive benefits of collaboration and co-operation in the multigrade classroom are emphasised. However, the available empirical literature tells a different story. Multigrade teachers are likely to teach their classes as if they were several mini monograde classes, leading to heavy demands on the teacher's classroom organisational skills. Furthermore, there is a decrease in the amount of direct instruction they can give to their pupils. This latter research evidence is almost exclusively drawn from developed country contexts, in particular from the USA, Australia, Holland, and England. In developing country contexts, there is evidence of an impoverished physical environment, but very little is known about how multigrade teaching compares to monograde teaching. The present study attempts to partially fill this gap.

RESEARCH APPROACH AND METHODS

This small-scale qualitative study seeks to compare instruction in multigrade and monograde classrooms in the Turks and Caicos Islands. The underlying hypothesis is that multigrade teachers, because of the way in which their classrooms are organised, are likely to be sensitive to differences in pupils' levels of attainment. This awareness will filter through to the way in which they plan and deliver instruction. Monograde teachers, by contrast, will be more likely to treat their class as one homogenous group and build in less differentiation. The hypothesis has been influenced by previous research in the Caribbean showing that monograde primary school teachers tend to teach to the high attainers in the class and make little use of paired work, peer tutoring, or co-operative learning (Kutnick *et al.*, 1997).

In the study, a combination of classroom observation and interview has been used in order to address the following two research questions:

- What differences are there between multigrade and monograde teachers in the way they organise, plan for, and teach their classes?
- How are these differences likely to impact on learning opportunities for pupils?

The fieldwork that forms the basis for the study was conducted over a two-week period in February 2002.

Sampling

There were two levels of sampling: the school level and the classroom level. In the first instance, purposive sampling was employed in order to identify five schools as sites for the research. Two of these were multigrade schools and three were monograde schools. Some basic information regarding the schools in the final sample is shown in Table 2.2 below:

Table 2.2 *Sample of schools in the study*

School	School type	No. pupils	No. teachers	Teacher-Pupil Ratio	Location
School A	Monograde	127	8	1/16	North Caicos
School B	Monograde	218	15	1/15	Grand Turk
School C	Monograde	287	14	1/21	Grand Turk
School D	Multigrade	55	4	1/14	North Caicos
School E	Multigrade	48	3	1/16	Middle Caicos

This sample represents half of the total number of state primary schools. The two schools on North Caicos were selected because they are similar with respect to the socio-cultural background of their students and their level of physical and human resourcing. The multigrade school has two grades per class. The schools on Grand Turk are fairly typical of larger schools serving more urban communities. The Middle Caicos school is a small multigrade school on an outlying island, with three grades in each of the classes in Grades 1–6.

The sample of teachers and classes was selected after discussion with the headteacher of each school. The main criteria used were that at least half of the classes observed should be in the core subjects of language and mathematics, teachers should be Turks and Caicos Islanders wherever possible, and the observations should focus on classes in Grades 1–6. The kindergarten classes were excluded from the study because they follow a different curriculum from the rest of the school. Grade 6 classes were actually sampled as little as possible because teachers were already focusing on the end-of-school leaving examination. The number of multigrade and monograde classes observed is shown in Table 2. 3 below:

Table 2.3 Number of classes observed by subject

Subjects	Monograde	Multigrade	Totals
Language arts	5	5	10
Mathematics	5	3	8
Science	2	1	3
Social studies	0	1	1
Totals	12	10	22

In the monograde classes, a total of 11 teachers were observed and interviewed (one teacher was observed twice). All of these teachers were female, and eight were trained teachers. The average length of teaching experience was 20 years, with a low of 3 years and a high of 30 years. In the multigrade classes, a total of 5 teachers were observed and interviewed; 4 of these teachers were female and all but one was trained. The average length of experience in the multigrade schools was 11 years, with a low of 8 years and a high of 13 years.

Data collection

Data were collected for the study through classroom observations, interviews and field notes. Lessons were observed in their entirety (most lessons are 45 minutes in length) and I took detailed notes on the activities of the teacher, together with an indication of the timings of different stages of the lesson. I also included a description of the kinds of activities in which the students were engaged, and the grouping patterns in which they were involved.

After the lesson was over, I usually interviewed the teacher immediately. The interviews lasted approximately 20 minutes and were taped. The purpose of the interview was twofold. First of all, I wanted to give the teachers an opportunity to cast light on the lesson that had just been taught and assess its typicality. Secondly, I wished to probe in depth aspects of the teacher's practice as they related to the research questions. After some reflection on the lesson itself, the interviews were generally structured around the following seven themes:

- Planning, resources and assessment
- Discipline issues
- Views on collaborative work
- Working with the range of pupil ability and interest
- Role of the learner in learning process
- Teacher's perceived relationship with the children
- Views on multigrade and monograde classes.

In addition, I took field notes and photographs focusing on the general school and classroom environment. I wrote up all the notes from the lessons within two days of conducting the observations. The taped interviews were also transcribed during the period of fieldwork. This was to ensure that the flavour of the observations and interviews was captured at the time.

Data analysis and presentation

The categories that emerged from the review of the literature were used in order to make sense of the data obtained from both the observations and the interviews. These categories are as follows:
- Classroom organisation
- Lesson planning
- Assessment
- Grouping for instruction
- Pupil dependence and interdependence.

The data were subsequently analysed in order to see to what extent they illuminated the different categories. Where possible, different types of data were drawn on as sources of evidence related to each area of interest. For example, teachers' views on how they worked with pupils across the range of ability could be related to classroom observations around grouping and pupil co-operation. The results of the analysis are presented in relation to each of the categories

DIFFERENCES IN PEDAGOGY

This section presents the findings in relation to the first research question:

- What differences are there between multigrade and monograde teachers in the way they organise, plan for, and teach their classes?

Classroom organisation

As far as classoom organisation is concerned, the multigrade and monograde classrooms are similar in terms of the number of pupils and the general seating arrangement, with pupils in rows facing the blackboard (with one multigrade exception). There is also no evidence that multigrade teachers operate in a particularly resource-poor environment in the Turks and Caicos Islands. This is in contrast to studies conducted in other developing country contexts. However, while there are similarities, one key difference is in the delineation of different grade levels in the seating arrangement in multigrade classes. In all the classes observed, each grade level in the class is roughly seated together and is readily identifiable by the teacher as constituting a particular grade. This contrasts with the generally mixed-ability seating arrangements in the monograde classrooms. A second difference is that the multigrade classes are more likely to have self-access materials available (four out of five multigrade classrooms had self-access materials, compared to six out of eleven monograde classrooms). The higher prevalence of self-access materials in the multigrade classrooms suggests that independent work is more likely to be promoted in these settings.

Planning

When planning, both multigrade and monograde teachers use the curriculum guides and textbooks that are provided by the ministry. These materials follow a graded structure. The difference is that all the multigrade teachers have to produce separate plans for all the grade levels that they teach. This contrasts with monograde teachers, who only plan for one grade level. Multigrade teachers generally regard this as an onerous task. One multigrade teacher comments that she 'would prefer to teach a monograde class with fifty pupils in it'. This is because of the requirement to produce separate lessons and the work that this creates. This attitude to planning echoes previous research on teacher attitudes towards multigrade teaching. On the plus side, however, producing plans for the different grade levels does seem to force multigrade teachers to think about the different ability levels in the class, at least in relation to the grade groupings. All the multigrade teachers in the sample refer to the issue of differentiation, while only two monograde teachers comment on this aspect of their practice. One multigrade teacher, for example, talks about the importance of planning lessons around the interests of pupils and tying the work to the local community:

> I just make up activities that will get their attention.. I think about things around them and the community here. It's such a closed community there are many things they haven't heard of. In planning any lesson I will try to broaden their knowledge and give them things that would keep their attention.

Assessment

Not surprisingly, the approach to assessment in both multigrade and monograde classes is underpinned by a graded paradigm. The main focus is on summative assessment of grade level material. Multigrade teachers therefore have to write more than one grade level test at the end of term, and this adds to their workload. Multigrade teachers appear to be more likely to consider individual pupil progress when planning and implementing their assessment activities (four out of five multigrade teachers mention individual difference in their interviews, compared to three out of eleven monograde teachers). For example, one of the multigrade teachers in the sample speaks of working with pupils independently in order to assess their strengths and weaknesses and then help them according to their level. She does not think that this would be possible in a monograde class unless she grouped them in some way and then worked with a group. She comments that one-to-one attention may be one reason why pupils in multigrade classes do better than pupils in monograde classes.

Grouping for instruction

In terms of grouping for instruction, the monograde classes generally begin with a whole class introduction followed by independent seatwork. There is no evidence from the classroom observations that monograde pupils work together in pairs or in small groups. Monograde teachers tend to like to ensure that pupils work alone and in silence during seatwork. By contrast, pupils in multigrade classes more frequently work in groups. Of the ten multigrade classes observed, six have at least two groups working independently for most of the lesson. This independent groupwork occurs when the teacher is giving direct instruction to one grade level group. While this is happening, the other grade(s) work on their own with work that the teacher has pre-prepared. This grade-by-grade approach to instruction is also found in multigrade classroom environments in other parts of the world. The majority of multigrade teachers in the sample (three out of five) believe that these grouping arrangements advantage their pupils in comparison to those in monograde class. This is because their pupils get exposure to work at different grade levels, which can both reinforce and extend their learning opportunities.

Independence and interdependence

With respect to working independently, a large amount of individual seatwork was observed in monograde classes, but this is very much directed by the teacher. Pupils are expected to work through exercises in the textbook and then to have them corrected before moving on to the next set of exercises. There is very little evidence of pupil autonomy. By contrast, in the multigrade classrooms there is greater evidence of pupils engaging in independent work. In part, this may be because the teacher cannot work with all the grades at once. For example, in a language arts lesson with Grades 4, 5 and 6, pupils in Grade 5 were seen going to get dictionaries to assist them with their reading comprehension without any direction from the teacher. In interviews, the multigrade teachers mention several areas in which they like to see pupils being more independent, including doing extra work at home, asking questions in class, and using self-access materials.

Pupil *interdependence* is extremely uncommon in monograde classrooms in our sample. In two classes, teachers actually direct pupils not to share when doing their work as 'this is cheating'. By contrast, when interviewed, monograde teachers tend to talk positively about the potential benefits of collaborative learning. Most mention the value of peer teaching for both maths and reading lessons. One of the teachers however, gives an indication of why so little collaborative work may have been observed in the monograde classes:

> Socially we would develop a whole lot better with that (collaboration). For now the classroom is set up as teacher centered here. If the programme is set up for child centeredness where you move at the pace of the children and around the needs of the children, that can work. But the timetable and the setting where everyone has to be doing the same thing at the same time. It works well in some instances, for example project work, but as an ongoing thing it doesn't work in this setting.

In all the multigrade classes where two or more groups work independently of each other, there is at least some interaction between pupils. This is observed to occur within the grade level group that is not receiving direct instruction from the teacher. The nature of the observational data collected means that it is not possible to be certain if this interaction is task related or not. However, judging by the teacher's response, the pupils who are working in their grade levels groups are normally engaged with classwork. When interviewed, all the multigrade teachers mention the importance of the judicious use of collaborative work in their classes, and three teachers actually identify pupil interaction as something that is engendered by the multigrade classroom.

LEARNING OPPORTUNITIES FOR ALL?

The second research question asks what impact the differences in pedagogy might have on learning opportunities for pupils in multigrade and monograde classes. This question cannot be tested empirically, but the above analysis suggests five ways in which learning opportunities may differ in the two types of classroom and how this might impact on the progress of low-, medium-, and high-attaining pupils.

Reduced direct instruction

Pupils in multigrade classes are exposed to less direct instruction from the teacher than pupils in monograde classes. In subjects where grade-level instruction is common (such as language arts and mathematics) multigrade pupils may receive as little as half the direct instruction as their monograde peers. However, since monograde teachers spend a lot of time delivering grade-level content to the middle and higher attainers in the class, the impact of this reduction in instructional time may not actually be detrimental to the progress of pupils at the lower levels of attainment. Even for those pupils achieving at higher levels, other features of the multigrade classroom may to some extent offset this reduction in direct instruction as we will see below.

Access to the curriculum

A low-attaining pupil in the higher grade of a multigrade classroom has incidental exposure to the curriculum for the lower year group, both during whole class instruction and when working in groups. This could lead to the reinforcement of concepts that have been poorly understood in earlier grades. Low attainers in monograde classes rarely get a chance to revisit earlier grade level material. Similarly, high attainers in the lower grade level have some exposure to the work of upper grade level(s). As a result, they are stretched in ways that do not happen in the monograde classroom where there is a focus on the material for one grade level.

Learning to learn

Independent work is positively encouraged in the multigrade setting. Where reference materials are available, this is likely to help the pupils to develop their learning-to-learn skills. There was evidence of this in the multigrade class where pupils were observed accessing and using dictionaries. By contrast, pupils in monograde classes mainly spend their time either receiving direct instruction from the teacher or engaging in seatwork. In the latter, they are normally expected to work as if they are under test conditions. Monograde pupils were rarely observed accessing self-study materials, and the materials were less likely to be available anyway.

Effects of peer instruction

This usually occurs informally when multigrade pupils are working in a grade level group that is not being directly instructed by the teacher. Their learning is therefore more likely to be 'scaffolded' (in a Vygotskean sense) by their peers. This increase in pupil interaction is likely to maximise learning opportunities for pupils of all levels of attainment (Veenman, 1995; Miller, 1999c; Colbert, 2002). By contrast, in monograde classes pupils almost invariably work either as a whole class or individually. They get almost no opportunities to interact with their peers without the presence of the teacher and so are exposed to only one source of instructional input and support.

Impact of small group instruction

Teachers in multigrade classes are much more likely to engage with pupils intensively in small groups. By contrast, monograde teachers either engage with pupils as a whole class or, more infrequently, as individuals. Small group tuition in the multigrade class possibly gives pupils more opportunities to ask for clarification from the teacher if they do not understand. This may be of particular help to the low-achieving pupil who is not confident to ask questions in front of the whole class. This increase in small group instruction also potentially offsets the reduction in direct instruction that has already been identified as a feature of the multigrade classroom.

CONCLUDING COMMENTS

The first conclusion that can be drawn from this study is that multigrade practice has the potential to inform and enrich monograde practice. Many of the teaching approaches employed by the multigrade teachers in this study are transferable to the monograde classroom with little or no modification. Policy makers in TCI have traditionally seen multigrade classrooms as a temporary aberration, waiting to be consolidated into single grade level groups as soon as population sizes were sufficient to employ one teacher per grade level. There is a need to examine these perceptions carefully in the light of the results obtained here. One strategy would be to undertake further research that examines practice in multigrade and monograde classrooms.

This research may then help educators to develop a deeper understanding of approaches to differentiating instruction in different classroom contexts.

A second conclusion is that there is an urgent need for curriculum reconstruction that challenges the graded paradigm. One obstacle to a teaching approach that is more inclusive of pupil diversity is the graded curriculum and related graded resource materials. In the Turks and Caicos, these materials offer little scope for working with pupils at different levels of cognitive development. The curriculum therefore needs to be reconceptualised in order to facilitate differentiation of instruction. This would be of benefit to pupils in either type of classroom. Examples of curricula that might offer more scope for differentiation in the Caribbean context come from Belize and Jamaica (Berry, 2002). A recent example from a very different context, Vietnam, can be found on the multigrade research project website at http://www.ioe.ac.uk/multigrade (Vu *et al.*, 2002).

A third and final conclusion is that teachers in all primary classrooms would benefit from exposure to training and other forms of support in order to help them to innovate in their instructional approaches. While multigrade teaches do appear to use a wider variety of instructional strategies than monograde teachers, these strategies are often not well developed. For example, there are no instances of multigrade pupils engaging in structured groupwork or pairwork activities in the sample. Teachers should be more aware of the range of pupils' learning needs in their classrooms and the variety of teaching and learning strategies that are appropriate to meeting these needs. An appropriate training programme, such as that described by Berry (1998; 2002), could be developed on island and delivered in-service on an ongoing basis.

REFERENCES

Aikman, S. and Pridmore, P. (2001) Multigrade schools in 'remote' areas of Vietnam. *International Journal of Educational Development*, 21 (6), 521–536.

Bennett, N., O'Hare, E. and Lee, J. (1983) Mixed-age classes in primary schools: a survey of practice. *British Educational Research Journal*, 9 (1), 41–56.

Berry, C. (1998) Improving reading attainment in a small island state. *Reading*, 31(1), 25–28.

Berry, C. (2001) Achievement effects of multigrade and monograde schools in the Turks and Caicos Islands. *International Journal of Educational Development*, 21 (6), 537–552.

Berry, C. (2002) Multigrade teaching: implications for the continuing professional development of teachers in the Caribbean. In E. Thomas (ed.), *Teacher Education: Dilemmas and Prospects*. London: Kogan Page, 183–192.

Birch, I. and Lally, M. (1995) *Multigrade Teaching in Primary Schools*. Bangkok: Asia-Pacific Centre of Educational Innovation for Development.

Brown, K.G. and Martin, A.B. (1989) Student achievement in multigrade and single grade classes. *Education Canada,* 29 (2), 10–13.

Caribbean Development Bank (1997) *Appraisal Report on Further Education in the Turks and Caicos Islands* (AR 97/8 TC). Caribbean Development Bank.

Carron, G. and Chau, T.N. (1996) *The Quality of Primary Schools in Different Development Contexts*. Paris: UNESCO.

Colbert, V. (2002) Improving the access and quality of education for the rural poor: The case of the New School in Colombia. Paper delivered at the conference 'Education for All: Enhancing quality and ensuring excellence', Institute of Education, University of London, 22 November.

Collingwood, I. (1991) *Multiclass Teaching in Primary Schools: A handbook for teachers in the Pacific*. Apia, Western Samoa: UNESCO Office for the Pacific States.

Commonwealth Secretariat (1997) Teacher education modules for multi-grade teaching modules 1–9 (DRAFT). London: Commonwealth Secretariat.

Dodendorf, D.M. (1983) A unique rural school environment. *Psychology in the Schools,* 20 (1), 99–104.

Fulford, B., Been, G., Williams, D. and Jones, G. (1996). Report on a review of the PINSTEP project in the Turks and Caicos Islands, 17–21 June 1996. Barbados: Overseas Development Agency.

Hargreaves, E. (2001) Assessment for learning in the multigrade classroom. *International Journal of Educational Development,* 21(6), 553–560.

Hargreaves, E., Montero, C., Chau, N., Sibli, M. and Thanh, T. (2001) Multigrade Teaching in Peru, Sri Lanka and Vietnam: an overview. *International Journal of Educational Development,* 21 (6), 499–520.

Her Majesty's Inspectorate (HMI) (1978) *Primary Education in England*. London: Department of Education and Science.

Knight, E.E. (1938) A study of double grades in New Haven city schools. *Journal of Experimental Education,* 7 (1), 11–18

Kotze, H. (2000) Struggling no more. An evaluation of Molteno's multigrade foundation phase classroom model. Braamfontein, Johannesburg, South Africa: The Molteno Project.

Kutnick, P., Jules, V. and Layne, A. (1997). Gender and school achievement in the Caribbean (Serial No. 21). London: Department for International Development.

Little, A.W. (1995) *Multi-grade Teaching: A review of research and practice*. London: ODA.

Little, A.W. (2001) Multigrade teaching: towards an international research and policy agenda. *International Journal of Educational Development,* 21 (6), 481–498.

Little, A.W. and Berry, C. (2005) Mixed-age classes in inner-city London primary schools: an exploratory study. In A.W. Little (ed.) *Education for All and Muligrade Teaching: challenges and opportunities,* Amsterdam: Springer.

Lungwangwa, G. (1989) *Multi-grade Schools in Zambian Primary Education: A report on the pilot schools in Mkushi District*. Report number 47. Stockholm: SIDA Education Division.

Mason, D.A. and Burns, R.B. (1996) Teachers' views of combination classes. *Journal of Educational Research*, 89 (1), 36–45.

Mason, D.A. and Burns, R.B. (1997). Reassessing the effects of combination classes. *Educational Research and Evaluation*, 3 (1), 1–53.

Mason, D.A. and Good, T.L. (1996) Mathematics instruction in combination and single grade classes: an exploratory investigation. *Teachers College Record*, 98 (2), 236–265.

McEwan, P. (1998) The effectiveness of multigrade schools in Columbia. *International Journal of Educational Development* 18 (6), 435–452.

Miller, B.A. (1991) A review of the qualitative research on multigrade education. *Journal of Research in Rural Education*, 7 (2), 3–12.

Miller, B. (1999a) *The Multigrade Classroom: A resource for small, rural schools. Book 2*. Oregon: Northwest Regional Educational Laboratory.

Miller, B. (1999b) *The Multigrade Classroom: A resource for small, rural schools. Book 4*. Oregon: Northwest Regional Educational Laboratory.

Miller, B. (1999c) *The Multigrade Classroom: A resource for small, rural schools. Book 5*. Oregon: Northwest Regional Educational Laboratory.

Miller, B. (1999d) *The Multigrade Classroom: A resource for small, rural schools. Book 7*. Oregon: Northwest Regional Educational Laboratory.

Miller, E., Forde, G. and Smith, O. (1994) *A Review of Primary and Secondary School Performance in the Turks and Caicos Islands*. Jamaica: Millrowe Consultants.

Ministry of Education, Turks and Caicos Islands (MoE) (1999) *Five Year Education Development Plan 1999–2004*. Grand Turk: Ministry of Education.

Multigrade Research Project Website, http://www.ioe.ac.uk/multigrade (accessed 25 November 2002).

Nielsen, D.H., Gillett, E. and Thompson, E. (1993) *Multigrade Teaching in Belize: Current practice and its relation to student achievement*. Belize: Ministry of Education.

Pratt, C. and Treacy, K. (1986) *A Study of Student Grouping Practices in Early Childhood Classes in Australian Government PRIMARY schools* (Co-operative Research Series No. 9). Nedlands: Education Department of Western Australia.

Psacharopoulos, G., Rojas, C. and Velez, E. (1993) Achievement evaluation of Colombia's *Escuela Nueva*: is multigrade the answer? *Comparative Education Review*, 37 (3), 263–276.

Rishi Valley Education Centre (2000) *Report of Second National Workshop on Planning and Implementation of Multigrade Programmes*. Rishi Valley, Andhra Pradesh: Rishi Valley Education Centre, Krishamurti Foundation India.

Rowley, S.D. and Nielsen, H.D. (1997) School and classroom organisation in the periphery. The assets of multigrade teaching. In D.H. Nielsen and W.K. Cummings (eds) *Quality Education for All: Community oriented approach*, 183–212. New York and London: Garland Publishing Inc.

Schiefelbein, E. (1991) *In Search of the School of the XXI Century: Is the Colombian Escuela Nueva the right pathfinder?* Santiago, Chile: UNESCO Regional Office in Latin America and the Caribbean/UNICEF.

Thomas, C. and Shaw, C. (1992) *Issues in the Development of Multigrade Schools.* Washington, DC: World Bank Technical Paper 172.

UNESCO (2001) *A Handbook for Teachers of Multigrade Classes (Volume 1).* France: UNESCO.

UNESCO/APEID (1989) *Multigrade Teaching in Single-Teacher Primary Schools.* Bangkok: Asia and the Pacific Programme of Educational Innovation for Development.

Veenman, S. (1995) Cognitive and noncognitive effects of multigrade and multi-age classes: a best-evidence synthesis. *Review of Educational Research*, 65 (4), 319–381.

Veenman, S., Lem, P. and Winkelmolen, B. (1985) Active learning time in mixed age classes. *Educational Studies*, 11 (3), 171–180.

Veenman, S., Voeten, M. and Lem, P. (1987) Classroom time and achievement in mixed age classes. *Educational Studies*, 13 (1), 75–88.

Vu, T.S., Pridmore, P., Nga, B., My, D. and Kick, P. (2002) *Renovating the Teaching of Health in Multigrade Primary Schools: A teacher's guide to health in natural and social sciences (Grades 1, 2, 3) and Science (Grade 5).* Hanoi, Vietnam: British Council/National Institute of Educational Sciences.

World Education Forum (2000) *The Dakar Framework for Action.* Paris: UNESCO.

CHAPTER THREE

A MULTIGRADE APPROACH TO LITERACY IN THE AMAZON, PERU

School and community perspectives

PATRICIA AMES

INTRODUCTION

Multigrade schooling in Peru, as in other developing countries, is wide-spread and serves a large segment of the population. There are currently 23,419 multigrade schools in the country representing 73% of the total number of public primary schools. In rural areas, 9 of every 10 schools are multigrade and 70.6% of rural students attend them (Montero *et al.*, 2002).

Despite the number of multigrade schools no consistent pre- or in-service training is offered to teachers. Material conditions in which multigrade schools operate are usually poor, and there is a lack of support from central or regional offices for such schools. In addition, the rural context that characterises most multigrade schools is often neglected by policy makers, curriculum designers and even teachers.

This chapter is based in an ethnographic study of a rural multigrade school in the Peruvian Amazon. The case study allows us to uncover how, despite the lack of training, resources and support, teachers develop a range of strategies to cope with the multigrade classroom. In researching these strategies and comparing them with others found elsewhere it is possible to highlight the advantages and disadvantages of these strategies and the points that deserve further attention. One particularly important consideration is the need to incorporate children's social contexts, and particularly their ways of learning outside school, since some of these features can be especially useful for multigrade classrooms.

Because of the importance that literacy learning has for Peruvian rural population,[1] I choose to focus my attention in this area. The study draws on two theoretical perspectives which highlight the social nature of literacy and learning. On the one hand, I use the framework provided by the New Literacy Studies (NLS), which considers literacy as a social practice, implicated

A.W. Little (ed.), Education for All and Multigrade Teaching: challenges and opportunities, 47–66.

in power relations and embedded in specific cultural meanings and practices (Street, 1995; Barton, 1994; Barton and Hamilton, 1998; Bloch, 1993). On the other hand, I use socio-cultural theories of learning which emphasise the importance of meaning and social context and move from a traditional conception of learning focused mainly in coding and decoding skills to one that focuses mainly on the social nature of literacy learning and practices (Czerniewska, 1996; Stromquist, 1997; Crawford, 1995; Fosnot, 1996; Steffe and Gale, 1995). According to both perspectives, this study addresses not only the multigrade school, but also other domains in the life of rural children, such as home and community, in order to understand the complexities of literacy learning (and learning in general).

Both perspectives provide a useful framework to address the social context of students, and also to question the traditional graded division inside schools (the monograde model), which tends to be considered as the ideal or normal by most educational systems. Indeed, looking through the lens of these social and educational perspectives, it appears that a particular view of literacy involves particular teaching methods. These particularities apply not only to ways of teaching literacy, but also to the school's instructional organisation, an issue that is especially important in this study. Links can be established, for example, between a technical approach to literacy and the long-dominant focus on literacy in schooling based on skill dimensions of reading and writing. Educational perspectives (e.g. developmentalist, connectivist) that see literacy as a set of isolated skills that can be arranged into a skill hierarchy and therefore taught as a series of steps tie in well with a division of children by ages and grades in which different skills will be taught step by step.

NLS, meanwhile, represents new conceptions that see literacy not merely as a technical matter, but as a socially and ideologically embedded practice. This conception matches with a shift in educational perspectives towards a meaning-centred approach (e.g. emergent, constructivism, whole language approach, critical literacy) and a reflection on social and cultural practices in which literacy learning takes place.

These theoretical perspectives enable us to see multigrade schools in new ways. The shift towards meaning in teaching and learning literacy makes it possible to involve children of different ages and grades in shared activities. Both despite and because of their differences, children's social interaction offers a rich opportunity for learning experiences. Multigrade classrooms, which used to be considered a problem from the point of view of the monograde curriculum and instructional strategies, can be reconsidered as viable and enriching educational environments.

This potential shift is illustrated by this chapter. The chapter presents a brief overview of the Peruvian educational context, highlighting how recent changes in educational policy have opened up possibilities for multigrade teaching, while simultaneously posing several limitations. Then, the multigrade school is analysed, with particular reference to teachers' classroom management strategies, their conceptions about literacy learning and the advantages and disadvantages of each strategy used. The fourth part addresses the learning context outside the classroom to highlight features that can enhance the potential of multigrade classrooms. The final part presents some conclusions.

THE INSTITUTIONAL CONTEXT: TRANSITION AND CHANGE

In 1993, the General Assessment of Peruvian Education (MED, 1993) showed severe problems in the quality of education offered in schools. As a result, the Ministry of Education has introduced several changes in the school system since 1996 as part of a Special Programme to Improve the Educational Quality of Primary Education (MECEP). The main changes can be summarised as follows:

- a new pedagogical approach (NEP), strongly based in constructivism theories of learning, child-centred and active pedagogy
- a new curriculum programme, which moves from a single-grade curriculum programme to programmes by cycles, each cycle comprising two consecutive grades (1 and 2, 3 and 4, and 5 and 6)
- in-service training for primary teachers in the new pedagogical model
- the distribution of new books and educational materials.

These changes convey new concepts of learning and teaching, as well as new ways of organising teaching and curriculum. Although multigrade schools were not specifically considered in the design of the programme, it opens up several possibilities for them. The introduction of curricular programmes by cycle instead by grade could help curricular planning in multigrade classrooms, since teachers of two grades have to deal with only one curriculum programme when working with two grades of the same cycle.

Several features of the new pedagogical model are consistent with the multigrade classroom. First, the call for child-centred pedagogy facilitates the use of self-learning strategies, which can help the teacher to focus his or her attention on other groups or individuals. Second, the recognition of peers as resources of learning can promote peer-tutoring and group work, again liberating time for the teacher to focus on given groups or individuals whilst at the same time providing support for group work. Third, the use of active learning strategies promotes flexibility in the use of different activities, moving from mechanical and time-consuming activities such as dictation and copying. Fourth, there is a recognition of the importance of children's cultural and social context in the learning process, which allows the design of meaningful learning activities for children of diverse social and cultural backgrounds, as those found in rural areas.

The provision of educational materials can also provide useful resources for learning activities. They are of special importance when working with several grades and in schools previously deprived of educational aids. Finally, the provision of in-service teacher training allows teachers to update their knowledge of new pedagogical approaches and strategies.

In principle, then, the recent policy changes are consistent with the multigrade classroom. However, the implementation of the policy has posed several limitations. The most important is the lack of attention that the multigrade school itself receives. In-service training has been based on examples and strategies from the monograde classroom, with no reference to adaptations needed in the multigrade classroom. The same can be said of curriculum planning, where there is a lack of clear strategies to adapt the curriculum for more than one grade. Educational materials such as workbooks have been designed on a grade basis, and other types of materials which could be more useful for multigrade classroom, such as non-graded material, have not been considered in their design. The second limitation is the confusion that the teachers feel in a context of change, with new learning and teaching paradigms, terminology and methodological strategies. Many teachers consider the short training they have received as insufficient to enable them to manage all this new information and the new approach. In particular, multigrade teachers feel confused since no explicit guidance was given on adapting these proposals to multigrade classrooms. In this situation, many teachers return to the (traditional) pedagogical strategies they are more familiar with, or try to mix new and old strategies to face the multigrade classrooms while retaining the single-grade classroom as their main reference point.

THE SAN ANTONIO SCHOOL:
MULTIGRADE CLASSROOM MANAGEMENT STRATEGIES

The school of San Antonio is a three-teacher school providing the six years of primary education, with each teacher responsible for two grades. When a teacher is (not infrequently) absent a teacher may be responsible for three or four grades. Since the research was conducted over two consecutive school years, I had the opportunity to analyse the strategies of five teachers (three in the first year and two more in the second year, who came to replace two of the previous three).

An analysis of multigrade classroom management practices among these five teachers shows that two strategies (teaching separate grade groups and whole-class teaching) are predominant, although a third (a combination of both) is used by two teachers for some specific activities. These are presented in Figure 3.1. In the following sections, I will discuss the characteristics, strengths and constraints of each strategy and relate them to multigrade teaching methodologies developed in other contexts.

Figure 3.1 Multigrade classroom management strategies

1 Teaching the two grades as separate groups (differentiation of levels)	2 Whole-class teaching of the class as one grade group (no differentiation of levels)	3 Whole-class teaching first, then split into separate groups according to different levels

Teaching separate grades

The first strategy for managing multigrade classrooms treats each grade as a separate group; therefore each group has different activities. This strategy follows a monograde model and is most clearly used by Olga[2] (Grades 1 and 2).[3]

Conceptions about literacy and literacy levels among children influence this strategy, as the teacher herself recognises. For Olga, first graders must learn to write, whilst second graders already have some notions of this and can copy and write. She therefore feels forced to choose this strategy because of the students' different literacy levels.

A particular conception about literacy underlies this apparently forced choice. As literacy is seen as a set of hierarchical and graded skills, teaching must take into account the level of development of coding and decoding skills. Children who are learning to write do this through copying bits of written signs before proceeding to more complex activities, such as reading and writing texts. Children who already have some coding/decoding skills can copy longer passages and lesson contents and begin to read.

If literacy is understood as a communicative and social practice, however, children with different levels of coding and decoding skills could engage in joint activities, such as shared reading, producing written texts with the help of older children, etc. What seems inevitable to this teacher is only so because of her approach to literacy.

As a permanent way of managing multigrade classrooms, this strategy has limitations. The most obvious is that the teacher must divide her time and attention between two grades, so children receive less direct teaching and teacher support.

This situation becomes more problematic in cases, like Olga's, where there is no lesson plan outlining the time to be dedicated to each group. For example, the record for one day clearly shows an unequal distribution of time: of a total of three hours, 29 minutes were dedicated to common activities (worship, singing, roll call), while 33 minutes were dedicated to Grade 1, 51 to Grade 2 and 90 to Grade 3.[4] First graders, therefore, received the least direct attention that morning.

This situation would be less problematic if the children were engaged in some learning activities that did not require the teacher's attention. The first graders, however, frequently awaited for attention for between 30 minutes and an hour. They spent most of the time copying syllables and words, a mechanical, time-consuming activity that could last the whole morning.

It can be questioned whether children need direct teaching all the time and lose out if time is split between two groups. Good planning could allow the teacher to devise learning activities for each grade group and rotate among the groups to provide support. Similar amounts of time could be dedicated to each group, and time without direct teaching would be dedicated to learning activities that children could conduct on their own (see for example UNICEF/MOET, 1998). Self-learning is a strategy that has proven useful as a way of avoiding having children remain unattended and unengaged in activities; instead, they are engaged in learning without the teacher's direct supervision.[5] Another common strategy is to have some children act as monitors, directing the activity whilst the teacher is busy with another group[6] (UNICEF/MOET, 1998; Collingwood, 1991).

A second limitation of this strategy is that it neither takes advantage of the students' diversity nor recognises peers as resources for learning. Because the children are engaged in separate activities, they do not support each other, but concentrate on their own grade's task. As explained above, multigrade teaching strategies have used monitoring from older children to help younger ones. Another fruitful use of children's diversity is group work in which older or more skilled children provide support for younger ones. Olga, however, does not use any of these strategies; nor does she encourage the children to support one another. Nevertheless, the children do this on their own, seeking support from peers who are also friends, siblings or cousins.

Children help each other largely on the basis of their own learning strategies outside school (see below). Such support is made possible within the classroom because of the flexibility of seating arrangements. The students sit in rows undivided by grade and are free to choose their seats. They also can move freely around the classroom most of the time and seek help from older children. Some children also take initiatives to overcome grade divisions. One example is Vivian (Grade 1), who decided on her own to undertake second-grade activities of which she felt capable. The teacher was flexible about such decisions.

Whole-class teaching

The other four teachers mainly used the second strategy in their multigrade classrooms, treating both grades as one group and delivering the same activities to all, without differentiation. Grade groups working under this strategy are Grades 3 and 4 and Grades 5 and 6.

Literacy is again playing a role in this strategy. Once the children have some coding and decoding skills, teachers are not so worried about delivery of discrete skills by separating grades. However, teachers differ greatly in their reasons for following this strategy. Thus, Cesar, Penny and Maria explain their choice in that children 'already know how to write' and thus can engage in the same activity despite their grade, putting the emphasis again in the coding and decoding skills dimension. By contrast, Mario explains what he considers a central reason: that children with different skills and abilities can help each other when doing the same exercise despite their grade. He seemed to envisage a more social and communicative view of literacy, in which children with different levels of coding and decoding skills could engage in joint activities and learn from that exchange. This is further reinforced by using intensively mixed-grade working groups which allow more opportunities to interact as well as a wide range of activities and resources in the classroom. In this sense, Mario, as well as Maria, moves from traditional activities such as copying, dictation, drill and repetition, widely used by Penny and Cesar, to more active strategies, involving the participation of children, providing different and new tasks to accomplish, and trying to develop meaningful situations rather than mechanical exercises.

The option of treating both grade groups as one solves the problem of dividing time and attention between two groups, as all children received direct attention from the teacher almost all the time. It also saves time for the teachers, as they prepare only one lesson for the whole class. This way of managing the multigrade classroom is facilitated by the new curriculum structure, which groups two grades into one cycle and sets out a common group of competencies to be developed during a two-year cycle. If curriculum contents are not carefully planned, however, the risk is that the children will study similar contents for two consecutive years. This is likely because of the constant turnover of teachers in multigrade schools.

Whole-class teaching also addresses diversity in the classroom, making it an aid for teaching and learning. As noticed above, since children from different grades and abilities work together on the same topics and activities, they can support each other. This is all the more feasible when the seating pattern does not separate the children by grade, as was partly the case in Grades 5 and 6 and even more possible when children worked in groups, as in the Grade 3 and 4 classroom. Some teachers, such as Penny, Mario and Maria, recognise and encourage working groups as a useful strategy for encouraging children to support each other when doing a particular task.

In these arrangements, then, student diversity could enhance peer tutoring, either in same-grade or mixed-grade groups. The flexibility to allow children to talk and move around the classroom is also necessary for peer tutoring, especially when children are seated in rows. Although this flexibility is observed in some classrooms (Maria, Mario and Olga), in others children's movements and talking are more strictly controlled (Penny and Cesar), limiting their interaction and the possibility of receiving help from their classmates.

There are some disadvantages, however, when the whole-class teaching strategy is used most of the time. Collingwood (1991) points out that this approach is usually very teacher-centred. This is especially true in the case of Penny and Cesar, and less so in that of Maria and Mario, who combine teacher-centred approaches with group work. An additional disadvantage that Collingwood points out is that the entire lesson is aimed at the average child in the room. Differences of level (either across grades or within grades) are not addressed. Younger and/or lower-achieving children may fail to keep up with the work, whilst high achievers and/or older children may become bored if the activity is too easy for them. The same is true of the group-work strategy, as observation showed that some children fail to appropriately carry out the activity, but their particular needs were obscured by the performance of the group as a whole. This demonstrates the need for individual attention and work as a complementary strategy for group work.

As Collingwood acknowledges, however, whole-class teaching has an important place in multigrade classrooms and could work particularly well in some areas. He also points out some advantages of whole-class teaching. One, which I mentioned when addressing peer interaction, is that working together for part of the day can improve children's relationships with one other. Another is that the children benefit from an exchange of ideas, opinions and skills far broader than those in monograde classrooms, constituting an enriching experience for children at all levels.

Combining whole-class teaching with level differentiation

A third strategy for managing multigrade classrooms combines activities for both grades as one group that is later divided to develop specific activities at different levels of complexity according to grade or level. This strategy is not predominant among any of San Antonio's teachers, but is sometimes used by Mario and Maria, especially when they develop the same topic for the whole group but also set extension activities, using graded workbooks for maths and language or assigning mathematics exercises with different levels of complexity according to grade. These two teachers are also the ones whose major concern is the development of thinking and learning in their students. To achieve that, they are in search of meaningful activities, in which the exchange between children of different levels of coding and decoding skills is not necessarily a problem but a possibility, as explained in the previous section.

This strategy allows direct teaching of both grade groups and does not split the teacher's time or attention as the first strategy does. Because this strategy acknowledges different grade levels among children, it also allows the development of specific activities according to grade, in contrast with the second strategy. Differentiation of levels, however, is still tied to grade differences. There may also be level differentiation among children within the same grade, which is not recognised if specific activities are designed only on the basis of grade. To overcome this problem, Collingwood (1991) suggests the use of different criteria creating small groups according to different subjects and activities: mixed-ability groups, same-ability groups, same-grade groups and social groups (by compatibility). These different groupings can be used not only to allow differentiated activities according to level (either within or across grades), but also to engage children in activities across levels.

What strategy works?

A brief summary of the three strategies, above, illustrates how a view of literacy as a set of graded skills forms the basis of the decision to split grades in the first- and second-grade classroom. However, the option does not seem to benefit Grade 1 children very much,[7] as they receive less attention and more mechanical tasks, making their literacy learning rather tortuous, mechanical and almost empty of clear purpose beyond the mastery of coding and decoding skills.

The whole-class strategy seems to be more effective in the cases observed, as the teacher's time and support are not divided. It also allows for a more flexible approach to literacy learning, and gives way, at least in some cases, to the development of a more social and communicative view of literacy. It engages children from different grades in common activities and expands their opportunities to experience peer tutoring and social interaction as part of their literacy learning process, especially with the use of working groups as part of whole-class teaching. However, mechanical tasks such as copying and drill are also present when using this strategy as well as a technical view of literacy.

A combined strategy, still scarcely developed, offers the benefits of whole-class teaching, but also allows teachers to address the particular needs of each grade group. It introduces the possibility of flexibility and shift between strategies and thus a more dynamic classroom environment.

Looking at these classrooms it is interesting to notice that the strategies observed are in fact in use in other multigrade schools, although not always with the same results. The teaching of separate grades, for example, is a central feature of the Multigrade Teaching Project of UNICEF/MOET in Vietnam (see Son and Pridmore this volume), whilst the whole-class approach is more common in projects such as *Cursos Comunitarios* in Mexico (Fuenlabrada *et al.*, 1996). A combination of whole-class teaching and differentiation by levels has been recommended by Collingwood (1991) and Cash (2000) as part of multigrade strategies and is also being explored by the UNICEF/MOET project in Vietnam (see Son *et al.*, 2002; Son and Pridmore this volume). These projects also use complementary strategies such as monitors, careful planning of time spent with each grade and self-learning strategies, among others, which enhance the advantages of a particular strategy or respond to the possible limitations it has.

It is remarkable then, that the Peruvian teachers observed in this study had not been trained in multigrade methodology. They had to rely on their initiative and creativity to manage multigrade classrooms. While this resulted in approaches similar to those taken by teachers elsewhere, they could gain and improve their teaching if they could draw on knowledge of similar situations and alternative strategies.

The relative flexibility introduced by the NEP helps teachers try new strategies. The freedom to develop more suitable strategies is fruitful, as it enables teachers to explore and improve their own teaching. The complete lack of support or guidance, however, makes the task overwhelming for some. This suggests that while teachers do not need a step-by-step recipe, they do need orientation and opportunities to reflect upon what learning entails and the possibilities offered by multigrade classrooms.

Literature on multigrade teaching usually does not pinpoint a particular strategy as the most effective way of managing the multigrade classroom. Instead, it calls for flexibility, combining different strategies according to the characteristics of the topic, subject or activity (Commonwealth Secretariat, 1997; Collingwood, 1991; UNESCO, 2001). As has been shown, each strategy has advantages and disadvantages. These have been presented in a general way, but the nature of the activity or topic also poses further advantages or disadvantages. Certain strategies, such as work groups, may be useful at certain times, but individual learning needs also require attention, and group performance may conceal particular individual problems or achievements. Literacy learning also requires flexibility, because while children can engage in literacy activities beyond literacy levels, as individuals they approach literacy in different ways. Different children also master particular literacy skills at different paces, even in the same grade.

San Antonio's teachers tend to follow a single methodology instead of shifting from one strategy to another depending on the subject. Their approach to the multigrade classroom could benefit from a more flexible perspective. Previous conceptions about teaching as instructional delivery and literacy as a rigid set of coding and decoding skills, however, still prevent some teachers from exploring the possibilities. Another restriction is the scarce use of children's background in mixed-age groups outside the classroom, a central feature in their learning at home and community, which is addressed below.

LEARNING OUTSIDE THE SCHOOL

Guided participation and mixed-age groups

Children in San Antonio perform various tasks in the home and community to support domestic and productive work. Their work contributes not only to family survival, but to the mastery of domestic, agricultural or fishing skills in preparation for adulthood. In this sense, the life of San Antonio's children is similar to that of many other children in rural communities who are involved in productive and domestic activities from a very early age. These activities and the way children learn to do them indicates four central characteristics of learning at home: the importance of observation, practice as a mean of developing skills, the development of a sense of autonomy and responsibility and the multi-age nature of the learning process.

Indeed, children learn at home mainly through their direct participation and observation of the activities carried out by adults and older children, who support them in the process. Children receive progressively more complex tasks, according to their capacity, thus developing their skills until they can carry out the activity independently. A sense of responsibility for the task undertaken, even simple ones, is always fostered by caretakers, as well as the sense of autonomy to carry it out. In the context of home and community then, children learn in a supportive and purposeful context and in constant interaction with others. This last feature is of special interest for the discussion of multigrade schooling, since this interaction with others occurs in what I call mixed-age groups, composed sometimes of adults and children and sometimes of older and younger children.

Thus, an important characteristic of the home as a learning environment is its multi-age nature. This is observable not only inside homes, but also in the groups that children establish outside the home as part of their daily activities. Many of these activities are carried out with the company of other children, a feature of particular interest for this study. Sibling and peer groups have been considered by other studies (Ortiz and Yamamoto, 1996; Anderson, 1994) as an important socialising agency in rural communities. Children in San Antonio share their time with siblings, but also with other children who are relatives and/or neighbours. They spend several hours per day in groups in which ages ranged from 3 to 12 years, since older children are usually accompanied by their younger siblings. Mixed-age groups, therefore, are part of the daily experience of children in San Antonio.

The relationships among children of a wide age range are usually very good. Older children are very patient with and affectionate towards younger ones, although they are also authoritative voices. They can give orders and instructions to younger children, who tend to be obedient. Play is a common and frequent activity among children, who do it not only at particular times, but also in the middle of their tasks. When they go fishing or carry water, because they go with other children, they take the opportunity to play a bit or perform the work as play. Although important, play is not the only activity in which mixed-age groups engage. Among siblings and relatives, caring for each other is a regular activity (e.g. dressing a little girl, bathing a little boy, feeding a younger sibling). Through play and care, children also learn from each other. While bathing at the river, for example, a 6-year-old girl caring for her 4-year-old sister may teach her to swim. Boys fishing in the lake teach each other what they know about fishing as they do so. While helping her mother with the cooking, an older child may show a younger one how to do some tasks. Children also enjoy teaching babies new words and identifying progress in their oral language development. Older children sometimes play school with younger ones and teach them as teachers. When doing homework, children are helped not only by their mothers, but also by older siblings to do it.

The children in San Antonio, then, have many experiences of playing, learning and working in multi-age groups. In relation either with adults or with other children, the multi-age nature of the interaction seems essential to the learning process. A kind of scaffolding strategy, in which the older person helps the child progressively master the activity, appears to be used not only by parents, but also by older children in multi-age groups. Children also learn how to interact with each other despite age differences and not only with children of the same age.

This feature is fundamental to the particular school context in which children are formally educated: the multigrade school. In the multigrade classroom, children of different ages and grades study together. Their previous experience in mixed-age groups could be a resource for teachers and teaching strategies for these classrooms as well as for the literacy learning process. However, observations of multigrade classes in San Antonio schools showed that teachers were not always prepared to take advantage of or even to recognise this resource.

Literacy outside the school: home and community practices

The difficulty teachers face in recognising the resources children bring to the classroom is particularly marked in relation to the literacy practices at home and in the community, which go unrecognised by most teachers. Indeed, the prevalence of a dominant discourse that had constructed the rural areas in developing countries as 'deprived of literacy' and rural people as mainly non-literate (Godenzzi *et al.*, 2000; Maddox, 2001) has had an impact on teachers' preconceptions about rural villagers, who are seen as offering limited support for children in their learning process.

A closer look into the daily life of the community revealed that literacy is used in a variety of ways and is related to different purposes. Looking at the written landscape, local organisations, religious events, access to and participation in health and education services and relationships with public institutions in general has shown a wide range of activities involving literacy. In the community, literacy is used intensively by local organisations in which villagers participate. Literacy plays a central role since these organisations have to deal with different kinds of documents related to the organisation of the community life. Literacy practices identified in the community show that they are strongly linked with the relationship that villagers maintain with external and public institutions, and in general with the Peruvian State. This is expressed not only at the collective level, through local organisations, but also when villagers approach public institutions individually. Written documents used in this relationship follow specific formats (official letters, health cards and charts, minutes books, identity paper applications, all with pre-designed formats) usually imposed by external institutions. Although external institutions impose a great part of this literacy, villagers appropriate it and use literacy for internal purposes, such as village organisation and accounting related to the communal labour force. In the community domain literacy is mainly used by adults (except in religious uses), particularly male adults at the collective level. Finally, literacy is considered a central tool for maintaining and improving one's status in relation not only to the state, its institutions and the market, but also with other social groups in the region, and in general to attain a position in the stratified social structure that characterises Peruvian society. Literacy, then, conveys multiple meanings for the rural villagers of San Antonio, not only at the local level but also in the context of the broader society to which they belong.

In the context of the home, literacy is also present in several ways. Close observation of nine households showed that literacy plays a role in organising domestic life, with the writing of shopping lists and short messages; in personal communication, such as letters to relatives outside the village and in affective relationships, through the use of love letters. Literacy serves recreational and informative purposes, and one can find the occasional reading of newspapers, magazines, school textbooks and the Bible, even when the distribution of the first two is confined to cities and bought by the villagers during their trips to the city. Despite the extended use of literacy at home, it appears to be mainly used by adults and youths. The occasions on which adults and children become involved together in a relationship with the written word in the home are usually related to school homework. In contrast with the ways of participation followed by children in other learning activities, doing homework seems to be shaped by school ways of organising instruction. When doing homework, mothers follow a traditional teacher–pupil pattern of interaction, use traditional teaching strategies such as copying and dictation, and emphasise the correctness of reading and writing. The formality and school features of doing the homework do not appear in spontaneous literacy events neither they do during the more informal learning at home related with domestic of productive tasks. It therefore seems that parents consider the literacy learning process to be more formal, separated from their daily uses of literacy and requiring the schooled way to teach it rather the kind of strategies used at home to learn other abilities. Teachers certainly encourage this point of view when asking parents to practise copying, dictation and multiplication with their children.

Both teachers and parents seem to ignore the fact that children are already involved in a relationship with the written word in which they try to find its purposes and meanings. Literacy for children is seen as strictly related to school and formal literacy learning. Children must learn literacy, but they are not expected to participate in literacy events at home beyond the school's formal requirements. Parents do not seem to consider involving children in less structured literacy events as part of the children's literacy learning.

Children working out a relationship with the written word

Nevertheless, children appear actively engaged in building an understanding of the written word beyond formal instruction. They try to deal with literacy in a more unstructured way, following their own interests and curiosity. This becomes clear in their relationship with written signs, when they use knowledge from their daily experiences to understand the forms and functions of written language. Through several exercises conducted with children, it was evident that they carefully observe and scrutinise the uses of literacy in the community and family life. Thus, when doing an exercise about the written signs in the village and stating the use of written signs in general, children emphasised the commercial use, as it is the most observed by them. When dealing with labels of cans and food products, children rely in the uses they see at home or in television advertisements to get clues before actually decoding written signs. Therefore, when approaching the written word, children draw from all their experiences with it, even if these experiences involved them indirectly. But they are also very keen to explore further uses of the written word and to create new literacy events. Some examples arose as part of our relationship: one was caused by the temporary presence of a typewriter in my home. During their frequent visits children decided to explore it and wrote their names, brief affectionate messages and songs they knew from the TV or the school. Another event was caused by me: I asked a group of children to write original stories on their own to check their writing skills. However, they became so enthusiastic with the task that they kept producing stories the following days and in further visits. In their stories, children used local characters (especially local animals), situations and scenarios of their daily life (the river, the forest), oral expressions and structure and the sense of humour so valued in their community for oral exchanges.

These and many other examples illustrate how children use what they know about literacy and language to cope with the written word. Both their formal learning and the informal ways in which they approach literacy become a resource upon which they build their literacy learning. Despite this ongoing learning process the resource is barely acknowledged by the teachers.

CONCLUSION

I started this chapter with a brief outline of the recent innovations in the Peruvian school system. I highlighted how, despite the positive features that have been opened for improving multigrade teaching, these changes have not considered explicitly the particularities and needs of multigrade classrooms. However, and despite the lack of training in multigrade methodology, teachers use various strategies to cope with the multigrade classrooms. In presenting and discussing each strategy it became evident that there are advantages and disadvantages in each case. Disadvantages are more acute when only one strategy is in use and when there is a lack of flexibility to mix strategies. In the same sense, different pedagogic styles might enhance or limit the potential of each strategy. Furthermore, positive features of multigrade classrooms seem to decay because insufficient attention is paid to children's context and experiences, which can constitute a resource upon which new learning can be developed.

Teachers fail to take advantage of children's experiences that can be particularly useful for multigrade classrooms. One of the most important of these features is the rich experience of children in multi-age groups in other learning situations outside the school. Thus, in the context of home and community, children are used to playing, learning and working with other adults and children of different ages. The multi-age character of this interaction is what makes learning possible in such a context. The multigrade school and teachers might take advantage of this if more attention was given to children's lives outside the school walls. The same happens with literacy learning, since the school sees it as a formalised set of exercises removed from their context of use and thus rely heavily on copying, drill and repetition. Moreover, teachers ask parents to develop this treatment of the written word at home, when doing the homework. Nevertheless, an examination of the home and community context shows that literacy is present in the daily life of children in a variety of ways that are not exploited by teachers. Literacy is used for a variety of purposes and conveys multiple social meanings for rural villagers and their children. Children are keen to find the very role that literacy plays in their social world with all the knowledge they can get from their daily life. They do not live in a world without letters. On the contrary, they live in a world where literacy is central to organising the household, communicating with others, expressing affection or getting information, organising community life through local organisations, establishing a relationship with public institutions and the state, and securing a position and identity in a given society.

Multigrade schools can benefit if more attention is paid to the ways teachers create alternatives to cope with the challenges to teach more than one grade. But teachers also need to recognise and dialogue with the local ways of learning and the local ways to use literacy. A social approach to literacy allows that bridge to be built. It shows that learning can and does happen in multi-age groups, that children can learn from each other and from others, and that they have local resources to approach literacy not only as a set of graded steps, but as a real communicative and social practice. If the school moves also in that direction and takes advantage of the social experience of children, learning in multigrade schools could be substantially improved. To achieve that, we have to move from labelling homes and social backgrounds as 'deficits', and start looking at how different cultural and social experiences can enrich rural children's learning in the context of a multigrade classroom.

NOTES

[1] The importance that rural villagers give to literacy (and to the school as the main place to acquire it) is related to historical, political and social aspects that I developed elsewhere (Ames, 2003, 2002).

[2] All personal names have been changed.

[3] Although this strategy is used by one of the five teachers at this school, it is widely used by teachers in Peru, as previous research in other schools has shown (see Ames, 1999, 2001).

[4] These activities add up to 3 hours and 25 minutes because part of the time (29 minutes) considered for Grades 1 and 2 overlapped as the teacher was supporting both grades by checking notebooks, making a clear distribution of time for each grade impossible.

[5] Self-learning has been developed especially as part of the *Escuela Nueva* programme in Colombia and adopted by several projects in Latin America (see Psacharopoulos *et al.*, 1992; Reimers, 1993; Ministerio de Educación de Guatemala, 1996; Subirats *et al.*, 1991).

[6] This strategy was observed in a one-teacher school in the area.

[7] Indeed, of the eight children in Grade 1 that year, only two were promoted to Grade 2 and only one of them was able to write and to read a bit.

REFERENCES

Ames, P. (1999) 'El poder en el aula: un estudio en escuelas rurales andinas'. In Tanaka, M. (ed.) *El poder visto desde abajo: educación, democracia y ciudadanía en espacios locales* (pp. 267–334) Lima: Instituto de Estudios Peruanos.

Ames, P. (2001) ¿*Libros para todos? Maestros y textos escolares en el Perú rural.* Lima: Consorcio de Investigaciones Económicas y Sociales Instituto de Estudios Peruanos.

Ames, P. (2002) *Para ser iguales, para ser distintos: Educación, escritura y poder en el Perú.* Lima: Instituto de Estudios Peruanos.

Ames, P. (2003) 'Multigrade Schools in Context: Literacy in the home, the community and the multigrade school.' PhD dissertation, University of London, December.

Anderson, J. (1994) *La socialización infantil en comunidades andinas y de migrantes urbanos en el Perú.* Documento de trabajo N°1. Proyecto de innovaciones pedagógicas no formales. Lima: Fundación Bernar Van Leer–Ministerio de Educación.

Barton, D. (1994) *Literacy: An introduction to the ecology of written language.* Oxford: Blackwell.

Barton, D. and Hamilton, M. (1998) *Local Literacies: Reading and writing in one community.* London: Routledge.

Bloch, M. (1993) 'The uses of schooling and literacy in a Zafimaniry village'. In B. Street (ed.) *Cross-cultural Approaches to Literacy* (pp. 87–109) Cambridge: Cambridge University Press.

Cash, T. (2000) 'Models of multigrade teaching'. Paper delivered at Symposium on Multigrade Teaching, Maharagama, Sri Lanka, 21 September.

Collingwood, I. (1991) *Multiclass Teaching in Primary Schools: A handbook for teachers in the Pacific*. Apia, Western Samoa: UNESCO Office for the Pacific States.

Commonwealth Secretariat (1997) *Teacher Education Modules for Multi-Grade Teaching*. London: Commonwealth Secretariat.

CONAFE (1996) *Educación Comunitaria Rural: Una experiencia mexicana*. Mexico DF: Consejo Nacional de Fomento Educativo.

Crawford, P. (1995) 'Early literacy: emerging perspectives'. *Journal of Research in Childhood Education*, 10 (1): 71–86.

Czerniewska, P. (1996) 'Learning to read and write in English'. In N. Mercer and J. Swann (eds.) *Learning English: Development and diversity* (pp. 76–106). London: Routledge and Open University Press.

Fosnot, C.T. (1996) 'Constructivism: a psychological theory of learning'. In C.T. Fosnot (ed.) *Constructivism: Theory, perspectives and practice* (pp. 8–33). New York: Teachers College Press, Columbia University.

Fuenlabrada, I., Taboada, E. and Rockwell, E. (1996) *Curriculum e investigación educativa. Una propuesta de innovación para el nivel básico/ Cursos Comunitarios: Una primaria alternativa para el medio rural*. Documento DIE 47, México: DIE.

Godenzzi, J., Flores, E. and Ramirez, E. (2000) 'Quiero tomar la palabra: Comunicación e integración de las niñas en la escuela, la familia y en la comunidad'. Paper presented to: II Conferencia Nacional de Educación de las niñas rurales, 28–29 de Setiembre, Lima.

Maddox, B. (2001) 'Literacy and the market: the economic uses of literacy among the peasantry in north-west Bangladesh'. In Street, B. (ed.) *Literacy and Development. Ethnographic perspectives* (pp. 137-151) London: Routledge.

Ministerio de Educación de Guatemala (1996) *La escuela rural guatemalteca en los albores del tercer milenio: Génesis de una Nueva Escuela Unitaria*. Memoria técnica de la experiencia piloto. Guatemala: Ministerio de Educación.

MED (Ministerio de Educación, Peru) (1993) *Diagnóstico general de la Educación*. Lima: MED, Banco Mundial, PNUD, GTZ, UNESCO-OREALC.

Montero, C., Ames, P., Cabrera, Z., León, E., Chirinos, A. and Fernández Dávila, M. (2002) *Propuesta Metodológica para escuelas unidocentes y/o con aulas multigrado*. Documento de trabajo No. 18. Lima: Ministerio de Educación.

Ortiz, A. and Yamamoto, J. (1996) *Un estudio sobre los grupos autónomos de niños a partir de un trabajo en Champacchocha, Andahuaylas*. Documento de trabajo. Proyecto de innovaciones pedagógicas no formales N°1. Lima: Fundación Bernar Van Leer – Ministerio de Educación.

Psacharopoulos, G., Rojas, C. and Velez, E. (1992) *Achievement Evaluation of Colombia's Escuela Nueva: Is multigrade the answer?* World Bank Working Paper 896, Washington, DC: World Bank.

Reimers, F. (1993) 'Promoting education for democracy in Latin America: innovations to provide quality basic education with equity' (unpublished paper). Boston: Harvard University.

Schiefelbein, E. (1993) *En busca de la escuela del siglo XXI: ¿Puede darnos la pista la escuela Nueva de Colombia?* Santiago: UNESCO/UNICEF.

Steffe, L. and Gale, J. (eds) (1995) *Constructivism in Education*. Hillsdale, NJ: Lawrence Erlbaum.

Street, B. (1993) *Cross-Cultural Approaches to Literacy*. Cambridge: Cambridge University Press.

Street, B. (1995) *Social Literacies: Critical approaches to literacy in ethnography and development*. New York: Longman.

Stromquist, N. (1997) *Literacy for Citizenship: Gender and grassroots in Brazil*. Albany, NY: State University of New York Press.

Subirats, J., Nogales, I. and Gottret, G. (1991) *Proyecto escuela multigrado. Evaluacion de su desarrollo en areas rurales de Bolivia*. La Paz: UNICEF-CEBIAE.

UNESCO (2001) *A Handbook for Teachers of Multi-Grade Classes*. Volumes 1 and 2. Paris: UNESCO.

UNICEF/Vietnam – Ministry of Education and Training (MOET) (1998) *Multigrade and Bilingual Education in Classes in Primary School in Vietnam*. Hanoi: MOET.

Vu, T.S., Pridmore, P., Nga, B., My, D. and Kick, P. (2002) *Renovating the teaching of health in multigrade primary schools. A teacher's guide to health in natural and social sciences*. Hanoi: British Council/National Institute of Educational Sciences.

CHAPTER FOUR

MULTIGRADE TEACHING IN LONDON, ENGLAND

CHRIS BERRY AND ANGELA W. LITTLE

INTRODUCTION

Multigrade teaching refers to settings where a single teacher has sole responsibility for two or more grades of students simultaneously. Multigrade may be contrasted with the more familiar monograde teaching, in which a single teacher teaches a single grade or class at any given time. Various terms are used in different countries to describe multigrade settings, e.g. multigrade, mixed-year, combination class, vertical grouping, family grouping, composite class, split class, double-graded class, unitary schools. We will use the term multigrade in this chapter, although 'mult-iage' or 'mixed-year' are the terms more usually employed in the UK literature.

In most countries the provision of learning opportunities via multigrade teaching is not a matter of pedagogic choice for teacher, parent or community. It is a necessity that arises in local contexts with particular demographic characteristics. These local contexts share a global significance in so far as the achievement of the global targets for Education for All will, in many countries, occur only through the provision of multigrade teaching. In these contexts the stark choice for households and communities is not whether children should attend a multigrade *or* a monograde school. It is between attending a multigrade school or no school at all. While compulsory education legislation in industrialised countries obviates this latter, extreme, choice, there are parallels that can be drawn between multigrade teaching contexts in industrialised and developing countries.

This chapter describes research we carried out into multigrade learning provision in schools in an inner city area of London. The study is located within the existing research literature on multigrade teaching in England and elsewhere. The study seeks to find out the extent of multigrade teaching in 'key stages' 1 and 2. It also explores teacher perceptions of the challenges, opportunities and pedagogical implications of this form of classroom organisation compared to single-age classes.

67

A.W. Little (ed.), Education for All and Multigrade Teaching: challenges and opportunities, 67–86.
© 2007 *Springer.*

MULTIGRADE TEACHING IN ENGLAND

In England, the most recent data from the Department of Education and Skills indicate that in 2000 25.4% of all classes in primary education were classified as 'mixed-year' and 25% of all students were studying in mixed-year classes (DFES, 2002).

Research into the extent and effects of multigraded classroom organisation has been undertaken in England in schools serving two rather different types of local context. The first is the rural sparsely populated community served by a school with low student enrolments, the 'small school' (Cornall, 1986; Galton and Patrick, 1990; Francis, 1992; Vulliamy and Webb, 1995; Hargreaves *et al.*, 1996; Hayes, 1999; OFSTED, 2000; Ireson and Hallam, 2001). These studies offer favourable conclusions about multigrade organisation, frequently connected to the 'family atmosphere' engendered by the small school environment. The second is the urban, densely populated, community served by a school, in which some, but probably not all classes are multigraded. This latter research literature is outlined below.

An important milestone in the development of attitudes towards multigrade classroom organisation in larger schools in England was the publication of a survey by Her Majesty's Inspectorate of Schools (HMI, 1978), *Primary Schools in England*. In their sample, about a quarter of children were in multigrade classes in schools whose enrolments would have permitted single-age year groups. Of these, about half consisted of classes containing two year groups of roughly equal numbers. HMI reported that not only was achievement lower in multigrade than in single-age classes, but also teachers were less able to appropriately match tasks to student abilities. This led to the recommendation that multigrade classes were something to be avoided if possible.

Other research published at about the same time (Galton and Simon, 1980) as part of an observational study found that students in 'double-grade' classes (i.e. classes containing two year groups) tended to achieve less than their counterparts in single-grade classes, but the differences found were not significant. Small differences in teacher–student interaction patterns and degree of pupil involvement were also found. Students in the multigrade classes tended to concentrate on their work less, and to spend more time on 'routine' interactions and waiting for the teacher. These multigrade classes were all formed as a response to fluctuating enrolment in otherwise single-grade organised schools.

Bennett *et al.* (1983) argued that the results of the HMI study should be treated with caution because, amongst other things, it conflated different multigrade contexts, particularly relating to urban and rural schools. They conducted a study of 936 schools, 619 (66%) of which had some kind of multigrade grouping. Of these, 37% were in rural areas, 32% in urban areas, and 27% were in suburban areas. While in rural schools most classes were organised for multigrade teaching, in urban and suburban schools the figure was closer to 20%. Seventy per cent of the schools in the sample reported that they had been forced to move to multigrade classroom organisation because of falling rolls, staff cuts, or uneven intake. They found a very wide variety of multigrade organisational patterns – 213 to be exact.

The most common criteria used to assign pupils to multigrade classes were age and ability. Teachers of pupils in Years 3–6 were more likely to be opposed to multigrade organisation than teachers of reception, Year 1, or Year 2 pupils. For teaching purposes, pupils in multigrade classes were rarely grouped according to age. Much more common was grouping by ability or individual assignment. Heads of both mixed and single age schools agreed that multigrade classes place more stress on the teacher, require more preparation, and need more resources. They saw advantages in terms of flexibility of staff, children and space. Heads in schools with multigrade groupings believed that younger children get sufficient teacher attention, older pupils do not resent younger pupils, and that multigrade classes provide grater stability and security for pupils.

The initial survey was followed up by case study interviews in selected schools (Lee, 1984). These indicate that heads and their staff make conscious decisions to avoid introducing multigrade classes. They may put up with uneven class sizes, or reorganise classes every year, putting pupils into new peer group arrangements. The majority of teachers interviewed felt that the defining characteristic of the multigrade class was the ability range, followed by the age range, and then the maturity level of pupils. However, when probed further, the majority felt that in reality the ability range in the multigrade class did not differ significantly from the ability range in a single-age class. Furthermore, most of the teachers reported that they did not change their approach to teaching when confronted by a multigrade class. They organised pupils into groups on the basis of ability and continued to use whole-class approaches. The majority of teachers who were interviewed felt that multigrade grouping offered possible social advantages to children.

Since the 1980s research on multigrade schools in England and Wales has focused on grouping practices. Hallam *et al.* (2003) surveyed 2,000 primary, junior and infant schools in England and Wales and reported that 47% of schools had some or all mixed-age classes (i.e. multigrade schools). The student grouping practices used within these schools were similar to those used in schools without multigrade classes. Within-class ability grouping was used most frequently in both types of school in mathematics and English, whereas mixed-ability groups were most frequently used for other subjects. The use of different 'setting' practices varied in mathematics in the two types of school. Same-age setting involves taking children from different classes of the same age to form groups based on ability. Cross-age setting involves taking children from different classes to form groups based on ability, regardless of age. In monograde schools cross-age setting was used less often than same-age setting, whereas in multigrade schools cross-age setting was used more often than same-age setting. In a linked study on the influences of changes in grouping practices Hallam *et al.* (2004) found that many schools had changed their grouping practices in response to government guidelines in the National Literacy Strategy recommending more whole-class teaching. The guidance was that for 75% of the Literacy Hour children should be taught together. Additional guidance was given for multigrade classes: reduce the time of whole-class teaching with more time for group teaching; increase group time and retain whole-class time by increasing the total amount of time; use an additional adult to provide simultaneous teaching or support; set by ability across a number of classes. The guidance included the possibility of 'two-year rolling programmes'. In schools with mixed-age classes 'grouping practices, in the main, were developed to facilitate teaching to single-year groups, although in some cases cross-age setting was being adopted' (Hallam *et al.*, 2004: 137).

Over the last 20 years there appears to have been a reduction in the percentage of schools with some multigrade classes (Bennett *et al.*, 1983; Hallam *et al.*, 2003). But, as we saw earlier, around a quarter of the total number of classes in England at the primary level are multigraded. And over the same period the challenges for multigrade teachers may have actually increased. Since the introduction of the Education Reform Act of 1988, curriculum content and delivery have been increasingly prescribed by central government authorities. Most of the curriculum frameworks are based on the implicit assumption that pupils are organised into single-year groups. The literacy and numeracy strategies, for example, provide objectives and content for each year group separately with, as we saw above, some guidance for mixed-year classes (see for example Department for Education and Skills, 2002). Similarly, schemes of work produced by the Qualifications and Curriculum Authority (QCA) to support the teaching of other core and foundation subjects are also generally organised for delivery to a single-year group (QCA, 2002). In addition, mandatory Standardised Assessment Tests (SATs) at the end of both Key Stages 1 and 2 reinforce this year-group based curriculum structure. In classrooms where pupils' ages span more than one year group there may well be some impact on the work of the teacher, both in relation to lesson planning and curriculum delivery. In view of the continuing high proportion of mixed-grade classes in the system as a whole the amount of curriculum advice provided centrally seems rather limited.

ATTITUDES AND PEDAGOGICAL IMPLICATIONS: A STUDY IN LONDON

Our research explores headteacher and teacher attitudes towards multigrade classes in terms of their perceived opportunities and challenges, and the pedagogical implications of this form of organisation. It concludes with a series of recommendations made by headteachers and teachers.

The study focuses on multigrade classes in Key Stages 1 and 2, as this is where the influence of the national curriculum has been strongest. The area that was selected for the study faces challenges to educational quality typical of several other inner-city London areas. These include high teacher turnover and pupil mobility, a relatively large proportion of students with English as an additional language, and several areas of significant socio-economic disadvantage (e.g. eligibility for free school meals). The Local Education Authority (LEA) in question has a population of 55 primary schools, the majority of which admit children to a seven-year span of primary education (i.e. one 'reception' year plus six primary years).

We initially surveyed the population of schools with a questionnaire, and received responses from 30 schools. Of these almost a quarter (12 schools), indicated that they were operating with multigrade classes. Out of 111 classes in Key Stages 1 and 2 in these twelve schools, 35 were multigrade. Assuming an average class size of 30 pupils, this means that at least 1,000 pupils in the LEA are being taught in multigrade classes. Without exception, multigrade classes in these schools are organised out of necessity.

The initial questionnaire survey was followed by the main study. This consisted of interviews with teachers in ten of the 12 schools identified in the initial survey. We asked about the perceived opportunities and challenges of multigrade classes in comparison to single-age classes, and the pedagogical implications of this form of organisation. The main findings are presented below.

Challenges associated with multigrade teaching

The most commonly perceived challenges fell into three categories: curriculum organisation, ability range and assessment.

Curriculum organisation

In all but one of the schools one or more teachers identified curriculum organisation as a problem for multigrade classes. Indeed, some 24 teachers/headteachers out of the total of 47 identified the curriculum as a major constraint. One teacher explains:

> The problems have become … manifold since the inception of the National Curriculum, which is written, or seems to be written, per age group of the children. Therefore the testing and expectations of the outcomes is age-group-wise. So having a multigrade class puts greater constraints on a teacher to try and cover two areas of the National Curriculum. I felt it really heavily back in 1998. I had an evenly mixed group of Year 2s and Year 3s. I had to teach to the National Curriculum tests at the end of the year with half the group (i.e. the Year 2s working towards the Key Stage 1 tests) whilst still trying to manoeuvre onwards … and that to my mind was almost impossible.

Some teachers acknowledged that the 'two-year curriculum cycle' offered one way around the problem of the age-graded nature of the curriculum. In this form of curriculum organisation teachers spread a subject curriculum across two calendar years. Pupils in different year groups begin the cycle at two different points. It is common in the foundation subjects. However, even here there could be major problems posed by the previous curriculum progression of pupils.

Ability range

The second most commonly mentioned problem was the breadth of the ability range posed by the multigrade class. Fourteen teachers and three headteachers perceived this to be a problem. A typical comment is that:

> If you have very low achievers in the younger age group, you will find in a class you might need to have about eight different groupings. It becomes a problem if you don't have a lot of classroom support because those low achievers in the lower age group might actually lose out a lot. It also means that the middle range and the top range might kind of lose out, because you can't give everyone the individual support they actually need in the classroom.

Although the breadth of the ability range was mentioned by teachers of grade combinations from the youngest to the oldest, eight teachers highlighted the particular difficulties faced in the combinations of the earliest years, Reception and Year 1, and Year 1 and Year 2:

> Year 1–2 … that's probably one of the hardest classes in this school to teach because you've got children coming right up from reception with children

who have had a year of reception and a year of Year 1 and the difference between those children is really difficult to tie up at times.

Assessment

The third most commonly perceived problem posed by multigrade classes was the constraint imposed by the Key Stage Standard Assessment Tests (SATs) that affected some but not all year groups. SATs are taken by all Year 2 and Year 6 children towards the end of Key Stages 1 and 2 respectively. The teachers who raised this issue were teachers of Years 1–2 or 5–6. No teacher responsible for 3–4 saw SATs as a problem.

A teacher in one of our sample schools explained the issue in some detail:

> With the pressure of Key Stage 1 SATs you've got 7 year old children expected to read a booklet, which I think is quite testing for age 7 children. You've also got children just out of reception and doing sound work and initial sounds and you're trying with the literacy hour to tie up the two. I think it's very difficult. I taught Year 5 and 6 and I think also that's got negativity in that Year 6s are geared so much towards SATs and I think quite a testing level again for 10/11 year olds. You really do end up, no matter how much you disagree ... gearing a lot of your work towards those tests and the types of questions they are going to be asked. I think the Year 5s really lose out quite a lot, for the Year 5 curriculum first of all, and also some of the creative side.

Another explained that the 'build up' to the tests stretched over many months. The formal assessments start in the January and become very intense in May.

Opportunities in multigrade classes

The three most commonly cited opportunities were: cognitive stretching/ modelling, peer tutoring and behavioural stretching/modelling.

Cognitive stretching/modelling

The most frequently mentioned response was the opportunity for cognitive stretching and modelling of the younger, less able and lower achieving children. One headteacher described the stretching process in graphic terms:

> It does give an opportunity for younger children ... to keep up with the more able children within the school. So they get a chance to work at a slightly higher level because they're pushed, pulled or dragged along by their classmates.

Other teachers expressed the same general idea as 'stretching', 'modelling', 'moving on and developing', 'extending', 'looking up and emulating'. Of the 24 teachers and headteachers who spoke of cognitive stretching, the majority (16) referred to specific grade combinations. Six spoke of the advantages for Year 5 in Year 5–6 grade combinations; and six for Year 1 in Year 1–2 combinations. The remaining four taught various combinations of Years 2, 3 and 4.

Peer tutoring

The opportunity for peer tutoring afforded by multigrade teaching was highlighted by 13 of the teachers. Although peer tutoring is a strategy that is used in straight classes, it seems to be perceived as a particularly appropriate teaching/learning strategy in the multigrade class:

> The older children get to discuss what they already know and that sort of cements their knowledge even further, and the younger children get to look up to these other kids and think wow they can do this, I can do this as well. And especially, when kids explain to kids, it's so much better.

For this teacher and several others peer tutoring benefited both the pupil 'tutor' or 'mentor' and the pupil 'learner'. Another teacher reinforces the point but emphasises the principle that the gap between the peer 'tutor' and peer learner should not be too great. 'The levels have to be close to each other and that's when it works. If the top ones are too far away from the bottom ones, it's just unmanageable'.

Behaviour stretching/modelling

Twelve teachers identified behaviour stretching/modelling as an opportunity in multigrade classes. In other words, the older pupils model appropriate behaviour for the younger.

An important consequence of behaviour modelling is the continuity and stability it affords to the social structure of the multigrade class. Because children learn appropriate ways of behaving in class from older children they in turn are in a position to provide role models to the newcomers in the following year. Since half of the class is already familiar with the teacher's expectations and class routines the structure reinforces continuity and provides a 'settling effect' on the younger children. Four teachers identified the benefits not only for the children themselves but also for the teacher.

However, it should be noted that the stability and continuity take effect only when pupils are kept in multigrade classes for two or more years. In most of our schools, with both mixed and single age classes, pupils followed various routes through mixed and single age-classes.

Preference for mixed or single-age classes

Having explored the perceptions of both the problems and opportunities posed by multigrade classes, teachers and headteachers were asked for their preferences in teaching. A majority – some 24, including five headteachers – expressed a clear preference for single age-group classes'. However, six teachers stated that they preferred to teach multigrade and 12 (including two headteachers) said they did not mind either way. A further two said they did not really know, one never having taught any other type of class and the other being content with her current multigrade class. Another two qualified their responses by saying that multigrade teaching worked fine when it was based on the ability not the age of the child and when the class was responsive to direction. 'Multigrade doesn't really enter it.... I prefer a class that will be responsive'.

Teaching approach in mixed- and single-age classes

We asked whether multigrade classes require a different teaching approach to single-age classes. The most common response is that multigrade classes require a similar approach to straight classes. Ten of the 13 respondents in this category refer to differentiation either explicitly or implicitly. This is the skill of tailoring instruction to meet the needs of the range of children in the class. For these interviewees, this skill is the same in both a multigrade and a single-age class. Underlying this response is the view that the range of needs in the multigrade class is no different from that in a straight class.

The main difference identified lies in the wider age range in multi-grade classes. Respondents express the view that the younger pupils in a multigrade class can be a lot less socially and cognitively mature than the oldest. As a consequence, the teacher needs to work harder to ensure that there is no bullying or pecking order, that everyone understands the school routines, and that the range of emotional needs are met. In addition, the teacher has to make sure that she presents material in a way that will stimulate and interest this range of pupil maturity. One further response in this category refers to the older year group in a multigrade class, and the need to ensure that they understand that they are not doing work that is meant for a lower year group.

Planning

We also asked what is involved in planning for a multigrade class. The main responses related to integrating curriculum frameworks, planning over a two-year cycle, and planning up or down (differentiating) from one curriculum framework.

Integrating frameworks
In this category teachers referred to the need to consult more than one curriculum framework when planning for a multigrade class. This occurs because frameworks are usually year-based. Integration meant reviewing the curriculum objectives for respective year groups, bringing together the material linked with similar objectives, then differentiating the tasks in relation to the objectives for the different year groups. For some teachers this posed a challenge. They refer to the difficulties of juggling two sets of objectives and/or topics in their planning. The following response is typical of this group:

> Well it's a pain because you've got all your planning folders for different subjects and for your year group and then of course if you've got a multigrade group you're then having to look at twice the amount of paperwork and you're needing to show that on your plans. Normally on the plans we're showing for the differentiation of different groups but then with a multigrade group class you're then showing the differentiation for the ability groups but also for maybe your Year 2s and your Year 1s, so it is a lot more work on the teacher.

However, there are also five teachers who do not view the juggling of two curriculum frameworks as such an onerous task. This is because the objectives and/or topics in the different curriculum frameworks are linked in some way. In fact, for two of these teachers working with two frameworks is actually beneficial because this means that they have more to select from when planning for the range of pupils in the class.

Two-year cycle
Nine of the schools in the sample operate with a two-year curriculum cycle in at least some subjects. This means that for year groups 5 and 6, for example, in year A the Year 5 curriculum will be followed, and in year B the Year 6 curriculum will be followed. This is an attempt to ensure that pupils moving between multigrade and single-age classes cover the entire curriculum.

In seven schools a two-year cycle is adopted in science and in some or all of the foundation subjects (history, geography, art, information and communication technology (ICT), design and technology (DT), music and physical education), but not in literacy or numeracy. Sometimes, constructing the two-year cycle in a foundation subject can cause difficulties. One teacher describes her attempts to construct a two-year cycle in design and technology:

> And when I organised that so that we could do it in our school it was a nightmare, because we've got new 'units of work'. Say, for instance, there's one on book making and it's for Year 4 in the QCA scheme. So the Year 3s do it in the Year 3/4 class, the Year 3s will be doing that. And of course the Year 3s without any Year 4s in the class have to do that unit when they're in Year 4. It involves using craft knives and things like that. Which I think could be dangerous if the children weren't being supervised properly when it was used. I mean there's a lot of difference between the physical capabilities of a Year 3 child and a Year 4 child and how sensible they are when it comes to using sharp knives and things like that.

Differentiation
In this category teachers refer to differentiation and 'planning up' and 'planning down'. Planning 'up' refers to using the objectives for the older year group and extending them, with differentiated tasks to meet the needs of the younger/less able children, while planning 'down' is the opposite. A problem when planning down, especially in a Year 5/6 class, is how to adequately prepare the Year 6 pupils for the SATs examination. One teacher mentions that she has proposed to the school that in the core subjects, they always plan up in the Year 5/6 class, thereby repeating the Year 6 material twice. This proposal had not yet been accepted. In a second school, Year 6 pupils in the mixed Year 5/6 class are being taken out of their class to have additional instruction to prepare them for SATs.

Grouping for instruction

When asked how they group pupils for instruction, the majority of teachers and heads reported that they use same-ability grouping just as they would in a single-age class. A smaller number talked about age as a possible criterion under certain circumstances.

Ability
This means that the higher ability pupils would go into one group, the medium ability into another group, and so on. This grouping would take precedence over any consideration of pupils' ages or year groups. Over half of these responses (14) refer to literacy and/or numeracy as the subjects in

which ability grouping is most likely to happen. This is in line with the guidelines for teaching these two subjects in the literacy and numeracy frameworks.   It would appear that if ability is used as a criterion, then this cuts across year group boundaries,   with some of the lower year group being placed into the high ability group, and some of the higher year group being placed into the lower ability groups.

Age
The majority of the responses that refer to age as a grouping criterion (10) do so in the context of having same-age groupings. Frequently mentioned (by five respondents) is the need to separate year groups for SATs preparation. This comes up in relation to both Year 2 SATs and Year 6 SATs. One respondent comments:

> When I had the 5/6s, towards the end of the first half of the, before SATs anyway, I did move them. I had them in ability groups until then. As we were getting up towards SATs, the last few weeks that I was actually focusing on revision, tried to avoid it but you always get caught up in the 'oh my God we'd better prepare'. So I did actually sit the Year 6s together and Year 5s together so that I could actually concentrate on the Year 6s and the Year 5s could do different things.

Two of the other responses that refer to the need for same-age teaching mention the social development of children. One of these mentions the sex education instruction in a multigrade class, and the other talks about the problems of doing role play with children who are of different ages. The other responses in this category refer to deliberately mixing age groups for peer teaching purposes.

Effective teaching strategies in multigrade classes

Most respondents express the view that there is no difference in the teaching strategies employed in multigrade and single-age classes. For these teachers, the age/year group of the pupils in the class is not a factor that they take into account when they are *teaching* (the story may well be different when they are planning).

The second most commonly cited teaching strategy is putting pupils into pairs. This echoes the responses to the question on opportunities above. For a number of the respondents, this includes pairing by ability so that a higher ability pupil can assist or instruct a lower ability pupil. When this is the case, the year group of the children is not necessarily a key factor.

Only a handful of respondents in this category make explicit why pairwork might be particularly appropriate in a multigrade class. One teacher comments that a lower achieving older child can have his or her confidence built up by working as the tutor for a younger pupil. A second teacher makes the point that a multigrade class make it less embarrassing for a lower achiever in the lower year group to be a 'tutee' because they can take direction from an older child.

MAIN FINDINGS

The main findings may be summarised as follows. At least one-fifth of the inner London schools that we studied have multigrade classes. The most common combinations of classes are Years 1–2, 3–4 and 5–6. Multigrade classes are formed out of necessity rather than pedagogic choice. Local education authorities require schools to admit students in line with their 'published intake'. Simultaneously legislation prevents schools forming classes with more 30 pupils per class. Seven of the ten schools have published intakes that require groups of one and a half or two and a half classes. While three others have published intakes consistent with single-age classes, uneven enrolments caused by local population movements create a need for single-age classes.

Teachers are quick to identify a number of challenges posed by the multigrade classes. The most commonly mentioned is the age-graded structure of the National Curriculum and the associated expectations of curriculum coverage and assessment/achievement targets. This issue is circumvented in the foundation subjects in some schools through the use of curriculum plans spanning two years of study, not one. But this approach also poses challenges, since pupils have different single/multiple grade histories. The second most commonly mentioned problem is the range of ability of pupils in those multigrade classes that have not been selected on the basis of ability homogeneity. A third constraint arises from the pressure of the Years 2 and 6 Key Stage tests on provision for Years 1 and 5 respectively in mixed 1–2 and 5–6 classes.

Teachers are equally quick to identify the positive learning and teaching opportunities posed by multigrade classes. The most commonly mentioned is the opportunity for cognitive stretching of the younger, less able and lower achieving pupils. This is expressed variously by teachers as 'stretching', 'modelling', 'moving on and developing', 'extending', 'looking up and emulating'. The second most commonly mentioned is the opportunity for the use of peer tutoring learning strategies. While such strategies are not unique to multigrade classes, the strategy appears to work particularly well in the heterogeneous ability, age and experience contexts of the multigrade class. Unlike the cognitive stretching, which appears to benefit mainly the less able, the lower achieving and the younger, peer tutoring is perceived to benefit all pupils. The more able, higher achieving and older pupils 'cement' their learning through teaching and helping others. The less able, lower achieving and younger pupils look up to and learn from others. A third commonly mentioned opportunity is 'behaviour stretching' or the opportunity to learn appropriate social behaviours from the role models offered by others. These confirm the benefits identified by others (e.g. Veenman, 1995; Ireson and Hallam, 2001).

When invited to express a preference for teaching a multigrade and single-age class, a majority of teachers expressed a preference for the single-age class. However this needs to be set alongside a small minority who expressed a preference for multigrade classes and a large number (14) who expressed no preference. All teachers accept the existence of multigrade classes and the need to teach in them without question.

Teachers identified similarities and differences in their approaches to multigrade and single-age classes. A significant number – 13 – said that their approach to a multigrade and single-age class was the same. 'Differentiation' of tasks to match the ability level of individual pupils formed the essence of their teaching strategies whether the class was mixed or single-age. Others identified differences. The three main differences focus on ways of handling the broader age range, the need to 'pitch' instruction at appropriate levels and the additional curriculum planning required for the multigrade class.

Not all multigrade classes produce an age range that is broader than a straight age class. Indeed, where age is the basis for allocating pupils to classes, the multigrade class will enjoy a narrower age range. Where the age range is greater teachers work hard to ensure that pupils of different social and cognitive levels are integrated into a single social unit. This involves, *inter alia*, the prevention of bullying of younger by older pupils and of pecking orders, ensuring that all pupils learn and practise class and school routines and presenting learning material in a way that stimulates and interests the full range of pupil maturity.

Teachers identify three specific approaches to curriculum planning: (i) integrating frameworks, (ii) the use of two-year cycles and (iii) different-iation. In the first, teachers attempt to marry or integrate two single-year curriculum frameworks into one, by matching objectives and/or topics. In the second, teachers develop a two-year cycle for one or more curriculum subjects. In the third, teachers work to one curriculum framework in terms of its objectives and adapt tasks in relation to the objective to suit the ability/achievement levels of the pupils.

It is most common for pupils to be grouped for instruction by ability in multigrade classes, across age boundaries. This occurs most frequently in literacy and numeracy where ability grouping is the strategy that is suggested in government documents. Where year group is used as the basis for grouping, this is often as an administrative device to allow the teacher to focus attention on a Year 6 or Year 2 class which needs coaching for the SATs.

TEACHER AND HEADTEACHER RECOMMENDATIONS

At the end of the interviews, teachers and headteachers were invited to make recommendations on how mixed-age teaching might be made more effective. They were invited to make recommendations both for teachers and headteachers of other schools and for government authorities.

Among the 47 respondents seven teachers had no recommendations to make, either because they failed to see it as a major issue, or because of inexperience or because 'individual teachers have individual approaches'. In a further seven cases five teachers and two headteachers recommended 'avoiding mixed-age classes if at all possible'. The headteacher of one school said:

> The nicest thing that could happen would be if you have not got enough children to justify paying for two teachers then money should be provided. If we had enough money we could have our Year 5 children in two small classes or put them all together and have two teachers.

But the majority of teachers and headteachers concluded that mixed-age classes would remain a feature of many urban schools and made four main suggestions with implications for local authorities and national authorities.

Curriculum frameworks and materials

An overwhelming majority, some 29 teachers, made practical suggestions about how curriculum frameworks and materials could be or needed to be adapted – in some cases quite radically – to meet the realities of the mixed-age classroom.

The basic concern was that the National Curriculum, both for core subjects and foundation subjects, was organised according to age. Curriculum provision for mixed-age classes required an enormous amount of additional curriculum planning input on the part of both schools and teachers. Three teachers were able to identify isolated examples of documents – some produced by the QCA, and some by the local authority –

that facilitated curriculum planning for mixed-age classes. These included documents published by the QCA in Physical Exercise and Music for Years 3/4 and 5/6.

A few teachers spoke specifically about the literacy and numeracy strategies and identified aspects of the current materials that could be developed, preferably by curriculum experts in QCA. One teacher explained how the current literacy materials could be 'pulled apart and made into a book, organised under subject headings, suitable for her current Year 5/6 class this year'. Others, however, claimed that the suggestions for teaching the literacy strategy to mixed-aged groups amounted to just 'a couple of pages'.

It is a similar picture in numeracy. One teacher claimed that the objectives for numeracy could be read across the Years 1–3 and Years 4–6 grade groups and that this facilitated differentiated work with two age groups. The problem she faced was that her class was Years 3–4. While this did not pose insurmountable problems she needed to spend time that a single-age grade teacher would not in reconstructing her curriculum plans.

A teacher who had been trained in New Zealand and accustomed to the New Zealand primary education curriculum structure commented on the over-prescriptive nature of the English National Curriculum in terms of the content of what should be taught in each grade. She contrasted this with a skills-based curriculum.

> Why not have a progression of skills that children move through from simple order of thinking up to higher order? You could be teaching the same higher order level in History or in Geography or in Science. Here in England it seems very discrete.

Another called for a 'broader approach' that did not demarcate all schemes of work by year group. A headteacher explained:

> In the exemplar schemes of work I think QCA should give a little more thought to the poor teacher or coordinator who's trying to work with mixed-year classes. Having said that, it would be difficult for someone in QCA to know what was going on for that child in the previous year and what is correct for a child in a Year 3–4 class. Perhaps the answer is to be less stringent: don't demarcate all your schemes by year group … perhaps a broader approach. A general lower junior programme would include these things and the schools would have to get those things included within the two years…. Having plans and frameworks is a godsend for several reasons. It does mean you know exactly what the children should be taught and that is an advantage in terms of quality assurance. But somewhere in the middle … don't demarcate everything by year group because it just does not work. We still end up having to spend a lot of time unpicking and putting certain topics into one year and making sure it does not appear the next year.

While all the teachers recommended that curriculum objectives and tasks should be rethought for mixed-age groups, they also recognised the variety of grade combinations that exist in schools, the varied routes of progression of children through single-age and mixed-age classes and the changing nature of split-class combinations over time. Hence, a scheme of units developed by the QCA or the LEA for Years 1–2, 3–4 and 5–6 would not suit a school that had to run a 2–3 or 4–5 class. Children who were in a split 1–2 class in their Year 2 might find themselves in a Year 3–4 class the following year alongside children who had come from a straight Year 2 class. The Year 3–4 curriculum would need to recognise both possibilities. A school with a straight Year 4 class one year might find itself with a 3–4 the next. Could both the straight and the mixed-age class be accommodated within a single curriculum plan or map for the whole school?

Whatever the difficulties involved in creating support and guidance for every situation all teachers were of the view that the national curriculum authorities should make more of an effort to recognise the mixed-aged nature of many classes and the additional curriculum planning and delivery burden this placed on teachers and headteachers. Specifically teachers would welcome:

- Sample plans for all terms of work in the numeracy strategy for mixed-age classes (as is done for the single-age grade groups)
- Clearer specifications of the skill progressions expected across age groups, with the possibility of substituting the development of one set of skills in one content area with that in another
- More examples of differentiated tasks in relation to objectives both within and across grades
- A broader curriculum demarcation that identified expectations across two or more years rather than single years
- The dissemination of curriculum frameworks and tasks through the internet.

Teacher training and professional development

Eleven teachers spoke of the desirability of further professional development in mixed-age teaching. For some this was training/development that could be organised at the school level and might be thought of as peer support or mentoring – talking to other teachers, observing another teacher doing it, and asking 'how do you manage this? how do you manage that?'

For most others however more formalised training, both at pre-service and in-service levels was considered desirable.

> I've never seen any information about teaching mixed-age classes. Obviously there should be something in teacher training about it. I really did not know it existed until I came to this school.
> If you are training to teach in a primary school you should have one teaching practice in a mixed-age class.
> I'm new to the mixed-age system. It's hellish, diabolical. People shouldn't assume that because you have been teaching for a long time that you can understand a new system just like that.

In sum, the teachers and headteachers recommended school-level support from fellow teachers, in-service professional development courses, and exposure to mixed-age teaching during pre-service training and teaching 'practice'.

School organisation

Six teachers made recommendations on school organisation and resources that went beyond curriculum and teacher education. These were:
- A national policy on mixed-age classes, including advice on best practice on age group combinations
- Allow repetition of a year to ensure mastery of the skills necessary for progression to the following year
- Additional teaching resources
- Additional curriculum materials for classroom learners.

Research

Finally, and without prompting by the researchers, four teachers recommended two areas for further research. For ease of presentation these are presented here as research questions: What are the children's perceptions of the opportunities and benefits of being in a multigrade class, and does this change as they move up the school? How do same-age children who have been the 'older' and 'younger' children in their respective multigrade classes previously compare cognitively and socially?

REFERENCES

Aikman, S. and Pridmore, P. (2001) Multigrade schools in 'remote' areas of Vietnam. *International Journal of Educational Development*, 21(6), 521–536.

Bennett, N., O'Hare, E. and Lee, J. (1983) Mixed-age classes in primary schools: a survey of practice. *British Educational Research Journal*, 9(1), 41–56.

Collingwood, I. (1991) *Multiclass Teaching In Primary Schools: A handbook for Vanuatu*. Apia, Western Samoa: UNESCO.

Cornall, J.N. (1986) The small school: achievements and problems. *Education Today*, 36(1), 25–36.

Department for Education and Skills (DfES) (2002) http://www.dfes.gov.uk/statistics/DB/SBU/b0222/030-t6.htm.

Department for Education and Skills (DfES) (2000) *Framework for teaching Mathematics: Reception to year 6*. Nottinghamshire: DFES Publications.

Department for Education and Skills (DfES)(1998) *The National Literacy Strategy: framework for teaching YR to Y6*. Nottinghamshire: DFES Publications.

Francis, L.J. (1992) Primary school size and pupil attitudes: small is happy? *Educational Management and Administration*, 20(2), 100–104.

Galton, M. and Simon, B. (eds) (1980) *Progress and Performance in the Primary Classroom*, London: Routledge and Kegan Paul.

Galton, M. and Patrick, H. (eds) (1990) *Curriculum Provision in the Small Primary School*. London: Routledge and Kegan Paul.

Gupta, D., Jain, M. and Bala, N. (1996) *Multigrade Teachin: Status and implications*. Delhi: National Council of Educational Research and Training.

Hallam, S., Ireson, J., Lister, V. and Chaudhury, I.A. (2003) Ability grouping practices in the primary school: a survey. *Educational Studies*, 29(1), 69–83.

Hallam, S., Ireson, J. and Davies, J. (2004) Grouping practices in the primary school: what influences change? *British Educational Research Journal*, 30(1), 115–140.

Hargreaves, L., Comber, C. and Galton, M. (1996) The national curriculum: can small schools deliver? Confidence and competence levels of teachers in small rural primary schools. *British Educational Research Journal*, 22(1), 89–99.

Hayes, D. (1999) Organising learning in multigrade classes: a case study about a multi-task lesson. *Curriculum*, 20 (2), 100–109.

Her Majesty's Inspector of Schools (1978) *Primary Education in England*. London: Department of Education and Science.

Institute of Education Multigrade Project website: http://www.ioe.ac.uk/multigrade.

Ireson, J. and Hallam, S. (2001) *Ability Grouping in Education*. London: Paul Chapman Publishing.

Jarousse, J.-P. and Mingat, A. (1991) *Efficacité pédagogique de l'enseignment à cours multiples dans le contexte africain*. Dijon: IREDU-CNRS: University of Dijon.

Lee, J. (1984) Vertical grouping in the primary school: a report of a study by Lancaster University on behalf of the Schools Council. *School Organisation*, 4(2), 133–142.

Little, A.W. (1995) *Multigrade Teaching: A review of research and practice.* Education Research, Serial No. 12, Overseas Development Administration.

Little, A.W. (2001) Multigrade teaching: towards an international research and policy agenda. *International Journal of Educational Development*, 21(6), 481–497.

Lungwangwa, G. (1989) *Multi-grade Schools in Zambian Primary Education: A report on the pilot schools in Mkushi District.* Report number 47. Stockholm: SIDA Education Division.

Martin, A.B. and Brown, K.G. (1989) Student achievement in multigrade and single grade classes. *Education Canada*, 29, 10–13.

Mason, D.A. and Burns, R.B. (1996) Teacher's views of combination classes. *Journal of Educational Research*, 89, 36–45.

Mason, D.A. and Burns, R.B. (1997) Reassessing the effects of combination classes. *Educational Research and Evaluation* 3(1), 1–53.

McEwan, P.J. (1998) The effectiveness of multigrade schools in Colombia. *Educational Development*, 18, 435–452.

Office for Standards in Education (2000) *Small Schools: How well are they doing?* A report by OFSTED based on the data from inspections and national test results. Online. Available http://www.ofsted.gov.uk/publications/index.cfm?fuseaction=pubs.summary&id=837 (accessed 20 September 2004).

Pratt, C. and Treacy, K., (1986) *A Study of Student Grouping Practices in Early Childhood Classes in Western Australian Government Primary Schools* (Cooperative Research Series 9). Nedlands: Education Department of Western Australia.

Psacharopoulos, G., Rojas, C. and Velez, E. (1993) Achievement evaluation of Colombia's *Escuela Nueva*: is multigrade the answer? *Comparative Education Review*, 37(3), 263–276.

Qualifications and Curriculum Authority (QCA) website: http://www.standards.dfes.gov.uk/schemes3.

Veenman, S., Lem, P. and Winkelmolen, B. (1985) Active learning time in multigrade classes. *Educational Studies*, 13, 75–89.

Vulliamy, G. and Webb, R. (1995) The implementation of the national curriculum in small primary schools. *Educational Review*, 47, 25–41.

CHAPTER FIVE

MULTIGRADE TEACHERS AND THEIR TRAINING IN RURAL NEPAL

TAKAKO SUZUKI

INTRODUCTION

Multigrade teaching has never been recognised officially in the education system in Nepal (CERID, 1988). However, large numbers of teachers find themselves responsible for multigrade classes. Although statistics are not collected routinely about the extent of multigrade teaching, a Joint Secretary of the Ministry of Education announced in 1989 that approximately 60% of schools in Nepal required multigrade teaching (CERID, 1989). This chapter describes the context of multigrade schools and teachers in Nepal, highlights issues of access, quality, efficiency and equity associated with multigrade schools, describes in-service training for multigrade teaching and analyses the impact of this training on teachers and classrooms.

COUNTRY CONTEXT

Nepal is a small country located on the southern side of the Himalayas, bordering on India to the east, west and south and on China to the north. The country is divided into three geographical regions, defined by their altitude: the Terai, the lowland along the southern side of the country, the snow-capped Himalayan mountains, whose altitude reaches up to 8,848 metres, in the north, and the mid-hills situated between the Terai and the Himalayan region where altitudes range from 610 to 4,877 metres. The Terai occupies 23% of the nation's territory, the mountain region occupies 35% and the hill region 42%. In 2001, the population was just over 22 million. According to the 1991 National Census, about 47% of the total population lives in the Terai, 7% in the mountains and 46% in the hills. This field research was conducted in two districts in the hills.

Nepal is predominantly an agricultural country. However, the range and productivity of crops cultivated in the rugged terrain on the steep slopes in the mountain and hill regions are limited. The physical features dividing the country pose a major obstacle to the development of transport, prevent the formation of markets and consequently force people to perpetuate closed,

87

A.W. Little (ed.), Education for All and Multigrade Teaching: challenges and opportunities, 87–102.
© 2007 *Springer.*

self-supporting economies (JICA, 1993). Thus 90.82% of the population live in rural areas, according to the 1991 Census. The estimated GDP per head in 1999/2000 was US$244 (HMG, 2001). About 40% of the population live in absolute poverty (EFA Committee, 2000).

Nepal is a Hindu kingdom with an 86.5% Hindu population (HMG, 2001). The census of 1991 lists 60 castes and ethnic groups in the country. The social structure of the population is characterised by two principal divisions: a vertical hierarchy between socio-professional and caste groups and a horizontal tribal division between ethnic groups. Although Nepalese is the official national language, and was in 1991 the mother tongue of 50% of the total population (HMG, 2001), there are 36 official languages reported in the census and 70 languages or dialects reported by researchers (Gurung, 1998). Partly because of the linguistic diversity, the literacy rate in the country remains quite low. According to recent estimate by the MOE (Ministry of Education), only 48% of the population of 6 years and over was literate in 1997 (EFA Assessment Committee, 2000). Moreover, and probably affected by Hindu tradition, there is a significant gender difference in the figures. Of the total literate population in 1991 (39.6%), the literacy rate among males was 54.5%, but the rate for females only was 25.1% (HMG, 2001).

ACCESS, QUALITY, EFFICIENCY AND EQUITY

Access and teacher supply

Over the past five decades, low enrolment rates have been the most significant issue in education in Nepal. The political priority for the quantitative expansion of primary school education has resulted in a sharp increase in enrolment in the five grades of primary school. Although schools have been established and more children have been enrolled, the supply of teachers has not matched the rapid increase in the number of schools and students. As a result, it is not possible to allocate one teacher to every grade of primary in every school. Consequently, a teacher is often responsible for two or more grades simultaneously. Despite the successful increase in the numbers of both schools and students, the teacher/school ratio has remained at 4.0 between 1989 and 1996 (MOE, 1996, 1997, 1998, 1999b; MOEC, 1990, 1992; MOECSW, 1993, 1994, 1995; MOES, 2000). The gap between the number of teachers required to allocate one teacher per grade and the actual number of teachers available between 1985 and 1998 has widened in the 1990s, compared with the 1980s. The teacher/school ratio has decreased from 4.0 in 1996, to 3.9 in 1997 and 3.8 in 1998 (MOE, 1998, 1999b; MOES,

2000). The education budget for 1999–2004 for physical facilities is US$32 million, allocated to the construction of 5,400 new classrooms. During the same project period, positions for additional teachers were to be frozen (MOE, 1999a). This would imply that the number of teachers responsible for more than one grade would increase over the period.

The teacher/school ratio in rural areas is slightly lower than the national average. The primary school teacher to school ratio in urban areas is 5.3 (MOES, 2000). Urban schools have, relatively speaking, enough teachers for the primary grades. However, less than 10% of all primary schools are located in urban areas. Thus only a limited number of schools have enough teachers for all primary grades. Teacher shortage and de facto multigrade schools are found in most parts of the country. For example, in the two districts selected for this research – Nuwakot and Kavre, located near the Kathmandu valley – 94.7% (2000) and 84.7% (2001) of primary schools are multigrade (calculated from District Education Office (DEO) Nuwakot, 2000a, 2000b; DEO Kavre, 2001).

Quality and internal efficiency

Student learning achievement is particularly low in the three core subjects, Nepalese, mathematics and social studies (MOE, 1999a). Student learning achievement is consistently related to the amount of time available for teaching and learning. It also depends on how this time is used (Lockheed et al., 1991). Students in multigrade classrooms tend to have less learning time than those in monograde classrooms. In Sri Lanka, for example, the working time of students in a multigrade class is estimated at around half of those in an equivalent monograde class (Hargreaves et al., 2001). In multigrade classes, students have to compete for materials and limited space in the classroom. They receive less of the teacher's time and attention. This implies less reinforcement of what they have learned (Hargreaves et al., 2001). In Malaysia, students are often left on their own in a classroom while the teachers go and teach in other classes (Sulaiman, 1989). In Vietnam, efficient use of time is problematic. The multigrade school day is short, on average 2 to 3 hours per day, with 5 days a week (Hargreaves et al., 2001). The efficiency with which teachers and students utilise time in multigrade classes is likely to be crucial in improving student achievement.

In 1995, the internal efficiency of primary education in Nepal was as low as 46%, a problem caused mainly by high repetition and dropout rates (MOE, 1999a). Students in multigrade schools tend to be neglected when a teacher is responsible for two or more grades. While a teacher teaches one grade, students of other grades are left alone without any work. Students often walk long distances to school carrying heavy textbooks. They often sit doing nothing in a dark, tiny classroom while they wait for the arrival of their teacher. This discourages students from coming to school, reducing the internal efficiency of the school even further.

Equity

Achievements in Nepalese primary education show marked variation by gender. In 1998, the Net Enrolment Rate was 70.5% for all children, but only 61.2% for girls. The completion rate for the primary level in 1998 was 53.0% for all students, but only 41.9% for girls (MOES, 2000). The internal efficiency in 1995 was 46% for all, but only 40% for girls (MOE, 1999a). When parents cannot afford to send all of their children to school, sons are sent to school and daughters remain at home until the family can afford to send them to school (Stash and Hannum, 2001). Sons may be sent to private schools, which are believed to be better than public schools, but girls are sent to the cheaper local public schools. When girls are sent to school with limited resources, they are often sent to the schools nearest to their house in the village, which are often multigrade. For example, in a Village Development Committee (VDC) area in Kavre district, the majority of the children are admitted to large monograde schools. Boys attend private schools more often than girls and more girls than boys enrol in multigrade schools (Suzuki, 2003). Multigrade schools are an alternative for girls who cannot enrol in the larger monograde schools.

Caste and ethnic hierarchical systems continue to perpetuate social inequality despite national legislation outlawing caste discrimination (Stash and Hannum, 2001). Urban affluence and access to education reinforce certain castes with superior status, reproduce elites and limit educational opportunities for the others. Only 21 out of 60 caste/ethnic groups are above the national average for primary and secondary school attainment (Gurung, 1998). Hata (2001) concludes that the hierarchy of caste/ethnic groups has a consistent correlation with student learning achievement and student school attainment. One of the reasons for the low enrolment and high dropout rates of low castes and minorities has been identified as the distance between schools and home in the remote areas where these communities often settle (Sellar *et al.*, 1981). Therefore, small schools have been constructed for communities in remote areas, and these are often multigrade. These multi-grade schools are a measure to incorporate minorities who cannot enrol in larger monograde schools. The data from the VDC of Kavre district shows that a majority of students from minority ethnic groups and low castes attend multigrade schools, while high castes and the major ethnic groups enrol in monograde and private schools (Suzuki, 2003). Furthermore, it has been observed that, with some caste/ethnic groups, dropout rates increase when the share of one group declines in a school (Hata, 2001). Low-caste and minority dropout happens mostly at primary school level (Hata, 2001). Improvements in the quality of primary multigrade schools are crucial for improving the conditions of education for low castes and minorities.

NATIONAL POLICIES AND STRATEGY FOR MULTIGRADE TEACHING

Multigrade teaching never obtained the status of a formal component of the education system of Nepal (CERID, 1988). Despite the absence of a clear policy in support of multigrade teaching, the Nepalese government has been implementing in-service training as a strategy to improve the quality of multigrade teaching.

Since 1956, a series of five-year plans has been produced in Nepal. Related to the World Conference for Education For All (WCEFA) held in Jomtien in 1990, the main policy priority of the eighth plan (1992–1996) was the improvement of literacy and universal primary education in rural areas (JICA, 1993; Matsumoto, 1998). Approximately 14% of the national budget has been regularly allocated to education throughout the 1990s. Primary education is the most significant sub-sector of the education sector. Accordingly, the Basic and Primary Education Project (BPEP) was initiated in 1992 in order to improve access to, and quality and management efficiency of, primary education (Bajracharya et al., 1998). The targets of the eighth plan were revised for the ninth plan (1997–2002) (EFA committee, 2000). Primary education remains one of the main priorities. Basic and primary education is to be expanded to achieve free and compulsory education throughout the country. Measures will be taken to achieve equitable education, ironing out social, ethnic, gender, as well as regional disparities. And provisions are to be made to provide primary education in the different languages of the country (Bajracharya et al., 1998).

In order to expand primary education to disadvantaged communities, and despite any clear policy statement on multigrade teaching, the second phase of the Basic Primary Education Project (BPEP) included a commitment to an 'improvement in teaching practice in the classroom through the provision of recurrent training and timely provision of supplementary materials designed for multigrade instruction' (MOE, 1999a: 16). BPEP started with 19 districts and eventually expanded to all 75 districts of Nepal. Multigrade teaching was included as one of the key features of the second phase of BPEP.

MULTIGRADE TEACHING TRAINING

The Multigrade Teaching Training component of BPEP provides ten-day in-service teacher training courses for multigrade and monograde teachers. The material for these courses was developed by the Primary Teachers' Training Unit (PTTU). The training is held at the Resource Centres and run by district trainers, who were themselves trained through the cascade system by national master trainers.

The content of the training material is divided into ten sections, each of which is planned for coverage in one day of the 10-day course. The material has the following four objectives (PTTU, 1998: 1):

- To prepare or plan educational activities required for multigrade teaching
- To prepare Self-Learning Activity (SLA) required for multigrade teaching
- To manage classes in a way conducive to multigrade teaching
- To teach the students in two or more classes simultaneously.

These objectives, especially the third and fourth, are very general. Moreover, at no point in the objectives or in the training content is an ideal model of multigrade teaching presented.

Yet the training material includes three key components that are intended to increase effectiveness in the organisation of multigrade class (PTTU, 1998). The most significant is the T and AM classes. The training material encourages multigrade teachers to differentiate their multigrade classes as a main teaching class (T) and other additional classes. Before starting teaching the main class, a teacher should provide self-learning activities (SLA) for the additional class(es) and nominate a student as monitor (M) to supervise the class during the absence of the teacher. The teacher should then concentrate on the main class during the rest of the lesson period. This main teaching class is named 'T' class after 'teacher.' These additional classes are named 'AM' classes after teacher 'absence' and student 'monitor'.

The second is called Self-Learning Activity (SLA). The teacher is to provide 'activities given to the students in order to involve them in teaching and learning activities during the absence of the teacher from the classroom' (PTTU, 1998: 98). A significant amount of the training material is devoted to SLA, although the distinction between SLA and activities given to students while the teacher in present or activities given as homework is not made. The reasons for providing SLA and the amount of SLA which is to be set are not stated in the training material.

The third is the selection of a monitor to take care of the class during the absence of the teacher from the classroom while he/she is teaching in another classroom. The teacher is expected to provide the monitor with clear directions as to his/her task and, where appropriate, with an answer sheet. In many multigrade schools in rural Nepal the students from different grades do not share the same classroom space. They are seated in different classrooms and the teacher has to move frequently between rooms. The presence of a monitor substitutes for the absence of the teacher from the classroom.

METHODS

In order to evaluate the effectiveness of the training programme on teachers and their practices in the classroom, research was conducted in Nuwakot and Kavre districts from July 2000 to March 2002. In June–July 2001, District Education Offices conducted Multigrade Teaching Training for all primary teachers in resource centres in these districts. All of the 108 teachers were called for a ten-day in-service training course in multigrade teaching, and 98 teachers participated. The research reported in this chapter was part of a broader study (Suzuki, 2003).

In order to examine the impact of the training, evidence was collected before, during and after the training. Before the training, 14 primary multigrade schools were visited. Fourteen headteachers and 33 teachers were interviewed. Five teachers were selected from the 33 and their classrooms were observed for a further week at their schools. These five would subsequently be followed up after the training. At the beginning of the training, 87 out of the 98 participating teachers completed a questionnaire about their attitude to and practice of multigrade teaching. Eight of the 98 trainees had followed a training course on multigrade teaching previously.

During the training, 'practice teaching' of the trainees was observed. This was assessed in relation to the training curriculum and provided an indication of the 'competence'. On the final day of the training, all 98 trainees filled out self-evaluation forms designed to measure 'knowledge' levels of the trainees in relation to the training curriculum.

After the training, the classroom practice of the five selected trainee-teachers was observed in their schools for one week to assess their 'performance' after the training. The term 'performance' rather than 'competence' is used to distinguish what the trainee-teachers were doing in their classrooms from what they had previously demonstrated they were capable of doing during the training course. The results of the analysis of the post-training observations of the five selected trainee-teachers were cross-checked with the views expressed in a focus group discussion of all the course trainers.

THE PRACTICE OF MULTIGRADE TEACHING OBSERVED
BEFORE THE TRAINING

Despite the prevalence of multigrade teaching, a model of monograde teaching dominates the structure of the education system. The national curriculum is structured grade-wise (MOE, 2000). Textbooks and teachers' guides are issued grade-wise. Classrooms are built grade-wise. Besides the in-service training, multigrade teachers are mostly unsupported and not prepared to teach in multigrade classrooms. Consequently multigrade teachers struggle to teach in the gap between their own multigrade reality and the universal monograde norm – not knowing what to do. They organise multigrade teaching their own ways (Wright, 2000). As a result, the practices of multigrade teaching in classrooms vary from classroom to classroom.

Prior to the training, the organisation of multigrade classes varied widely. Five different patterns of multigrade teaching organisations were identified. In pattern 1, teachers divide their whole teaching time during one day between the number of grades they have to cover, and teach each grade individually. This means that teachers avoid multigrade teaching by shortening the length of each period and simply abandoning some grades for part of each school day. Multigrade teaching is invisible.

Four other patterns are more visible. These are shown in Figure 5.1. In pattern 2, teachers divide the lesson period of a multigrade class into two equal time sections and teach each grade separately, as if they were teaching two monograde classes. They do not provide SLA.

Figure 5.1 Patterns 2, 3, 4 and 5 of the organisation of a multigrade class during one lesson period

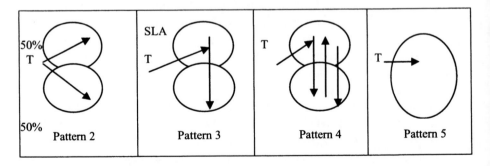

In pattern 3, one class is considered the main class to be taught, and the other is treated as an additional class. This conforms to the T and AM classes

advocated in the training curriculum. In the additional class, teachers assign Self-Learning Activity (SLA) during the first few minutes of the period, before going to teach the main class. Some appointed a monitor and others did not. At the end of the lesson, the teacher often comes back to the additional class to check the work of students.

In pattern 4, teachers visit different classes frequently during the same lesson period. The teachers provide SLA whenever they leave one grade. By visiting and checking all grades frequently, they supervise the student activity on SLA.

In pattern 5, the teachers identify two or more grades as a whole class and teach them together as a monograde class without any differentiation among the grades. Subjects whose curriculum is not organised by grade, such as sports, music and arts, are often taught in pattern 5. All students of different grades receive direct teaching from the teacher and their activities during the lesson are fully supervised.

THE KNOWLEDGE GAINED THROUGH THE TRAINING

Table 5.1 presents the responses of the trainees to questions about their multigrade teaching practices at the beginning (N=87) and end (N=98) of the training.

Table 5.1 Knowledge concerning multigrade teaching before and after the training

Category	Components	The number of trainee-teachers	
		Before (%)	After (%)
Organisation	Pattern 1	1 (1)	0 (0)
	Pattern 2	5 (6)	0 (0)
	Pattern 3	15 (17)	22 (22)
	Pattern 4	1 (1)	2 (2)
Methods	The provision of SLA	27 (31)	37 (38)
	The appointment of a monitor	17 (20)	64 (65)
	Others	14 (16)	25 (26)
	Total number of trainees	87	98

Note Multiple responses generate percentages (rounded) that total more and less than 100%

Table 5.1 indicates a number of differences in the trainees' responses before
and after training in relation to the training curriculum intentions. The most
marked shift, from 20% to 65%, was in the percentage of trainees who said
that they would appoint a monitor to supervise work in the additional class.
No teachers said that they would adopt organisational patterns 1 and 2 in the
future. There is a slight shift in the percentage of those who said that they
would provide SLA.

Not all knowledge of these three training components was new to all.
Eight trainees had taken the training previously and several trainees reported
using pattern 3 organisation, the provision of SLA and the appointment of
the monitor even before the training. However, the following individual
comments indicate that the training stimulated the trainees.

> I was using the methods (learned in the training) before the training, but I did not
> know fully how to manage them well. This training gave me self-confidence to
> manage my classes effectively.
>
> (Kavre-23)

> I will adopt the techniques learned in the training, as well as use my previous
> experience and knowledge.
>
> (Nuwakot-B28)

Some trainees did acquire new knowledge through the training, but did
not accept what they have learned in the training as desirable practice.

> (Multigrade classes should be) supervised by a monitor in one class and taught by the
> teacher in another class, but I do not think this technique is useful.
>
> (Nuwakot-K3)

> (I will) prepare SLA and arrange for a monitor, but if the monitor is given the answer
> keys, he/she copies the answers and does not learn well. Consequently he will fail the
> examinations. Therefore, alternative methods should be taken.
>
> (Nuwakot-B3)

The opinions expressed by the trainees indicate that acceptance and likely
adoption of the training messages is not guaranteed. Nonetheless the
evidence suggests that the trainees acquired new knowledge during the
training or recalled and strengthened things learned previously. The training
has stimulated the trainees.

COMPETENCE ACQUIRED THROUGH THE TRAINING

During the training, twenty-one trainees demonstrated their multigrade
teaching. Six trainees were current multigrade teachers, three were monograde

teachers with previous multigrade experience and 12 were current monograde teachers with no previous multigrade experience. Table 5.2 presents the training curriculum components demonstrated in the practice teaching during the training.

Table 5.2 shows that most trainees, including monograde teachers who had never taught multigrade classes, had developed the competence to apply the knowledge introduced by the training course. Eighteen (86%) of the trainees were capable of organising two or more grades with T and AM classes, differentiating the main teaching class and the additional class and provided SLA for the AM class (pattern 3). Significantly, all trainees provided SLA to keep all grades occupied at the same time. Fifteen (71%) trainees appointed a monitor, although only 5 (33% of the 15) trainees provided the monitor with instructions on what the monitor should do.

THE PERFORMANCE IN CLASSROOMS AFTER THE TRAINING

In the five classrooms selected for observation before the training, two trainee-teachers changed their practice of multigrade teaching. Before the training, trainee Nuwakot-B3 taught two or more classes sequentially with no distinction between T and AM classes and no provision of SLA. After the training, she differentiated T and AM classes, provided SLA and appointed a monitor, who followed by instructions and used answer keys given to him. Students in each of the classes for which she was formally responsible at any given time were provided with learning opportunities whether she was present in their classroom or not. Before the training, trainee Kavre-12 also had not distinguished T and AM classes and had not given SLA while he was teaching in another grade. After the training, he still did not distinguish his teaching classes into a main and additional class and taught each class in turn, in equal amounts of time. But he provided SLA for the grade which he could not teach before starting teaching the other class. When he finished teaching the first, he checked on the SLA before starting teaching the other. Prior to training, both trainee-teachers had considered themselves

Table 5.2 Practice teaching during the training

Lesson demonstrators	Lesson duration (minutes)	Class organi- sation	Provision of SLA	Appoint- ment of a monitor	Instructions for the monitor
training content	undefined	AM, T classes	√	√	√
multigrade (B-2)	15	AM, T classes	√	√	
multigrade (B-3)	17	frequent visits	√	√	√
multigrade (B-21)	24	ad hoc	√		
multigrade (B-22)	24	AM, T classes	√	√	
multigrade (B-26)	25	AM, T classes	√	√	√
multigrade (B-28)	26	AM, T classes	√		
multi-monograde (B-5)	17	AM, T classes	√	√	
multi-monograde (B-13)	22	AM, T classes	√		
multi-monograde (B-23)	21	AM, T classes	√	√	√
monograde (B-1)	17	AM, T classes	√		
monograde (B-4)	15	AM, T classes	√	√	
monograde (B-6)	22	AM, T classes	√		
monograde (B-7)	18	AM, T classes	√	√	
monograde (B-8)	15	AM, T classes	√·	√	
monograde (B-9)	20	frequent	√	√	√
monograde (B-10)	23	AM, T classes	√	√	
monograde (B-11)	15	AM, T classes	√	√	
monograde (B-12)	25	AM, T classes	√		
monograde (B-14)	21	AM, T classes	√	√	
monograde (B-20)	25	AM, T classes	√	√	
monograde (B-n/a)	9	AM, T classes	√	√	√
Total	21		21 (100%)	15 (71%)	5 (33% of 15)

responsible only for one class at a time, even though the timetable indicated they were responsible for two or more. Now both trainee-teachers were aware of responsibility for two or more classes simultaneously.

The other teachers demonstrated no change in the way they organised their multigrade classes. They continued to demonstrate responsibility for only one class at time. However, they had changed some practices and had been influenced by the content of the course that had emphasised 'doing and learning' teaching. Natural materials, experimentation, teaching materials including wooden alphabet cards and alphabet pocket cards, as well as original handmade materials were observed being used in the classroom. These trainees did not transfer what they had learned about organisation of classes into their classrooms but they would appear to have been attracted by other content in the course. Physically visible contents such as the 'doing and learning approach' had attracted their attention and been transferred to the classroom.

During the focus group discussion, trainers reported that 'class organisation' and 'the monitor appointment' had improved among the trainees in both districts. They reported that after the training, some teachers organised teaching by distinguishing the T and AMT classes, gave instructions to the monitors systematically and assigned more SLA. These reports confirm and extend the results from the observation of the five classes selected for observation before and after the training.

CONCLUSION

The in-service Multigrade Teaching Training course stimulated the trainees. Although the training curriculum was not new to some trainees, they still acquired new knowledge, and others recalled existing knowledge through the training. Most trainees also acquired the competence to demonstrate the newly acquired knowledge in the practice teaching during the training course. However, demonstration of skills during in-service training and practice in the classroom are two different things. And we need to question what impact, if any, there will be on the learners in the classes. If teachers are not re-organising their classes and taking responsibility for providing learning opportunities for all their students then the learning time and achievement of students is unlikely to increase. As Table 5.3 shows, the key problem is not how to make trainees gain knowledge and competence through the training but how to actualise it in their classrooms.

Table 5.3 The scope of the impact of the training

Result of training	Impact on classroom
Knowledge gained by trainees	Change
Competence gained by trainees	Change
Classroom performance by trainees	Little change
More learning time for their students	No change
Improvement of their students' learning achievement	Change unlikely

The difference between the two trainee-teachers who changed their practice and the other three who did not change involves not only the motivation of individual trainees but their context of multigrade teaching. It is important to understand the organisation of the schools in which they teach. For example, teachers in a school organised along the lines of pattern 1 cannot change their classroom performance by themselves. As each class is treated as a monograde class, the whole structure of multigrade teaching in the school must be changed. And this is a decision for the school head, supported by local supervisors. The follow-up support and monitoring by educational supervisors should be emphasised more to link the knowledge and competence gained during training to classroom practice.

This chapter concludes that training can have an impact on the trainee-teachers but the transfer of this impact to students in the classroom is questionable. A major concern for the future is how to bridge the gap between newly-acquired teacher competence and their performance in the classroom.

REFERENCES

Bajracharya, H., Ratna, Thapa, B., Kumar and Chitrakar, R. (1998) *Trends, Issues and Policies of Education in Nepal.* Kathmandu: CERID, Tribhuvan University.

CERID (Research Centre for Educational Innovation and Development) (1988) *Multigrade Teaching in Primary Schools of Nepal* (Parts 1–3). Kathmandu: Tribhuvan University.

CERID (Research Centre for Educational Innovation and Development) (1989) *Multigrade Teaching in Primary Schools* (report of a national training workshop on 4–8 July 1989). Kathmandu: Tribhuvan University.

DEO (District Education Office) Kavre (2001) *Educational Destination 2058.* Dhulikhel: DEO.

DEO (District Education Office) Nuwakot (2000a) *School Leaving Certificate Examination Nuwakot: At a Glance.* Bidur, Nuwakot: DEO.

DEO (District Education Office) Nuwakot (2000b) *Teacher Selected Form 2000.* Bidur, Nuwakot: DEO.

EFA Assessment Committee (2000) *Education for All: The Year 2000 Assessment: Nepal country report.* Kathmandu: MOE.

Gurung, H. (1998) *Nepal Social Demography and Expressions.* Kathmandu: New ERA.

Hargreaves, E., Montero, C., Chau, N., Sibli, M. and Thanh, T. (2001) 'Multigrade teaching in Peru, Sri Lanka and Vietnam: an overview'. *International Journal of Educational Development*, 21, 499–520.

Hata, H. (2001) 'The study on the educational gap among Nepali caste/ethnic groups and its factors'. *Education and Development*, 12–26.

HMG (His Majesty's Government of Nepal) (2001) *Statistical Year Book of Nepal 2001.* Kathmandu: Central Bureau of Statistics.

JICA (Japan International Cooperation Agency) (1993) *Country Study for Development Assistance to the Kingdom of Nepal* (country report). Tokyo: JICA.

Lockheed, M.E., Verspoor, A.M., Bloch, D., Englebert, P., Fuller, B., King, E., Middleton, J., Paqueo, V., Rodd, A., Romain, R. and Welmond, W. (1991) *Improving Primary Education in Developing Countries.* Washington, DC: Oxford University Press for The World Bank.

Matsumoto, T. (1998) 'Education in Nepal'. In Y. Hirosato (ed.), *Structure and Features of Educational Development Process in Developing Countries: In Search of Asian Models and Future Prospects* (pp. 181–208). Nagoya.

MOE (Ministry of Education) (1996) *Educational Statistics of Nepal 1994.* Kathmandu.

MOE (Ministry of Education) (1997) *Educational Statistics of Nepal 1995.* Kathmandu.

MOE (Ministry of Education) (1998) *Educational Statistics of Nepal 1996.* Kathmandu.

MOE (Ministry of Education) (1999a) *Basic and Primary Education Program (BPEP2), Program Implementation Plan, 1999–2004.* Kathmandu.

MOE (Ministry of Education) (1999b) *Educational Statistics of Nepal 1997.* Kathmandu.

MOEC (Ministry of Education and Culture) (1990) *Educational Statistics of Nepal 1989.* Kathmandu.

MOEC (Ministry of Education and Culture) (1992) *Educational Statistics of Nepal 1990.* Kathmandu.

MOECSW (Ministry of Education, Culture and Social Welfare) (1993) *Educational Statistics of Nepal 1991.* Kathmandu.

MOECSW (Ministry of Education, Culture and Social Welfare) (1994) *Educational Statistics of Nepal 1992.* Kathmandu.

MOECSW (Ministry of Education, Culture and Social Welfare) (1995) *Educational Statistics of Nepal 1993.* Kathmandu.

MOES (Ministry of Education and Sports) (2000) *School Level Educational Statistics of Nepal 1998*. Kathmandu.

PTTU (Primary Teachers' Training Unit) (1998) *Multigrade Teaching Training Manual (For the Teachers)*. Sanothimi, Nepal: DOE, BPEP.

Sellar, P.O., Sprague, D. and Miedema, V. (1981) *U.S. Aid to Education in Nepal: A 20-year Beginning (project impact)*. Washington DC: Agency for International Development.

Stash, S. and Hannum, E. (2001) 'Who goes to school? Educational stratification by gender, caste, and ethnicity in Nepal'. *Comparative Education Review*, 45, 354–378.

Sulaiman, M.M.B. (1989) 'Malaysia'. In PROAP (ed.), *Multigrade Teaching in Single Teacher Primary Schools* (pp. 40–45). Bangkok.

Suzuki, T. (2004) 'Multigrade teachers and their training in rural Nepal: practice and training'. Unpublished PhD thesis, Institute of Education, University of London.

Wright, W.N. (2000, 17–21 July) 'Belize experience of multigrade teaching'. Paper presented at the Commonwealth Secretariat Regional workshop on multigrade teaching, Gaborone, Botswana.

CHAPTER SIX

PREPARED FOR DIVERSITY?

Teacher education for lower primary classes in Malawi

ALISON CROFT

INTRODUCTION

Every class contains a diverse range of children – children who vary by age, academic achievement, personality, and many other factors. But how does teacher education prepare teachers for the diversity they will face in their classrooms? This chapter looks at how teacher education in Malawi and other developing countries prepares teachers for diverse classes including multigrade classes. Between education systems, the factors that constitute important pupil variance for teachers and policymakers differ. A group of teachers in Albania considered a child's temperament a significant source of diversity: viewing children as 'sanguine' or 'phlegmatic' for example. The degree of diversity found among pupils in one class also differs between national education systems and between regions and schools within these systems. The Malawian government's objective that 'Average age range in a class will reduce from 10+ years to 5 years' (Ministry of Education, 2000: 15) illustrates the considerable age diversity that sometimes exists even in predominantly single-grade classes.

Teachers are most likely to be aware of pupil diversity when they have an overtly multigrade class or when there is a policy of including more children in education and the school population is therefore changing. In some countries, often the poorer countries in sub-Saharan Africa, national policies aiming to provide 'Education for All' (EFA) have encouraged large numbers of additional children to enter school. Many of these were unable to attend previously and are therefore significantly overage for the first grade in which they must start their school careers. Children entering school in these circumstances are likely to be poorer than those in previous pupil cohorts. In other countries the few remaining children to be brought into the school system are those from ethnic minorities including nomadic groups, those living in remote areas, and disabled children (UNESCO, 1990). Multigrade is sometimes introduced as the only viable school provision. The challenge

A.W. Little (ed.), Education for All and Multigrade Teaching: challenges and opportunities, 103–126.
© 2007 *Springer.*

of EFA is therefore the challenge of educating more diverse groups of pupils in either single or multigrade classes (Little, 2001).

Education systems have traditionally been structured so that pupils with diverse levels of academic achievement are treated differently: for example, organising schools by ability, setting or streaming within schools (Burton, 2003) or lengthening the academic cycle for the most able. At primary level in particular, differentiation is usually less structured and expressed pedagogically (Burton, 2003) with teachers differentiating the curriculum pupils experience to a greater or lesser extent, and more or less consciously. Teachers and schools are encouraged or constrained in their responses to pupil diversity by the curricular flexibility allowed by the state. Examination 'backwash' means that the flexibility allowed in learning objectives is a powerful influence on the potential extent of differentiation.

Some national systems give an expected range of achievement for a particular grade, while others expect that most pupils will achieve above a certain level. School systems in developing countries often require pupils to pass an examination at the end of the year in order to be promoted to the next grade. The opportunity to repeat is therefore a form of differentiation as pupils are seen to need a variable number of years to master the curriculum. Pupils in each grade are treated as a homogenous group able to follow a tightly prescribed curriculum for the academic year, set out in teachers' guides (Hargreaves, 2001). Malawian lower primary guides give the pace, content, and methods for teaching and learning for every lesson, allowing little opportunity for differentiation for urban or rural pupils, or for higher- or lower-achieving pupils.

Different understandings of equity in schooling could partly explain these differences between school systems, and therefore the limited transfer from an automatic promotion to a promotion-based system of pedagogical reforms which help teachers respond to diverse pupil needs. Under the Malawian system, and other similar systems, treating pupils in a particular grade as an homogenous group is considered equitable and resonates with traditions of giving equal treatment to children of a certain age or developmental stage (Serpell, 1993). The *de facto* aim of primary schooling is to select the few pupils who will go on to secondary school. In Malawi, at present, there is competitive entry to secondary school as there are places for only some of those who complete primary school.[1] In this ostensible meritocracy all children should theoretically be given access to the same curriculum, but the issues of whether and how the curriculum should adapt to include them have not been given much consideration. The school system gains its legitimacy from providing a chance to all children, and yet there does not appear to have been much debate about concepts such as equal opportunities, equal outcomes and equity (Gipps and Murphy, 1994). Instead, children should be given a 'second chance' and allowed to repeat a year if they fail. Efforts to reduce repetition to increase the internal efficiency of the school system have been ill-understood by Malawian primary teachers, who see not allowing repetition as unfair to children (Wolf *et al.*, 1999). Promoting a child before they are ready will set the child up to fail, and therefore discriminates against children who, through poverty, were not able to attend for the whole year. In the longer term, however, repetition often means that pupils do not progress far through the school system. As they get older their time becomes more valuable to families who cannot afford to keep them in school (Rose, 2002).

Education is therefore constructed as a process through which children are tested to see if they are worthy, by dint of a combination of ability and perseverance, to benefit from further study and ultimately the rewards of the few well-paid formal sector jobs (Serpell, 1999). This construction precludes much adaptation to the needs of individuals or sub-groups within classes (Bernard, 2000); a child who does not succeed was either not ready for school, otherwise incapable of benefiting from the curriculum or too frequently absent. The curriculum leads up to assessment and selection of individuals, rather than the curriculum and its implementation being judged by an assessment of how much all pupils have learnt. There is therefore little teaching tradition of significant differentiation to the diverse learning needs of pupils within a grade, and this 'gradedness' persists even in multigrade classes (Hargreaves, 2001). Multigrade teaching appears to be inevitably double the work of single grade teaching carried out less effectively and is therefore seen as 'inferior' (Birch and Lally, 1995). Benveniste and McEwan argue that to implement the cooperative learning, peer tutoring and use of self-instructional textbooks typically recommended for multigrade classes would be a 'revolution at the core' of 'educational practice in rural areas of developing countries' (2000: 35). To move from the existing situation to one in which the teacher is expected to help each child make as much progress as they are able in a school year – whatever the starting and finishing levels – is a considerable conceptual and practical leap. Some change is needed, however. The increasingly diverse classes found in the era of EFA are straining a system that views equity simply as exposure to the same curriculum, repeated as often as necessary. Repetition stretches already scarce resources, causes even larger classes and a further deterioration in quality (Croft 2002b).

As well as harsh economic reality, attitudes to individualism or collectivism in broader national cultures also shape the attitudes to differences between individual pupils reflected in some developing country school systems. In highly individualistic Western societies teachers are used to encouraging and responding to individual differences. They see a multigrade class as only a degree more diverse than a single-grade class:

> In a sense, all teaching is multiclass teaching. Even in a straight class with just one year group, there is always a considerable range of interests, abilities, maturity and needs. No two children can be considered as being at the same level in all areas.
>
> (Collingwood, 1991: Chapter 1)

In its purest form, progressive pedagogy celebrates individuals, allows them to learn at their own pace and to follow their own interests in order to meet their educational needs (e.g. Plowden, 1967 cited in Gillard, 2000). The influence of this pedagogy in UK and US primary schools has declined (e.g. Marcus, 1999), but current emphasis on multiple intelligences and different learning styles (Gardner 1993) keeps pupils' diverse needs in teachers' minds although the curriculum is far more tightly prescribed. Nevertheless, the language of progressive pedagogy is still popular in donor technical support to developing countries (Alexander, 2000) where certain interpretations of child-centred pedagogy (sometimes reduced to a *pot-pourri* of methods involving visual aids, individualised programmes, 'activity' and 'group work') are assumed to be the best solution for all schools (Croft, 2002a). Rather than being child-centred in this way, teachers in Malawian lower primary classes appear to be more children-centred as they respond to the situation of learners as a group. They attempt to build a sense of community among the learners to cope with challenging conditions, partly by appealing to communal values, such as social co-operation, found in the wider society (Croft 2002a). Although writing on donor efforts to reform education in India, Alexander's comments have broader application:

> it is not yet clear how far an individualistic, enquiry-based ideology is compatible with either the deeply rooted collective orientation of Indian primary teaching or the unassailable fact of very large classes.
>
> (Alexander, 2000: 546)

Where teaching is generally conducted to the class as a whole, and individualism is not encouraged, pedagogy that successfully includes a wider range of children in school learning is likely to develop differently from that in Western primary schools.

How diverse teachers consider their classes to be, and the extent to which they consider it to be their responsibility to address this diversity therefore depends on local expectations as a part of the whole culture of teaching and learning. The pressure of EFA is felt particularly in large lower primary classes, and, to improve quality, teacher education is frequently recommended, for example as a way of improving teachers' 'capacity and will' (Benveniste and McEwan, 2000) to implement multigrade education. The success of this teacher education will partly depend on how it understands and develops from teachers' existing conceptions of diversity, equity and learning, and their current practices.

This chapter looks at the preparation that primary teachers have in their initial teacher education (ITE)[2] to respond to various forms of pupil diversity, including diversity resulting from multigrade schooling. This is done by first looking at the extent to which teachers are prepared to teach diverse classes in the teacher education curriculum as documented in a number of countries. Secondly, an example from Malawi shows how pupil diversity is regarded in three rural primary schools where student teachers were learning from experienced qualified teachers.[3]

MULTIGRADE TEACHER EDUCATION

Multigrade pedagogy and inclusive education – resources for all teachers

Pupils in multigrade schools are often from remote communities, or otherwise live on the margins as members of ethnic and linguistic minorities (Aikman and Pridmore, 2001; Hargreaves *et al.*, 2001). So, too, the teachers in these schools are also often marginalised. This can affect their access to professional development, as well as creating problems in the supply of teacher support materials, such as teachers' curriculum guides (Lungwangwa, 1989). In ITE the inclusion of multigrade teaching 'is complicated by the fact that not all teacher graduates will experience such teaching' (Birch and Lally, 1995: 59). Even when included it is not always given the status of being examined and can be 'resented by students because it is considered to be a preparation to teach in the remotest parts of the country a situation they would like to avoid at any cost' (Lungwangwa, 1989: 34).

Despite its marginalisation, preparation to teach diverse classes, such as multigrade classes, is crucial if EFA is to be achieved. Several writers (e.g. Little, 2001; Thomas and Shaw, 1992) have commented that while multigrade education has at various times and places in developed countries been chosen for pedagogic reasons as the best way of organising the classes in a school, in developing countries it is seen as second-best, and only used when single-grade schooling is not thought feasible. Despite this, pedagogy often associated with multigrade teaching and learning is a potential resource for all teachers, including those who throughout their careers teach single-grade classes (Birch and Lally, 1995; Berry, 2001; Little, 2001).

Similarly, developments in inclusive education (emerging from the disability rights movement) increasingly recognise that where teachers and schools adapt to successfully teach a greater diversity of pupils, there are potential benefits for all pupils:

> Regular schools with this inclusive orientation are the most effective means of...achieving education for all; moreover, they provide an effective education to the majority of children and improve the efficiency...of the entire education system.
>
> (UNESCO, 1994: Salamanca Statement, Section 2)

For example, video-based teacher development in Lesotho (Mariga *et al.*, 1997) focused on disabled children but with an understanding that 'difference' was not limited to children with obvious physical impairments. In one session teachers were asked to produce an action plan for their school which would include (a) enabling a class teacher to spend time giving extra help to certain pupils, and (b) creating a bank of resource materials for example, worksheets and teaching aids. Teaching strategies that allow teachers to work with different groups at different times, and periods of independent pupil learning mediated by teaching/learning resources are also typical of multigrade pedagogy (Benveniste and McEwan, 2000).

While multigrade pedagogy is therefore considered to have lessons for all teachers about treating pupils as individuals with different learning needs, there are also general lessons from inclusive pedagogy that can be applied if a teacher works in a multigrade class during her career. The following review of a number of teacher education programmes will explore the extent to which their curricula cover multigrade pedagogy and differentiating teaching and learning.

Initial teacher education curricula

The Multi-site Teacher Education Research (MUSTER)[4] Project recently conducted extensive research on primary teacher education in five countries. The following comments consider the documented curricula of four teacher education programmes that MUSTER studied. The preparation of teachers for multigrade teaching and other diversity varied between countries not only in its extent but also in the ideology of difference that it appears to reflect.

In South Africa, one programme considered by MUSTER researchers was the Bachelor of General Education and Training (BAGET) Programme at the University of Durban Westville. While not appearing to overtly address the issue of multigrade education, this degree programme was introduced partly to better prepare students to 'address teaching and learning in multilingual, multicultural settings' (Samuel and Pillay, 2002: 31) and to be educators in a range of workplaces, not only schools. Included in the programme were 'seven modules designed to integrate themes from a range of educational theories and apply them critically to the Durban context' (Stuart, 1999: 17). These included one entitled 'Identity and Diversity'. Here, diversity is foregrounded as an essential issue in education. The general pedagogical underpinning of the programme promotes critical reflexive practice. It expects student teachers to develop their own 'personal working theories', to 'actively experiment, challenge and present alternative conceptions of teaching and learning' (Samuel and Pillay, 2002: 37).

By contrast, a trial syllabus of a three-year Education Studies programme as part of initial teacher education in Ghana lists 'multigrade teaching' as one of a number of 'classroom management techniques' although no further details are given. In general, diversity is treated in a more traditional way than in the BAGET programme. The Ghanaian syllabus includes a unit entitled 'Exceptional children in Basic Schools in Ghana' with a related objective that student teachers will be expected to 'identify factors responsible for learning disabilities and remedial measures to be taken' (Teacher Education Division, 1998: 2). The use of the terms 'exceptional' and 'remedial' along with a further objective that the students will understand 'normal child development' suggest a course that will see certain pupils as having 'special' needs, rather than all children as having 'individual needs'; integrated rather than inclusive education (Stubbs, 2002). Integrated education responds to difference by giving the appropriate 'remedy' to pupils hoping that they will then be able to learn as their peers at the expected level set for their class. Therefore, this approach to differences in learning abilities might not be easily adaptable to multigrade teaching.

Lesotho has many multigrade classes, particularly in the mountains where difficulty travelling requires small local schools. Mathot (1994) wrote that the National Teacher Training College did not teach specific courses on multigrade teaching at pre- or in-service level, even though 36% of all primary school teachers worked in schools where the number of classes was less than the seven years of primary schooling. Lesotho has, however, been developing an inclusive school system. A revised ITE primary education diploma curriculum was introduced in 1998 and this refers to working with diverse learners. For example, 'reaching all pupils' was one of four concepts to be introduced in a 'teaching methods' module, and there was also a module on special education in which the educational implications of inclusive education were one of four key areas (Lefoka and Ntoi, 2002). The curriculum as documented did not appear to clearly address the issue of multigrade teaching but teachers were receiving some in-service support from District Resource Teachers on 'ways of dealing with multi-standard classrooms' (Lefoka et al., 2000: 23).

Unlike Lesotho, Malawi does not have a large proportion of multigrade classes, but lower primary classes are typically large and very diverse, most obviously multi-age. MIITEP (Malawi Integrated In-Service Teacher Education Programme) was introduced in the wake of an expansion in primary education. It gave a route to qualified teacher status for additional staff taken on to teach the million or so extra pupils who enrolled in schools in 1994 (Ministry of Education/UNICEF, 1998). An analysis of the Foundation Studies (FS) course shows that there is some formal preparation for responding to pupil diversity but no apparent mention of multigrade or multi-age teaching.

A unit on preparing lesson plans suggests an awareness of various pupil needs in presentation: 'Slow learners may benefit a lot if they are shown real objects, flash cards, maps, charts, pictures, diagrams, books and models' (TDU,[5] 1996a: 67). It does not, however, provide any structure for planning to meet different learning needs in whole-class teaching, group or individual work. Instead, FS appears here to teach that planning is aimed at the level of the class as a whole:

> How bright is the class? The brightness of pupils will determine how much time should be spent on a topic.
>
> (TDU, 1996a: 10)

Teacher questions during the lesson help to monitor progress and 'find out pupils' difficulties' (TDU, 1996a: 32). This appears to be the progress of the class as a whole as well as of specific pupils, as the example record of a week's work shows:

> Students responded to oral and written exercises very well.... Only Jane and Peter found problems. This was because they missed the two previous lessons and could therefore not make meaning of what was being taught easily. These two will be helped outside school hours.
>
> (TDU, 1996a: 17)

The approach therefore appears similar to the Ghanaian programme with a normative view of child development based largely on 'Western sources of some decades ago' (Stuart, 1999: 18). Intelligence is presented as a single 'overall capacity' (TDU, 1996b: 405). Pupils are expected to work at the grade level and there is limited extra support for those who cannot keep up perhaps because they have poor attendance or a sensory impairment. Problems are largely located within the individual; 'Basically learning difficulties are personal defects which make it difficult for the learner to interpret and understand instruction' (TDU, 1996b: 415). Nevertheless, teachers 'have the responsibility of helping all the children in their classes so that they all learn. Less bright pupils need more help than the brighter ones' (TDU, 1996b: 405).

The FS course suggests few specific differentiation strategies. For 'gifted' children these include working 'in a group of their own in order to learn at their own pace', being given extra work and 'content and activities that can challenge their abilities' (TDU, 1996b: 425). Space is limited but in a three-page unit on physical impairments there are only four suggested teaching strategies (e.g. avoid drawing attention to disability). There is a focus on defining and characterising pupils' difficulties (labelling) rather than exploring how to help particular children when teaching them. Towards the end the FS course gives brief general advice on pupils' diverse learning needs:

> The teacher should use various methods in each lesson as different pupils learn better with different methods. The teacher should deal with children as individuals
> - reward pupils according to their abilities
> - give content that is suitable for the whole class
> You must know that the knowledge of individual differences in children helps the teacher to manage his/her class well.
>
> (TDU, c.1997: 1206)

Given the large lower primary classes, it is unclear how teachers can give attention to individuals and to know all the pupils as individuals. A unit on large classes advises using a mixture of mixed-ability and same-ability groups so that teachers can distribute their help to pupils effectively and so that pupils can help each other.

Despite aiming to 'focus on the core content and skills needed to become an effective teacher' (TDU, 1996b: iii) the FS course seems to mainly teach theoretical knowledge about learning and individual differences rather than either passing on much 'teacher craft knowledge' (Zeichner et al., 1987) or providing opportunities to explore inclusion, exclusion, difference, diversity and equity as a critically reflective practitioner.[6] MIITEP does not therefore appear to fully prepare teachers for the diverse classes they are likely to face or prepare them to adapt their teaching to possible multigrade classes.

This review has considered the degree to which the documented curricula of four initial teacher education programmes prepare their graduates for teaching multigrade and for pupil diversity in general. There is little mention of multigrade teaching even where multigrade classes are common. There are more references to pupils' special or individual needs, such as physical or learning difficulties. The extent to which the general pedagogy of the programme emphasises reflecting on and adapting teaching strategies to the variety of schools and the many different pupils that teachers are likely to meet in the course of their careers is important. Most programmes apparently see certain pupils as 'special' and requiring special treatment to help them integrate into school, whereas the South African example appears more inclusive, and expects the school and the school system to adapt to successfully teach more diverse pupils. The documented teacher education curriculum is, however, only one of many influences on teachers' practice. The following section looks in detail at the degree of diversity that is acknowledged and responded to in a small number of Malawian lower primary classes where student teachers were working alongside experienced teachers.

TEACHING AND DIVERSITY IN MALAWIAN LOWER PRIMARY CLASSES

Primary education in Malawi

Malawi is one of the poorest countries in the world and provides an extreme example of the challenges of providing EFA where resources are severely constrained. The challenge of implementing the 'Free Primary Education' introduced in 1994 fell heaviest on lower primary sections of schools when over a million extra pupils enrolled, many of them in Standard 1 (equivalent of Grade 1). Resources are most stretched in lower primary classes because schools tend to favour the higher classes when allocating the limited teaching staff, classrooms, furniture and stationery that they receive. Pupils who have nearly 'made it' to secondary school are seen as the best investment for the school and broader community.

Officially, Malawi does not have a high proportion of multigrade classes as population density is sufficient in most areas to support single-grade classes at least in lower primary standards. Despite this, several of the conditions under which multigrade teaching often arises (Little, 2001) operate in Malawi. For example, difficulties with posting teachers to rural schools, lack of cover for teacher absence, and a shortage of classrooms in the rainy season result in classes being combined. These are frequently classes in the same grade, but can be classes from consecutive grades. Sometimes teachers supervise the two grades in different classrooms. Multigrade pedagogy could therefore be useful in these situations, and could also help alleviate the problem of very large lower primary classes (60 to 100 is common for single classes, combined classes can be close to 200 pupils). Small classes of twenty or fewer pupils are common in rural middle and higher grades where there is a tendency to avoid multigrade classes although these would allow lower primary classes to be split and given a fairer share of a school's teachers. In unofficial multigrade classes therefore, as well as in their single-grade classes, Malawian lower primary teachers commonly face a diverse range of pupils.

The following analysis describes the range of pupils who are already included in Standard 1 classes in three schools in Southern Malawi, and the strategies that their teachers use. It is based on 15 lessons taught by five experienced, locally respected qualified teachers, and three MIITEP student teachers who work with them.[7] Ultimately, teachers' existing strategies for working with diversity are a good place to start in implementing Education for All rather than selection of the few. Multigrade pedagogy in Western cultures usually includes differentiated education programmes for individuals and/or groups in a class. What will Education for All look like in a less individualistic culture, with much larger classes, and fewer resources with which to provide these programmes? Part of the answer appears to be that teachers think about their classes as composed of different sub-groups, and teach in ways that address some of the needs of these sub-groups.

Pupil diversity in Malawian lower primary classes

Socio-economic status is a major contributory factor to many aspects of pupil diversity. It has many potential effects on children, including the following:

- The age at which they start school
- How regularly they attend school
- Whether they feel hungry in class, and are malnourished over the longer term
- Whether they have warm clothes in winter
- Whether they have paper and pencils.

All of these affect the progress that they are able to make in their learning. The official school starting age is 6 years but there is considerable age diversity within a class with both underage and overage pupils common in lower primary classes. In line with Kadzamira and Chibwana (2000), the present study found evidence for lower primary classes functioning as unresourced childcare, also fuelled by an expectation that young children would get accustomed to school by attending intermittently as 'listeners' (Marshall, 2003) before formally enrolling.

Irregular school attendance frequently means that pupils fail a grade and have to repeat it. There is seasonal variation in attendance linked to the demands of agriculture, but also variation from day to day. In one class, for example, there was a 25% 'turnover' in pupils present from one day to the next. Children's time is valuable to poor families and where school quality is low, parents would rather their children assisted with household chores than go to school and learn little of use (Chimombo, 1999):

> the difficulties families face in financing their children's school attendance is leading to a situation of 'stuttering education' (Rosentahl/Nov 99). This is a problem for the child who makes little progress over an extended period, and for the school which finds itself dealing with classrooms full of children of many ages who come and go as finances at home permit.
>
> (Bernard, 2000: 9)

Many families found it hard to provide sufficient food and clothing for their children, which affects pupils' attendance and concentration in class. In a sample of 400 children present in lower primary classes, 51% had had no solid food before walking or running to school (Croft, 2002b). Long-term malnutrition leads to increased ill-health, including increased incidence of sensory impairments. Where there is insufficient money for food there is also insufficient money to supplement the scarce resources in lower primary classes – many children had no books, pencil or paper with which to learn to read and write.

Poverty therefore has many interrelated effects on primary education in Malawi which together mean that formal schooling by no means includes all children. Difficult teaching and learning conditions mean that it is hard to provide an education of sufficient quality in the lower standards. This creates a vicious circle in which, as more children need to repeat, class size increases and quality further deteriorates, thus stoking further repetition and making classes increasingly diverse in age and school experience.

Teachers' responses to absenteeism, lack of teaching and learning materials and hunger

There were several ways in which teachers respond to the effects of poverty. Mr Banda,[8] a qualified teacher (QT), used code-switching to Chichewa to check comprehension in English lessons, as a way of helping infrequent attenders to follow the lesson. Most of the teachers in the study talked about the effect of absenteeism on pupil learning, and schools tried to promote attendance by discussing absenteeism with parents.

Although schools officially provide stationery this only infrequently filters through to lower primary classes. Teachers sometimes found a spare pencil or two to give to children who had only paper, let children practise the early stages of writing on the ground, and allowed pupils to fetch pencil and paper from siblings in other classes. The schools in the study did not have school feeding programmes at the time so again schools could do little in this regard. The rest of this section will focus on factors more within the teachers' realm of control, i.e. how teachers used various strategies in their lessons to work with a multi-age class of boys and girls, and how they attempted to keep them participating in the lesson despite difficult teaching and learning conditions.

Boy volunteers and 'shy' girls

A male student teacher (ST), Mr Moyo, discussed a number of sub-groups in his class: boys, girls, able, less able, rich and poor, children who volunteer to answer and those who are shy, and those who imitate what others are doing. He described how he called on volunteers and non-volunteers to answer, and that he concentrated on 'duller' pupils, not only the 'clever' ones from 'clever families'. When asked whether he made any difference in his teaching between girls and boys, he answered that, 'Most of the girls are shy'. He tended not to call on them to answer in class because waiting for them to answer delayed the lesson too much. Mr Moyo seemed to locate the problem of under-achievement in children or their families, while still feeling some degree of responsibility to counter this.

Under-age pupils

Teachers frequently discussed under-age pupils. Mr Banda took the under-age learners to the back of the class to learn to write in the sand, to aid their learning but also 'so that they must not disturb their friends'. A student teacher, Mrs Mponda, addressed questions of an appropriate level to young disruptive pupils to draw them into the lesson when they were 'making noise'. Although she was feeling some frustration at having under-age children in her class, another student teacher spoke of her efforts to make them feel at home. I observed her whispering 'coaching' comments to support a young child who she had called up to the front of the class to answer a question. Variety was seen as key here:

Because if you can use one method sometimes pupils become bored,
especially lecture method, they become very tired, and they start making
noise, but if you use group method, discussion, and then back to other method,
and they cannot tire until the lesson end.

The same student teacher used choral repetition and choral answering by
groups rather than always the whole class so that she could 'see if they are
participating in the lesson'. Croft (2002a) describes in detail how teachers
used songs instead of punishment for class control, encouraging participation
and building positive relationships in the class. The use of an oral teaching
style in this situation suggests a different kind of learner-centred pedagogy
than that described in MIITEP.

In urban areas under-age learners are becoming more common, while
in these rural schools it appears that a few young children can make
maintaining control in challenging circumstances even more difficult. For
teachers, under-age pupils are a significant problem, although they form only
a small proportion of pupils. Whereas for policymakers and planners, the
large percentage of over-age pupils puts additional stress on an already
strained system. The teachers try to encourage under-age children to
participate, but the current curriculum and organisation of schooling are not
designed for very young children.

Using age diversity: over-age learners, 'learning from friends' and group work

The benefits of age diversity, particularly when organising learning through
co-operating groups of pupils, is an argument in favour of multigrade
education. Despite being in the majority, older learners did not receive
explicit mention in my interviews with teachers. The teachers did however
appear to respond specifically to over-age learners. They were chosen for
certain roles within the class, most formally as monitors, known as 'class
leaders'. In one class the monitor was the oldest boy. Older girls sometimes
performed certain practical duties, such as cleaning up a younger child's
vomit. In one school there were fixed groups where older children were
leaders. In other classes where groups were used, for example to share
textbooks, these appeared to be friendship groups which formed on the day,
and were more likely to be homogenous by age and gender. There was
some limited differentiation of the curriculum in individual 'seatwork',
mostly through additional tasks set for more able children. For example, in
mathematics lessons, if a child was able to write numbers 1 to 15 from

memory, they were then allowed to proceed to working out sums written on the board.

Teachers also expected that pupils would 'learn from friends', i.e. their fellow pupils. These were often the older, more able pupils who were also sometimes repeaters. During whole-class teaching, the teachers followed a pattern of first asking the whole class to answer or repeat in chorus. For example, in one English lesson Mrs Mponda moved a book onto a table and asked, 'Where's the book?' At first only some pupils answered, but the response built with the second and subsequent times of asking. Typically, teachers would next ask a pupil to answer individually (hereafter referred to as a 'focus pupil'). They usually asked the more able/older pupils to answer as a demonstration for the younger/less able children, and perhaps also to give the more able pupils a greater challenge, as they had fewer prior examples. Mrs Chapita (ST) explained how she had learnt this technique from an experienced qualified teacher, and then made sense of it in terms of what she had learnt at college:

> At first we learned it from Mrs Phiri, we are told that if you want to demonstrate you take a child to demonstrate to his friends, and then at the TTC we are told, because nowadays the curriculum is pupil-centred, not teacher-centred.

Mr Banda (QT) noted the difficulty of keeping all the class involved during a lesson on writing numerals. To maintain interest, he slightly altered the task set to different focus pupils and the location of their demonstrations to the rest of the class:

> I changed the activity slightly because in the class there are some pupils who were not attending [to] the lessons so, ... it is very difficult to go individually that's why I conducted various activities. For one to write in the air so that everybody who is in the classroom will see what somebody is pretending to write.... on the board here is where in the class each and every pupil [can see what the pupil] has written on the board.

Here, the tension between working with individuals, but also maintaining all pupils' participation in a large class is made explicit.

The use of learning from friends was further explained by Mrs Gama, another qualified teacher:

> If one pupil fails it, we must choose another pupil to help her friend. Yes. That is our style. We don't want to feed them everything.

She was the only teacher who suggested an explicit link between large classes, group work and learning from friends:

> For large classes you must have enough teaching and training of teachers and have the pupils within groups, giving them different activities [unclear]. Choose the leaders to help you. That is how we handle large classes. We must prepare our work in advance. Prepare enough work for the pupils. If you prepare less work, most of the time the pupils will just play [unclear] but if you involve them in different activities, they learn more even from their friends.[9]

This second comment suggests a use of age diversity closer to progressive Western pedagogy for multigrade classes.

Teachers therefore appear to differentiate their treatment of older learners to facilitate their classroom management, and for more academic reasons when constructing the text of the lesson during whole-class teaching. There is some adaptation to different ability levels, most commonly by asking more challenging questions, earlier on in a teaching sequence, or sometimes by setting more demanding extension work. This, however, is limited by the curriculum in a system that expects all children in a class to be at a certain 'standard'. The children were formed into groups in many lessons, but this was sometimes little more than a seating strategy, or for sharing textbooks. While pupils did appear to learn from watching other pupils point to the relevant picture as they shared these textbooks, there did not appear to be the substantial use of group work that technical advisers to education in developing countries often call for. Instead, the older and more able learners provide examples during whole-class teaching from which other pupils can hopefully learn. How well teachers know their pupils in order to appropriately differentiate their treatment of them, is now considered.

Teachers' knowledge of their pupils

In order to help pupils learn, it would seem likely that the more the teacher knows about their diverse needs and their current and previous learning the better, as suggested in the MIITEP Foundation Studies course. Even if the needs of an individual are not addressed individually, but as part of a sub-group of the class, it is necessary for the teacher to know enough about a child to mentally assign them to a group.

Teachers had strategies for seeing how the pupils responded to the lesson. Mrs Gama (QT) asked her class to come to the front of the room so that:

> I can see that this one is not doing the activity, this one is playing, so if I say, 'Jump!', everybody jumps. Where [as] if they stay in the back...they will just play.

At the end of a lesson, another teacher asked those who had 'Good' or 'Very good' written on their marked work to stand up while the rest of the class clapped them. Here, a rough assessment of how the class has done is combined with rewarding those who have done well. As with many teaching strategies observed these seemed to be partly about class management as well as about knowing how well pupils were following the lesson.

Discussions with teachers showed that they had detailed knowledge of individual pupils, and sometimes also spoke to their parents and visited their homes. There were limitations however to the teachers' knowledge of the pupils, which is understandable given the numbers and shifting class population. Firstly, an expatriate education adviser who had observed a large number of lessons in Malawi considered that it was the regular attenders who became well-known to teachers. Teachers tended to teach to this core, who were expected to pass at the end of the year. This is understandably rational behaviour, when faced with an impossible task, to settle for a task that is within reach, but it does have significant implications for achieving Education for All, in current Malawian conditions. Secondly, it is not clear how much unregistered 'listeners', and other under-age irregular attenders, affect the teacher's ability to get to know the learning needs of pupils, for example, their 'hidden disabilities', such as hearing and visual impairments. Thirdly, in a large class there is a danger that a little knowledge of pupils can lead to teacher stereotyping of learners, where they are seen as part of a homogenous sub-group (Burton, 2003), rather than as individuals with their own profile of strengths and weaknesses. While all mainstream teachers must group pupils to a degree, the issue is to avoid gross generalisations where possible. For example, when teachers view girls as shy and taking up valuable class time to answer they are likely to call on them infrequently, and therefore reinforce the stereotype and the inequity.

Individual help

The most focused response to pupil diversity is help from a teacher, addressed to a particular child when they are having difficulty with part of the curriculum. The question and answer to individuals and chorus that constitutes the bulk of most lessons does address individuals, but this is done in public and might, as noted above, be less accessible to certain sub-groups in the class. Also, the reasons teachers elicit responses from individuals during whole class teaching are numerous; it is not all about engaging with that individual's learning needs (Pryor, 1999). There are two ways in which pupils receive individual help.

Firstly, combining classes means that while one teacher leads the lesson, the second, and sometimes third teachers, can circulate around the room giving help to individual children. This was observed regularly at two schools where student teachers team-taught with qualified teachers. Secondly, children stay behind after lessons to have extra help, often to counter irregular attendance:

> today they learned ordering numbers, from 1 to 10, modelling numbers from 6 to 10, so if there come new pupils, if I ask them, for example, tomorrow, model these numbers or write these missing numbers in this number, they fail ... so it's difficult teaching the new pupils today, the other new pupils tomorrow.
>
> (Mrs Gama, QT)

As well as being common in the schools in the study, several student teacher autobiographies[10] mention staying behind after school, which suggests that this is something that has been widely practised for many years.[11]

This analysis has shown that these teachers try to make lessons accessible and challenging to the different sub-groups in the class during whole-class teaching. Teachers also seemed ready to physically group children in many lessons although this was largely a seating strategy and all groups did the same task at the same time. Some individual help was given to pupils with their academic work. Although tasks set were rarely differentiated by ability, the presentation of a task could be adjusted to individual need as teachers responded to any difficulties pupils were experiencing, in or after class. The teachers appeared to know the pupils in their own class reasonably well, but were also often teaching pupils they knew less well, such as intermittent unregistered attenders and pupils from other classes. This limited the extent to which they could address pupils' needs, as did the dearth of material resources and the curriculum's lack of suitability for under-age learners.

DISCUSSION

How does the teaching style described above relate to the approach to pupil diversity presented in MIITEP? Student teachers on MIITEP spent most of their time working in schools. Those included in the above study were able to work with and learn from qualified experienced teachers. The messages they received in schools and in the Foundation Studies course have important similarities and differences. Similarities include teachers' responsibility to help all children learn by varying teaching methods, challenging more able children, questioning pupils during the lesson to monitor progress, and giving individual help after lessons. Differences include a strong emphasis on visual aids in MIITEP and no apparent advice on teaching multi-age classes with high absenteeism.

There was also little or no mention of multigrade pedagogy in the curricula reviewed. Some space was given in MIITEP and other teacher education curricula to teaching pupils with 'special educational needs'. Most of the teacher education curricula reviewed appeared to express a 'graded' pedagogy in which a certain level of achievement counts as success, and a few 'special' children need extra help to stand a chance of achieving this. The focus in MIITEP on labelling pupils leaves little room for suggesting teaching approaches. These pupils' differences seem to be over-privileged so that potential links between the pedagogy of inclusive education and multigrade pedagogy are missed.

In schools, however, student teachers were learning to use a largely oral teaching style to encourage the participation of young pupils and irregular attenders, while also using and challenging older and more able pupils in whole-class teaching. 'Learning from friends' was an important theme in teacher discussions. In progressive and multigrade pedagogy this might occur through cooperative group work (Berry, this volume), while in these Malawian schools it largely occurs in whole-class teaching. This resonates with Pryor's comments based on empirical work in the UK. He gives a typology of teacher intentions when giving feedback on pupil responses. One intention is 'To create a text which might be appropriated by other pupils by eliciting, or paraphrasing the focus pupil's text' (1999: 1–2). Pryor suggests that children who learn well in larger teaching groups are those who can acquire knowledge from the teacher and also from their peers and then make it their own. If pupils learn from others' responses, then the Malawian teachers' comments about 'learning from friends' are probably a local way of expressing this theory.

Certain children might, however, be excluded by this teaching style. Pryor talks about the children who are not as good as their peers at learning by appropriation. As is often the case in large classes the time allowed to individual pupils to respond was short (Galton et al., 1996). This is likely to disadvantage less able and less confident pupils. Teachers are unable to afford the 'luxury' (Rubagumya, 1994) of time for pupils such as 'shy' girls to answer, suggesting that large classes might differentially impact on girls' participation in whole-class teaching and learning. The practice of keeping such children behind is a way of accommodating diverse learning styles to a degree. This pattern of providing individual help outside class has been found in studies of other school systems where whole-class teaching takes up much of lesson time (Volet, 1999).

As discussed above, the collective orientation of most teaching appears to at least partly result from the broader socio-cultural context as well as from a graded curriculum and difficult school conditions. Teachers in the study were concerned about the lack of physical resources, over-crowding and under-age learners. One teacher commented 'The teacher can't teach properly, you can't do it in a good way ... if the class is crowded.' Croft (2002a) argued that human resources and the resources of oral culture become comparatively more important in this situation, leading to a teacher-intensive pedagogy that is sometimes criticised for being too teacher-centred. The findings of the study of Malawian classes suggest that pedagogy that focuses on pupils' diverse needs is likely to develop differently in different contexts. The teaching strategies described above show what is possible in large classes with few material resources in a relatively collective culture (Croft, 2002a, 2002b). These strategies contrast with the resource-intensive individualised strategies for multigrade and other diverse classes that have developed in smaller, better-resourced classes in more individualistic Western cultures. Further research is needed to see how and to what extent more resources could help teachers in countries such as Malawi develop their teaching so that all children can learn.

CONCLUSION

The central question of this chapter is how prepared new teachers are for the challenge of including more diverse pupils in primary school learning in order to make EFA a reality. If all children are to be educated, repetition as the major structure for differentiating the curricular journey that pupils take through the school system is no longer affordable for individuals or for societies. This chapter has shown something of the complexity of teachers' approaches to pupil diversity in lower primary classes. Much of the pedagogy suggested in teacher education programmes for teachers working to implement EFA in developing countries has its roots in progressive Western primary practice which addresses diversity by striving to treat pupils as individuals. In large classes the guidance a teacher can give individually is stretched thinly, and teachers compensate for this by providing extra help after class. Some teaching strategies respond to the needs of various sub-groups of pupils within the class. With limited teaching and learning materials, a teacher-intensive rather than a resource-intensive pedagogy tends to develop. The 'graded' nature of the curriculum does, however, limit teaching addressed at pupils' diverse needs.

To implement EFA it will be necessary to enlarge the rationale for schooling and perhaps to challenge the 'gradedness' of schooling. In order to do this, it is important to understand the current beliefs and practices of teachers and all those involved with schools. These can be used as a starting point to imagine local pedagogy that can respond to multigrade and other diverse classes. Teacher education and development has a clear role to play here.

NOTES

[1] Pupils with the highest academic achievement therefore receive an extended curriculum, another form of highly-structured differentiation. With increasing economic development the selection point comes later, but schooling is usually understood as a competitive process to a greater or lesser degree.

[2] ITE includes pre-service programmes for those entering teaching as well as programmes for those wanting qualified teacher status after working as unqualified teachers.

[3] This is drawn from Croft, 2002b where further details are given. It is a sub-study of the MUSTER (Multi-site Teacher Education Research) Project, funded by DFID.

[4] The MUSTER Project is based on collaboration between educational research institutes in Malawi (CERT, University of Malawi), Ghana, Lesotho, South Africa, Trinidad and Tobago and the University of Sussex Institute of Education. There were four main strands to the research: the costs of teacher education, the college context, curriculum issues, and the process of becoming a teacher.

[5] Teacher Development Unit.

[6] The writers were pushed to develop the materials quickly and clearly felt themselves constrained by the student teachers' limited English; 'recall', 'recognise' and 'retain' are all defined in the text (TDU, 1996b: 414).

[7] This was deliberately a study of 'good' practice as reported by local advisors and headteachers. The classes chosen were not experiencing the most difficult conditions in Malawi at the time, but neither were they all particularly well-resourced. The main research methods used for the findings reported here are lesson observation and audio-recording followed by teacher interview on the same day (Croft, 2002a).

[8] Pseudonyms have been used.

[9] This was said when she spontaneously discussed how much she had learnt from working at a school supported by two former DFID programmes, the Primary Community Schools Programme and Malawi School Support Systems Programme.

[10] Malawi MUSTER Project data.

[11] There are issues of equity of access to help that is given less formally outside lesson time. Girls, orphans or poorer pupils might have to hurry home to work. Older girls might also not feel comfortable if left alone with a male teacher (Leach *et al.*, 2000).

REFERENCES

Aikman, S. and Pridmore, P. (2001) Multigrade schooling in 'remote' areas of Vietnam. *International Journal of Educational Development*, 21(6), 521–6.

Alexander, R. (2000) *Culture and Pedagogy: International comparisons in primary education.* Oxford/Malden: Blackwell.

Benveniste, L.A., and McEwan, P.J. (2000) Constraints to implementing educational innovations: The case of multigrade schools. *International Review of Education*, 46(1/2), 31–48.

Bernard, A.K. (2000, 26–28 April) Education for All and children who are excluded. In *Thematic Studies*. World Education Forum, Dakar, Senegal. Paris: UNESCO.

Berry, C. (2001) Achievement effects of multigrade and monograde primary schools in the Turks and Caicos Islands. *International Journal of Educational Development*, 21(6), 537–552.

Birch, I. and Lally, M. (1995) *multigrade Teaching in Primary Schools*. Bangkok: Asia-Pacific Centre of Educational Innovation for Development, UNESCO Principal Regional Office for Asia and the Pacific.

Burton, D. (2003) Differentiation of schooling and pedagogy. In S. Bartlett and D. Burton (eds), *Education Studies: Essential issues* (pp. 42–71). London: Sage.

Chimombo, J.P.G. (1999) Implementing educational innovations: A study of Free Primary Education in Malawi. Unpublished PhD thesis, Brighton: University of Sussex.

Collingwood, I. (1991) *Multi-class Teaching in Primary School: A handbook for teachers in the Pacific*. Apia, Western Samoa: UNESCO Office for the Pacific States. Available online: http://k1.ioe.ac.uk/multigrade/fulltext2collingwood.htm (accessed 21 July 2004).

Croft, A.M. (2002a) Singing under a tree: Does oral culture help lower primary teachers to be learner-centred? *International Journal of Educational Development*, 22(3–4), 321–327.

Croft, A.M. (2002b) *Pedagogy in school context: An intercultural study of the quality of learning, teaching and teacher education in lower primary classes in Southern Malawi*. Unpublished DPhil thesis, Brighton: University of Sussex.

Galton, M., Hargreaves, L. and Pell, A. (1996) *Class Size, Teaching and Pupil Achievement*. Leicester: NUT/University of Leicester.

Gardner, H. (1993) *Frames of Mind: The theory of multiple intelligences*. London: Fontana.

Gillard, D. (2000, Autumn) The Plowden report. *Forum*, p. 120.

Gipps, C. and Murphy, P. (1994) *A Fair Test? Assessment, achievement and equity*. Buckingham/Philadelphia: Open University Press.

Hargreaves, E. (2001) Assessment for learning in the multigrade classroom. *International Journal of Educational Development*, 21(6), 553–60.

Hargreaves, E., Montero, C., Chau, N., Sibli, M. and Thanh, T. (2001) Multigrade teaching in Peru, Sri Lanka and Vietnam: An overview. *International Journal of Educational Development*, 21(6), 499–520.

Kadzamira, E.C. and Chibwana, M.P. (2000) *Gender and Primary Schooling in Malawi*. IDS Research Report, vol. 40. Brighton: Institute of Development Studies (177 pages).

Leach, F. and Machakanja, P. with Mandonga, J. (2000) *Preliminary Investigation of the Abuse of Girls in Zimbabwean Junior Secondary Schools.* Education Research, vol. 39. London: Department for International Development (82 pages).

Lefoka, J.P. and Ntoi, V. (2002) *Primary Teacher Education in Action: A peep into the TTC Classrooms at the National Teacher Training College, Lesotho.* MUSTER Discussion Paper, vol. 29. Brighton: Centre for International Education, University of Sussex (42 pages).

Lefoka, J.P., Jobo, M., Khiba, R., Liphoto, N., Mapuru, P., Molise, M., Moeti, B., Moorosi, M., Nenty, H.J., Ntoi, V., Qhobela, B., Sebatane, E. and Sephelane, T. (2000) *Lesotho: A baseline study of the teacher education system.* MUSTER Discussion Paper, vol. 8. Brighton: Centre for International Education, University of Sussex (83 pages).

Little, A.W. (2001) Multigrade teaching: Towards an international research and policy agenda. *International Journal of Educational Development*, 21(6), 481-497.

Lungwangwa, G. (1989) *Multigrade Schools in Zambian Primary Education: A report on the pilot schools in Mkushi District.* Education Division Documents, vol. 47. Stockholm: Swedish International Development Authority (86 pages).

Mariga, L., Phachaka, L., and McConkey, R.. (1996) *Preparing teachers for inclusive education,* Maseru: Special Education Unit, Ministry of Education, Lesotho.   Available: http://www.eenet.org.uk/key_issues/teached/video_feedback.shtml (accessed 26 July 2004).

Marcus, J. (1999) Where lessons are scripted. *Times Educational Supplement,* 29/10/1999. Available: http://www.tes.co.uk/search/search_display.asp?section =Archive&sub_section=News+%26+opinion&id=306791&Type=0 (accessed 26 July 2004).

Marshall, J.H. (2003) Grade repetition in Honduran primary schools. *International Journal of Educational Development*, 23(6), 591–605.

Mathot, G.B. (1994) *Survey of one-teacher schools and multi-grade classes in Lesotho.* Maseru: Primary Education Section, UNESCO.

Ministry of Education Malawi (2000) *Education Policy and Investment Framework (PIF).* Lilongwe: Ministry of Education, Sports and Culture (51 pages).

Ministry of Education/UNICEF (1998) *Free Primary Education: The Malawi experience: a policy analysis study conducted by the Ministry of Education in collaboration with UNICEF.* Lilongwe, Malawi: Ministry of Education.

Pryor, J. (1999) Analytical working notes from the Primary Response Research Project. Brighton, University of Sussex.

Rose, P. (2002) *Cost-sharing in Malawian primary schooling: From the Washington to the post-Washington consensus.* Unpublished DPhil thesis, Brighton: University of Sussex.

Rubagumya, C.M. (1994) Language values and bilingual classroom discourse in Tanzanian secondary schools. *Language, Culture and Curriculum*, 7(1), 41-53.

Samuel, M. and Pillay, D. (2002) *Face-to-face initial teacher education degree programme at University of Durban-Westville, South Africa*. MUSTER Discussion Paper, vol. 31. Brighton: Centre for International Education, University of Sussex (51 pages).

Serpell, R. (1993) *The Significance of Schooling: Life journeys in an African society*. Cambridge: Cambridge University Press.

Serpell, R. (1999) Local accountability to rural communities. In F.E. Leach and A. Little (eds), *Education, Cultures and Economics* (pp. 111–39). New York/London: Falmer.

Stuart, J.S. (1999) *Primary Teacher Education Curricula as Documented: A comparative analysis*. MUSTER Discussion Paper, vol. 3. Brighton: Centre for International Education, University of Sussex.

Stubbs, S. (2002) *Inclusive Education: Where there are few resources*. Oslo: Atlas Alliance/Norwegian Association of the Disabled.

Teacher Development Unit (TDU) (1996a) *Student Teacher's Handbook 1 (1st draft version)*. Domasi, Malawi: Malawi Institute of Education.

Teacher Development Unit (TDU) (1996b) *Student Teacher's Handbook 2 (1st draft version)*. Domasi, Malawi: Malawi Institute of Education.

Teacher Development Unit (TDU) (undated – circa 1997) *Student teacher's Handbook 4 (1st draft version)*. Domasi, Malawi: Malawi Institute of Education.

Teacher Education Division (September 1998) *Education Studies for Three-year Post-secondary Teacher Training Colleges (Trial Edition)*. Accra: Ghana Education Service.

Thomas, C. and Shaw, C. (1992) *Issues in the development of multigrade schools*. World Bank Technical Paper, vol. 172. Washington: World Bank (47 pages).

UNESCO (1990) *World Declaration on Education for All*, Jomtien, Thailand. Available: http://www.unesco.org/education/efa/ed_for_all/background/jomtien_declaration.shtml (Accessed 25/5/04).

UNESCO (1994) *The Salamanca Statement and Framework for Action on Special Needs Education*, Salamanca, Spain. Available: http://www.unesco.org/education/pdf/SALAMA_E.PDF (accessed 26 July 2004).

Volet, S. (1999) Learning across cultures: Appropriateness of knowledge transfer. *International Journal of Educational Research*, (31), 625–43.

Wolf, J., Lang, G., Mount, L.B. and VanBelle-Prouty (1999) *Where policy hits the ground: Policy implementation processes in Malawi and Namibia*. SD Publication Series, v Technical Paper no. 95. Washington: ABIC/U.S. Agency for Development (94 pages).

Zeichner, K.M., Tabachnik, B. and Densmore, K. (1987) Individual, institutional, and cultural influences on the development of teachers' craft knowledge. In J. Calderhead (ed.), *Exploring Teachers' Thinking* (pp. 21–59). London: Cassell.

CHAPTER SEVEN

ADAPTING THE PRIMARY MATHEMATICS CURRICULUM TO THE MULTIGRADE CLASSROOM IN RURAL SRI LANKA

MANJULA VITHANAPATHIRANA

INTRODUCTION

This chapter is based on an action research project in multigrade schools in a rural Education Zone in Sri Lanka from April 2000 to February 2002 (Vithanapathirana, 2005). It presents the major findings of an intervention to improve multigrade teaching. The intervention is set within the context of the Sri Lankan education system and the place of multigrade teaching within it.

THE COUNTRY CONTEXT

Sri Lanka is an island in the Indian Ocean with a land area of about 65,610 km². It is a multi-ethnic and multi-religious country. The population was estimated at 18.7 million in 2002. Sri Lanka, known earlier as Ceylon, was traditionally an agricultural economy, with tea and rubber being the main export crops. By the 1990s the manufacture of garments had become the main source of export income. Sri Lanka is considered to be a middle-income developing country. The per capita income figure for 2002 was US$840. The war persisting for more than two decades in the north-eastern parts of the country has pulled down the rate of development in Sri Lanka. The average GDP per capita growth rate is 3.4 for the period of 1990–2002.

Sri Lanka has shown a considerable improvement in terms of social development and thus has acquired a Human Development Index of 81. The impressive figures of literacy, infant mortality, fertility, population growth and life expectancy have contributed to the overall social development of the country. The under-5 mortality rank is 130 and the total fertility rate is 2.0.

127

A.W. Little (ed.), Education for All and Multigrade Teaching: challenges and opportunities, 127–153.
© 2007 Springer.

The annual population growth rate for the past 20 years is estimated to be 1.2. The life expectancy at birth is 73 years. The adult literacy rate is 92% with the rate for males being 94% and 89% for females (UNICEF, 2004).

RESPONSIBILITIES OF THE GENERAL EDUCATION SYSTEM

Responsibility for the education system lies with several bodies. The formulation of recommendations for educational policy is the responsibility of the National Education Commission (NEC) since 1991. The responsibility for education administration was devolved in 1997. The National Ministry is responsible for the overall monitoring and review of the development of general education implemented by the eight Provincial Offices, 92 Zonal Offices and 302 Divisional Offices. The decisions and guidelines developed by the Provincial Ministries cascade down to the schools through the Zonal and Divisional Educational Offices.

The National Institute of Education (NIE) is entrusted with sole responsibility for curriculum development for general education. The curriculum specialists of the Primary Education Department of the NIE design and develop the primary curriculum and involve practising teachers in their work. Different committees take responsibility for developing subject curricula. Draft versions are tested in schools and then finalised after a series of review discussions with teachers, teacher educators and curriculum specialists. Further, several committees including the Academic Affairs Board and the Council of the NIE subject the new curricula to review and approval before they are implemented. The centralised curriculum development ensures uniformity of standards of the intended curriculum across the whole country. The curriculum development process of the NIE is supported by international donor agencies.

The modes of teacher education are two: initial and continuing. The responsibility for implementing initial teacher education lies with the national colleges of education and universities. The continuing teacher training component is introduced by the NIE and the faculties and departments of education in universities in addition to the provincial education offices, teacher colleges and teacher centres. Teacher education curricula for both initial and continuing other than for the courses that are conducted by the universities are developed by the NIE.

The responsibility for educational research is entrusted to (i) the universities, (ii) the National Education and Research and Evaluation Centre affiliated to the Faculty of Education, University of Colombo, and (iii) the NIE.

Central government is the main source of funding for education in the country. During the 1990s the government spent on average 10% of the national budget on education, accounting for 3% of the GDP, which is less than the 3.5% average for Asia and 3.9% for developing countries. It has even declined further, to about 8% in 2001. In addition external resources from multi-lateral and bi-lateral aid are provided. The major proportion of the recurrent expenditure, nearly 75%, is spent on teacher salaries. The next highest share is spent on school textbooks, followed by school uniforms, which are distributed free to all students (NEC, 2003).

ACCESS TO PRIMARY EDUCATION

The Constitution of Sri Lanka affirms the need for complete eradication of illiteracy and assurance of the right to universal and equal access to education to all citizens. The achievements made in terms of human development in Sri Lanka could be mainly attributed to the provision of non-fee levying or free education policy introduced since 1945. Education for 5–14-year-olds has been legally compulsory since 1998. One of the major attempts made with regard to improving access to educational opportunities is the provision of a primary school for all children within 2 km of their homes and a secondary school within a distance of 4 km. There are 9,826 government schools in the country (Ministry of Human Resource Development, Education and Cultural Affairs, 2002).

Sri Lanka's achievement in reaching gender parity in primary education reflects the impact of implementation of free education for more than 50 years. The net enrolment ratio is 97 for both sexes (UNICEF, 2004). Out of the total number of schools which offer primary education 97% are co-educational (School Census, 2002).

Education imparted through the mother tongue is another factor that contributed to the high rates of literacy. Of the schools 70.9% are Sinhala medium schools, 28.5% are Tamil medium schools and a small number are bi-media schools.

MULTIGRADE TEACHING IN SRI LANKA

In Sri Lanka education policies have generally addressed aspects of monograde teaching. Multigrade teaching has not been a recognised option for providing education in Sri Lanka. The school census database of the Ministry of Education does not include statistics on the prevalence of multigrade teaching and there the criteria for identification of multigrade schools have not been defined. Multigrade teaching has been 'invisible' (Little, 1995). The only teacher education resource for multigrade teaching is a single small module produced by the NIE for its distance teacher education course.

The existence of multigrade teaching in Sri Lanka had been reported by several educationists either directly or indirectly. Ekanayake (1982) reported the incidence of 'multigrade schools' as 33% of the total number of schools. Baker (1988), who did a study of a disadvantaged district in Sri Lanka, reported the existence of a considerable amount of 'multiple class teaching' in small schools. Abhayadeva's (1989) estimate in the late 1980s indicated that 24% of schools had multigrade teaching. Little (1995) reported that one-teacher schools accounted for 2% of the country's schools and that two-teacher schools accounted for 5% of all schools in 1991. Sibli (1999), based on the 1997 school census, indicates that 12% of schools have three or less teachers.

Vithanapathirana (2005) estimated the incidence of multigrade teaching through a secondary analysis of school census data based on teacher deployment guidelines. The teacher deployment guidelines are constructed on the basis of a predetermined Teacher/Pupil ratio. Accordingly schools with less than 114 students in the primary grades are compelled to function with less than one teacher for each grade.

If a school has four or fewer teachers assigned for the five primary grades it faces the likelihood of having at least one multigrade class within the primary grade span. Hence, some classes will comprise two or three grades some of the time. Unfortunately, the official data on teacher numbers do not separate the primary from the post-primary grades of schooling. The estimates presented in Table 7.1 are based on 'schools having four or fewer teachers' rather than 'schools having four or fewer teachers in the primary grades'. Table 7.1 shows the number of schools with four or fewer teachers in Sri Lanka by province and by district, based on the 1998 school census. It shows that all provinces and districts of the country have schools that needed to adopt multigrade teaching. The percentages ranged from 7.57% to 30.78%. Highest prevalence figures were from Northern, Eastern and Sabaragamuwa provinces.

The overall estimate for Sri Lanka was 18%. Nevertheless the estimate in Table 7.1 does not include the schools having more than five teachers to serve in both primary as well as in secondary grades but facing situations of multigrade teaching due to non-availability of five teachers for the five primary grades. This could be considered therefore as a minimum estimate of the extent of multigrade teaching.

Table 7.1 Schools with four teachers or fewer in Sri Lanka, 1998

District/Province	Schools with four teachers or fewer	(%)
Western	**140**	**9.49**
Colombo	22	4.98
Gampaha	44	7.62
Kalutara	74	16.19
Central	**286**	**18.69**
Kandy	79	11.47
Matale	66	20.63
Nuwara Eliya	141	44.06
Southern	**92**	**7.57**
Galle	63	12.80
Matara	10	2.54
Hambantota	19	5.74
Northern	**361**	**30.78**
Jaffna	135	32.92
Kilinochchi	32	38.09
Mannar	49	56.32
Vavunia	103	58.86
Mullativu	42	45.65
Eastern	**259**	**28.83**
Batticoloa	123	41.74
Ampara	89	22.42
Trincomalee	47	19.50
North Western	**160**	**12.29**
Kurunegala	122	12.88
Puttalam	38	10.73
North Central	**149**	**19.15**
Anuradhapura	100	27.54
Polonnaruwa	49	22.79
Uva	**147**	**17.60**
Badulla	101	17.57
Monaragala	46	17.69
Sabaragamuwa	**257**	**21.61**
Ratnapura	117	19.63
Kegalle	140	23.60
Total	**1851**	**18**

The need for multigrade teaching seems to be growing with the increase in number of 'small schools'. In 2002, 47.7% of schools had less than 200 students and 27.4% of schools had less than 100 enrolled. If these schools are to be provided with one teacher for each grade the cost would be very high. However, the recent reform proposals by the NEC has suspended the closure of any school due to its size, as the majority of the 'small schools' serve as the only avenue of educational opportunity for children in small remote communities (NEC, 2003).

In addition to the reported prevalence there have been a few other studies on multigrade teaching carried out in Sri Lanka. Abhayadeva (1989: 2) has pointed out that 'a single grade with multi-levels could be conceived as operating in a multigrade framework'. In another study Jayawardena (1995) revealed that the mean achievement levels for mathematics and mother tongue (Sinhala) of Grade 5 students in rural multigrade schools were 20.32% and 19.79% respectively, which was found to be lower than with students in urban monograde schools. However, multigrade teaching could be considered as an under-researched area in Sri Lanka.

THE DESIGN OF THE STUDY

The study design arose out of a literature review on action research. The definition of action research by Cohen and Manion (1994: 218) is 'a small-scale intervention in the functioning of the world and a close examination of the effects of such intervention'.

The multi-phased design was influenced by Elliott's model (1991) and included the 'general idea', followed by 'reconnaissance', preparation of a general plan, implementation of 'action steps', and the monitoring of implementation and effects. The final design comprised three main phases with two main steps within each phase.

Phase 1: Fact-finding about multigrade contexts and teaching
(i) obtaining an understanding of the characteristics of multigrade teaching, school contexts and multigrade teachers
(ii) understanding multigrade teaching practices and the challenges involved.

Phase 2: The intervention on multigrade teaching
(i) visualising and developing the innovation for multigrade teaching
(ii) implementing the intervention, in collaboration with teachers.

Phase 3: The assessment of the intervention
(i) assessing the impact on the students
(ii) exploring teacher satisfaction.

RURAL MULTIGRADE CONTEXTS

Step one of Phase 1 comprised a three-month 'condensed fieldwork' to survey the contextual characteristics of multigrade schools in a rural education zone. Dehiowita education zone was selected for its high prevalence of schools with four or fewer teachers among the zones of the Sabaragamuwa province. Although the Northern and the Eastern provinces of the country had the highest number of schools with four or fewer teachers (see Table 7.1) the areas were inaccessible due to the civil war.

The sample comprised 38 schools having permanent multigrade classes. These sample schools were either 'fully-multigrade' with all classes in the school functioning as multigrade classes or 'partially-multigrade' with some of the classes functioning as multigrade while others functioned as mono-grade classes. The proportion of 'partially' multigrade schools was larger (60.5%) than the proportion of 'fully' multigrade schools (39.5%).

The field visits revealed that access to multigrade schools was difficult because of distances, difficult terrain and poor/irregular public transportation facilities. The majority of the sample schools were located 10–15 km from the nearest urban centre. Only 50% of the sample schools could be accessed by public transport.

The following case study illustrates the inconveniences due to poor transport facilities faced by a school principal who was also a multigrade teacher.

> A principal of a school situated 10 km from town on a hilly terrain, arrives 45 minutes late daily in spite of travelling on the first bus of the day. In the afternoon he had to either walk 3 km to the next junction to take a bus or wait for two more hours for the next bus going to town to pass the school. He travels to this school from another direction in the town for which he has to take another bus from the town. He spends a considerable number of hours each day in commuting to this school.

However this school was the most accessible for the students of the nearby villages.

The classroom space of the majority of the samples was adequate but poorly maintained. The major shortcoming regarding building facilities was the absence of decent teacher residential facilities.

Table 7.2 illustrates the distribution of sample schools by the number of primary students in the school. It shows that 50% of the sample schools had less than 50 students, 18.5% had between 50 and 100, and 23.7% had 100 to 200 students. Even larger schools, with enrolments of 200–350 students, had some multigrade classes.

Of the 38 sample schools 17 had post-primary classes. One of the schools had grades up to Grade 13, another 11 had grades up to Grade 11. Of the remaining 10 schools some were attempting to upgrade from primary only toinclude post-primary grades, and others were in the process of being down graded and losing some of their grades.

Table 7.2 Student numbers of sample schools

Number of students in the school	Number of schools	%
Less than 50	19	50.0
50–100	7	18.5
101–200	9	23.7
201–300	1	2.6
301–350	2	5.2
Total	**38**	**100.0**

The following conditions were found to promote the need for multigrade teaching in the 38 schools.

1   Schools with persisting low enrolment, mainly located in villages with sparse populations and thus entitled to four or fewer teachers only. These schools were mostly Sinhala medium primary schools.

2   Schools facing shortages of teachers due to a deficient supply of teachers and compelled to form multigrade teaching classes despite their

entitlement to monograde teaching. These schools are mostly Tamil medium schools and are situated within commercial plantations.

3   Schools which continue to lose popularity due to reasons such as downgrading as a result of the rationalisation process and/or teacher shortages. This results in a decrease in student numbers in the secondary grades and is later reflected also in the primary grades. This in turn causes such schools to lose their entitlement for teachers for monograde teaching in both the primary and secondary grades.

4   Schools located within growing communities, having decided to expand the grade range for the small number of students in the upper grades face situations of non-entitlement to teachers for monograde teaching. These schools are mostly Tamil medium plantation schools.

5   Schools which barely have teacher entitlement for monograde teaching face multigrade needs when subject to teacher absenteeism. Absenteeism could be due to long leave such as maternity or sick leave, and/or frequent intermittent days of leave for problems related to residential facilities and commuting to school. This condition arises in schools of both media and all school types. Out of the 38 schools with permanent multigrade teaching needs, 26 schools were faced with teacher absenteeism on the day of the visit. Six schools were found to be functioning as single-teacher schools on the day of the visit due to the absenteeism of other teachers.

In these schools multigrade teaching was a necessity rather than a choice and arose for three main reasons:
• non-entitlement for teachers to implement monograde teaching due to smallness of student enrolment
• teacher deployment disparities due to teacher deficits, reluctance of teachers in serving some of the remote schools and ad hoc transfers
• teacher absenteeism due to personal problems, lack of residential facilities, transport failures, rain and/or teachers taking long-term leave for maternity, study, or medical leave.

Teachers avoided the recognition of their situation as multigraded. The term 'multigrade teaching' was not in use. Teachers did not recognise that they adopted multigrade teaching and they did not identify themselves as multigrade teachers. A majority of the teachers considered that they were officially responsible for one grade group while 'taking care' of an additional grade group until more teachers were supplied. Frequently the grade groups were arranged separately whether in different classrooms or one. The teachers indicated that they addressed each grade separately during instruction, which was highly inconvenient and resulted in teacher fatigue.

Of the teacher sample 87.0% were trained teachers. The percentage of untrained teachers was 8.7%. The remaining 4.3% were undergoing training at the time of the study. Out of the trained teachers, the majority had undergone training through distance mode by NIE. When considering their teaching experience the majority (about 80%) had more than five years. Those with 5–10 years and 11–15 years, were 32.6% and 30.4% respectively. The proportion of teachers with 16–20 years, 21–25 years and over 25 years of experience were 4.3%, 13.0% and 2.1% respectively. The teachers were rarely supervised. The education authorities seem to purposefully ignore the multigrade schools because they were unprepared to address the situational needs of such schools.

Table 7.3 summarises the grade combinations for the 43 multigraded classes for which teachers were responsible in the 38 sample schools. The table indicates the higher prevalence (in 30 classes) of two-grade combinations. 'Consecutive' grade combinations are more frequent than 'discrete' combinations among both two- and three-grade combinations (in 37 classes). Teachers indicated that the grade combinations of multigrade classes were very flexible due to frequent teacher absenteeism and *ad hoc* teacher transfers. Effective timetables were not developed to manage the teacher resources of the specific multigrade settings.

THE PRACTICES OF MULTIGRADE TEACHING

Step two of Phase 1 was designed to study multigrade teaching practices in three schools selected from among the 38 schools. The schools were selected to represent three conditions prevailing in schools having multigrade teaching needs (conditions 1, 2 and 3 above).

Within-case and cross-case analysis showed that the quality of teaching in the three schools was poor. The common approach to multigrade teaching adopted by teachers may be considered a 'quasi-monograde' type (Little, 2004). Through this approach each grade was addressed separately by the teacher one after the other. Instruction was mainly limited to mathematics and

Table 7.3 Number of grades combined, by grade combinations and number of classes

No. of grades combined	Grade combinations	No. of classes	%
Two grades	Consecutive combinations of 1+2, 3+4 and 4+5	25	58.1
	Discrete combinations of 3+6, 1+5, 2+4 and 1+4	5	11.5
Three grades	Consecutive combinations of 1+2+3 and 3+4+5	10	23.5
	Discrete combination of 2+3+5	1	2.3
Four grades	Consecutive combination of 1+2+3+4	1	2.3
All five grades combined	Consecutive combination of 1+2+3+4+5	1	2.3
Total		**43**	**100.0**

mother tongue. The teachers did not structure their teaching according to the graded syllabi and the teacher guidebooks provided by the government. Teaching was based mainly on the student textbook assignments. The lessons were limited to brief instructions for textbook assignments. Students were expected to engage in self-study until such time as the teacher returned to correct the answers after focusing attention on other grade/s and/or attending to general administrative tasks in schools. Hence, these lessons did not include time for concept building and teacher-guided learning. The students spent a large proportion of school time idling. The low quality of teaching affected teacher and student motivation and attendance negatively.

The observations of teachers and classes led to the definition for multigrade teaching as:

> Multigrade teaching is a teaching situation where a single teacher is responsible for instructing more than one grade level, either adjacent or discrete, on a fixed or temporary basis, depending on the needs of the school, with or without teachers recognising themselves as multigrade teachers.

The teachers stated a range of difficulties faced by teachers as a result of serving in multigrade schools. These included:

1   Instructional challenges such as

- Bridging the gap between the widely accepted monograde instruction and needs of multigrade classes
- Addressing different ability levels of students in different grade groups simultaneously
- Addressing the multigrade situations without support or feedback.

2   Fulfilment of multiple roles, such as being a teaching principal and surrogate parent for students amidst challenges of teaching several grades at the same time.

3   Meeting professional development needs due to lack of awareness of the available opportunities due to isolation.

AN INNOVATION FOR MULTIGRADE TEACHING THROUGH CURRICULUM ADAPTATION

The curriculum innovation for multigrade was designed in Phase 2, step one through a two-stage process. The vision for primary education is the laying of a suitable foundation for the acquisition of the knowledge, skills and attitudes necessary for day-to-day life, the world of work and further learning (MOEHE, 2000: 1). The national primary curriculum extends for five years. The present curricula are one-year graded and no acknowledgement has been made in the guidelines of the needs of multigrade teaching situations. Only a broad statement is made to the effect that curricula could be adapted to suit the specific conditions prevailing in the schools.

Analysis of the primary mathematics curriculum

The first stage of Phase 2, step one was an analysis of the primary curriculum to assess the possibility of developing a way to address the problems of quality of teaching resulting from poor lesson planning. This stage was focused on mathematics.

The organisation of the mathematics curriculum was studied through interviews with curriculum developers of the NIE and the Primary Mathematics Project (PMP) and analysis of a range of documentary materials.

Content of the mathematics curriculum

The mathematics curriculum content has a topical organisation within and across the one-year graded structure. Table 7.4 shows that the scope of the content for the five grades is centred around eight broad topics and 25 specific topics. It illustrates the topics addressed in each of the five grades by 'X' marks.

The distribution of topics shows three patterns across the grades. First, certain topics, i.e. pre-number concepts and counting, are found to be addressed only in Key Stage 1 and these could be considered as pre-mathematical competencies. Second, there are topics addressed across the entire range of the primary grade span, i.e. number concepts, number patterns, addition, subtraction, measurement (length, distance, volume, time), money, solids, plane figures and spatial concepts. Third, there are topics that need higher thinking skills and hence are arranged in the second and third Key Stages, i.e. fractions, decimals, roman numerals, multiplication, division, measurement of area, directions, right angle, tables, graphs and problem solving. These patterns indicate the hierarchical and the cyclic nature of the curriculum.

Nanayakkara (personal communication) elaborates on this aspect indicating that each topic is visited and revisited several times during a year and throughout the entire primary cycle in increasing depth. The content areas of all grades are interlinked so that it is necessary for the child to complete the work in the lower grade before going on to the higher grade. It is also emphasised that inter-subject and intra-subject integration is promoted and encouraged.

The content is generally divided into two components: the 'essential component' and 'desirable component'. Of these the 'essential component' is considered to be compulsorily mastered by all children (MOEHE, 2000).

The mathematics curriculum model

The primary mathematics curriculum of Sri Lanka has been constructed by setting its objectives that were capable of evaluation. Hence, it conforms to the 'objectives-driven' curriculum model by Tyler (1949, cited in Ross, 2000: 118). With the reforms, an additional framework was built into the curriculum which is termed the 'competency-based' curriculum. The 'competency-based' curriculum could be considered an improvement of the 'objectives-driven' model. The five basic competencies given in the curriculum guidelines are the competencies in communication; the competencies related to the environment;

Table 7.4 Curriculum blueprint for mathematics Grades 1 to 5, 1999

Broad topic	Specific topic	KS1		KS2		KS3
		Gr1	Gr2	Gr3	Gr4	Gr5
Pre-number concepts	Sorting	X	X	–	–	–
	One-to-one correspondence	X	–	–	–	–
	Ordering	X	X			
Number	Counting	X	X		–	–
	Number concept	X	X	X	X	X
	Number patterns	X	X	X	X	X
	Fraction	–	–	X	X	X
	Decimals	–	–		X	X
	Roman numerals	–	–	–	X	X
Mathematical operations	Addition	X	X	X	X	X
	Subtraction	–	X	X	X	X
	Multiplication	–	–	X	X	X
	Division	–	–	X	X	X
Measurement	Length and distance	X	X	X	X	X
	Weight	X	X	X	X	X
	Volume and capacity	X	X	X	X	X
	Time	–	X	X	X	X
	Area	–	–	–	X	X
Money	Identification and transaction	–	X	X	X	X
Shapes and space	Solids and plane figures	X	X	X	X	X
	Right angle	–	–	–	X	X
	Directions	–	–	X	X	X
	Spatial concepts	X	X	X	X	X
Data handling	Tables and graphs	–	–	X	X	X
Problem solving	Problem solving	–	–	X	X	X
Number of topics		12	14	17	21	21

Source: Primary Mathematics Project, 1999
Key: KS = Key Stage; Gr = Grade

the competencies in ethics and religion; the competencies related to the use of leisure and recreation and the competencies in learning to learn.

Instructional methods for primary curriculum implementation
The modes of instruction to implement the 'competency-based' new curriculum are 'guided play', 'activities' and 'deskwork'. A mix of 'guided play' and 'activities' is promoted in the Key Stage 1, while a mix of 'guided play', 'activities' and 'deskwork' is promoted for Key Stage 2. For Key Stage 3, a combination of activities and deskwork is recommended (MOEHE, 2000).

Student assessment strategies
The new curriculum promotes informal methods of assessment based on 'Essential Learning Competencies' (ELCs). The layout of the ELCs for each Key Stage have made the evaluation task less complicated and more effective. Formats for recording assessment information are given in teacher guides. Teachers are expected to be committed to ensure that the majority of the children master the ELCs of a particular Key Stage prior to moving to the next (MOEHE, 2000). Although the ELCs are not separately listed under different subjects but are included in a common list, ELCs related to mathematics could be identified.

Curricular materials
The main curricular materials produced for primary mathematics were the syllabi, the teacher guides, student textbooks and student workbooks. All curricular materials were produced in both national languages. The format of the syllabi cum teacher guide is designed to provide guidance for teachers as a series of detailed lesson plans.

The components of the revised lesson formats included the unit title for each grade, lesson title for each grade, time duration for the lesson, a statement of the lesson objectives, a list of the teaching resources required, essential mathematical vocabulary to be taught and explained to pupils, introductory activities to teach the pupils the concepts involved in the lesson, activities and mathematical games for group work to consolidate pupils' learning, extension activities for fast learners and suggestions for the support of slow learners and suggestions for assessment and follow-up work to ensure that pupils have learned and understood the concepts used.

The framework of the primary curriculum illustrates the underlying assumption that all teachers are engaged in monograde teaching. The curricular materials do not address the extra demands made on the teachers faced with multigrade teaching needs.

The innovative strategy developed for multigrade teaching
The second stage of Phase 2, step one was the development of the innovative strategy. In developing an innovative strategy the main objective was to address the major issues affecting the quality of multigrade teaching revealed through Phase 1, Step 1. Issues included the need for lesson planning on the topics in the syllabi, concept formation in students, student engagement in appropriate grade level activities, and the need to minimise student idle time and teacher fatigue. The development of the strategy was influenced by the experimental approach on the spiral curriculum described by Laukkanen and Selventoinen (1978) and the whole-class approach' by Mason and Burns (1996: 36–43). The innovation planned in this study attempted to address the same subject across two or more grades. The outline of the strategy was to include a whole-class introduction, gradual development of the lesson to suit both the grades and to assign different grade level assignments. This innovative strategy was planned in collaboration with the curriculum developers at the NIE.

INTERVENTION THROUGH COLLABORATION

Step two of Phase 2 involved a small-scale intervention with 18 teachers in 10 rural multigrade schools over a period of seven months. The intervention was made in two consecutive cycles following the action research cycle designed by Kemmis and McTaggart (1988). Each cycle comprised four stages: (i) planning, (ii) action, (iii) monitoring with facilitation and (iv) reflection. Intervention was made after obtaining consent from and raising awareness about the intervention in school principals and zonal education officers.

The planning stage involved organising workshops and field visits. The action was mediated through workshops held at the Teacher Centre of the Education Zone and teachers implementing the lessons planned at the workshops by the teachers in their respective schools. The monitoring and facilitation was carried out by the researcher through several rounds of visits to intervention schools and during workshops. Each cycle ended with individual and group reflections.

Carr and Kemmis's (1986: 136) descriptions of types of relationship between outside facilitators and practitioners was helpful in negotiating the collaboration with the multigrade teachers during the intervention. The 'technical action research' model where practitioners test the applicability of findings generated elsewhere, while the researchers provide practitioners with ideas and strategies for improvement and further study of the situation, was a starting point for the intervention.

In order to support the teachers in lesson planning in mathematics, a co-facilitator, who is a primary mathematics curriculum developer was invited for the workshops. One-day workshops were held on selected days of weekends. All workshops were observed by an observer who was not a participant in the intervention. Data collection was done by the researcher through tape recording the workshop proceedings, interviews with teachers and record keeping. Written reflections and observers' notes were also added to the range of sources of data.

Cycle 1: Introducing the lesson planning strategy and making individual attempts to plan lessons

After a formal inauguration session with zonal officers, principals and teachers of the intervention schools the first task of the facilitators was to elicit current practices and problems of multigrade teachers. With this background the innovative strategy was introduced. In order to implement the strategy the following is the sequence of activities agreed in collaboration with the teachers.

1   Familiarising with the subject content of the graded syllabi pertaining to the grade combination of the multigrade class.

2   Selecting similar topics from the graded syllabi of the grade combination.

3   Selecting the objectives under the specific topics to be covered for each grade.

4   Re-sequencing the two or more sets of objectives selected from different grades in a logical sequence where a gradual advancement of the lesson could take place.

5   Clustering the re-sequenced objectives for suitable number of lessons considering time allocations and students' ability levels.

6   Organising the content of the re-sequenced objectives to include an intro-duction to the lesson at a level suitable for grade combination and to develop the lesson horizontally and vertically to meet different needs of grade levels.

7   Allocating suitable assignments for different grades/ability levels.

8   Concluding the lesson by directing the students of different grades to extend their learning depending on their different levels.

Teachers were expected to implement the strategy in their respective schools. The observations made during the school-based facilitation and reflections during Cycle 1 revealed that teachers appreciated the usefulness of the innovative strategy and were enthusiastic to adopt it.

Example 1

I used to arrange the two grade groups separately and teach separately following the mathematics textbooks. Since I began participation in the multigrade workshops, I realized the following as shortcomings of my former practices (i) one group would idle and make a lot of noise while I teach the other grade group (ii) it is inadequate to teach only through referring to textbooks.

(Vijaya)

Example 2

I used to move from one classroom to another to address the two grades that I was responsible for, because these were housed in separate classrooms. After the suggestion made at the workshop, I arranged both grades in one classroom because then I could teach them together. It is a great consolation for me as well as to my students.

(Nirmala)

Example 3

I frequently face the situation of teaching all five grades in the primary, due to various reasons. The method that I adopted was to first assign work to Grades 5, 4, 3 and 2 one after the other and be with the Grade 1 students because they need a lot of support. As a result of participation in the workshops now I combine Grade 1+2 and Grade 3+4+5, and now I have organised my class into manageable units and do lessons in common considering them as multigrade classes.

(Kusuma)

However, the number of lessons planned by each teacher was small and teachers indicated that they were unable to manage lesson planning as the adaptation of monograde curricula was difficult. The following example highlights one of the specific difficulties faced by teachers in planning lessons adopting the innovative strategy.

> In School 3, Sumanawathi explained her difficulty adopting the innovative strategy due to the mismatch of the sequence of topics in different grade level syllabi. The example she forwarded was the topic 'two dimensional shapes' for Grades 2 and 3. The advice she has received at the in-training sessions were to implement the curricula sequentially. However, when trying to combine similar topics according to the study intervention she faced the difficulty of mismatch of sequence of the topics across the grades. The topic sequence of Grade 2 syllabus indicates topic 2 as three-dimensional shapes and topic 8 as two-dimensional shapes, whereas in Grade 3 syllabus, both two and three dimensional shapes are included in topic 11.

The problem Sumanawathi raised was important because it brought to light the need for support in selecting and combining objectives from graded syllabi which do not have the same topic sequence. After two rounds of visits to the schools for monitoring and facilitation the first cycle ended with a workshop for reflection and re-planning for Cycle 2.

Cycle 2: Collaborative lesson planning to prepare exemplary lesson plans

Cycle 2 of the intervention commenced with a collaborative lesson planning workshop. The teacher group with the support extended by the facilitators prepared a set of lesson plans based on the innovative strategy for the coming school term. Out of the set of the lesson plans, the combination of the grade-wise specific objectives for four mathematical operations are given in Table 7.5. The combination of the objectives was made possible by using the grid prepared by the PMP curriculum developers to view the topic objectives across the grades.

Figure 7.1 shows a lesson plan developed by the team that addresses the topic of 'addition' for Grades 4 and 5. It highlights the nature of the whole-class introduction and the lesson development adopting the ideas of the innovative strategy. Figure 7.2 shows a lesson plan developed for the topic of 'time'.

Table 7.5 Combination of specific objectives for multigrade teaching for selected grade combinations for the four mathematics operations

Topic	Grade combination of the lesson	Specific objectives for each grade
Addition	1+2+3	1 Adding two sets of objects, sum not exceeding 9
		2 Adding two numbers, sum not exceeding 99, without carrying over
		3 Adding two numbers sum not exceeding 999, without carrying over.
	1+4	1 Adding two sets of objects, sum not exceeding 9
		4 Adding two numbers sum not exceeding 999, without carrying over
	4+5	4 Addition of two numbers sum not exceeding 999 with carrying over at unit's and ten's places
		5 Addition of two numbers sum not exceeding 9999 with carrying over at unit's and ten's places
Subtraction	2+3	2 Subtraction from a number not greater than 20
		3 Subtraction from a number not greater than 99 without bringing forward
	4+5	4 Subtracting from a number not greater than 999 with bringing forward from not more than two places
		5 Subtracting from a number not greater than 9999 with bringing forward from not more than two places
Multiplication	3+4	3 Multiplication by 2 and 3 using practical methods
		4 Multiplication by 4 using practical methods and then using numbers
Division	3+4	3 Dividing two digit numbers by 2 without remainder
		4 Dividing two digit numbers by 2 and 3 without remainder
	4+5	4 Dividing three digit numbers by 2 without remainder
		5 Dividing three digit numbers by 3 without remainder

Figure 7.1 A section of a lesson plan developed by the team on
the topic of addition for Grades 4 and 5

Grades: 4 and 5

Topic: Addition

Specific objectives

Grade 4: Add two numbers sum not exceeding 999 with carrying over at unit's and
ten's places

Grade 5: Add two numbers sum not exceeding 9999 with carrying over at unit's and
ten's places

Resources: Dienes apparatus or Ekels (singles and bundles of ten), number cards, place
value charts and assignment cards

Step 1: Whole-class introduction

- Recall addition by writing single digits on the board up to sum not exceeding 50.
- Group the class into about four groups disregarding the grade level. Give each
group a place value chart with two columns, Dienes apparatus (small cubes
and rods) or Ekels (singles and bundles). Encourage a competition between
groups where one group shows two numbers with number cards while the
other group adds them.

**Step 2: Teacher-led lesson development sequentially to meet different needs of
grade levels**

Sub-step 1:
- Write three digit number which will add up with carrying over at unit's place
on the board.
- Ask a volunteer to come up and add them. Repeat this three or four times.

Discuss with the students.

Sub-step 2:
- Write three digit number which will add up with carrying over at unit's place
and ten's place on the board.
- Ask a volunteer to come up and add them. Repeat this several times.

Figure 7.2 A lesson plan developed by the team for the topic of time for Grades 2
and 3

Grades: 2 and 3

Topic: Time

Specific objectives

Grade 2: Consolidate knowledge about time associated with daily activities.

Grade 5: Know the number of days in each month.

Resources:

Step 1: Whole-class introduction

Students are made to sing and act a song about a clock.

Step 2: Teacher-led lesson development sequentially to meet different needs of grade levels

- They are asked questions on the content of the song. Cards with the words of the song are given to the students. Questions are posed.
- A brief discussion about the daily routine and special annual events.
  Examples: Coming to school at the seven in the morning; closure of school in the afternoon; having dinner at seven in the evening; New Year and Christmas festivals.

Step 3: Assignment of different grade level student activities

The following group activities are suggested:

- Grade 2: Students are led to write the times in a table giving events closely associated with their life.
- Grade 3: Divide the students into groups and ask them to find the number of days in each month and record.

The team implemented the lesson plans in their respective schools in the two-and-a-half-month school term, during which time the researcher made one round of visits to schools for monitoring and facilitation.

THE IMPACT OF THE INTERVENTION

In Phase 3 the impact of the intervention was assessed in two steps over seven months and across two dimensions. The first was its impact on student achievement; the second, its impact on the teachers.

A quasi-experimental model was adopted to assess the impact on student achievement. It involved a pre- and post-one-control group design. Three mathematics achievement tests were constructed using questions from the NIE item bank in collaboration with the leader of the curriculum development team. The post-test was a parallel test of the pre-test. Students in both intervention and control groups were tested before and after the intervention.

Table 7.6 presents the results of the linear regression analysis of mathematics 'gain in score' for the Grades 3, 4 and 5 students of the intervention and control groups (Plewis, 1997). In the regression model The 'gain in score' was considered as the response variable. The linear regression analysis was performed using SPSS version 7.

Table 7.6 Results of the linear regression analysis of the mathematics 'gain in score' of students in Grades 3, 4 and 5 in intervention and control schools

	Grade 3		Grade 4		Grade 5	
	B	T	B	T	B	T
	1.38	−.83	5.89**	.36	3.69**	1.86
Constant	0.67		0.43		1.22	
Adjusted R square	0.21		0.24		0.21	
F	1.91		18.77**		20.22**	
N	43		58		74	

Table 7.6 shows that, with the exception of Grade 3, the intervention had significant positive impact on student achievement in mathematics. The F values for Grades 4 and 5 (18.77 and 20.22 respectively) indicate the significance of the differences between the variables in the model. The differences between the means of the 'gain in scores' of control and intervention groups (denoted by *B*) for the Grades 4 and 5 are significant at p=.000 level indicating the positive impact of the intervention.

The non-significant effects of the Grade 3 scores may be explained post hoc by a possible 'ceiling effect' of the test instrument due to the high performance levels of both the intervention and control groups in the pre-test. The relatively high attainment levels shown by Grade 3 may have been a result of the implementation of country-wide primary education reforms. The reforms were introduced to Grade 1 country-wide in 1999 and the Grade 3 students in this study had been in Grade 1 in 1999. The implementation of the reform was emphasised and schools may well have focused special attention on this particular grade group. By the end of Grade 2 they had also been subjected to assessment of the Essential Learning Competencies just two months before the implementation of the pre-test for the study. However, it is interesting to note that while the achievement levels of Grade 3 intervention group showed an increase at the post-test the control group showed a decline in the same. This difference could be explained as a result of the intervention. The teachers in both intervention and control schools responsible for Grade 3 faced problems in implementing the new Grade 3 curriculum in a multigrade mode. This was because the curriculum was new to them and also they were not conversant with multigrade teaching methods. However, this problem may have been overcome in the intervention schools through the supportive actions for the teacher, whereas the control schools did not receive any such support.

On average the model explains over 20% of the variance (as shown by adjusted R square). It is an indication of the existence of influence of other variables on the model. The sample size is denoted by N which includes the number of subjects under both intervention and control schools. The sample size takes the values of 43, 58 and 74 for the Grades 3, 4 and 5 respectively.

The outcomes of the impact assessment on the teachers indicated that the intervention was a success. The teachers found the innovative strategy for multigrade teaching was effective and it addressed their problems related to instruction of two or more grades simultaneously. More importantly it helped to change their negative beliefs in multigrade teaching. All the teachers indicated that they were highly satisfied with the understanding and skill in multigrade practice they acquired through participation in the intervention.

Follow-up studies of the intervention need to be made to assess the sustainability of the intervention. A follow-up on one of the schools was done through project LATIMS in 2003. A further study will be launched through the LATIMS project during 2005/6.

FOR THE FUTURE

This study points to several recommendations for policy and research on multigrade teaching.

Recommendations for policy

Policy recognition of multigrade as a teaching option
This study bears evidence to justify a claim to recognise and support multigrade teaching by education policy as an option for teaching in Sri Lankan schools due to its de facto prevalence.

Teacher capacity building
If multigrade teaching is to be implemented effectively it needs to be introduced to initial and continuing education courses.

Recommendations for research and development

Re-sequencing the topics of the syllabi and preparing exemplary lesson plans
The significance of the pedagogical innovation suggested by this study reveals the necessity to adapt existing curricula. This could address the long neglected need to address multigrade teaching in the school curriculum.

Towards this objective, the re-sequencing of the curriculum content by Key Stages and preparing exemplary lesson plans for the mathematics curriculum commenced in 2003 through the project LATIMS (Learning And Teaching In Multigrade Settings) sponsored by DFID. Further re-sequencing work will be undertaken in one other curriculum area.

Capacity building of the teacher educator
Capacity building of teacher educators is a necessity because multigrade teaching has not been a recognised teaching strategy in Sri Lanka and has therefore not received emphasis within any teacher education course.

Researching multigrade teaching
Since multigrade teaching is an under-researched area, both large-scale and small-scale research has to carried out. Studies to establish prevalence in all

provinces could be carried out by the Provincial ministries of education. Small-scale studies on classroom innovations for multigrade practice and learning should be encouraged among teachers facilitated by Teacher Centres.

REFERENCES

Abhayadeva, C.M. (1989) *Development of Multigrade and Multilevel Teaching Strategies towards Qualitative Development of Primary Education in Sri Lanka*, Sri Lanka: National Institute of Education.
Baker, V.J. (1988) *The Blackboard in the Jungle: Formal education in disadvantaged rural areas, a Sri Lankan case.* Netherlands: Eburon Delft.
Carr, W. and Kemmis, S. (1986) *Becoming Critical: Education, knowledge and action research.* London: Falmer Press.
Cohen, L. and Manion, L. (1994) *Research Methods in Education* (4th edn). London: Routledge.
Ekanayake, S.B. (1982) National case study – Sri Lanka. In *Multiple Class Teaching and Education of Disadvantaged Groups: India, Sri Lanka, and the Philippines.* Bangkok: UNESCO: 40–77.
Elliott, J. (1991) *Action Research for Educational Change.* Philadelphia: Open University Press.
Jayawardena, A.A. (1995) A study of the factors affecting the educational achievement of students in multigrade schools in disadvantaged areas in Sri Lanka. Unpublished PhD. University of Colombo. Sri Lanka.
Kemmis, S. and McTaggart, R. (eds) (1988) *The Action Research Planner* (3rd edn). Australia: Deakin University Press.
Laukkanen, R. and Selventoinen, P. (1978) *Small Schools and Combined Grades in Finland, Centre for Educational Research and Innovation.* Pros: OECD.
Little, A. (1995) Multigrade teaching: a review of research and practice. *Education Research*, Serial Number 12, London: Overseas Development Administration.
Little, A.W. (2001) Multigrade teaching: towards an international research and policy agenda, London. *International Journal of Educational Development*, 21(8), 481–497.
Little, A.W. (2004) Learning and teaching in multigrade settings. Background paper for UNESCO (2005) *EFA Global Monitoring Report 2005. Education for All: The quality imperative* Online. Available HTTP:http://portal.unesco.org/education/en/ev.php-URL_ID=36184&URL_DO=DO_TOPIC&URL_SECTION=201&URL_PAGINATION=20.html (accessed 18 January).
Mason, D. and Burns, R.B. (1996) Teachers' views of combination classes. *Journal of Educational Research*, 89 (1), 36–45.
Ministry of Education and Higher Education (MOEHE) (2000) *Guidelines for the Implementation of the Primary Education Reform.* Sri Lanka: MEHE.

Ministry of Human Resource Development, Education and Cultural Affairs (2002) *School Census*. Sri Lanka: Ministry of Human Resource Development, Education and Cultural Affairs.

Nanayakkara, G.L.S. (1996) *Discussion Paper on Primary Curriculum Reform in Sri Lanka*. Sri Lankan: National Institute of Education.

National Education Commission (2003) *Proposals for a National Policy Framework on General Education in Sri Lanka*. NEC: Sri Lanka.

Plewis, I. (1997). *Statistics in Education*. London: Arnold.

Primary Mathematics Project, Sri Lanka (1998) *Inception Report Primary Mathematics Project*, 13 June 1998. Sri Lanka: PMP.

Primary Mathematics Project, Sri Lanka (1999) *Curriculum Blueprint for Grade 1–5 Mathematics*. Sri Lanka: National Institute of Education.

Ross, A. (2000) *Curriculum: Construction and critique*. London: Falmer Press.

Sibli, M. (1999) *Multigrade Teaching in Sri Lanka: Country paper presented at the Oxford symposium on multigrade teaching in 1999*. Oxford University.

Thomas, C. and Shaw, C. (1992) Issues on the development of multigrade school. *World Bank Technical Paper* (Issue 72). Washington, DC: World Bank.

UNICEF (2004) *The State of the World's Children 2004*. New York: UNICEF.

Vithanapathirana, M.V. (2005) Improving multigrade teaching: action research with teachers in rural Sri Lanka. Unpublished PhD thesis. Institute of Education, University of London.

CHAPTER EIGHT

IMPROVING THE QUALITY OF HEALTH EDUCATION IN MULTIGRADE SCHOOLS IN VIETNAM

T. SON VU AND PAT PRIDMORE

INTRODUCTION

Multigrade teaching, where a teacher takes instructional responsibility for students of more than one grade level, has long been a feature of the primary education system in Vietnam, but over the last decade it has been expanded to help achieve Universal Primary Education (UPE). Now that UPE has been declared the Government has turned its attention to improving the quality of the primary education provided. This chapter reports on a study conducted in the Northern Highlands of Vietnam to improve the quality of health teaching in multigrade schools.

This chapter firstly presents some background on the primary education system in Vietnam with special reference to health education and the multigrade context. It reviews the findings from mini case studies of learning and teaching in multigrade schools. These showed that teachers were using passive pedagogy and had an excessively heavy workload from planning and delivering separate lessons to each grade in their classroom at the same time. Secondly, the chapter describes a piece of action research conducted with teachers to improve teaching quality and reports on the impact of the intervention. Finally, it draws out some of the implications for policy and practice.

PRIMARY EDUCATION IN VIETNAM

The Socialist Republic of Vietnam is a very low-income country in Southeast Asia. The total population of the country is about 76 million (according to the 1989 national census) and is made up of 56 different ethnic groups, of which 88.26% are ethnic Vietnamese known as *Kinh* (Nguyen and Ngo, 2002). The country has large areas of mountainous highlands covered

A.W. Little (ed.), Education for All and Multigrade Teaching: challenges and opportunities, 155–168.
© 2007 *Springer.*

by forests where there are many isolated hamlets with populations from ethnic minority groups (Nguyen and Ngo, 2002).

Primary education is compulsory and the country declared Universal Primary Education (UPE) in 2000 on the basis of a 70% children enrolment (Pham, 2000). Primary education comprises five years of schooling from Grade 1 to 5 and children are supposed to enter Grade 1 at the age of 6 years (MOET, 1995a). At the end of each school year class teachers assess students' achievements not only in terms of marks in each subject but also in relation to their behaviour and the moral values that they exhibit. The teacher then decides whether they can be promoted to the next grade or have to repeat the same grade. At the end of Grade 5 students take the primary level final examination in Vietnamese language and mathematics. Those who pass can enter the lower secondary school while those who fail have to repeat Grade 5.

Table 8.1 shows that in recent years the number of primary students has been around 10 million in more than 300,000 classes. Repetition and dropout rates have been gradually decreasing but at around 70% educational efficiency is not high. The need to improve the quality of teaching and learning in the classroom has been highlighted by the Ministry of Education and Training (MOET), which has started a process of educational renovation. As a result, the new National Primary Curriculum (NPC), called the National Curriculum Year 2000, with sets of textbooks and instructional materials written for each grade (MOET, 2002), is being developed grade by grade, starting with Grade 1.

Table 8.1 Primary education statistics in Vietnam

Items	1999–2000	2000–01	2001–02
Total number of schools	13,387	13,738	13,897
Total number of classes	322,041	319,508	315,070
Total number of classrooms	203,898	211,810	216,392
Total number of students	10,063,025	9,741,413	9,311,010
Student–class ratio	31–25	30–52	29–55
Percentage of repetition	3.27%	2.79%	2.29%
Percentage of drop-outs	5.00%	4.67%	3.67%
Total number of complete primary students	1,733,537	1,746,801	1,889,274
Educational efficiency* (E)	69.64	70.88	74.42
Total number of teachers	340,871	347,833	353,804
Teacher–class ratio	1.06	1.09	1.12

Source: The Centre of Information Management, MOET
Key * No. of Grade 5 completers/No. of students entering Grade 1, five years earlier

Schemes of work follow a prescribed plan to be used by all teachers in all primary schools. The official language of instruction is Vietnamese, which is the mother tongue of the majority *Kinh* ethnic group (NIER, 1999), but some provision has been made for schools in ethnic minority areas to use a bilingual programme. There is also provision for teachers to use one lesson a week for teaching content that is relevant to the local culture and circumstances of the students. Multigrade teachers have been given some degree of flexibility in how they deliver the curriculum in their classrooms (NIER, 1999) but no advice on how to adapt the NPC to the multigrade situation.

In the 2002/3 school year students in the first grade of the primary level and the first grade of the lower secondary level started learning the new curriculum with new textbooks. This new curriculum will gradually be rolled out year by year so that by the 2006/7 school year the whole school population will be following it (Government of Vietnam, 2000). The overall aim of this educational renovation is to develop students' competencies in thinking and in practical skills. To this end it concentrates on changes in the teaching and learning methods to help make students more creative in their learning and develop their potential as autonomous, self-directed learners.

Within the curriculum the aim of health education is to improve health, including the physical and spiritual health of the individual, the community and the society (MOET, 2000). This aim is to be achieved through the provision of basic knowledge about health, nutrition and the environment and recognition of the role of health in the life of the student and his/her family and community. The health curriculum has been developed using a concentric design with four main themes: (i) the human body and personal hygiene, (ii) environmental hygiene, (iii) nutrition, and (iv) prevention of some common diseases (see Table 8.2). These themes are repeated throughout the primary grades so that grades share common topics but each grade has some differentiated content and different learning objectives.

The curriculum suggests that because health knowledge and skills are mainly formed through practice and activities teachers should use a range of teaching methods, such as discussion, group work, games, investigations and solving of real life problems. In addition, a hygienic school environment is seen to play an important role in forming good health habits and students need skills to spread these to other members of the family and the community through their lifestyles and communications (MOET, 2002; 2000). Health education needs to be implemented through health instruction, extra-curriculum activities and a healthy environment. It is also stressed that health education needs to be spread from the school to the wider environment, to families and communities.

Table 8.2 Structure of health syllabus

Themes	Grade 1	Grade 2	Grade 3	Grade 4	Grade 5
Human body hygiene	x x	x x	x x	x x	x x
Environmental hygiene	x	x	x x	x x	x x
Nutrition	x x	x x	x x	x x	x x
Prevention of diseases	x	x	x	x x	x x

Source: Government of Vietnam: The Decision No. 2957/GD-DT, 14.10.1994

MULTIGRADE SCHOOLING

The history of multigrade teaching in Vietnam may be traced to a time when village scholars taught local children of various ages and levels together (Nguyen, 1996). After liberating the colonised country from the French in 1945, the Vietnam Democracy Republic Government emphasised the elimination of illiteracy. The 'literacy broadcasting movement' stretched across the country up to the remote and mountainous areas (MOET, 1995b). In ethnic minority areas volunteer teachers who came from the lowlands followed the government's encouragement to seek out students in remote hamlets to teach. Small schools located close to the homes of local people were considered suitable for the mountainous and isolated communities and there were many classes with a small number of students of different levels and ages (MOET, 1995b). In 1959 the number of teachers in one-teacher schools in Vietnam was reportedly 1,169 (6.6% of the total number of primary teachers) and the number of students was 76,579 (7.6% of the total number of primary students) (UNESCO/IBE, 1961, cited in Little, 1995). However, at this time very few ethnic minority children attended school – only 3.24% of the ethnic minority population (MOET, 1995b).

In 1991 the MOET/UNICEF Multigrade Teaching Project was launched (MOET, 2000). Over the next ten years it established a wide network of multigrade classes in sparsely populated areas to encourage parents to send their young children to school at the compulsory age of 6 years and to help meet the serious shortage of teachers in disadvantaged areas (MOET, 2000). These multigrade classes have helped MOET to provide primary education to children in difficult areas who would not otherwise be able to go to school. Nine years after its launch the Project had covered 39 provinces and supported 144,791 students in 6,313 classes and 6,332 teachers (MOET, 2000).

In the 2000/1 school year, multigrade schools were found in 49 out of the total number of 61 cities and provinces in Vietnam. In the country as a whole there were 7,990 multigrade classes, representing 2.5% of the total number of primary classes and 169,662 multigrade students, representing 1.74% of the total number of primary students. Although the overall percentage of multigrade classes is not high, in some of the high mountainous areas multigrade classes are considerably more prevalent. For example, the percentage of multigrade classes in Son La Province is 13.3% and in Baccan Province it is 14.94%. In Hoabinh and Bacgiang Provinces, where the case studies and action research were carried out, the percentages of multigrade classes were 7.73% and 2.67% respectively (MOET, 2000).

Because multigrade schools were established to provide education to children living in small communities the size of multigrade classes depends on how many children of each grade level there are in the community in any given school year. The combination of grades in any one class also varies according to the number of pupils enrolled. Some schools combine two or three consecutive grades whilst others combine non-consecutive grades. There are slightly fewer students in multigrade than in monograde classes. For example, in the 2000/1 school year the average number of students in each single-grade primary class was 30.52, whereas it was 21.78 in multigrade classes (MOET, 2000).

Multigrade schools face many problems. There is a serious shortage of the teachers who are qualified at the standard required by MOET for multigrade teaching (NIER, 1999) and according to MOET there are no formal training programmes in multigrade teaching in teacher training colleges (MOET, 2000). Because of the remoteness of the areas where multigrade schools are typically located, multigrade teachers often do not have regular access to updates on new teaching methods or opportunity to share teaching experiences with colleagues or adequate supervision and management (MOET, 1995b). There is no specific curriculum for the multigrade setting and a lack of teaching and learning materials for multigrade teachers and students. There is often a language barrier between teachers and students because most qualified teachers are Vietnamese-speaking Kinh whilst most ethnic minority students do not have the chance to learn and use the Vietnamese language before going to primary school. The proportion of ethnic minority teachers is only 15% of the total number of the local primary teachers (NIER, 1999). Although multigrade teachers generally have good relationships with the community, families are too poor to be able to support the school financially or give time to provide voluntary teaching services (Vu, 2002).

THE STUDY

The aim of the study was to increase understanding of how health education was being taught in multigrade classes in Northern Vietnam and to develop a more effective approach to teaching it. This aim was addressed by developing case studies of current classroom practice to identify factors that were reducing teaching quality and then using action research with teachers to develop a more effective teaching model (Vu, 2005).

Case studies of teaching and learning

Data from classroom observation of teaching, interviews with teachers and school managers and timetables and lesson plans were collected between April and October 2000. These data were used to inform mini case studies of teaching and learning for health in 23 multigrade schools in Hoabinh and Bacgiang Provinces. These schools were selected so that the sample included schools in different contexts and with differing levels of support from the MOET/UNICEF Multigrade Teaching Project.

The case studies showed that in developing the weekly timetable teachers generally taught subjects that required heavy teacher input, such as maths or Vietnamese language, to one grade group whilst the other group(s) were doing subjects that required light teacher input, such as health education or art. In some cases, however, health education lessons were timetabled for all grades in the class at the same time, but with each grade group following the curriculum for their own grade.

To organise the teaching and learning, teachers in these schools adopted the 'quasi monograde' strategy promoted by the MOET/UNICEF Project for all subjects except for physical and moral education and music. This strategy involved teaching each grade separately but at the same time, which was achieved by giving short bursts of direct teaching to each grade in turn whilst the other grades worked on activities set by the teacher. The teacher generally stayed about five minutes with a grade group before moving on to the next group. During this five minutes the teacher gave information and asked questions to check understanding and factual recall before setting a task for individual, independent learning that was then supervised by a grade group monitor. Occasionally small group tasks were given but these rarely challenged students to think or to work collaboratively. Teaching was strongly teacher led and controlled and relied heavily on students learning by rote the content provided in the textbooks or written by the teacher on the blackboard.

At best this model enabled students to spend a good percentage of time on task, albeit learning passively. At worst students finished their task quickly and wasted time waiting for their turn with the teacher. Many of the potential benefits of multigrade teaching that come from increased opportunities for cross age/grade/gender interactions and peer support of learning were not being accessed. Teachers spent many hours after school preparing separate lessons for each grade group for each timetabled period and then faced an exhausting day moving constantly between the grade groups.

Action research to improve the teaching of health

Action research is a process of innovation, change and problem solving that helps people to act more intelligently and skilfully. It is a process in which researchers and practitioners are partners in doing research for better practice (Elliott, 1992; Trespeces, 1993). In this study action research was chosen to help develop a more effective model of teaching health education in multigrade classes because it could enable average teachers working in average classrooms (rather than master-teachers in demonstration classrooms) to find their own solutions to everyday practical problems and lead to immediate improvement in their practice.

The action research was carried out from November 2000 to April 2002. It involved three stages: (i) a three-month preparatory phase, followed by (ii) an action research phase to develop and trial the new model for teaching health, and (iii) a follow-up phase during which the effectiveness of the new model was evaluated and discussed.

Stage 1: The preparatory stage

The necessary permissions were obtained at all levels for the action research and intervention and control groups were set up. Five teachers of multigrade classes with Grades 4 and 5 students and three headteachers from schools visited for the case studies were invited to form the action research group to develop the new teaching model for health and implement this intervention in their classes. Vu Son acted as a facilitator for this group and Grade 4 and 5 classes were chosen to reduce the barrier to learning caused by lack of competence in Vietnamese experienced by lower grades. These intervention classes were all in Bacgiang Province where the large number of multigrade schools made it possible to find five (Grades 4 and 5) classes to act as a control group in the evaluation of the intervention. The intervention and control classes were located in the same mountainous district and the intervention and control classes were matched for economic, social and educational status of the parents and standard of training of the teachers. In all these classes the majority of pupils belonged to ethnic minority groups. During the preparatory phase the evaluation design was agreed and the tools for data collection prepared.

Stage 2: The action research phase
This stage started with an initial workshop in Hanoi during which the action research group reviewed the case studies and identified one key issue from the findings that was reducing the quality of their health teaching. The group also reviewed the pedagogic requirements of the national curriculum. Taking these requirements into consideration alongside the findings from the cases studies they agreed that they wanted the action research to address the current lack of opportunities for active learning and collaborative learning in their own pedagogic approach to health education. During subsequent workshops held in Bacgiang Province the group looked at the national curriculum for health for Grades 4 and 5 and identified three topics that they could teach across these grades that were priority health issues in their school communities. These topics were: (i) Life and health, (ii) Good food at home, and (iii) Prevention of common digestive diseases (see Table 8.2). The group wanted the new model of teaching health to meet the requirement of the national curriculum by developing students as autonomous, self-directed learners able to make decisions for themselves and by developing their capacity to use what they learned in the classroom to take action to improve health at home and in the community. To achieve this aim Vu Son introduced the group to an enquiry-based approach to health education known as Child-to-Child (Pridmore and Stephens, 2000). The group then adapted this approach to fit their own context so that they could teach a health topic over two consecutive lessons with linked homework tasks. The first lesson was to provide information on the health topic. The linked homework was to develop students' observation and critical thinking by finding out more about the topic at home or in the community. The second lesson was to provide opportunities for students to make a plan of action they could carry out to promote health at home, at school and in their community. The linked homework was for students to carry out their plan of action and this was to be briefly evaluated and the topic revised at the start of the next lesson. The group agreed on how to use different student groupings during each lesson. They would start with some whole-class teaching followed by small-group activities in same grade or mixed-grade groups before bringing the class together to share and review their work and the end of the lesson.

During the intervention the students in the intervention group were taught the three topics using the new model for teaching health whilst students in the control group were taught the same topics using the passive teaching pedagogy that their teachers normally used. Students in the control group were taught the same topics in the more conventional way which focused on children learning health messages.

Diagrams to illustrate the new model of teaching health (enquiry-based approach and the format for grouping students during a lesson) are given in Chapter 9 of this book, where we report on a subsequent exercise conducted by the National Institute of Educational Sciences (NIES) in Hanoi in collaboration with teachers to further adapt the health curriculum for multigrade teachers in Vietnam. This exercise adopted the model for teaching health topics previously developed by the action research group reported on in this chapter.

Once the new teaching model had been agreed, the group wrote lesson plans for teaching the first of the three health topics and tried them out with their classes. Members of the action research team observed each other teaching these topics and gave feedback. At the end of the first cycle of action and reflection the whole group came together for a local workshop to exchange experiences, review progress and make further adjustments to the model before developing the lesson plans for the next topic. This cycle of action and reflection to improve the model was then repeated twice more until all three health topics had been taught. A final workshop was held in the field to draw together and share the findings from the study.

Stage 3: Evaluating the model
Before any teaching started a knowledge test was given to all students in both the intervention and control classes to assess their initial level of knowledge on the three health topics. The same test was administered again immediately after the third topic had been taught. Teachers kept reflective diaries after each teaching session about what they felt had gone well or not so well during the lesson and the discussions they had during their workshops were recorded and analysed. Students were also invited to share their views on the new teaching model.

The knowledge test was designed to cover the main health messages taught and required students to make decisions relating to behaviour and lifestyle concerning their own health, other people's health and health in society. Table 8.3 shows that the mean gain scores for the intervention group were 14.17 (Grade 4) and 13.64 (Grade 5) compared to mean gain scores for the control group of 10.54 (Grade 4) and 10.43 (Grade 5).

Table 8.3 Mean total tests scores for intervention and control students

	Grade 5		Grade 4	
	Intervention group (n = 45)	Control group (n = 44)	Intervention group (n = 42)	Control group (n = 52)
Pre-test	Mean = 6.69 (SD = 4.85)	Mean = 5.82 (SD = 2.26)	Mean = 3.48 (SD = 3.67)	Mean = 4.89 (SD = 3.15)
Post-test	Mean = 0.33 (SD = 5.99)	Mean = 16.25 (SD = 6.53)	Mean = 17.64 (SD = 7.50)	Mean = 15.42 (SD = 7.02)
Gain scores	Mean = 3.64 (SD = 6.40)	Mean = 10.43 (SD = 6.87)	Mean = 14.17 (SD = 5.10)	Mean = 10.54 (SD = 8.31)

The difference in test scores between the intervention and control groups was found to be significant at the 0.05 level. Students in the intervention group therefore gained significantly more knowledge than those in the control group. The mean test scores also show that girls in the intervention group made almost as much progress as the boys (mean scores of 13.33 for girls and 15.00 for boys), whereas girls in the control group made much less progress (mean scores of 7.88 for girls and 13.19 for boys). These findings may suggest that girls were more confident and able to learn better through the collaborative small-group learning tasks used in the intervention group than those in the control group, who were taught using more formal and traditional teaching methods.

The test scores were also subjected to linear regression analysis and the results, shown in Table 8.4, confirmed that the difference between the gain scores remained consistent even when the effects of gender, age, ethnicity and school year were controlled for. In the table of coefficients, the large β coefficient value for the Grade 5 intervention and control groups ($\beta1=0.313$), indicated that the strongest unique contribution to explaining the gain scores was made by the intervention/control variable. This variable made a statistically significant contribution to the prediction of the gain scores with a Sig. Value of 0.012 (< 0.05).

Table 8.4 also shows that β coefficient values for gender, ethnicity, age and primary school years were 0.008, 0.117, (–)0.183 and (–)0.025 respectively. However, these variables made no statistically significant contribution to the variance in the gain scores because the Sig. Values are 0.942, 0.293, 0.089 and 0.830 respectively (> 0.05). These findings would imply that at least a small part of the differential gain between the experimental and control group was due to the other variables in the model. The β coefficients value for the gender variable of grade 4 is 0.230, and the

Table 8.4 Regression analysis of the gain scores by group

Variables in the model	R square		R. square change		Sig. F change	
	Grade 5	Grade 4	Grade 5	Grade 4	Grade 5	Grade 4
Gender, age, ethnicity and school year	0.029	0.113	0.029	0.113	0.065	0.029
Intervention/control group	0.101	0.174	0.072	0.061	0.012	0.012

Coefficients						
Variables in the model	Standardised (β)		T		Sig. T	
	Grade 5	Grade 4	Grade 5	Grade 4	Grade 5	Grade 4
Intervention/control group	0.313	0.255	2.580	2.556	0.012	0.012
Gender	0.008	0.230	0.073	2.352	0.942	0.021
Ethnicity	0.117	0.140	1.058	1.417	0.293	0.160
Age	0.183	0.101	1.723	1.036	0.089	0.303
Five primary school years	0.025	0.092	0.216	0.926	0.830	0.357

Sig. T Value for gender variable is 0.021 (< 0.05). This indicates that for Grade 4 gender makes a significant difference to the prediction of the gain scores.

The results shown in Tables 8.3 and 8.4 suggest that the new model of teaching health used with the intervention group was more effective in terms of knowledge gain than the normal passive pedagogy used with the control group. This finding is corroborated by classroom observations of teaching and discussions recorded during the review workshops with the action research group. Teachers reported that their students had learned more, liked to work collaboratively on group tasks and stimulated each other to share their ideas. The new model had helped to increase students' confidence and feelings of self-worth.

Teachers also reported that the new model helped them manage a multigrade class more easily. Despite initial uncertainty about delivering the curriculum more flexibly and allowing students additional freedoms in the classroom during the group activities, the teachers' confidence increased as the action research continued, their skills in handling the class developed and they became accustomed to using the enquiry-based approach and using a variety of student groupings. Moreover, they found that their students were able to take action to promote health and that their relationship with the students improved.

DISCUSSION AND CONCLUSIONS

This study has demonstrated that action research can be used with multigrade teachers to improve the quality of teaching and learning for health in remote and disadvantaged rural areas of Vietnam. The point to stress here is that the teachers in the action research group were average teachers working in average classrooms. They were not master teachers in demonstration schools. The model they developed may be more easily spread to other teachers in similarly resource-poor schools. It is important to recognise, however, that further spread of the innovation would depend on teachers being able to set up their own peer support structures or micro-circles of learning. Such structures enable teachers to learn from each other through observing classroom teaching and sharing experiences whilst they are developing the skills and confidence needed to deliver the new model. Although teacher managers may be tasked with setting up support structures for teachers we must not forget that in remote areas many teachers are not well managed or supported and need to set up support structures for themselves.

This study has implications for more effective teacher training and teacher support. In Vietnam teachers are not trained to be innovators and experimenters; rather they are trained to deliver a uniform, tightly controlled and heavily prescribed National Curriculum. Although the Ministry of Education and Training (MOET) has acknowledged the need for multigrade teachers to be permitted to deliver the curriculum more flexibly such notions do not fit easily into the current mind set of most teachers. MOET will need to take further action to raise awareness and sensitise teachers to this new policy and to the degree of flexibility permitted. Such action will also need to be targeted at education officers at all levels of the system so that teachers can get informed support for flexible delivery and have their confidence and self-esteem raised so that they are willing and able to innovate. This study has shown that action research with teachers can empower teachers to be more flexible and innovate to improve the quality of their teaching.

This study also has implications for further curriculum development. It has demonstrated that health education can be a useful entry point for improving the quality of teaching and learning in multigrade classes because health topics easily lend themselves to being taught across different age and grade levels. In this study the action research group had some technical support from Vu Son in re-sequencing the National Curriculum so that the teachers could more easily see the areas of overlap between topics and grades. However, there is a bigger role here for curriculum developers to work alongside teachers to make multigrade teaching easier by presenting the entire curriculum in a format that helps teachers to plan lessons for multigrade classes. Teachers also need support in developing their ideas for student useful activities and group tasks that can enable students to take control of their own learning both individually and collaboratively. These issues are taken up and developed further in Chapter 9.

Health is also a good entry point for further curriculum development because the local environment (including the students themselves) provides a rich source of learning materials and stimuli for teaching health but teachers need to be sensitised to the learning materials around them in the environment. Although the enquiry-based approach adopted by the action research group helped students to develop the required skills and competencies it needed more time than the traditional passive pedagogy that focused on students simply learning health messages. In this study teachers used the one lesson a week given in the curriculum for locally relevant content to supplement the time given to health teaching. This allowed them to use the enquiry-based approach that enabled students to link knowledge to life and move from theory to practice. Seeing students taking health action is a good way to increase young people's agency in the eyes of their teachers and their parents. Teachers felt that selecting topics that reflected local health proprieties and concerns was a good use of the 'window' in the curriculum set aside for local content and that it increased the relevance of the curriculum and helped to bring the school and the community closer together. This has important implications for schools that serve small communities where it is crucial for the well-being of the school and the community that a strong link is established.

In conclusion, multigrade teachers in remote rural schools live and work in very complex and challenging teaching and learning contexts. To improve the quality of their teaching we need to make multigrade teaching easier by finding ways to present the curriculum in a more user-friendly manner, by providing improved training and support and more flexible and interactive learning materials. This chapter has demonstrated that action research with teachers can make a significant contribution to improving teaching quality by developing new teaching models grounded in real life contexts and that health education is a useful entry point for innovation and change.

REFERENCES

Elliott, J. (1992) *Action Research for Educational Change*. Milton Keynes: Open University Press.

Government of Vietnam (1994) *The Decision No. 2957/GD-DT, 14.10.1994*. Hanoi: MOET.

Government of Vietnam (2000) (Vietnamese National Parliamentary Decision of renovating the popular curriculum. *The Parliamentary Decision No. 40/2000/QH10*. Hanoi: MOET.

Little, A. (1995) *Multigrade Teaching: A review of research and practice*. Education Research Serial No. 12. London: Overseas Development Administration.

MOET (1995a) *Materials under the Law of Primary Educational Compulsory*. Hanoi: MOET.

MOET (1995b) *50-year Development of Education and Training (1945–1995)*. Edited by H.Q.Tran. Hanoi: Giaoduc Publisher.

MOET (2000) *The Recapitulate Conference of Multigrade Teaching and Bilingual Education Project for 10 Years*. Daklak: MOET.

MOET (2002a) *The National Primary Curriculum*. Hanoi: Giaoduc Publisher.

MOET (2002b) *Education Statistics*. Hanoi: Ministry of Education and Training, Centre for Educational Management Statistics.

NIER (1999) *An International Comparative Study of School Curriculum*. Tokyo: National Institute for Educational Research.

Nguyen, D.T. (1996) *The History of Vietnam Education before the August Revolution, 1945*. Hanoi: Giaoduc Publisher.

Nguyen, Q.T. and Ngo, D.T. *et al*. (2002) *The Centre of Maps and Pictures*, Hanoi: MOET.

Pham, M.H. *et al*. (2000) *10-year Literacy and Universal Primary Education (1990–2000)*. Hanoi: National Policy Publisher.

Pridmore P. and Stephens, D. (2000) *Children as Health Educators: A critical appraisal of the Child-to-Child approach*. London: ZED Books.

Trespeces, F. (1993) *Educational Action Research: a practitioner-oriented research process*. Philippines: SEAMEO INNOTECH.

Vu, T.S. (2002) Multigrade teaching in Vietnam and challenges for multigrade teaching. *Education Journal*, 31. Hanoi: Vietnam.

Vu, T.S. (2005) 'Improving teaching and learning for health in multigrade schools in Vietnam'. Unpublished PhD thesis. Institute of Education, University of London.

CHAPTER NINE

ADAPTING THE CURRICULUM FOR TEACHING HEALTH IN MULTIGRADE CLASSES IN VIETNAM

PAT PRIDMORE WITH T. SON VU

INTRODUCTION

Multigrade schools play a crucial role in helping countries reach the Millennium Development Goals to reduce poverty by increasing access to education, especially for girls. These schools are often located in remote and disadvantaged areas of the world where teachers live and work in very difficult circumstances with little support from the education system. The multigrade teachers' workload is increased because they are teaching across more than one grade level in one timetabled period using national curriculum materials that are generally developed with the needs of monograde[1] classes in mind. The curriculum content is presented grade by grade and textbooks are written for teachers to lead whole-class learning through direct teaching. Such monograded presentation of the curriculum greatly increases the work-load for teachers, who have to single-handedly take on the work of adapting the curriculum for use in their multigrade classrooms.

This chapter asks whether it is fair to expect multigrade teachers to take on this heavy burden and explores how curriculum developers might work with teachers to help share the burden. It reports on a curriculum development exercise undertaken between June 2001 and May 2002 by the National Institute of Educational Sciences (NIES) in Hanoi, in collaboration with multigrade teachers, in response to concerns that multigrade teachers spend too much time preparing lessons and that the quality of the teaching–learning interactions is frequently poor (APEID, 1995; Aikman and Pridmore, 2001; Hargreaves et al., 2001; Son, forthcoming). In this exercise curriculum developers reorganised the primary curriculum for health and developed lesson plans for multigrade teachers using an enquiry-based approach. The reorganised curriculum and piloted lesson plans were then included in a guide to teaching health for teachers of multigrade classes (Son et al., 2002). The aim was that this guide would act as a model for adapting the curriculum in other subjects to meet the needs of multigrade teachers. We would like to acknowledge the strong support given to this initiative by Dr Chau, Director of NIES, and by the British Council in Hanoi.

169

A.W. Little (ed.), Education for All and Multigrade Teaching: challenges and opportunities, 169–191.

This chapter firstly provides background and context to multigrade schooling in the Northern Highlands of Vietnam to explore some of the barriers to delivering good quality education in these settings. It then describes how the curriculum exercise was conducted and presents the reorganised curriculum for health and examples of lesson plans. Finally it addresses the wider picture in which curriculum reform is only one component of a package of interventions that need to be applied simultaneously to achieve improved teaching and learning in multigrade settings.

MULTIGRADE SCHOOLS IN VIETNAM

Vietnam is undergoing a long process of 'renovation' known as doi moi, in order to move from being a centrally planned economy to a multisectoral market-based economy managed by the state. In this process special attention has been paid to improving quality and access to primary education to help reach national economic and social development goals. There has been some success, especially in urban areas, and the government has declared Universal Primary Education on the basis of 70% enrolment. However, improvement in rural areas has lagged behind and the Ministry of Education and Training (MOET) is now challenged to meet the commitment[2] of 'Ensuring that all children, particularly girls, children in difficult circumstances and those belonging to ethnic minorities, have access to and are able to complete primary education that is free, compulsory and of good quality' (EFA Goal 3, UNESCO, 2000 para 7). To help reach this commitment MOET has been promoting multigrade schooling for children in sparsely populated areas. Multigrade schools have enabled thousands of children in economically and socially disadvantaged areas to have a formal education and this is the only type of school they will have access to in the foreseeable future. However, multigrade schooling is viewed as a necessity rather than a choice, a condition that, as Little (2004) points out, itself impacts on the quality of the provision.

The need to improve the quality and relevance of multigrade schooling

According to MOET (2001), 2.5% of primary classes (with 169,662 students) were multi-grade. Although this prevalence is not very high overall, the majority of these schools are clustered in remote areas where the correlation between multigrade teaching and disadvantaged children has led to calls for improved quality and relevance of teaching and learning in these schools. A study of multigrade schools in the Northern Highlands of

Vietnam by Aikman and Pridmore (2001) showed that teacher education offered little opportunity for guided trial or experimentation with new approaches to promote independent and collaborative learning. Most teacher trainees were only able to observe expert 'master teachers' in well supported 'demonstration' schools. There was no explicit recognition that new approaches are embedded in a totally different and new methodology of teaching and learning where the teacher is no longer the source of all knowledge but expected to facilitate independent and collaborative learning. Consequently, few teachers were able to use their training in the real life context of their school and were not followed up and supported to help them do so.

This study also revealed a lack of sensitivity in the curriculum and in teacher training to ethnic minority students' knowledge, socio-cultural environment, language and styles of learning and few teachers were able to use the so-called '15% window' in the curriculum to develop locally relevant content. Some of these challenges arise from the government policy of sending the best qualified teachers, most of whom are urban Vietnamese (*Kinh*), to multigrade schools where students come from ethnic minority groups and do not speak Vietnamese well. Such teachers often have a weak understanding of the language, culture and community where they are placed.

The MOET/UNICEF model of multigrade learning and teaching

Multigrade classes are not new in Vietnam. They have been present in rural areas for a long time, and many teachers have been specially trained to teach in them. Multigrade demonstration schools have arisen from a 10-year collaboration between MOET and UNICEF, starting in 1991, to develop training modules for multigrade teachers (UNICEF, 1998). Multigrade training follows a cascade approach and focuses primarily on classroom organisation skills. A team of staff at MOET have trained master teachers to work in the demonstration schools and in key training teams delivering short courses at Provincial level. At the District level in-service training is provided for some teachers in the summer break and at community level there is some professional development for multigrade teachers based in the centre school of school clusters. Teachers are taught to prepare a lesson plan for each grade in their class for each lesson, and to teach each grade separately but in parallel. This is achieved by giving short bursts of direct teaching to one grade group at a time whilst the other grade groups get on with individual or group tasks set by the teacher (often referred to as holding activities.)

Case studies of multigrade classroom practice in the Northern Highlands of Vietnam by Vu (2005) showed that many teachers were using the MOET/UNICEF model of classroom organisation, dividing the class into single-grade groups and teaching either different subjects or the same subject to each group in turn. This quasi monograde model was very exhausting for the teachers, who needed to be constantly moving between grades, checking progress and setting new tasks. The quality of teaching was found to be variable, but teaching was always teacher-initiated and directed and learning was passive. The best teachers managed to keep students on task most of the time although the tasks were not always sufficiently challenging, and young students became demotivated when left for too long between visits from the teacher. Group-work rarely engaged students in collaborative learning, but frequently involved students in the same grade group taking turns to read out loud or take turns writing on the board. Each grade group generally had a monitor who would stand in front and keep peers on task when the group was doing a holding activity. Teachers often described this as 'peer tutoring'. Teachers complained about the wide range of age and ability in their classes and the long hours they spent writing separate lesson plans for each grade. They said this doubled, tripled or quadrupled their workload and was demoralising. The monograded curriculum materials made it difficult for them to plan any whole-class or mixed-grade teaching.

ADAPTING THE NATIONAL CURRICULUM FOR PRIMARY SCHOOLS TO THE MULTIGRADE TEACHER

The curriculum development exercise was conducted in four steps:

1 Reorganising the Natural and Social Science and Science subject content.
2 Developing a new model for teaching health topics and writing lesson plans.
3 Field testing the lesson plans.
4 Writing and disseminating the teachers' guide.

Step 1: Reorganising the Natural and Social Science and Science content

In Vietnam all primary schools follow a national curriculum which is delivered over a total period of 165 weeks of term time spanning years 1 to 5.

This curriculum is designed and controlled centrally by MOET with set textbooks for each grade level, a prescribed daily timetable for lessons and a national school calendar. During the 1990s the national primary curriculum came under growing criticism for failing to prepare students for the world of work and life as moral citizens. Much of the content was considered to be superfluous, or not sufficiently relevant (see Chau writing in Hargreaves *et al.*, 2001). The national primary curriculum has subsequently been 'renovated' and the new Primary School Curriculum 2000 (MOET, 2002) aims to address the former shortcomings. It seeks to develop students' competencies in critical thinking and practical skills and stresses the need for renovation of teaching and learning methods to develop students as self-directed and creative learners.

For the purpose of the curriculum exercise it was decided to make a start with Natural and Social Sciences (for Grades 1, 2, 3) and Science (for Grades 4 and 5). The intention was that this reorganised curriculum could then act as a model for reorganising the other curriculum subjects in the future. In the National Curriculum document the content is presented by grades, themes and topics, as shown in the extract presented in Figure 9.1. The three themes shown here are introduced in Grade 1 and repeated through Grades 2 and 3 with a broadening and deepening of the topics. The first theme then continues through Grades 4 and 5 but the other two themes are replaced by two new themes – Materials and Energy, Plants and Animals.

To adapt the new curriculum to the needs of multigrade teachers a working group was set up led by Vu Son from NIES with representatives from NIES, MOET and the Research Centre for Ethnic Minority Education. Pat Pridmore from the Institute of Education in London was the technical adviser. Two members of the working group who had experience in developing the new Natural and Social Science and Science curriculum reorganised the entire content for this subject to show the topics spread across the five grades.

The reorganised curriculum is illustrated in Figure 9.2 with an example taken from the topics on safety. This figure shows that repeated development of the theme can now be clearly seen as well as the areas where grades could most easily be combined for whole-class teaching.

It is important for multigrade teachers to be able to see the entire primary grade span because in Vietnam grade combinations vary from year to year according to student enrolment. A teacher with Grades 1 and 2 in the class one year may have Grades 2, 3 and 5 the next year – or any other combination. Most classes have two or three grades but some have four or even five and there is no set pattern to the combination of grades that any

Figure 9.1 Part of the National Primary Curriculum (2000) for Natural and Social Science to show how it is presented in the curriculum document

Grade 1 One period a week for 35 weeks = 35 periods

Theme 1: Human beings and health

Sub-themes: Physique and hygiene; safety and prevention of disease

Topics:
- The human body and senses (outside characteristics of the human body, the ability to be conscious of things in the surroundings; personal hygiene and sense organs; oral hygiene).
- The need to eat clean food and drink clean water.

Theme 2: Society

Sub-theme: The family

Topics:
- Family: members of the family (grandfather, grandmother, father, mother, brothers, sisters).
- House (home address, places for eating, sleeping, working, learning and receiving guests) and necessary household utensils. The need to keep the house clean. Safety at home (preventing and avoiding burning, cutting of fingers, or electric shock).
- Classroom: members of the classroom, utensils used in the classroom, keeping the classroom clean and tidy.
- Hamlet, village, commune, street or road where one is living, scenery and daily activities of the people. Road safety and communication.

Theme 3: Nature

Sub-themes: Flora and fauna; sky and earth

Topics:
- Plants and animals: some common plants and animals (names of species, characteristics, benefit or adverse effects on human beings).
- Some natural phenomena: sun, wind, storm, hot, cold.

Figure 9.2 Part of the Natural and Social Science and Science curriculum showing how the topics on safety were reorganised across all five grades

Theme: Human beings and health. Sub-theme: Safety and disease prevention
Grade 1   **Safety at home** Know how to avoid getting burnt, cut, or electric shock. **Traffic safety** Be alert while travelling along narrow paths between water-fields, or on river banks, around lakes, or up mountain cliffs. Know that it is lawful to walk on pavements or areas reserved for pedestrians and unlawful to play games, or football in the streets. Be aware of traffic rules at T-junctions, forks and crossroads.
Grade 2   **Safety at home** Be alert against food poisoning by not eating stale food. Know not to take medicines without instructions from doctors or parents. Know whom to call for in emergency. **Safety at school** Can take precaution against falling. Can realise the danger, not to play, stand, run or jump near dangerous places. **Traffic safety** Observe traffic laws (when walking or using private or public transport). Identify some traffic signs on roads and railways.
Grade 3   **Safety at home** Be alert against food poisoning by not eating stale food. Know not to take medicines without indications from doctors or parents. Know whom to call for in emergency **Safety at school** Take care against unexpected accidents caused by naughty playing. Avoid danger caused by contacting strangers. **Traffic safety** Observe traffic laws (when walking, cycling or taking public transport). Identify some traffic signs on roads and railways.
Grade 4   **Food safety** Be aware of the harm caused by stale, contaminated food, or under-cooked food.
Grade 5   **Safety in society** Avoiding drug abuse. Being conscious of the harm caused by cigarettes, liquor, drugs and heroin, etc. Being determined to refuse all invitations to use any kind of stimulants. Not being involved in transport or dealing of stimulants. **Know how to take medicine safely.**

teacher has in the class from year to year. The unpredictability of the grade combinations from one year to the next also means that teachers cannot use strategies such as two- or three-year curriculum spans, in which students enter the span at different points but the teacher teaches the same content to the whole class as in a monograde class.

Step 2: Developing a new model for teaching health topics and writing lesson plans

Having reorganised the curriculum for Natural and Social Science and Science a decision was made by the working group to select the health topics in this curriculum as the focus for developing lesson plans and writing a teacher's guide. The health topics were selected for four main reasons.

First, the cases studies of multigrade teaching had confirmed that even the most expert teachers were using largely passive pedagogy and that students needed more opportunities to meet the demands of the new National Curriculum in order that they should develop critical thinking and practical skills and become self-directed and creative learners. Where such passive pedagogy persists studies have shown that an enquiry-based approach to health education can be a useful entry point for reform (Phinney and Evans, 1992; Pridmore and Stephens, 2000), and that once teachers are convinced this approach can help them teach health more effectively they can use it to improve the quality of their teaching in other subjects (Gibbs, 1997). Health is also a good entry point for pedagogic reform in poorly resourced schools because the local environment (including the students' own bodies, their homes and community) is a rich source of learning materials. Moreover, healthy habits are something that students need to practise now, whilst they are still at school, as well as later when they become adults, and to do this they must learn skills as well as knowledge.

Second, it enabled the working group to build on the new model for teaching health developed by Vu Son through action research with multigrade teachers. This model used an enquiry-based approach together with whole-class, single-grade and mixed-grade groupings for teaching and learning. (This model is described further below.) This research showed that the new model could be implemented within existing resources and that once teachers and students developed skill and confidence in using the model and saw that it improved student achievement it transformed entrenched, negative attitudes to multigrade teaching.

Third, it is important to teach health in very poor communities because there is good evidence that healthy children learn better (Pollitt, 1995). This was clearly recognised by the parents interviewed by Aikman and Pridmore (1998) in remote communities in the Northern Highlands who wanted schools to teach about taking care of health and improved methods of farming. It was also recognised by the Provincial Director of Education from Son La, who commented that 'Teachers in isolated schools are not just required to teach children, they also have to take care of the children' (Aikman and Pridmore, 1998: 17). The truth of this statement is borne out by the fact that in many small communities the teacher is the only professional person living in the community and it is essential for them to feel confident to teach health effectively.

Fourth, health topics are rarely taught in remote multigrade schools, despite being crucial for school achievement, because health is a low status subject in the curriculum. Although MOET requires all teachers to deliver the full national primary curriculum, in practice multigrade students experience a reduced curriculum that often focuses on only two subject areas, maths and (Vietnamese) language, with some limited social studies. This is because schools lack textbooks and learning materials to cover all subjects and because teachers do not feel confident to teach health (Aikman and Pridmore 2001).

Having decided to work with the health topics in the curriculum, the starting point for developing linked lesson plans and homework activities was the need for students to achieve the objectives of the National Curriculum 2000. These objectives are to provide health knowledge and to establish skills so that the knowledge can be used by students to take care of their health and to develop a sense of responsibility about keeping the rules of personal hygiene and safety for oneself, family, school and native land. At the same time the working group needed to use a pedagogic model that would enable teachers 'to link knowledge of health and natural science with real life, local production; exploiting students' living experience' (MOET, 2002: 57). MOET (2002) has also emphasised the need for good health skills to be widely broadcast to other members of the family and the community through students' life styles and their communications with others.

To achieve these objectives the curriculum working group adopted the new pedagogic model for teaching health topics developed through Vu Son's action research with multigrade teachers. This model drew on an enquiry-based approach to health education known as Child-to-Child, which has been adapted and used in classrooms all over the world to teach health education effectively and promote children as capable citizens with rights and responsibilities for health (Pridmore, 2000, 2003). This pedagogic model can be roughly divided into four steps: Identify, Study, Act, Evaluate (and do it better next time). Figure 9.3 shows how these steps were spread over two lessons with homework activities that enabled students to link learning in school with learning at home and/or in the community and also plan and take action to improve health. This pedagogic model needed more time to cover each topic than the traditional passive learning model. This time was found by using the so-called 15% window in the curriculum (equivalent to one timetabled period a week) in which teachers are supposed to teach topics of their own choosing that are of local relevance.

Figure 9.3 The enquiry-based approach used to link the lessons

---

Lesson 1: Understanding the concepts and learning the main health messages. *Homework: Finding out more about the topic at home and in the community.*

Lesson 2: Discussing what students have found out and planning action they can take to improve the situation. *Homework: Taking action.*

Lesson 3: First 10 minutes only: feedback on action and brief revision of the topic.

Within the new pedagogic model the teacher started and finished each lesson with a short period of whole-class teaching to help students develop a strong sense of belonging to one class (rather than just to a grade group in a multigrade classroom). During each lesson the teacher introduced activities for mixed-grade as well as single-grade groupings to build on diversity of student ages, grades, ability and temperament to increase interaction and learning. These changes were designed to harness the potential benefits of multigrade schooling – improved development of psychosocial and civic skills and self-esteem (Colbert *et al.*, 1993) and cognitive skills, especially for less able students (see Berry, Chapter 2 in this book). The method used to group students for learning during a typical lesson is shown in Figure 9.4.

Figure 9.4 Example of student groupings used during a lesson

Step 1: Direct teaching to the whole class to facilitate feedback from last week's homework activity and to introduce the topic for today.

Step 2: Small group activities (single grade or mixed grade, etc.) with the teacher moving from group to group providing support.

Step 3: Direct teaching to the whole class to facilitate feedback from group-work, to ask questions to check that students have learned well and to set the homework activity.

This new model of teaching health has the potential to achieve the new curriculum objectives with the support of MOET, which has now permitted multigrade teachers a small degree of flexibility in the sequence in which curriculum topics can be delivered in the classroom. The curriculum-working group felt that this enquiry-based approach could realistically be taken up and sustained by the majority of teachers in average multigrade schools without additional materials or support because it builds on forms of teaching with which teachers are already familiar and only asks them to make small changes by introducing one activity each lesson. It also includes opportunities for students to collect health-related data and to pass on health messages and practise healthy behaviours (and avoid unhealthy ones) in their home, school and community.

The curriculum working group then scrutinised the reorganised curriculum for Natural and Social Science and Science to identify topics that could be taught across more than one grade and were also priority health issues in the areas where multigrade schools are most commonly found. The seven topics identified are shown in Figure 9.5.

Figure 9.5 Examples of health topics from the Natural and Social Science and Science curriculum that can be taught across grade levels

• Personal hygiene	Grades 1 and 2
• Taking care of our teeth	Grades 1 and 2
• Environmental hygiene	Grades 1 and 2
• Safety at home	Grades 1, 2 and 3
• Prevention of disease	Grades 3 and 4
• Nutrition	Grades 4 and 5

In applying the enquiry-based pedagogic model to teach a health topic the following process was followed. First a brief overview was written showing the main focus of each lesson. Second, the specific curriculum objectives for each grade were defined. Third, the two linked lesson plans and home-work activities were developed, starting with advice on lesson preparation and then a step-by-step account of how to organise learning and teaching with timings and groupings for each of the steps. This process is shown in Figure 9.6.

Step 3: Field-testing the lesson plans

The lesson plans and homework activities developed by the curriculum working group were field tested in ten rural multigrade schools in Backing Province by five teachers from the action research group working with five teachers who had no previous experience of the new model for teaching health. Two members of the curriculum working group, five head teachers and two external evaluators observed teachers implementing the lesson plans

Figure 9.6 Example of two linked lessons to teach Safety in the Home
(Grades 1, 2 and 3)

Overview
Lesson 1: Accidents at home: What is an accident? What causes accidents in the home?
Homework: Looking for dangers in the home.

Lesson 2: How to avoid accidents in the home.
Homework: Sharing what we have learned with our parents and friends and taking action to make our home safer.

Review: Feedback on action taken and revision of the topic.

Learning objectives: By the end of this sequence of lessons your students should:

	Grade 1	Grade 2 – same as Grade 1, plus:	Grade 3 – same as Grade 1 and 2, plus:
K N O W	• Many accidents occur at home, • The 5 most common accidents are: (1) burns and scalds from fires and cooking pots (2) poisons from bottles left in the wrong place (3) accidents with electricity from wires that are not properly protected (4) falls from trees or furniture (5) cuts from sharp things left where young children can reach them. • Nearly all these accidents can be prevented by being aware of danger and getting parents to notice it and by avoiding dangerous games that can cause eye and ear injuries.	• Who to call in an emergency and how to do it. • How to avoid danger – for example by not climbing trees or running and jumping dangerously. • The need to be alert to the danger of food poisoning.	• Most accidents can be prevented once it is understood that small students act and move differently from adults. • Crawling babies and young students just learning to walk are particularly at risk, especially from burns, scalds and poisons. • Children below school age cannot estimate the speed of moving vehicles and should be watched carefully. • Not to carry things that are too heavy. • Simple first aid can minimise the harm from accidents.

D O	• Regularly look around their home and remove causes of accidents not only for themselves but also for others, especially babies, young children and old people – or get their parents to notice the danger. • Practise safety rules for themselves and with friends.	• Avoid danger from falling, for example, by not climbing trees or running and jumping dangerously. • Keep medicines out of the reach of young students and not take medicines without indications from doctors or parents. • Avoid eating stale food.	• Watch babies and young children and teach them safety rules. • Apply simple first aid for burns, cuts and wounds. • Be aware of the danger of fire when cooking – do not put flammable things near cooking-stoves. • Take precaution against unexpected accidents from careless playing. • Make those who have an accident safe and comfortable while getting help.
F E E L	• Concern for those who have accidents and the need to care for them.	• Awareness of danger and responsibility for avoiding it and keeping themselves safe in the home. • Responsibility for making their homes as safe as possible.	• Concern and responsibility, alongside adults, to watch over others particularly younger students, and prevent unsafe behaviour.

Lesson 1: Understanding what an accident is and why accidents happen	
Preparation: For Activity 1, draw pictures on the board to show some common accidents such as a child falling from a tree and breaking his/her leg, or a child hitting his or her bare foot on a stone and making it bleed. Include some pictures of problems that are not caused by an accident such as a swollen face caused by toothache, an insect bite or diarrhoea.	
Introduction	*Whole class* Introduce the new topic: 'You are going to start a new topic today called 'Safety in the home'.
Activity 1 10 minutes	Show the pictures you have drawn on the board and lead a discussion using the following questions: Ask 'What problem is shown in each of these pictures?' Ask 'Which of the problems shown are caused by an accident?' Make sure students understand that accidents can take place anywhere, anytime, that there are lots of causes and that most accidents can be avoided.

(Continued)

Figure 9.6 continued

Activity 2 10 minutes	Ask: 'What accidents have *you* had at home?' List on the board. Ask 'What accidents have *other members of your family* had at home?' Add these to the list and add any more accidents that are common including cut fingers or toes, electric shock, burns from boiling water or fire, drinking poison, a fire breaking out at home, a young child or elderly person falling over. Discuss 'What are the most common types of accidents and who has each type of accident most often (e.g. young/old people, boys/girls)?'		
	Single grade groups		
Activity 3 10 minutes	*Grade 1* Copy the list of accidents. Discuss 'How do some children get burnt, break a leg, get an electric shock or cut their finger?'	*Grade 2* Discuss 'Why do some people get poisoned from eating bad food or drink?' List four reasons (e.g. drinking insecticide from an unlabelled bottle, eating food with flies on it.)	*Grade 3* Ask 'List the things in your home that can cause a fire.' Ask 'Why should we not put these near the fire?' Discuss 'What can cause fire to break out in your home?'
	Whole class Ask a spokesperson from each group to tell the class what they learned from their discussions.		
Homework	'Look around your home and make a list of 1) sharp things that can cause cuts 2) hot things that can cause burns 3) electrical appliances (and where they are stored and the state of the wire flex).'	'Look around your home and list poisonous things and say where they are kept.'	'Look around your home and list things that can cause a fire and say where they are kept.'

Lesson 2: What can we do to prevent accidents at home?
Preparation: Clean water, cloth and a bandage for Activity 3, Grade 3

Introduction	*Whole class* Take feedback from students on homework activities and discuss. Remind students that accidents happen unexpectedly and can happen anywhere – in the cooking area, the living area, the sleeping area or the playing area/garden.
Activity 1 15 minutes	*Mixed grade groups* Divide students into 3 groups with students from each grade in every group. Group 1 discuss 'How can sharp things in the home be kept safely?' Group 2 discuss 'How can hot things that cause burns and fires in the home be kept safely?' Group 3 discuss 'How can poisonous things in the home be kept safely?'

	Whole class Take feedback from each group in turn. Make sure all students understand the need to keep small children safe by watching them carefully and keeping dangerous things such as lamps and matches, fire, cooking pots and sharp things away from them. Make sure Grade 3 understand the need to be careful while cooking, to put the fire out before leaving the house and to keep inflammable items away from the cooking fire. Explain that dangerous behaviours can also cause accidents and give examples: running and jumping dangerously, climbing trees, games that can injure the ears or eyes.		
	Single grade groups		
Activity 2 15 minutes	*Grade 1* 'You are helping your brothers and sisters to make the evening meal and your little sister cuts her finger and screams with terror. Discuss what you will do.' *(Stay calm and call for your parents or an adult to help.)*	*Grade 2* 'Your young brother accidentally drinks something poisonous in the living area. You are playing in the garden with your friends when you see him staggering towards you in great pain.' Make a role play to show what you will do.' *(Quickly ask him what he drank, call for help and take him and some of the poison to the health worker.)*	*Grade 3* Ask your teacher to help you practise how to give simple first aid for a cut or a burn. *To treat a cut finger or toe (a) Wash the wound with clean water and soap (boiled and cooled water is best) (b) Dry the skin, cover the wound with a clean cloth and place a bandage over it. To treat a small burn (a) Cool burned area immediately by putting it into cold, clean water for at least 5 minutes (b) Do not remove anything that is sticking to the burn or put anything except cold water on it. If the wound or burn is more serious report it to an adult and help to take the patient to the health worker.*
	Whole class Take feedback from each group on their activities and summarise how to prevent and treat accidents at home.		
Homework	Ask students to tell parents or carers what they have learned about how to prevent and treat accidents at home and alert them to any dangers in the home so that they can make their home safer. Remind them to practice what they have learned and emphasise the need to watch younger brothers and sisters carefully to keep them safe. Ask Grade 3 to find four ways to make their homes safer.		

Lesson 3 (First 10 minutes only)

Review: Briefly revise how to prevent and treat accidents and take feedback on homework tasks. What action have students taken? What problems (if any) have they had? Ask students to suggest a promise they could make to continue taking safe measures at home. Students make the promise.

and interviewed them and their students to find out their views on the new model of teaching health. These findings are complemented by those of Vu (2005), which showed that teachers had been able to follow the lesson plans and facilitate the activities. Feedback was used to improve the plans.

Interview data revealed that teachers had initially lacked confidence in their ability to carry out the activities and were not comfortable with students moving around the classroom during lessons and talking to each other during groupwork activities. Students also felt uncomfortable with their new freedoms in the classroom. In time, however, both teachers and students became accustomed to health lessons being noisier and less controlled than other lessons. Students came to enjoy the variety of approaches used in the lessons and the way that the homework activities helped to link what they learned in the classroom with the reality of their lives. Teachers made sure that in mixed-grade groupwork each student had a specific task to do. One teacher started to creatively adapt the lesson plans with new homework activities based on mixed-grade interest groups. Teachers reported that the new model helped students develop better communication and groupwork skills (such as listening to each other, expressing their own view and encouraging shy students to participate) and made them more confident in the interactions with each other and with the teacher. These findings are again complemented by those of Vu (2005), which showed that students taught using the new model had significantly higher cognitive scores compared to those in a control group who had received traditional health teaching.

Step 4: Writing and disseminating the teachers' guide

As previously mentioned the curriculum exercise led to the writing of a guide to teaching health in the new primary curriculum for multigrade teachers that could be used as a model for curriculum reorganisation in other subjects. This guide is divided into two parts. Part 1 presents the monograded National Primary Curriculum 2000 for Natural and Social Sciences and Science and provides guidance for teachers of multigrade classes on how to develop a whole-school approach to promoting health. It explains how to organise teaching, to build a healthy school environment, to make good use of health services and to spread health knowledge and skills from the school to the community. Each chapter ends with workshop activities to help teachers improve current practice. Part 2 presents the National Curriculum 2000 for Natural and Social Sciences and Science reorganised for teachers of multigrade classes. It then gives the lesson plans for use in multigrade classes so that teachers can feel confident that they are covering key health topics required by the National Curriculum (Vu *et al.*, 2002). The teachers' guide has been well disseminated by NIES and the British Council.

DISCUSSION AND CONCLUSIONS

This chapter has highlighted the challenges to multigrade teaching posed by the monograded presentation of the National Primary Curriculum in Vietnam and by the expectation that all classes will cover the curriculum and meet the annual assessment targets for each grade level in the same way. Having to meet annual assessment targets that in practice are still overly concerned with graded learning objectives for knowledge makes it difficult for teachers to deliver the curriculum more flexibly. It also pushes them towards using quasi monograde curriculum strategies and teaching methods that focus on rote learning and recall of factual information. This needs to be challenged because a key principle for effective multigrade teaching is flexible delivery of the curriculum to enable teachers to respond to the increased diversity of student ages and grade levels in their class using a combination of curriculum strategies.

This chapter has described a curriculum exercise to reorganise the national curriculum for the subject Natural and Social Science and Science to meet the needs of multigrade teachers by making the spiral development of the themes more explicit by presenting the topics spread across all five grades and developing lesson plans for multigrade classes using a new pedagogic model for teaching health. The strength of this new pedagogic model is that it was developed and trailed by multigrade teachers working in average classrooms and not by master teachers in demonstration schools. A further strength is that it uses an enquiry-based approach with realistic links to daily life and local needs designed to make schooling become part of the social and cultural environment of the child – conditions which are well recognised to be crucial for good multigrade teaching (Thomas and Shaw, 1992).

Building on diversity and differentiation

This new pedagogic model seeks to help teachers build on the increased diversity of student ages, abilities, temperament, culture and language found in the multigrade classroom in Vietnam through increasing the opportunities for interaction and learning between students both within and across grade levels and between learning in the classroom and in the local environment.

The model is designed to achieve this through using a range of different teaching methods including whole-class teaching and collaborative groupwork activities differentiated for differentiated for different student groupings. As Berry and Little (see Chapter 4 in this volume) point out, combining these different methods provides increased opportunities for 'cognitive stretching' of younger and less able students as well as for social and personal development. By acting as role models older students can gain in confidence and self-esteem. Whole-class teaching and shared learning may also be attractive as a means of building up a sense of belonging to the class and strengthening values that are important in traditional, collectivist cultures such as that found in Vietnam (see Croft in Chapter 6 of this volume).

The new pedagogic model also builds on diversity by involving students and teachers in formative assessment at the end of the enquiry-based process when students are evaluating the action they have taken to improve health. There is much scope for further development of this component to develop teacher and student skill in assessing the process and outcomes of groupwork as well as student skill in self-assessment. It is beyond the scope of this chapter to explore the issue of 'assessment for learning' in any depth but the way in which formative assessment can improve students' learning needs to be more widely recognised. Hargreaves (2001) has argued that formative assessments are especially useful in multigrade classrooms, where students learn at different levels.

The opportunity to build on diversity is also being taken up elsewhere. A similar curriculum exercise is currently being conducted in Sri Lanka working on the curriculum for Mathematics (and building on action research conducted by Vithanapathirana – see Chapter 7 in this book) and also in Nepal working on the Environmental Science curriculum. The aim of this curriculum work is to develop accredited Teacher Education courses to be validated by Universities that recognise the professional development needs of teachers in multigrade teaching settings (see Little, Chapter 1 in this volume).

Continuing the work in progress

The curriculum exercise reported in this chapter should be regarded as work in progress to be further developed and expanded. In Vietnam scope and sequence charts need to be drawn up for all subjects to display the topics and objectives across all primary grades. In each subject the topics that can be taught to mixed-grade classes (through whole-class teaching with differentiated activities) need to be identified, and also the topics that must be taught to single grades only. These topics can then be put into a programme (scheme of work) for each multigrade class to indicate the sequence in which the topics should be taught to cover the main themes, units and essential learning objectives for that subject. Separate schemes of work need to be developed in each subject for classes with the most common grade combinations.

Pat Pridmore has recently taken this work forward with curriculum developers from seven countries in Sub-Saharan Africa which are now starting to adapt their national curricula for multigrade teaching. She has also worked with the Ministry of Education in Bhutan to help them adapt the entire primary curriculum for multigrade teaching. This experience has shown that in many developing countries there is some resistance to combining different curriculum strategies in the way that most effective multigrade teachers do in developed countries. The two strategies most commonly combined in developed countries are the quasi monograde strategy and two-year or three-year curriculum cycles, known as rolling programmes. In developing countries resistance to using multiple-year curriculum cycles appears to be based on firmly held beliefs about the need for learning to be incremental in nature and lack of flexibility in delivering the curriculum caused by annual, graded examinations that test student knowledge rather than competencies. Despite these concerns, multiple-year cycles have been introduced into multigrade demonstration schools in Zambia. In the absence of multiple-year cycles teachers resort to quasi monograde organisation, which increases their workload in planning and delivering separate lessons to each grade to a level that generally becomes unsustainable when there are more than three grades in the class.

In developed countries two-year curriculum cycles have been shown to work well in all subjects, except perhaps in reading and number work, which are more incremental in nature and where each grade is therefore usually taught separately. In a two-year curriculum cycle students in two consecutive grades are taught the same content at the same time but start and finish the cycle at different times. For example, in the first year of the cycle all students in a class with Grades 3 and 4 will work together through the Grade 4 syllabus for the chosen subject. When the Grade 4 students move up a grade at the end of the school year the Grade 3 pupils become Grade 4 but stay in the same classroom and are joined by a new set of Grade 3 students. The new class then work together through the Grade 3 syllabus for that subject. At the end of this school year Grade 4 have completed the two-year syllabus and leave the cycle whilst Grade 3 continues on for a second year, becoming Grade 4 students, and being joined by a new set of Grade 3 students.

Curriculum developers can help multigrade teachers to use multi-year curriculum cycles by providing expert advice on how best to sequence the units in the cycle. In the United Kingdom, for example, schemes of work are provided by the Ministry of Education for different combinations of grades. The scheme of work for the primary science curriculum shows how units can be sequenced over two years (six terms) for a class with Grades 1 and 2, a class with Grades 3 and 4, and a class with Grades 5 and 6. The sequencing of the units is different from the monograde syllabus but builds on the incremental nature of the units where needed (DFEE, 1998: 15). Additional guidance is also provided for teaching using multi-year curriculum cycles. For example, teachers are advised to make sure that the Grade 4 students are being stretched when they are studying the Grade 3 curriculum and to provide additional support for Grade 3 students when they are studying the Grade 4 curriculum. Teachers who have a wider range of grades in their class are advised to develop their own scheme of work using the scope and sequence chart to assist them.

Challenging deep-seated cultures of curriculum design

The concerns currently being expressed by some countries about using multiple-year curriculum cycles (and also modularised curricula) reflect deep-seated cultures of curriculum design. It is one thing to demonstrate that a national curriculum can be reorganised to address the needs of multigrade teachers. It is quite another thing to persuade Ministries of Education and their Curriculum Development Units to make adaptations that require them to allow considerable flexibility in delivery and trust their teachers to make good decisions. Effective curriculum adaptation for multigrade teaching also requires curriculum developers and teachers to acknowledge the diversity of learners in both monograde and multigrade classrooms and to respond to this diversity through differentiation of inputs and outcomes. As Little (2004) points out, accepting the principle of diversity requires a change in the philosophical, sociological, psychological and pedagogical theoretical base that informs the monograde organisation of the curriculum and acknowledges that the capacity to learn is open and not narrowly governed by notions of developmental stages.

And yet we must not forget that monograde schools have not always been with us. As Little (1995, 2001) reminds us, the monograde organisation of schooling has only been around for a couple of hundred years, before which schools were ungraded. If education systems were reoriented towards a multigrade norm with all teachers trained in multigrade and multilevel strategies, and if formative as well as summative assessment was built into the curriculum then all teachers would be able to deal more effectively with the full range of diversity that they can meet in any classroom. This is important because multigrade teaching is probably more prevalent than many policy makers, curriculum developers and teacher educators realise and it is here to stay for the foreseeable future. It is also important because multigrade is a daily reality in the majority of monograde schools, where teachers have to teach more than one class whenever colleagues are absent. A strong argument can be made for all teachers to be trained in multigrade and multilevel skills and education systems and for their national curricula to be reoriented towards a multigrade norm.

In light of the foregoing discussion, the recent renovation of the National Primary Curriculum in Vietnam might be viewed as a missed opportunity to radically rethink the basis on which the curriculum is predicated and promote a combination of curriculum strategies. However, the curriculum exercise can be viewed as one small step in the right direction. Even though attention in Vietnam has now moved on to renovation of the secondary school curriculum, we have to ask whether there is still scope for further reorganisation of the curriculum and the production of primary texts written with the self-studying learner in mind. For example, the lesson plans included in the teachers' guide produced from the curriculum exercise led by NIES could easily be adapted as a learners' guide so that students can take more control of their own learning and the teacher is released to facilitate that learning. It is important that such guides are not only designed to be used by individual children but by groups of children learning together with help from the teacher. This is because self-study can be lonely and boring for children and does not develop the range of lifeskills needed. It is also important that further exemplar materials are developed in collaboration with multigrade teachers and that teachers are encouraged to further adapt them to their specific context.

The need for further policy development to support a comprehensive package of interventions

This chapter has been largely concerned with the reorganisation of the curriculum to meet the needs of multigrade teachers. However, it is clear from the foregoing discussion that curriculum reform is only one component of a comprehensive package that is needed to improve the quality of learning and teaching in multigrade settings. This package must also include simultaneous efforts to develop self-study learning materials, teacher education in classroom management and facilitation of student-led activities, and formative assessment. It is unlikely that any single strategy will lead to significant improvements in student learning because synergy is needed between all of the components. Moreover, as Little (chapter 14 of this volume) points out, 'Surrounding these strategies is the need for national policies (for curriculum, materials, teacher education and assessment) that recognise, legitimate and support learners and teachers in multigrade settings.'

In Vietnam the Ministry of Education and Training is currently seeking to improve the quality of teaching and learning in disadvantaged areas with support from the World Bank. This focus has stimulated constructive debate and a favourable climate for further policy development to support the sort of comprehensive package detailed above and ensure more equitable treatment of multigrade teachers. Such a package should help multigrade teachers make the school part of the child's world and not representative of some remote institution that has little relevance for children or their parents It should also realise the full potential of multigrade schooling to contribute to poverty alleviation in some of the poorest areas of the world.

NOTES

[1] In monograde classes the teacher teaches students of only one grade in a timetabled period.

[2] This commitment was made by delegates at the World Education Forum on Education for All held in Dakar, Senegal in 2000.

REFERENCES

Aikman, A. and Pridmore, P. (1998) *Multigrade Teaching and Learning: A study of classroom practice and teacher education in northern Vietnam.* Research report. Hanoi: The British Council.

Aikman, S. and Pridmore, P. (2001) 'Multigrade schooling in remote areas of Vietnam'. *International Journal of Educational Development*, 21, 6, 521–536

APEID (1995) *multigrade Teaching in Primary Schools.* Bangkok: UNESCO.

Colbert, V., Chiappe, C. and Arboleda, J. (1993) 'The new school program: more and better primary education for children in rural areas in Colombia'. In H.M. Levin and M.E. Lockheed (eds) *Effective Schools in Developing Countries.* London: Falmer Press.

Gibbs, W. (1997) 'Evaluation of the Child-to-Child Programme in Zambia'. Unpublished report. London: The Child-to-Child Trust.

Hargreaves, E. (2001) 'Assessment for learning in the multigrade classroom'. *International Journal of Educational Development*, 21, 6, 553–560.

Hargreaves, E., Montero, C., Chau, N., Sibli, S. and Thanh, T. (2001) 'Multigrade teaching in Peru, Sri Lanka and Vietnam: an overview'. *International Journal of Educational Development*, 21, 499–520.

Little, A.W. (1995) *Multigrade Teaching: A review of research and practice.* Education Research, Serial No. 12. London: Overseas Development Administration.

Little, A.W. (2001) 'Multigrade teaching: towards an international research and policy agenda'. *International Journal of Educational Development*, 21, 6, 481–495.

Little, A.W. (2004) 'Learning and teaching in multigrade settings'. Paper prepared for the *UNESCO 2005 EFA Monitoring Report*. Online. Available at http://portal.unesco.org/education/en/file_download.php/548cfe4ac0864fcea6669 00c2144e4d1Little.doc (Accessed 10 March 2005).

MOET (2001) *Education Statistics*. Hanoi: Ministry of Education and Training, Centre for Educational Management Statistics.

MOET (2002) *Primary Curriculum*. Hanoi: Giaoduc Publisher.

Phinney, R. and Evans, J. (1992) 'From child to child: children as communicators'. In *Development Communication Report 78*, 7–9. Arlington, VA: Clearinghouse on Development Communication.

Pollitt, E. (1995) *Malnutrition and Infection in the Classroom*. Paris: UNESCO.

Pridmore, P. (2000) 'Children's participation in development for school health'. *Compare*, 30, 1, 103–113.

Pridmore, P. (2003) 'Children's participation: a critical review of Child-to-Child experience in Kenya and Vietnam'. *Journal of Anthropology in Action*, 10, 1, 15–24.

Pridmore, P. and Stephens, D. (2000) *Children as Health Educators: A critical appraisal of the Child-to-Child approach.* London: ZED Books.

Thomas, C. and Shaw, C. (1992) 'Issues in multigrade schools'. *World Bank Technical Paper No. 172*. Washington: World Bank.

UNESCO (2000) *The Dakar Framework for Action., Education for All: Meeting our collective commitments.* Adopted by the World Education *Forum* (Dakar, Senegal 2001). Paris: UNESCO.

UNICEF (1998) *An Evaluation of the Multigrade and Bilingual Education Project.* Hanoi: UNICEF.

Vu, T.S., Pridmore, P., Nga, B., My, D. and Kick, P. (2002) *Renovating the Teaching of Health in Multigrade Primary Schools: A teacher's guide to health in natural and social sciences (Grades 1, 2, 3) and Science (grade 5).* Hanoi, Vietnam: British Council/National Institute of Educational Sciences (Published in English and in Vietnamese).

Vu, T.S. (2005) 'Improving teaching and learning for health in multigrade schools in Vietnam'. Unpublished PhD thesis. Institute of Education, University of London.

CHAPTER TEN

EFA FOR PASTORALISTS IN NORTH SUDAN

A mobile multigrade model of schooling

SHEILA AIKMAN AND HANAN EL HAJ

INTRODUCTION

This chapter examines the challenges of providing access to good quality basic education for nomadic and semi-nomadic pastoralist children in the western region of North Sudan and the contribution of multigrade mobile schools to this end. From an examination of a model in the state of Northern Darfur in the northwest of Sudan, the chapter investigates whether the government's mobile multigrade school can be both responsive and sustainable to the changing contexts in which pastoralists live.

Estimates of numbers of nomadic and pastoralist children out of school worldwide are difficult to make because of an invisibility of pastoralist groups within national aggregated education statistics. This is compounded by an invisibility of pastoralists in educational policy making in all but a few national exceptions, such as Nigeria, Mongolia and more recently Kenya. Recent estimates put the numbers of nomadic and pastoralist children out of school at between 15 and 25 million (OxfamGB *et al.*, 2003).

Nomadic and semi-nomadic pastoralists today are considered to be marginalised and 'hard to reach' in terms of mainstream education provision. They are becoming a focus of donor attention with the growing awareness that Education for All (EFA) by 2015 will not be achieved unless particular efforts are made to ensure expanded access and retention for groups beyond the reach of mainstream provision. In North Sudan pastoralist peoples have some of the lowest enrolment and completion rates in the country. The Darfur region (including the states of North, South and West Darfur) has enrolment rates of approximately 24–25% and girls' enrolment is much lower than boys'.

A.W. Little (ed.), Education for All and Multigrade Teaching: challenges and opportunities, 193–213.
© 2007 *Springer.*

This chapter considers important dimensions to providing quality basic education that responds to the contexts in which the mobile pastoralist peoples of Western Sudan live, i.e. taking into consideration their mobility and the inadequate reach of centralised provision of public services such as education. It concludes that the current model for mobile schooling has much to commend it but that a 'one-size-fits-all' model for mobile pastoralist peoples cannot hope to cater for the diversity of their lifestyles and the changes that they are experiencing in their physical and social environments. However, as part of a multi-mode approach to providing a relevant and qualitative basic education for mobile and semi-mobile peoples the mobile multigrade school has much to offer. Such a multi-mode approach, however, is contingent on adequate and sustainable means of funding and resourcing education.

The first section of the chapter examines key dimensions of Sudanese politics and education policy making which have shaped the development of the Darfur mobile multigrade school. This is government-recognised schooling managed and run by Pastoralist Development Associations and local communities with support from OxfamGB. The second section describes the model and then briefly considers a range of other models of mobile schooling around the globe which have been established as a policy response to increasing access and retention to basic education for mobile peoples. The final section considers opportunities and constraints in the Darfur context (as it was in early 2003) for providing quality basic education through mobile multigrade schooling that is not only responsive to pastoralists' mobility but sustainable and flexible in the face of changing pressures on pastoralists' ways of life.

The field work for this chapter was carried out in February 2003, in collaboration with the OxfamGB education team in North Darfur. It draws primarily on unpublished reports and policy documents as well as semi-structured interviews with government officials at national, state and local levels, NGO staff, teachers and parents, as well as visits to mobile schools in North Darfur (one of which was temporarily camped in South Darfur), static schools and full primary schools in the Kutum Locality. The chapter does not attempt to be comprehensive or produce conclusions and recommendations that are generalisable. It attempts to set reflection on a small sample of mobile schools in a wider conceptual framework by drawing on a growing published literature and utilising unpublished reports and papers. Since the fieldwork was carried out serious conflict has closed the schools and we are acutely aware that the lives of the communities and children we worked with have since been uprooted and in some cases devastated.

SUDAN: THE POLITICAL AND EDUCATIONAL CONTEXT

Since Independence in 1956 Sudan has had only eleven years of peace. The Sudan Peoples' Liberation Movement/Army (SPLM/A) has controlled areas in the south of Sudan from where they have been fighting against the army of President Bashir's National Islamic Front, based in Khartoum. The conflict has often been described in religious terms, the Christian South fighting the Islamic North, but the conflict is more complex than this. Historically, the South's resources of oil, minerals, agricultural produce, cattle and timber have been exploited by the North, whilst the government in Khartoum stands accused of failing to develop the infrastructure, health and education systems in the southern regions.

The North–South conflict, which has lasted 19 years, has seriously damaged educational development in areas controlled by both the Government of Sudan and the SPLM/A. After stop–start negotiations a Peace Agreement was finally signed at the beginning of 2004. The civil war has resulted in 4 million people being displaced and as a consequence of droughts in the 1980s and 1990s, a decline in rural economies. The western states of Darfur have suffered severely from recurrent drought, food insecurity, tensions between pastoralists and agriculturalists and local inter-tribal conflict aggravated by a proliferation of small arms (SCF *et al.*, 1998; El Haj, 2002).

Pastoralists

Sudan is home to one of the largest pastoralist populations in the African Sahel – some 2 million (8.5% of the total population of Sudan). Most of these pastoralists inhabit the sparsely populated areas furthest from the centres of national economic and political power. Their livelihoods are vulnerable to recurrent shocks of drought and livestock epidemics. Increased drop-out from pastoralism as a way of life is exacerbated by recurrent drought and harvest failure, little access to basic services (health, water and education), tribal conflict over natural resources, conflict with agriculturalists over routes and access to pastures and low levels of participation and representation among the pastoralist community (OxfamGB, 2001). Conflict over land and tensions with agriculturalists and other tribal groups is often violent. A localized outbreak of inter-tribal conflict in March 2003 in Western Darfur led to the closure of schools in the Kebkabiya and Kutum areas and the subsequent escalation of violence has provoked widespread human rights abuses and large-scale flight of refugees over the border into neighbouring Chad. At the time of writing over a million people have been forced to flee their homes in Darfur and numbers of refugees crossing the border to Chad continue to rise from 100,000 in early June 2004. Just as the 20-year long civil war in Sudan nears a conclusion, a new refugee crisis has emerged which is today described as the world's worst humanitarian crisis (OxfamGB, 2004).

The dominant policy advocated by the Sudanese government during the 1960s and 1970s was the resettlement of nomadic pastoralists based on the assumption that pastoralism is incompatible with 'modern life' and that basic services, such as education – deemed necessary for incorporation into modern life – were difficult to provide to nomads (Egemi, 2001). More recently the government has begun to recognise the contribution of livestock production to the national economy, and that pastoralism supports 85% of the livestock sector in the Sudan. A conference in 2000 confirmed renewed economic interest in pastoralists and called for increased provision of basic social services to pastoralists, and increased co-ordination and networking between international non-governmental organisations (NGOs) and United Nations (UN) agencies involved in pastoral development and the promotion of pastoral organisations (Egemi, 2001). This new policy approach towards pastoralism as an economic asset is echoed in other African national policy developments and as Dyer and Kratli (forthcoming) note, in some countries the assumption that pastoralism is an inferior mode of production to agriculture is being questioned and instead being 'recognized as the most efficient and sustainable way of exploiting the natural reources of the drylands'.

Pastoralist communities in Sudan are involved in mobile livestock practices but the type and extent of their seasonal movement differs between groups, ranging from movement around permanent settlements to nomadism with no fixed base (OxfamGB, 2002). Mobile communities are changing their patterns of mobility and for a variety of reasons, including shortage of pasture and access to formal education, some women, children and old people have become semi-settled while the youth and men continue to move with the herds. These settlements or 'damras' are becoming focal points for permanent schools (Eisa, 2001).

Through the 1990s with support from NGOs, particularly OxfamGB and Save the Children-UK, pastoralists have begun to set up their own organisations to push for access to government institutions and to create means for lobbying for their rights with government agencies. The Pastoralist Development Association of Kutum is one such organisation and the Chairperson plays a very active role in lobbying for improved access and facilities in basic education for semi-settled and mobile communities in the region. Over 80% of the pastoralist community in Kutum are nomadic households who follow the availability of pasture and drinking water for their livestock (Abdulla Ibrahim, 2003).

Education

The Government of Sudan has made a commitment to raise the Gross Enrolment Ratio (GER) of children by 10% in order to reach EFA. However, according to UNESCO's 'Proposed Action Plan' of 2002, if present enrolment and retention trends continue the ratio of children in school will not increase but decrease by 8.1% from its 1999/2000 level by 2006/7. The GER for North Sudan also obscures low enrolment rates in rural areas and in pastoralist areas in particular. Reliable data is hard to get in Sudan but estimates indicate that around half of all students who enroll do not complete even four years of schooling.

Education reforms over the last 10 years have had serious implications for the provision of quality basic education. Because of the conflict between the north and south there has been no multilateral or bilateral support to education. Nevertheless in 1993 North Sudan underwent a self-imposed structural adjustment process and administrative and financial decentral- isation. For education this meant the devolution of financial responsibility from the centralised ministries in Khartoum to states and localities (mahalyas), which are now responsible for raising revenues for education and teachers' salaries. In many parts of the country, but especially in marginalised areas such as North Darfur with a dispersed and semi-nomadic population, the state has found it extremely difficult to raise revenue for education leading to severe shortages of teachers because of recruitment freezes and a situation of persistent late or non-payment of teachers.

Basic education in North Sudan comprises eight years divided into three cycles (Grades 1–3, 4–6 and 7–8). Secondary education (called Upper Secondary) is one cycle of three years. All children are taught in Arabic regardless of their mother tongue and the content is highly Islamised, with learning based on the Qu'ran (SCF-UK, 2003). Subjects taught in the first four grades of basic education include maths, Arabic, religion, geography, science and history and thereafter the curriculum becomes increasingly diversified including subjects such as English and integrated sciences. The curriculum is content-based with poorly articulated learning objectives for individual subjects. Teaching and learning is characterised by a whole-class and teacher-led approach. Child-centred or active learning has not been adopted, though UNICEF has carried out some training in this approach.

MOBILE MULTIGRADE SCHOOLING IN DARFUR

In an attempt to address the very low rates of participation of pastoralist children in formal education, the Ministry of Education developed a strategy in 1994 for nomadic education. Within the context of a new National Education Strategy (1992–2002) priorities for pastoralist education were outlined as the need to expand access, link education to socio-economic and cultural practices and to eradicate illiteracy by 2000. This resulted in 1999 in the establishment of 265 mobile nomadic schools which adhered to specific criteria (see Box 10.1) in western Sudan (Darfur and Kurdofan regions) which provided places for 11,625 pupils, of which 68.6% were boys (Egemi, 2001).

Box 10.1 The nomadic school model

• Offers the four years of basic education.
• The Government provides a salary for one teacher for each school on a 4-year contract.
• The teacher lives and moves with the community.
• Teachers:
o receive a 3-month training in delivering the formal curriculum, in primary health care, first aid and animal health;
o are recruited locally and must have completed their secondary education;
o receive incentives from the community to work in mobile schools as the government salary is not adequate.

Since their establishment these schools have faced many problems, including high levels of drop-out, poverty of learning materials and physical environment, wide gender disparity in enrolment and shortage of trained teachers. Many of the original 265 mobile schools have ceased to exist because of a lack of funding and support. In 2003 in North Darfur there were only 15 functioning mobile schools (of which OxfamGB supports 11) and of the estimated 24,000 school-age children in North Darfur only 10% of pastoralist children have access to schooling (personal communication Director of Education, Kutum Locality, 20 February 2003).

In this wider context the mobile multigrade school, then, provides only for basic education. It terminates in the middle of the second cycle of basic education at a point where the curriculum diversifies. Data from individual mobile schools indicate that there is a large dropout in the early grades. For the academic year 2002–3 117 children from 15 existing schools were expected to complete Grade 4 but, with a severe shortage of upper primary schools and little or no boarding facilities, few children from mobile schools are expected to continue with schooling beyond Grade 4. In 'complete' primary schools girls are particularly vulnerable to drop-out in Grade 4 (DFID, 2002); mobile multigrade schools make this vulnerability a sure thing.

The low completion rates of children attending the mobile schools reflect a lack of a coherent policy framework for pastoralist education as well as an inflexible model of schooling. Very low government per capita spending means that parents are expected to meet all costs of learning materials as well as supplementing teachers' salaries. The recent establishment of a separate administrative unit within the Federal State Ministries of Education for pastoral education indicates a certain level of government awareness of pastoralist education needs and tolerance towards them, but without funding from UNICEF and NGOs such as OxfamGB the Unit would not be able to function. The decline in the numbers of mobile schools since 1999 is a result of under-funding and reflects a broader neglect for pastoralist regions such as Darfur in general. Nevertheless, the situation belies a growing demand for schooling from parents and students, as witnessed by the recent formation of some entirely community supported mobile schools (personal communication Director of Education, Kutum Locality, 20 February 2003).

WHY MOBILE SCHOOLS?

Different forms of mobile school have been developed in Sahel countries and other parts of the world as a means of providing basic education for children living in mobile households in areas of low population density for whom static schools are inaccessible (Lugano and Abdi, 2003). Mobile schools are one of a range of responses taken to try to improve access and retention for mobile pastoralists in basic education. The mobility and semi-mobility of groups of pastoralists provides specific challenges to formal education, which is primarily physically organised around permanent buildings and settled communities. As Carr-Hill and Peart (2002) note, because of pastoralists' mobility as well as low density of population, decisions about where to locate schools is a difficult issue, whereas mobile schools follow the rhythm of pastoralist nomadic life.

Over several decades there have been a range of innovative approaches developed to respond to particular circumstances pertinent to different contexts. Boarding schools have been utilised in many places but with mixed results in terms of increasing access and retention for children of primary school age. In Wajir, Northern Kenya, for example, boarding schools for pastoralist girls have closed because of underuse (Lugano and Abdi, 2003). Parents may be very uneasy about leaving their children, and daughters in particular, in boarding schools where personal safety and quality of food and facilities are questionable. This concern has led to Darfur parents calling for girls-only boarding schools from Grade 4 and upwards (DFID, 2002). Other approaches to providing basic education have included radio and television education, for example in Nigeria (see Iro, 2002), and flexible literacy centres in Kenya (Lugano and Abdi, 2003).

Circumstances common to many nomadic groups include low population density, remoteness from centres of habitation, changing patterns of mobility, low levels of education in the pastoralist population, high labour demands on children in relation to herding and fetching water, and socio-cultural practices which differ from neighbouring, often agricultural, groups. Details of models of mobile schools are to be found in Kratli (2001), Carr-Hill and Peart (2002) and Dyer (forthcoming). We refer to a few of the best documented examples here.

In 1995 in North Eastern Province of Kenya, the Nomadic Primary Health Care, an NGO, set up a mobile schools project to overcome the exclusion of pastoralists to formal education and to increase formal school enrolment and reduce drop-out rates. A special curriculum was developed which emphasised developing the capacity of mobile teachers. These 'dugsi' schools were modelled on existing Quranic schools, which emphasised individual instruction and individual assignments (Lugano and Abdi, 2003). One teacher moved with a small family group in the way a Quranic teacher would and taught children and adults according to a timetable that fitted around household labour arrangements and long-distance mobility (Leggett 2001).

In northern Nigeria the government has for many years supported a community education programme which has included a component for nomadic peoples designed to increase access. It has prioritised training teachers who are willing to work and travel with split-movement and semi-sedentary groups. Though beset by problems due to the reluctance of non-nomadic teachers to travel and live a nomadic lifestyle, this programme has persisted (Tahis, 1997 and Ardo, 1991, both cited in Ezeomah and Pennells, 2000). Some other issues which have undermined the model include problems with the design of collapsible classrooms, inadequate supply and maintenance of tents, and limited provision of textbooks. In 1990 the national primary curriculum was adapted for nomadic schools to make it more culturally relevant but still retaining enough commonalities with the national system to comply with the national policy of integration and equity (Ezeomah, 1993 cited in Ezeomah and Pennells, 2000). But concerns have persisted over the use of traditional methods of teaching, and children's lack of knowledge or exposure to English, the language of the teaching modules and materials (Carr-Hill and Peart, 2002: 25).

In parts of Iran a programme to provide education for pastoral and nomadic people has been supported for several decades. By the 1970s hundreds of tribal schools had been built to improve access to schooling for pastoralist peoples and tent schools were provided for small groups of mobile households. At its peak the programme reached about 10% of tribal school-age children, 20% of whom were catered for in tent schools. The national standard curriculum was adopted but the methodology was distinct and the school day was two hours longer than the mainstream school day – 8.5 hours (see Carr-Hill and Peart, 2002). Shahbazi (forthcoming), describes the tent schools and training for the Turkish-speaking Quashqa'i people in south and southwest Iran: local teachers were given 12 months training then began their career with 'a tent, some chalk, a Persian dictionary and a box that contained materials for basic scientific experiments'.

Many of these innovative approaches have been short-lived. Ezeomah (1997), writing about single-teacher mobile schools in Nigeria, states that they largely failed for a combination of reasons, including lack of coherent government policy, ineffective administration, and non-nomadic teachers utilising an inappropriate curriculum and language of instruction. Challenges faced by the dugsi mobile schools in North Eastern Province of Kenya include lack of suitable teaching and learning materials and lack of incentives for teachers. Here, external factors have also played an important role; drought and unpredictable environmental conditions have driven the pastoralists far from their traditional grazing lands and have increased children's labour in the household and with the animals (Lugano and Abdi, 2003).

These and other experiments indicate that, 'with the exception of Iran, mobile schools have performed far below expectations' (Kratli, 2001: 3). In attempting to understand this apparent low performance the next section examines the Darfur mobile school as a multigrade school, an important but generally overlooked type of school.

MULTIGRADE TEACHING AND LEARNING IN DARFUR MOBILE SCHOOLS

The Darfur mobile school is a multigrade school, set up to provide schooling for small numbers of children travelling with their families in small groups. Low population density, high mobility and limited demand for schooling means that, with additional support from OxfamGB, a multigrade model can be highly appropriate, as the El Shiekh school illustrates (see Box 10.2).

The model is multigrade because one teacher has responsibility for more than one grade of children – in the Darfur case, for four grades of students. Multigrade teaching and learning is not specific to mobile schools but is found in many parts of the world, in particular in sparsely populated rural areas (see Little, 2001). However, there is very little research and very little policy which makes explicit reference to the resources and training necessary to achieve good quality multigrade teaching and learning. On the contrary, multigrade schools tend to be plagued by the belief that they are inferior to 'complete schools', that is schools where each grade has its own dedicated teacher (e.g. OxfamGB 2003, where interviewees concurred that multigrade was inferior).

The inferior status of multigrade stems primarily from its association with the poorest and least well resourced education settings, for example indigenous schools in the Amazon Basin and rural schools in Sindh, Pakistan. As Little notes:

teachers' perceptions of the multigrade classroom reflect academic and professional hierarchies that legitimize some types of educational practice and knowledge as more valuable than others ... multigrade teaching barely warrants a mention in international and national education research agenda, in teacher education curricula and materials ... and in education information networks.

(Little, 2001: 492)

Across the globe teacher training is oriented towards teaching in complete primary schools and teachers who find themselves in multigrade schools are given no training for coping with children spanning a wide range of abilities and ages, nor are they trained to adapt curricula designed for the one-teacher-per-grade ideal (Aikman and Pridmore, 2001; Ames, 2004).

Multigrade classrooms and schools are found worldwide and are not restricted to low income countries. There are multigrade schools and classrooms in high income countries with low population areas such as in parts of Scotland, Canada and Australia but there are also multigrade classrooms in cities, for example Inner London (see Berry and Little, Chapter 4, this volume) and in remote rural areas (see Aikman and Pridmore, 2001). The Darfur multigrade school, however, bears many of the hallmarks of 'second best' and marginalised schooling: poorly constructed classrooms with inadequate provision of teaching materials and inappropriate curricula, no training for multigrade teachers and an absence of ongoing professional support.

TEACHING IN A DARFUR MOBILE MULTIGRADE SCHOOL

The teachers and their training

When establishing mobile schools, and moreover when establishing multigrade (though not necessarily mobile) schools for people living in remote areas, the question of teacher recruitment is complex but key. The Darfur model has chosen to work as far as possible with teachers who are recruited from the locality, rather than insist on working with fully trained teachers who have to be enticed into the schools and find it hard to adjust to the mobile way of life. Low levels of education among the pastoralists mean that it is difficult to find 'local'

Box 10.2 El Shiekh Mobile Multigrade School

From November to May/June, the community of Ahmed Abdulla Jadulla pitch thei low mound-shaped tents in a shallow dry river bed within reach of water and pasture for their sheep and camel herds in the south of North Darfur state. The El Shiekh mobile school takes place under the trees where the children sit cross-legged on fibre mats and the blackboard is perched on an easel pushed into the sand. The children each have text books for their grade and the teacher has chalk and a collapsible chair. They move to another spot in the *wadi* as the afternoon sun penetrates the scrubby trees. In May/June the teacher packs the scant school possessions on a camel and together with the community follows the flocks of sheep and camel herds into South Darfur state, where they remain through the summer period. Wherever the community comes to rest the teacher initiates lessons under the trees.

In 2003 El Shiekh had a total enrolment of 31 children: 14 girls and 17 boys divided into two classes. The children enroll every two years and so in 2003 there were no Grade 1 children but one class of Grade 2/3 and one of Grade 4, both taught by the one teacher.

The El Sheikh teacher is from the Ahmed Abdulla Yadulla community and son of the chief, who himself went to school in pre-independence Sudan. To teach in this school he received three months of pre-service training over and above his secondary education. He signed a contract with the government for a four-year period during which time he is responsible for the school as well as primary health care for the people and animals in the community. He can choose whether to run adult literacy classes too.

He receives a meager and intermittent salary from the government but the school is supported by the community itself and by OxfamGB. By way of an incentive to work as the teacher and remain for the duration of his four-year contract, the teache received 40 sheep from OxfamGB when he began teaching and subsequently receives 10 sheep per year from the community. Without this incentive it is unlikely he would continue to teach, but with it he is likely to become a relatively wealthy herder by the end of his contract.

Via OxfamGB support the students receive the government text books for each grade and the teacher receives some basic teaching materials as well as a package of medicines and equipment to allow him to care for the basic health needs of both the community and their animals.

teachers and the few pastoralists who have completed secondary schooling are disinclined to stay in mobile communities, preferring to look for paid employ-ment in the urban areas, where they have already spent many years in order to complete their schooling. In the early years of the Darfur programme there were no female teachers (Eisa, 2001) though in 2003, of the 11 NGO-supported schools, two had female teachers, who receive the same incentives as the men. The reasons for the closure of many of the schools established in 1999 lie in a mixture of factors, including lack of local teachers and lack of government resources for the schools.

As with other mobile schools, the El Shiekh teacher had completed primary and secondary schooling and had received three months of training prior to signing his four-year contract with the Ministry of Education. The training emphasised how to teach the national curriculum for Grades 1–4 as well as modules in basic health and primary health care, veterinary care and use of basic medicines. The other mobile schools like El Shiekh functioning with NGO support receive quarterly monitoring visits but these do not offer educational or pedagogical support to teachers, who have to develop their own ad hoc ways of coping with the diversity of age and ability of the learners. These include dividing the grades between two sessions, with two grades in the morning and two in the afternoon, sometimes followed by adult literacy classes in the evenings. The teachers use a very teacher-centred, rote approach to teaching and learning which is in keeping with their own experiences of schooling and with the dominant pedagogical approach in Sudan at present (Aikman and El Haj, 2003).

El Shiekh school, therefore, illustrates some of the responsive and culturally sensitive dimensions to the mobile multigrade model in Darfur. Teachers, though not formally highly educated, are from the same cultural background as their pupils and are thus more likely to be sensitive to the values and ways of being and doing than 'outside' teachers with higher formal qualifications. The teacher, as probably the most highly trained or educated member of the community, is provided with some resources to attend to the basic health needs of both people and animals. However, this can put immense pressure on one individual.

Incentives

One of the issues raised in the wider literature on mobile schools (and schools in remote rural areas) is that of attracting and keeping teachers (see above). Not only is the mobile lifestyle unattractive to many but the dire lack of materials and resources allied with the low status of rural schools and the challenge of teaching multigrade classes means that incentives are crucial to the functioning of the schools.

As the Sudanese government's contribution to the running of the school is the teacher's salary and this is small and erratic, OxfamGB and the community itself provide incentives for the teacher to remain committed to the work. While OxfamGB provides an initial 40 sheep when the teacher signs his/her contract, the community provides ten sheep each year for four years. With the birth of lambs each year the teacher accumulates a sizable flock, which represents significant wealth within the pastoralist society. It also means that the teacher is integrated into the society of herders as his/her sheep are tended as part of the community flock. This particular incentive system is an effective response to the challenging realities of providing formal schooling for nomadic pastoralists.

The curriculum

Teachers have the autonomy to set up a flexible timetable which caters for their children's household labour commitments and a flexible calendar which fits the rhythm of seasonal movements. The mobile multigrade schools allow children to be taught in their own cultural and social environment but the curriculum does not reflect the cultural diversity of Darfur nor the multilingual nature of Sudanese society with its vast array of lifestyles and traditions (SCF-UK, 2003).

There is considerable discussion of the goals and purposes of nomadic education and their policies in terms of the ideological underpinnings and whether these are based in policies of assimilation and integration or self-development and cultural affirmation (e.g. Carr-Hill, forthcoming; Dyer, forthcoming). In the Nigerian context Ezeomah (2002) argues that the policy on nomadic education 'does not encourage assimilation but allows nomads to retain "the good aspects" of their culture and also contribute to Nigerian culture'. The tent schools introduced in Iran were part of a Tribal Education Programme presented as a move away from previous attempts to sedentarise nomadic tribes through the use of the standard national curriculum with a new methodology (cited in Kratli, 2001).

The Darfur mobile schools follow the national curriculum, which is imparted through national textbooks. In North Sudan the curriculum is not open for debate and the government maintains a strong control over what is taught, how this is taught and the religious orientation, though the signing of the Peace Agreements between the predominantly Muslim north and the Christian/non-Muslim south brings the issue of curriculum and national identity to the fore. The research carried out for this chapter showed that curriculum content and pedagogy was not a concern for parents, communities and Locality education officials, who instead focused their attention and energies on trying to ensure resources to keep the few functioning schools open (personal communication, Abdulla Sai Amour, Pastoralist Development Association of Kutum, 19 February 2003).

The rigid national curriculum does not, therefore, recognise the environment or knowledge of pastoralist children, and although teachers are local this is no guarantee that they will be able to or consider it appropriate to value this knowledge in the school. Without training and support teachers have no encouragement to teach in new ways more suited to their multigrade situation, for example by peer learning and small-group work. Instead teachers' innovativeness is limited to the timing of classes and combining grades, but this is ad hoc and they have received no training to challenge and adapt the rigid one-grade, one-syllabus and textbook curriculum structure.

In terms of responsiveness of the model the sections above have highlighted some strengths and weaknesses in its design and functioning. Being mobile the school is accessible to more children and especially girls, but there is high dropout, particularly among girls and even for those children who complete four years there are few opportunities to continue with primary schooling (Aikman and El Haj, 2003).

QUESTIONS OF SUSTAINABILITY

Tomorro School follows the model of one teacher and four grades of children. The teacher receives sheep as incentives and is very proud of his growing herd. However, in practice, the school is a stark contrast to El Shiekh School (see Box 10.2).

Tomorro contrasts with El Shiekh in terms of the sustainability of each as a multigrade school. One teacher with 188 students in any context is highly challenging (see Croft, 2002) but with 188 students at different levels of education, different ages and different abilities the teacher's task easily becomes one of survival. The very size of the school enrolment questions the added value which training in multigrade techniques can have. The teacher makes no attempt to combine grades but the physical layout of the school in discrete buildings for each grade effectively means that one teacher works with four different monograde groups. And with three of the grades considerably bigger than the total school enrolment in El Shiekh, Tomorro school is straining the multigrade model to breaking point.

Box 10.3 Tomorro Mobile Multigrade School

In 2000 the chief of the community successfully lobbied the government to create a mobile multigrade school and parents agreed to contribute to the salary for the teacher, a man from a sub-group of the same tribe as the villagers. Together the chief and teacher encouraged parents to send their children – boys and girls – to school, though boys outnumber girls in Grades 3 and 4 by 4:1.

There are no trees for shade in the *wadi* where the community was camped in February 2003 when we visited, but the community had constructed four thornbush huts in different parts of an open dry dusty field, one for each grade.

The school provides the teacher with a huge challenge: there are 188 students, of whom 36 are girls, ranging in age from 6 years to approximately 16 years old, divided into four grades. All the classrooms were roughly the same size and so Grade 1 with some 90 children were squeezed together in rows on the sand occupying most of the ground space. Grade 2 had 45 children, Grade 3 had 28 and Grade 4 had 23 (of whom only four were girls). The teacher teaches Grades 1 and 2 in the morning for two hours and moves back and forth across the hot scrub between the classrooms setting work and leading recitation. In the afternoon he does the same with Grades 3 and 4, each in their respective classrooms.

The teacher has a small hut where he lives and stores medicines for the community and their animals and runs adult literacy classes in the evenings. He is hoping that his new wife, also a teacher and from this community, will be able to help him with the enormous task he has, but it is not clear where her salary will come from as the government is committed to only one teacher per mobile school (Aikman and El Haj, 2003).

As a one-teacher multigrade model, the mobile schools are restricted to teaching only the first four years of basic education. The vast majority of students finish their education midway through the second cycle of three of primary education. The rationale for this is unclear but may be linked to the greater diversification of subjects from Grade 5 where the wide range of compulsory subjects would put excessive demands on one teacher with only a brief period of training. Statistics from Kutum Locality indicate that as complete primary schools are only available in permanent settlements few nomadic children continue their education. This raises the question of what learning outcomes are achieved in these four years and whether the quality of education experienced through Grades 1 to 4 is enough to promote independent learning in students. However, discussions by parents and pastoralist organisations about how to provide a meaningful basic education beyond Grade 4 for nomadic pastoralist children do not touch on expanding the mobile multigrade school, for example with more teachers, but revolve around how to fund boarding facilities at the few complete primary schools which exist in towns and *damras*. The boarding school model is familiar to elders from colonial times; no one has experienced mobile schools in any other form than exists at present and have no other models to help them identify alternatives or adaptations.

Financial sustainability of the mobile multigrade school even as it exists at present, not to mention new and more responsive models, is critical. With the onus for raising taxes and funding schooling on the education authorities at the Locality, the stark reality is a system in complete decay, with teachers rarely receiving their meagre salaries. This in turn puts pressure on parents to provide materials and incentives for teachers and to manage the schools. In Sudan decentralisation of the education system and funding has meant that, however willing the local education department might be to support and develop appropriate methods of achieving EFA and meeting pastoralist peoples' own demands for education, it is unable to do this because of a complete lack of resources.

The lack of a budget commitment to fund the mobile multigrade schools is related to a lack of policy commitment to pastoralist education. That the model is recognised by government does indicate some level of awareness of pastoralist peoples' lack of access to basic services. However, local government departments are disempowered through lack of resources and strong central control over curriculum and pedagogy. The lack of a policy framework to guide the development of pastoralist education is a serious drawback to providing relevant quality education and to the government meeting its commitment to achieving EFA.

There are also factors and changes in the external Sudan context which affect demand and supply of education as well as sustainability of models such as the mobile multigrade schools. There is a trend towards more movement along seasonal routes which pass through semi-settled *damras*. These *damras* are becoming focal points for complete primary schools and young women with babies as well as the elderly are increasingly living there all year round while the young men move with the herds. This raises the possibility of more children attending static schools, which offer more than four years of schooling. The impact of this on identity and way of life are huge and the effects of a national integrated curriculum on economic and socio-cultural change has not been assessed. Increasing conflict over recent years between pastoralists and agri-culturalists has also meant changes in the composition and size of mobile groups, which in turn has implications for the size and structure of multigrade schools.

CONCLUSION

This chapter has considered a model of schooling being implemented in a one-size-fits-all form in Darfur. The Tomorro School has illustrated the dangers of how the multigrade model of the one-teacher school can be misused if rigidly applied where conditions are unsuitable. If mobile schooling is to continue to be the way to provide access to basic education for pastoralist children and not become another model of mobile schooling which 'performs far below expectations' (Kratli, 2001: 30) then policy makers at all levels of government and in partner NGOs need to establish optimum conditions for its functioning to ensure good quality multigrade teaching and learning. Clearly the model as it stands has the potential to provide quality basic education for children in a small school such as El Shiekh. However, rising demand and continued lack of materials will continue to frustrate the work of the very dedicated teachers we met. The lack of educational opportunity beyond Grade 4 and the size of classes in Tomorro school are factors which severely undermine the efforts of teachers and students alike.

There is need for multi-modality provision which is flexible and adaptive and can cater for different sizes of school population (not a rigid one-teacher model), and changing and fluid patterns of mobility and settlement (not a choice between mobile or boarding). A rethink is needed about how to provide education for nomadic children which incorporates learning from good practice around the globe in terms of both the question of mobility (mobile schools/static schools) and the teaching and learning approaches within the school (multigrade/monograde).

A multi-modality approach to EFA for Sudanese mobile pastoralists might seem unrealistic in the context of the current education system in Sudan but if children are to achieve their right to education and Sudan is to fulfil its commitments made at Dakar then a dramatic increase in resources and a radical solution are needed. With Peace Agreements signed donors are poised to support education reform and innovation – to invest in peace. Donors are being called upon to support civil society initiatives in capacity building to reduce poverty and increase access to basic rights such as health, education and a safe environment so that the people of Sudan can begin the process of reclaiming their ways of life and livelihoods. The terrible irony remains, however, that the pastoralist peoples of Darfur are caught up in a humanitarian crisis on the eve of Peace for Sudan.

NOTE

The motivation for writing this paper came from a visit by the authors to several mobile schools supported by Oxfam in Feburary 2003 to document the model and examine its successes and challenges. Our thanks go to colleagues Madga Abdulla Ibrahim and Farrah El Hag Bello in Darfur in the El Fashir office of OxfamGB and to Abdulla Safi Alnour, chairperson of the Pastoralist Development Association, Kutum.

REFERENCES

Abdulla Ibrahim, M. (2003) 'Briefing note on Pastoralist Education, N. Darfur'. Manuscript. OxfamGB.

Aikman, S. and El Haj, H. (2003) 'Report on a visit to North Sudan Education Programme with a focus on pastoralist education, Darfur'. Unpublished report. OxfamGB.

Aikman, S. and Pridmore, P. (2001) 'Multigrade schooling in "remote" areas of Vietnam. *International Journal of Educational Development*, 21, 6, 521–536.

Ames Ramello, P.P. (2004) 'Multigrade schools in context: literacy in the community, the home and the school in the Peruvian Amazon'. Unpublished PhD thesis. Institute of Education, University of London.

Croft, A. (2002) 'Pedagogy in school context: an intercultural study of the quality of learning, teaching and teacher education in lower primary classes in Southern Malawi'. PhD thesis. University of Sussex, Brighton.

Carr-Hill, R. (2002 forthcoming) 'Nomadic groups and Education for All' in C. Dyer (ed.) *The Education of Nomadic Peoples: Current issues, future prospects.* Oxford: Berghahan.

Carr-Hill, R. and Peart, E. (2002) 'Study on education for Nomads and Pastoralists in Eastern Africa: review of the literature'. IIEP, UNESCO/IICBA, UNICEF/ESARO.

DFID (2002). *Seminar Report: Sudan Education – Building for Peace.* Draft report. 6 August.

Dyer, C. (ed.) (forthcoming) *The Education of Nomadic Peoples: Current issues, future prospects.* Oxford: Berghahn.

Dyer, C. and Kratli, S. (forthcoming) 'Education and development for nomads: the issues and the evidence. In C. Dyer (ed.) *The Education of Nomadic Peoples: Current issues, future prospects.* Oxford: Berghahn.

Egemi, O.A. (2001) 'Pastoralism in development policies and possible options in Sudan'. Unpublished OxfamGB report. Khartoum.

Eisa, S.I. (2001) 'Pastoral education experience in Sudan'. Paper presented at the Second Conference on Pastoralist Education, Khartoum, 29–30 December.

El Haj, H. (2002) 'Education in Sudan'. Presentation for the DFID Seminar on Education in Conflict situations. Sudan, 29 July.

El Hag Bello, F.O. (2002) 'Sustainability of community-managed projects in developing countries – the case of Kebkabiya Smallholders' Charitable Society (KSCS) in Western Sudan'. MA dissertation, University of Bradford.

Ezeomah, C. (2002) 'Social, economic and political activities of nomads and educational policy implementation for nomads'. Research report presented at the International Conference on Nomads. Nigeria, 16–19 January.

Ezeomah, C. and Pennells, J. (2000) 'Basic education for refugees and nomads. In C. Yates and J. Bradley (eds) *Basic Education at a Distance.* London: Routledge.

Iro, I. (2002) *Nomadic Education and Education for Nomadic Fulani.* Online. http://www.gamji.com/fulani7.htm (Accessed 6 December 2004).

Kratli, S. (2001) *Education Provision to Nomadic Pastoralists: A literature review.* Sussex, Institute of Development Studies Working Paper 126.

Leggett, I. (2001) 'Continuity and change in primary education in the pastoral districts of Kenya: a study of Wajir'. MA dissertation, University of London, Institute of Education.

Little, A. (2001) 'Multigrade teaching: towards an international research and policy agenda'. *International Journal of Educational Development,* 21, 6, 481–498.

Lugano, E. and Abdi, A.H. (2003) 'Learning and pastoralism: challenges of accessing education for nomadic pastoralists in Kenya: policy and practice'. Paper presented at Oxford Conference: The State of Education: Quantity, quality and outcomes. 9–11 September.

OxfamGB (2001) 'Sudan Programme – National Pastoralist Proposal 2002–2005', ms.
OxfamGB (2002) Sudan Programme 2002/2003, ms.
OxfamGB (2003) Peer Review, Mali Programme, ms.
OxfamGB (2004) http://www.oxfam.org.uk/what_we_do/where_we_work/sudan/emergency/appeal.htm.
OxfamGB *et al.* (2003) 'Achieving EFA through responsive education policy and practice for nomadic and pastoralist children: What can agencies do?' Advocacy Paper developed by participants at the OxfamGB Seminar on Pastoralist Education: Access to Quality and Relevance in Oxford. 8 September.
SCF-UK (2003) 'A situation of basic education in Sudan'. Save the Children-UK, ms.
SCF, Care International and OxfamGB (1998) 'Sudan: who has the will for peace?' Advocacy and lobby document. 22 October, ms.
Shahbazi, M. (forthcoming) 'The Quashqa'i, formal education and indigenous educators'. In Dyer, C. (ed.), *The Education of Nomadic Peoples: Current issues, future prospects.* Oxford: Berghahn.

CHAPTER ELEVEN

EXTENDING BASIC EDUCATION TO OUT-OF-SCHOOL CHILDREN IN NORTHERN GHANA

What can multigrade schooling teach us?

ALBERT KWAME AKYEAMPONG

INTRODUCTION

This chapter examines the impact of a form of multigrade schooling on increasing access to formal basic education for children in poor and remote settlements who are out of school. For such children, many of whom would never have been to school for reasons of poverty and remoteness, getting them enrolled in formal basic education poses a real challenge. By describing features of a programme which operates on multigrade teaching and learning principles and examining evidence about its impact on improving access to primary school and beyond, it is argued that the multigrade model holds a lot of promise for addressing the educational needs of this disadvantaged group.

Northern Ghana has socio-demographic characteristics typical of many poor deprived communities in sub-Saharan Africa. For example, it is an area with low socio-economic activity, high levels of poverty and scattered community settlements, all of which contribute to undermining access to conventional school systems. These characteristics have also, in the past, undermined government commitment to rapid expansion of primary education because of inadequate supply of trained teachers. In this chapter, it is argued that, rather than seeing these as obstacles hindering expansion of primary education, by introducing multigrade schooling it is possible to increase access without undermining quality.

The chapter is broken into four parts. The first part begins with a short historical overview of attempts to provide education for all children in Ghana and how this affected the Northern areas. The second part provides

A.W. Little (ed.), Education for All and Multigrade Teaching: challenges and opportunities, 215–238.
© 2007 *Springer*.

details about the socio-demographic characteristics of Northern Ghana and its impact on access to basic education. The third part describes 'the School for Life' programme. It describes how it uses principles of multigrade teaching and learning to offer children out of school a chance to access the regular basic education system. The fourth part of the chapter discusses School for Life's impact on access and examines costs and sustainability of this model of multigrade schooling. The conclusion pulls together key issues from the discussion to present lessons that might be learnt in using multigrade schooling in a difficult education delivery context.

EFA IN GHANA: THE HISTORICAL PERSPECTIVE

To understand just how important multigrade schooling is to the objective of reaching underserved populations with quality basic education in northern Ghana, it is necessary to understand how the development of primary education has created the set of conditions that has led to such a need. Thus this section examines some of the challenges of providing education for all children of school-going age in Ghana, from a historical perspective. Some of the early policies for increasing access to primary education in Ghana disadvantaged parts of the north. Later attempts to expand primary education more rapidly overtook the capacity to produce and retain teachers and led to the situation where many schools were unable to have their full complement of teachers. This situation still persists today and is much worse in northern Ghana (Akyeampong, 2004).

Making quality the basis for access

Colonial governments were the first to set the agenda for achieving compulsory primary education for all children of school-going age in Ghana (then called the Gold Coast) (McWilliam and Kwamena-Poh, 1975). Notably, it was Governor Gordon Guggisberg in the early 1900s who outlined 16 principles for achieving the goal of a comprehensive and expanded education system for the country. Of relevance to the theme of this chapter is his first principle, which stated that: 'primary education must be thorough and be from the bottom to the top'. The idea of a thorough primary education system meant that even when there were resources available for rapid expansion of primary education, and in Guggisberg's era there was enough to triple provision, nevertheless this was not allowed to happen because trained teacher demand could not be matched with supply to support accelerated expansion (McWilliam and Kwamena Poh, 1975). Quality was imperative and expanding access to primary education was done selectively on the basis of trained teacher availability and assurances that expanded facilities would not be underutilised. Consequently, schools were only built in areas with a sizeable population, and more importantly, if expanding provision could be matched with the supply of trained teachers.

Thus, at this early stage of Ghana's education development thinly populated areas, particularly in the north, with low population densities and scattered settlements were at a disadvantage with respect to planned primary expansion. Interestingly, the situation has not changed very much today. As we shall see later in this chapter, many areas in northern Ghana are still underserved with schools either because they are hard to reach, too distant from other catchments, or teachers would simply not accept postings there because of the few opportunities for social and economic advancement (Akyeampong, 2004).

Accelerated expansion of primary education: 1950s to 1966

The period beginning with the early 1950s and leading to self-government in 1957 witnessed the introduction of an accelerated development plan for education with special emphasis on increasing provision of primary education to all parts of the country. The plan envisaged a fee-free primary education of six years, followed by a four-year middle school education for which fees were to be paid (Addae-Mensah, 2000).

> A large number of new classrooms were built and much temporary accom-modation pressed into use, with the result that over 132,000 children began their primary schooling in January 1952, more than twice as many as in the previous year. By 1957 ... there were over 450,000 children in primary schools, about double the figure in 1951 ... taught by about 15,000 teachers (PTR 30:1). Primary enrolment in the North rose from 2,218 in 1945 to 23,340 in 1957 [but] was still only about 10% of the children of school-going age, compared with 60% of children in Accra (in the south) regularly attending school.
>
> (McWilliam and Kwamena-Poh 1975: 75)

Such enrolment gaps between the north and south was often blamed on the stricter control of the pace of expansion in the interest of 'quality' (McWilliam and Kwamena-Poh, 1975).

Fee-free and *compulsory* primary and middle education was first introduced in the 1960s by the first president of Ghana, Dr Kwame Nkrumah. In 1961, a new Education Act (Act 87) added urgency to the primary education expansion agenda. Section 2 of the Act stipulated that every child of school age was expected to attend a course of instruction in a school recognised for the purpose by the Minister of Education (Education Act 1961: Section 2). According to McWilliam and Kwamena-Poh (1975), the effect of the Act on primary education was greater than had been expected. 'Just before this, 1960–61, there had been 441,117 children in 3,514 public primary schools, but within two years both these figures had doubled, and by ... 1966 the total had surged on to 1,137,494 children attending 8,144 schools' (p. 101).

Notably, the rapid expansion of primary education far outstripped the supply of trained teachers, thus violating Guggisberg's first principle for education development. Following the overthrow of Dr Kwame Nkrumah in 1966, the issue of quality assurance re-entered the politics and policies of primary education development and slowed its growth. Primary enrolments started declining but this was more noticeable in northern Ghana where enrolments declined by about one-third (McWilliam and Kwamena-Poh, 1975).

The 1987 education reforms

By the mid-1970s the education system had started slipping slowly into decline, which prompted several commissions of inquiry to be set up to determine the causes for this and the way forward for recovery. This process led to the introduction of major educational reforms in 1987 as part of a national economic recovery plan. The reforms started with the restructuring of the school system, a process validated and accelerated by the global agenda of 'Education for All' following the Jomtien Conference in 1990. The most persistent criticism of the old education system had been its structure, in which pre-tertiary education lasted for 17 years and was considered inefficient, highly selective and margi-nalising the poor (Addae-Mensah, 2000). The new structure replaced the 6 years of primary, 4 years of middle and 7 years of secondary schooling with 6 for primary, 3 for junior secondary and 3 for senior secondary, thus shortening pre-tertiary education from 17 to 12 years.

In 1996 the government introduced an education sector policy plan known as 'Free Compulsory Universal Basic Education' (FCUBE). FCUBE represented the effort to ensure that all school-age children received free and compulsory quality primary education by 2005. It is now recognised that this goal is not attainable by 2005 (Ministry of Education, 2003). Nevertheless, the new policy was intended to create (a) motivation for a co-ordinated sector programme providing a framework for donor support to education, (b) promote educational decentralisation with greater recognition of the important role of community participation in school management for school improvement, and (c) improve access and participation especially through schemes that encouraged girls' participation at primary level (World Bank, 2004).

Contexts for multigrade schooling

The 1987 education reforms clearly produced successes in terms of improving access and participation at basic education level. Net enrolment ratio in primary education, which stood at 72.1% in 1988, improved to 84.1% by 2003. And from 1980 to 2000 the number of basic schools (primary and junior secondary) had increased from 12,997 to 18,374, representing an increase of about 50% (World Bank, 2004). But the expansion had also created by default or necessity the conditions for multigrade schooling, or made it more pressing.

First, the improvements in primary enrolments outstripped the supply and retention of trained teachers, thus 'forcing' schools to introduce 'multi-class teaching' (Ministry of Education, 2002). There are now a good proportion of primary schools with no trained teacher or just one teacher, as shown in Table 11.1. If we include schools with only two or three teachers, this proportion could even be higher. The reality in Ghana today is that teachers are more likely than ever before to face two or more classes which have pupils of mixed ability and different maturity levels. Coupled with the precarious demand and supply for trained teachers (Akyeampong, 2002), this means the phenomenon of multigrade teaching is now part and parcel of the teaching and learning experience in many public schools, and is not something that can be wished away. And as Table 11.1 suggests, the phenomenon is more common in the three northern regions.

Table 11.1 Public primary schools in the regions with one or no trained teacher

Region	No. of public primary schools	No. of schools with one or no trained teacher	Percentage
Greater Accra	799	10	1.3
Eastern	1,897	57	3.0
Volta	1,428	88	6.2
Central	1,235	38	3.1
Western	1,333	59	4.4
Ashanti	1,848	48	2.6
Brong Ahafo	1,423	74	5.2
Northern	1,432	219	15.3
Upper West	452	32	7.1
Upper East	378	27	7.1
Total	12,225	652	5.3

Source: Ghana Education Service, 2000/2001

Second, analysis of age/grade enrolments in public schools in Ghana indicates that 'in some grades, such as 4th, 5th, and 6th, children of the age appropriate for that grade are far outnumbered by older children ... and this is also true for grades eight and nine (JSS2 and 3)' (Ghana Ministry of Education/EMIS, 2002). This clearly calls for teachers to be equipped with the skills for facilitating learning for children of a highly diversified age group, and consequently with very different learning needs. Thus, already the age/grade enrolment in public schools (primary and junior secondary) makes an urgent case for equipping teachers with multigrade instructional skills.

Third, there is the problem of out-of-school children which is the focus of this chapter. Although the problem is nationwide (about 18% of Ghanaian children are out of school according to the Ghana Statistical Service (2000)), it is more acute in northern Ghana, where the number of children out of school is far greater than in the southern half of the country, both in the primary and junior secondary school age group. Census data indicates that this corresponds to 37.5%, 40.5% and 32.9% for Northern, Upper West and Upper East regions respectively.

At the primary level, there are 25 districts that have 22% to 30% of the children out of school. This is the lowest range. Most of these districts are located in the southern half, but there are few districts in the North that fall into this range. On the other end of the spectrum, there are 23 districts that have between 60% and 70% of the primary-age children out of school. Most of these districts fall in the Northern part of the country.

(Ghana Ministry of Education/EMIS 2002: 7)

Although the Ghana Ministry of Education recognises the provision of basic education for children out of school as a first priority (Ghana Ministry of Education/EMIS, 2002), it has yet to articulate a policy detailing how this might be achieved. In fact, many governments in developing countries have left the task of improving access to quality basic education in poor deprived and remote areas almost entirely to NGOs and other aid organisations (Miller-Grandvaux and Yoder, 2002; Akyeampong, 2004). But before we take a close look at how a multigrade school programme in northern Ghana might serve as a model for reaching underserved populations, it is worth highlighting some of the socio-demographic characteristics of the north to appreciate the importance of multigrade schooling in that context.

CHARACTERISTICS OF THE NORTH AND THE IMPACT ON SCHOOLING

Northern Ghana comprises three regions: Northern, Upper West and Upper East. These comprise about 40% of Ghana's land area. Northern Ghana is inhabited by about 10% of Ghana's population, representing a population density of less than 25 people per square kilometer. The majority (70%) of the workforce in the Northern region is employed in the informal agriculture sector, 10% are unemployed and the remaining 20% are economically inactive. In Upper East, approximately 80% of the workforce is employed in agriculture, and about 17% is economically inactive (Ghana Statistical Service, 2001). About 70% of Ghanaians who live below the poverty line also live in the north (Casely-Hayford, 2002). The literacy rate among adults is less than 5% and less than 40% of children up to 14 years attend school. This leaves about 60% of children out of school, the majority being girls. About 43% of girls between 6 and 11 years are out of school in the Northern region, 45% in Upper East and 27% in the Upper West (Ghana Statistical Service, 2001). Girls are particularly affected because of strong cultural beliefs about their role in society and concern about sexual harassment, especially where they have to walk long distances to school (Casely-Hayford, 2002).

The north, in general, struggles to make the necessary adjustments and sacrifices to meet the requirements of formal schooling (Akyeampong, 2004). There seem to be three factors which pose particular threats for the effective establishment of regular schools and which could be seen as contributing to the high incidence of children out of school.

First, there is low socio-economic activity and poverty. Because of these conditions, children either have to supplement their family's income through the provision of their labour in economic activities (e.g. farming) or have to fend for themselves by engaging in economic activities to support their basic food requirements (Casely-Hayford, 2000). Some parents counteract the in-compatibility of schooling with their economic needs by sending children below school age to school with older siblings who are expected to care for them while their parents work on their farms. Others, who cannot dispense of their children's labour at crucial periods of the farming season, are likely to withdraw their children and allow them back during lean sessions (CARE International/USAID, 2003). The sum effect is the high proportion of over- and under-age children at all the different grade levels in public schools, as well as a high proportion who are out of school. Undoubtedly, for any monograde teacher not trained in how to facilitate learning for children of such diversity in age and social maturity, this must pose a big challenge and lead to a worsening of learning outcomes.

The second is the problem of teacher supply and retention. Ghana suffers from acute teacher shortage at the primary school level and the situation again is particularly bad in the north (Hedges, 2002; Akyeampong, 2002). As noted earlier, most trained teachers are unwilling to accept postings to many parts of the country where they feel opportunities for personal and professional development are lacking. And even if they accept a posting they leave at the first opportunity (Action Aid REV, 2000; Akyeampong, 2002). To address the acute shortages in the north, Action Aid Ghana operates a Rural Education Volunteer (REV) scheme. The REV scheme recruits and trains (for 1–2 weeks) secondary graduates who hail from the north and sends them into schools in poor and deprived areas. REV recruits are secondary-school graduates who are spending at least a year at home to retake subjects they failed at senior secondary exams, hoping to improve their grades in order to gain admission into universities, teacher training colleges or polytechnics. Research suggests that these students do not become very effective classroom teachers. Most employ teacher-centred teaching approaches and, crucially, are unable to use the local language to explain basic concepts for lower primary pupils (CARE International/USAID, 2003).

Thirdly, the nature of community settlements in northern Ghana clearly presents difficulties for establishing regular schools. As Akyeampong (2004) has noted: 'these settlements tend to be small (sometimes comprising about 10 household units) … thus, finding appropriate locations for building schools to service reasonable size populations then becomes a real problem' (p. 44). And, given that distance to school is ranked with costs and child labour as major reasons for many children not attending school (Ghana Statistical Service, 1998), this explains the exceptionally high proportion of out-of-school children in northern Ghana.

The analysis points to the presence of a large number of children who will not be reached by formal education systems by the target date for universal primary/basic education, which in Ghana was originally 2005 but has been moved to 2015. These children live in scattered remote settlements where there are no schools, or the few schools that exist may have few or no teachers in them. Their families are likely to be very poor, compelling many to work from an early age on farms or herding animals. Often the children come from communities whose language may not be used as the medium of instruction, thus making early learning experience difficult and unproductive. It is these conditions which cause many children to drop and stay out of school or not enter in the first place. And, it is such an 'invisible' mixed-age group that the School for Life (SFL) programme targets to offer an alternative form of schooling that is not streamed by age, to enhance enrolment in public basic schools in northern Ghana.

MULTIGRADE SCHOOLING: THE SCHOOL FOR LIFE EXAMPLE[1]

Parts of northern Ghana fit the socio-demographic profile of populations which give rise to multigrade schooling as described by Little (2005,

Chapter 1 in this volume), namely 'areas of low population density where schools are widely scattered and enrolments low'. This section describes features of the School for Life (SFL) programme with particular emphasis on its 'multigrade charac-teristics' and presents evidence of how it is helping to extend quality basic education to out of school children living in poor and deprived communities.

School for Life (SFL): background and characteristics

School for Life evolved as a joint co-operation between northern Ghanaian community-based organisations and Ghanaian and Danish development activists. The Ghanaian development activists are organised under an umbrella organisation called Ghana Danish Communities Association (GDCA) whereas their Danish counterparts are members of a Danish NGO, Ghana Friendship groups in Denmark. Together they run three programmes, one of which is the SFL programme.

The programme's long-term vision is to enable the formal educational system to achieve and sustain increases in functional literacy and in the quality and equitable access to relevant basic education. This is seen as a means to address the problems of poverty, underdevelopment and gender inequality in northern Ghana (School for Life, 1998).

Originally, SFL was to cover about two-thirds of the population of northern Ghana, but because of violent conflicts in 1994 between two tribal groups, Konkombas and Dagombas/Nanumbas, the programme covered fewer districts than had been planned. By 2002 SFL was operating in 30 districts and had developed an instructional methodology based on mother tongue education. The mother tongue is used as both the literacy language in the class and as the language of instruction. In the Northern Region the programme operates in four languages.

SFL's school term runs from October to June(a nine-month cycle), which is the dry season. This avoids interfering with the major farming season when children will be required to help on the farms. Advocacy and animation work with parents stresses that classes will be organised at times to suit communities so that pupils will still be available to help their parents in the farms and in doing household chores (CARE International/USAID, 2003).

Instructional organisation and practice

The classes take place in the afternoons, usually from 2pm to 5pm. Afternoon schooling is an example of adapting education delivery to the cultural practices of a people; in this case children are able to offer the needed assistance to their parents by working on the farms or grazing sheep or cattle before going to school.

Table 11.2 provides a summary of the instructional organisation of SFL programmes. The programme targets the 8–15 years age group, although much younger and older children are known to enrol. After the nine-month programme children are expected to join mainstream schooling. Instruction focuses on three core instructional areas: literacy, numeracy with emphasis on problem solving, and writing, within a maximum class size of 25, which is expected to be composed of roughly the same number of boys and girls. This gender parity has, however, proved difficult to achieve (School for Life, 2001). Depending on community size a school can have one, two or three classes, which run in parallel. Each class has its own teacher. The low pupil–teacher ratio allows for improved teaching and learning and internal efficiency, which results in good levels of achievement.

Textbook to pupil ratio in SFL schools is 1:1. Instruction is sequential, with emphasis on the phonetic approach to language learning. The SFL instructional approach has been described as participatory, interactive and child-centred (in the sense that the teachers regularly use a question and answer teaching technique) (CARE International/USAID, 2003). Instructional activities are intended to provide opportunity for learning in groups, preferably by age group and ability level. Teachers are trained in child-centred pedagogy and the expectation is that they will organise some classroom learning around the different age groups.

The programme is multigrade because each teacher has responsibility for teaching a highly diversified age group, and therefore groups within the class require specific instructional attention. More importantly, the curriculum is not streamed according to a particular age group as one would find in monograde primary schools. Instead, classroom texts attempt to develop broad literacy, numeracy and problem-solving skills across a wide age range.

Children are expected to reach different levels of achievement depending on their ability and effort (Casely-Hayford and Akyeampong, 2002).

Texts in the three subject areas are organised to cover a wide range of knowledge, skills and understandings. Some portions require teachers to organise learning in groups, to discuss simple problem-solving strategies and offer explanations for local environmental problems, solve arithmetic tasks, etc. Content and skills are sequenced across a wide ability range under a single curriculum framework. Thus, the curriculum could even be described as 'monograde for a wide multi-aged group' – that is, if one considers that this is a single curriculum for just nine months.

Table 11.2 Instructional organisation

Characteristics	School for Life
Targeted population	8–15-year-olds
Type of location	Typical rural Peripheral
Programme equivalent in formal education	Designed to enhance enrolment in formal schools
Time to complete the programme cycle	9 months
Average no. of days attended by pupils in a year	274
Number of weekly school days	5 days in a week
Daily learning hours	3 hours
Average class size	25
Number of shifts	One

Subject texts include learning material that usually starts from the basics and extends to more challenging learning outcomes. It assumes that teachers will work their way through the text with *all* their students, but with the understanding that some will make faster progress than others. Thus the curriculum could also be described, as Little (2004) puts it, as a 'multi-year curriculum' because it is designed with consideration for the kind of basic learning requirements across a multi-year group (SFL, 2002). Inevitably, some learners will find some learning material more difficult than others. Therefore, for effective delivery, teachers would have to organise classroom learning in a manner which ensures that all pupils make progress appropriate to their social maturity, effort and abilities. In effect, the SFL curriculum design, like other alternative basic school programmes, is meant to encourage child-centred methods and permit multigrade teaching (Hartwell and Destefano, 2003).

This invites the question of classroom instructional organisation. Although this was not a direct research interest in the study of the SFL programme, some relevant observations were noted. From six classroom observations, we noticed that some teachers tried to pitch their questions according to pupils' ages. But, some pupils, especially very young ones, appeared to be left behind as lessons progressed. Occasionally, group work was used where pupils of a similar age, who usually sat near each other, discussed and shared their knowledge. Although, for effective delivery, much of the teacher–pupil interaction should have been organised according to the various age and ability levels in the classrooms, actual lesson delivery did not follow strictly this logic. This situation reveals the gap that often exists between curriculum aspiration and teachers' capacity to deliver it as intended. What was clearly evident, however, was that teachers did not seem inhibited by the presence of children of such a wide age range in their classes. It is difficult to draw firm conclusions about the multigrade character of SFL teachers' instructional practices just from a few classroom observations. What is remarkable, though, is the improvement in pupil learning outcomes that is achieved after nine months of instruction, which enables successful mainstreaming into different monograde levels in the formal school system. This issue is discussed further below.

SFL teachers: selection, training and support

Each participating community is responsible for nominating a volunteer trainee who must be literate in the local language and a resident of the community. The volunteer teachers (usually called facilitators) then undergo six weeks of intensive residential training, during which they are trained in the skills of using instructional materials to facilitate learning. In addition, they study the various texts used for teaching in SFL schools. Teachers are trained to work with the class as a whole group, but emphasis is placed on child-centred approaches to address individual learning differences and abilities. Interviews with SFL school supervisors and curriculum developers indicated that the teacher training placed a high premium on activity-based grouping of pupils, development of teaching and learning materials, and general primary teaching methods. Trainees are introduced to basic ideas about child development and their implications for organising teaching and learning. The training also introduces teachers to various questioning techniques to promote active participation of all pupils in lessons. Thus, an attempt is made to sensitise teachers to the variable learning needs arising from the wide age composition in the SFL classroom. Much of the teacher training pedagogy is consistent with the philosophy of multigrade teaching and learning because of the programme's attempts to address the learning needs of a highly diversified age group in the SFL classroom. However, one cannot describe the teacher training curriculum framework as multigrade. Instead, providers were incorporating ideas appropriate for multigrade teaching and learning. Trainers are drawn from Ghana Education Service (GES) district staff and SFL's own training staff.

When they begin teaching teachers are visited regularly (by motor bike) by SFL trained supervisors, usually two members per district. These supervisors offer further assistance and on-the-job training. Two field supervisors in the Gusheigu-Karaga district pointed out that this pedagogical support was crucial as they were able to give encouragement and offer practical suggestions to reinforce knowledge and skills that teachers acquire in their training. Such commitment to further professional development contrasts sharply with what pertains in the Ghanaian public school system. There, almost all resources are poured into residential training, which until recently lasted three years (it has recently been reduced to two years residential and one year out in school learning to teach), after which beginning teachers receive very little or no in-service training. Their welfare needs are often neglected by the communities or district education officials (Hedges, 2002; Akyeampong 2002). As Lewin and Stuart (2003) point out, in many sub-Saharan countries teacher training can be heavily front-loaded, leaving very little resources for organising continuous professional development activities for beginning teachers.

In the SFL Programme there is a high level of community involvement in hiring teachers. A five-member local committee ensures that teachers are adequately supported financially or in kind – through supply of foodstuffs or by providing labour on the teacher's farm (CARE International/USAID, 2003). This is intended to allow teachers to concentrate fully on teaching. Since, in effect, it is the local communities who hire teachers from their own community, commitment to their welfare comes naturally and has a reciprocal positive effect.

What makes the SFL model of multigrade schooling approach appealing is the fact that it is able, within nine months, to provide instruction to out-of-school children of a wide age range up to a standard which enables many to access and succeed in public monograde primary schools. In the remaining sections, we take a look at some of the more concrete evidence of its success in achieving this objective.

ISSUES ABOUT IMPACT, COST AND SUSTAINABILITY

First, we start with the impact on access and retention. Within a seven-year period the programme was able to cover about 26% of communities in the districts in which it operated (see Table 11.3), enrolled about 36,044 pupils and

Table 11.3 School for Life: Coverage in the Northern region

District	Total communities covered	Total communities in district	Coverage (%)
Gusheigu-Karaga	151	415	36.4
Nanumba	64	350	18.3
Saboba-Chereponi	76	408	18.6
Savelugu-Nanton	97	350	27.7
Tamale (rural)	89	350	25.4
Tolon-Kumbungu	57	350	16.3
Yendi	128	316	40.5
Zabzugu-Tatale	105	350	30.0
Total	**767**	**2889**	**26.5**

Source: SfL statistical document, 2001

mainstreamed 22,090 into the public school system, representing a transition rate of about 61%. Of those mainstreamed about 41% were girls and 59% boys (SFL, 2001). About 3,105 students dropped out, and about 11,000 SFL graduates were unable to access public primary schools. The main reason given for this was the difficulty in finding public primary schools within close proximity to local communities.

Official statistics from one district help to paint a picture of how far SFL graduates are able to go in the education system. Data provided by the Gusheigu-Karaga district education office in the Northern region revealed that about 6,089 SFL pupils who had successfully completed their programme were unable to find public primary schools nearby to attend (see Table 11.4). Some who were lucky enough to find a school were found to drop out because their parents could not pay the locally prescribed public school levies or provide school uniforms. Undoubtedly, the programme had improved access to basic education and beyond, to as far as senior secondary, but the inability to find

Table 11.4 Enrolment and transition into formal system:
Gushiegu-Karaga District (1995–2001)

Enrolment and transition	Total
Enrolled in SFL programme (male = 5107) (female = 3280)	8387
Completed SFL programme	7592
Dropped out of programme	795
Enrolled in public primary school (mainstreamed)	1023
Made the transition from primary to junior secondary	244
Made the transition from junior secondary to senior secondary	108
Enrolled in community schools	128

Source: Gushiegu-Karaga District Education Statistics (2002)

public schools within reasonable distance of communities still poses a major challenge. Some communities were responding, with assistance from the district office and SFL organisers, by initiating steps to set up public schools within their locality after School for Life had phased out its programme in the community (CARE International/USAID, 2003).

On learning outcomes, random testing of SFL pupils revealed that about a third of a given cohort of students could either (a) read very well and write on their own, (b) read fairly well and write a few words, (c) could read with some difficulty (SFL, 2001). Researchers for CARE International reported that district education officials and opinion leaders in the districts spoke highly of the programme and its successes (CARE International/USAID, 2003).

Upon completing the nine-month programme, pupils are tested and selected by district education officers for entry into public primary schools. Selection into the various grade levels is based on performance in a short test designed for the particular age/grade that pupils have been earmarked to enter. Through this process, SFL graduates are able to enter a range of grades from 1 to 5 or 6 (Casely-Hayford and Akyeampong, 2002).

Opinion leaders interviewed pointed out that some 'trained' teachers in public schools were not as dedicated as SFL teachers, and often absented themselves from school. Teachers in some public primary schools with SFL graduates pointed out that they were usually among their best students. In five public primary schools that were randomly sampled, it was possible to find 8 out of the top 10 in a particular class who were products of the SFL programme (Casely-Hayford and Akyeampong, 2002).

Costs

Just how do the costs for this multigrade programme add up? Analysis of costs can be divided into capital and recurrent. Usually building cost (capital) tends to be the most expensive, followed by infrastructural facilities such as desks, chairs and other facilities (e.g. playground equipment, toilet facilities, etc.). SFL helps in the construction of classroom blocks (a maximum of three classroom blocks) with labour for the construction usually coming from the community. Sometimes communities contributed about 15% of the total construction costs (CARE International/USAID, 2003).

Table 11.5 SFL programme cost profile

1 Operational costs	Amount in $
Teacher salaries per student	2.3
Textbooks per student	6.5
Other learning materials per student	2.9
Supervision	10.1
Continuous staff training costs per student	3.6
Other operating costs per student	5.8
Total operating unit cost	31.3
2 Capital and start-up costs	
Initial training costs per teacher	49.4
Furniture and facilities per classroom	154.0
Building construction per structure	5358.0

Exchange Rate: $1 = C8500
Source: SFL regional office, Tamale

For running costs, the biggest expenditure is the supervision of teachers (on-the-job training) followed by textbook production and supply, other operational costs, e.g. office supplies, and finally the cost of training SFL support staff. Teacher salaries are the lowest recurrent cost at $2.3 per pupil, which is less than one-tenth of teacher costs in the public school which are estimated to be about $27 per annum (CARE International/USAID, 2003). Even with a low pupil–teacher ratio (25:1), the unit cost for teaching is still considerably less than the cost to train and pay a trained teacher, which is estimated to total about $2,100 (recurrent) (Akyeampong, 2002).

The total operating unit of $31 is not significantly different from government-run schools, which have a total unit recurrent cost of about $39 (Orivel, 2002). This might suggest that the recurrent expenditure of the SFL programme is appreciable due mainly to the cost of teacher supervision and in-service support. But when looked at in terms of cost-effectiveness we reach a different conclusion. The difference is that in the nine months of instruction with the SFL Programme pupils (about 62% measured over six years) reach the third and fourth grade of formal schools. Government schools take up to three years to produce a fourth-grader, and, in lower grades, the dropout rate can be as high as 50%. And according to Hartwell and Destefano (2003), the cost of schooling a pupil who has Grade 3 or 4 ability is $50 for SFL, compared to $204 for government schools.

Nevertheless, given the often high number of SFL pupils who cannot access public schools because of distance, this means the costs per successful graduate in terms of access to basic education may be considered to be rather high. To reduce the waste, more needs to be done to improve access to public primary schools. For example, school-mapping exercises to build more public schools in the north should factor SFL programme sites, as well as programmes of similar nature in arriving at where to locate schools in the future. A more radical and, possibly, more costly alternative, would be to introduce boarding multigrade primary schools. To achieve economies of scale these schools will have to have high enrolments, probably of not less than 150 (see Lewin, Chapter 12 in this volume).

Sustainability

Although the SFL programme seems quite successful there are some doubts about its long-term sustainability. Elsewhere, Akyeampong (2004) has described and analysed SFL's partnership arrangement with local district authorities. From this analysis he reached the following conclusion:

> Although, SFL has had what may be described as fruitful links with some district education authorities for the purpose of mainstreaming its students into the formal school system, it has not entered into any formal working arrangements which would make it possible for them to share experiences and help develop local institutional capacity to sustain what had been started. This means that although it is helping to improve access and participation to basic education ... this alternative approach has not become part of the wider system plan for delivering basic education, and by implication, could not benefit from any local funding arrangement for supporting schools. In effect the programme was simply supplementing the formal system, thus doing little to encourage local governments to become more responsible for improving and maintaining the quality of their own system.
>
> (Akyeampong, 2004: 49)

Thus, the goal of alternative multigrade schooling systems such as the SFL should be to enter into formal partnership arrangements with district authorities so that these schools eventually become recognised as part of the formal school system. District assemblies in Ghana have been given oversight responsibility and resources to build and maintain schools (Akyeampong, 2004). Districts need to learn why the SFL model is successful in reaching children in hard-to-reach areas, and how it can support such initiatives to improve enrolment in formal basic schools. But, more importantly, district education authorities can learn from SFL how the multigrade curriculum can work, and adopt some of its practices in response to the perennial problem of teacher absenteeism and shortages in public schools.

CONCLUSION

It is important to point out that although SFL can be described as multigrade schooling, the programme designers do not refer explicitly to it as such. Thus although multigrade philosophy is what SFL practises it fails to receive due recognition and value as a viable alternative to monograde schooling, especially in reaching out-of-school children in deprived and sparsely populated regions. In fact, the tendency has been to describe schools where grades are mixed and the age range is wide as undesirable and requiring policy to correct the anomaly (Ministry of Education, 2002). This rather unfortunate perception arises because of the problem of state education systems unable to adapt their operations, programmes and structures to face and address the challenges of access to quality basic education in poor and hard to reach areas in society (Akyeampong, 2004). More needs to be done to raise the profile of effective 'innovative' approaches such as multigrade schooling and have them integrated into the larger system of basic education delivery. If we ignore the important role it can play, a large number of out-of-school children under similar circumstances as described in northern Ghana will not be reached by the target date for universalisation of primary education for all.

So, what can multigrade schooling as practised by SFL teach us about increasing access and participation in basic education to out-of-school children in areas typical of northern Ghana? At least five lessons can be learned.

1   The first is that a monograde schooling system is not the only answer to quality education provision for all children, especially in circumstances where there is high repetition or drop-out, or in areas where socio-

demographic conditions increase the likelihood of out-of-school children. As we saw at the beginning of this chapter, when earlier efforts in Ghana linked access strictly to quality, defined narrowly in terms of 1:1 trained teacher to class ratio, the policy disadvantaged the north for reasons that we have already discussed and need not repeat here. One can only think that if multigrade schooling had been embraced earlier, access to primary education in the north would have improved significantly and would not remain at the low levels we find today.

2   A lot about what we can achieve with multigrade schooling has to do with effective instructional organisation. This applies to whether two or more grades are combined and the teacher responsible for the mixed group has to use a curriculum designed with monograde in mind. Or whether the teacher is faced with a wide age range group and has to use a curriculum that does not differentiate by grade level and age.

3   Although SFL can provide us with an indication of how successful multigrade teaching and learning can be, further research is needed to understand it in depth, what its strengths and weaknesses are, and how it might be improved. But it seems from the limited evidence provided in the SFL example that when teachers are trained to see learners through multigrade lenses, they may see little problem and have little difficulty in helping children under such circumstances to learn effectively. We can only guess that because the SFL teachers have not gone through the traditional teacher training, which assumes monograde as ideal and desirable, they are more likely to be accepting of multigrade teaching and learning. The way forward is to introduce discourse on multigrade teaching and learning into teacher-training programmes and encourage action research into its practice. In this way we may begin to learn more about its appropriate application and enhance its acceptance as a viable system of education.

4   Without paying attention to the economies of scale in setting up multigrade schools, the costs can be relatively high. The maximum enrolment for an SFL school is approximately 75 students and, as the analysis of costs suggests, the recurrent operational cost is not very different from that of the regular public primary school that can enroll

about 200 students. The difference between the two is that, in the former the school is located at the heart of a small community, thereby reducing drop-out and the number of children out of school. In the latter, the public school is built to achieve economies of scale. Such schools are often located in places with no local community and are difficult to reach by children of some communities (Fobih *et al.*, 1999). The choice between these two options is not simple.

5   Perhaps the most important lesson from the SFL example is that multigrade schooling can contribute positively towards improving access and quality in basic education. In this case, it provides a model for reaching children who are out of school in poor and remote population areas. Multigrade schooling is not a panacea for all the problems developing countries face with regards to improving access to quality basic education, as Lewin (Chapter 12, this volume) points out. Rather, what it teaches us is that it can achieve much if teacher commitment, professional support for multigrade teachers, instructional materials (pupil textbook and teacher guides) and community commitment to the school are all high.

NOTE

[1] This section draws from the author's field research notes and School for Life programme documentation collected in a study which examined emerging good practices in reaching underserved populations with basic education in deprived areas in Ghana. It was carried out for CARE International with funding from USAID.

REFERENCES

Action-Aid REV (2000) 'Action Aid Pilot Education Survey: Draft Ghana Report'. Accra.
Addae-Mensah, I. (2000) *Education in Ghana: A tool for social mobility or social stratification?* The J.B. Danquah Memorial Lectures, April. Accra: Institute for Scientific and Technological Information.
Akyeampong, A.K. (2002) *Teacher Training in Ghana: Does it count?* Multi-Site Teacher Education Research Project (MUSTER). Country Report One. DFID

Educational Paper 49b. London: Department for International Development. Available from DFID website: http://www.dfid.gov.uk/pubs/default.asp (Accessed 19 January 2005).

Akyeampong, A.K (2004) 'Aid for self-help effort? A sustainable alternative route to basic education in Ghana'. *Journal of International Cooperation in Education*, 7, 1, 41–52.

CARE International/USAID (2003) *Reaching Underserved Populations with Basic Education in Deprived Areas of Ghana: Emerging good practices*. Accra and Washington, DC: CARE International/USAID.

Casely-Hayford, L. (2000) 'Education, culture and development in northern Ghana. Micro realities and macro context: implications for policy and practice'. Unpublished DPhil thesis. University of Sussex, UK.

Casely-Hayford, L. (2002) 'Ghana Education Sector Review Consultancy Area Report: General education, gender and the disadvantaged'. Accra: Ministry of Education.

Casely-Hayford, L. and Akyeampong, A.K. (2002) 'Strategies for reaching out of school children in rural areas in Ghana: Northern Ghana field research report'. Prepared for CARE International (Ghana).

Fobih, D., Koomson, A. and Akyeampong, K. (1999) 'Ghana primary school development: final evaulation of project performance'. Accra: Ministry of Education Commissioned Study.

Ghana Education Service (2002) *Kushiegu-Karaga District Education Statistics, Northern Region*. Ghana.

Ghana Ministry of Education/EMIS (2002) *Policy Briefs*. Accra.

Ghana Statistical Service (1998) *Core Welfare Indicators Survey Report*. Accra: Ghana.

Ghana Statistical Service (2001) *2000 Population and Housing Census: Summary report of final results*. Accra.

Hartwell, A. and Destefano, J. (2003) 'The challenge of achieving Education for All: quality basic education for underserved children.' EQUIP2 Issues Brief. Washington, DC.

Hedges, J. (2002) 'The importance of posting and interaction with the education bureaucracy in becoming a teacher in Ghana'. In *Researching Teacher Education: The Multisite Teacher Education Project*. Special Issue of the *International Journal of Educational Development*, 22 (3/4).

Lewin, K.M. and Stuart, J.S. (2003) *Researching Teacher Education: New Perspectives on Practice, Performance and Policy*. Multi-Site Teacher Education Research Project (MUSTER) Synthesis Report. DFID Educational Paper No. 49a. London: Department for International Development. Available from DFID website: http:// www.dfid.gov.uk/pubs/default.asp (Accessed 19 January 2005).

Little, A.W. (2004) *Learning and Teaching in Multigrade Settings.* Background paper for the Global Monitoring Report. Available online at http://portal. unesco.org/education/en/ev.php-URL_ID=36184&URL_DO=DO_TOPIC&URL_ SECTION=201.html

Little, A.W. (2006) 'Education for All: Multigrade realities and histories'. In *Education for All and Multigrade Teaching. challenges and opportunities,* Amsterdam: Springer.

McWilliam, H. and Kwamena-Poh, M. (1975) *The Development of Education in Ghana.* Second edition. London: Longman.

Miller-Grandvaux, Y. and Yoder, K. (2002) *A Literature Review of Community Schools in Africa.* Washington, DC: USAID Bureau for Africa, Office of Sustainable Development.

Ministry of Education (2002) *Meeting the Challenges of Education in the Twenty First Century: Report of the President's Committee on Review of Education Reforms in Ghana.* Accra, Ghana.

Ministry of Education (2003) *Education Strategic Plan 2003–2015 – Policy, Strategy and Targets.* Volume 1. Accra, Ghana.

Orivel, F. (2002) 'Education Sector Review Consultancy Report: Finance'. Accra: Ministry of Education.

SFL (School for life) (1998) *Project Document: Functional literacy programme for children.* Tamale, Ghana.

SFL (School for Life) (2001) 'Report from Educational Forum of School for Life', 19 April 2001. Tamale, Ghana.

SFL (School for Life) (2002) 'Final Report of the Mid Term Review Team: Functional Literacy Programme for Children'. Ghana: Ministry of Foreign Affairs/DANIDA.

World Bank (2004) *Books, Buildings, and Learning Outcomes: An impact evaluation of World Bank support to basic education in Ghana.* Washington, DC: Operations Evaluation Department (OED).

CHAPTER TWELVE

COSTS AND FINANCE OF MULTIGRADE STRATEGIES FOR LEARNING

How do the books balance?

KEITH M. LEWIN

INTRODUCTION

This chapter explores the financial and resource aspects of multigrade approaches to school and curriculum organisation in the context of low enrolment countries in Sub-Saharan Africa (SSA) and South and West Asia (SWA). There are several cost and efficiency related reasons to consider multigrade alternatives to monograde patterns of organisation. First, primary school curricula and the organisation of teaching and learning in the overwhelming majority of developing countries are shaped by monograde assumptions, whereby children are grouped by grade level in separate class groups. Where school size is small, this can lead to very low pupil–teacher ratios (and high recurrent costs per child) which may restrict access. Multigrade can reduce this problem. Second, repetition remains very high in many systems with low enrolment rates, and increases costs whilst reducing access. One reason for repetition may be rigid promotion criteria associated with progress through classes. Multigrade can allow more flexible progression, which might reduce repetition and also increase female enrolment. Third, there is scant evidence that quality and pupils' performance have increased as enrolments have expanded. If this is in part because monograde teaching strategies are poorly matched to learners' capabilities, then multigrade may offer opportunities to adopt more effective pedagogies and increase the time pupils spend learning. Fourth, the literature on multigrade schooling contains few contributions analysing costs and efficiency gains. Decisions to adopt multigrade need to be informed by estimates of the costs and probable benefits associated with different modes of multigrade.

This chapter is organised in seven parts. The first elaborates on types of multigrade organisation to clarify some of the options. The second profiles the different types of costs associated with educational provision. The third presents a model which can be used to estimate cost implications of

239

A.W. Little (ed.), Education for All and Multigrade Teaching: challenges and opportunities, 239–263.
© 2007 *Springer.*

Education for all programmes. In part four the special characteristics of multigrade schools are considered in terms of their possible impact on costs. Part five explores the relevance of multigrade strategies to systems which have many small schools and models different forms. Part six consolidates some observations on the costs of multigrade organisation. Lastly, a range of general issues are presented arising from reflection of the analysis offered.

WHAT KIND OF MULTIGRADE?

There are many different ways of organising learning and teaching in a multigrade classroom. Various examples are described elsewhere in this book. A schematic simplification of some of the main options can help frame discussion of costs. Figures 12.1 and 12.2 show some possibilities of how teachers and classes may be organised, and how students may be organised within classes.

In Figure 12.1 T represents a teacher, and the numbers in the class boxes represent pupils operating at different grade levels. Thus in Pattern A a single teacher takes responsibility for two separate class groups (Grade 1 and Grade 2 pupils) and teaches one class group (Grade 1) whilst the other class group (Grade 2) self-studies after a brief introduction. The dotted line represents supervision at a distance – i.e. the teacher is 'keeping an eye' on the second group, but is actually with the Grade 1 group for most of the teaching period. The second group could be set up to make use of peer learning strategies where pupils support each other to complete learning tasks in the absence of the teacher. This differs from simple monograde only in so far as the unattended group has structured learning tasks. The pupils remain in their grade groups. The teacher teaches one grade and supports the other.

Figure 12.1 Patterns of multigrade organisation

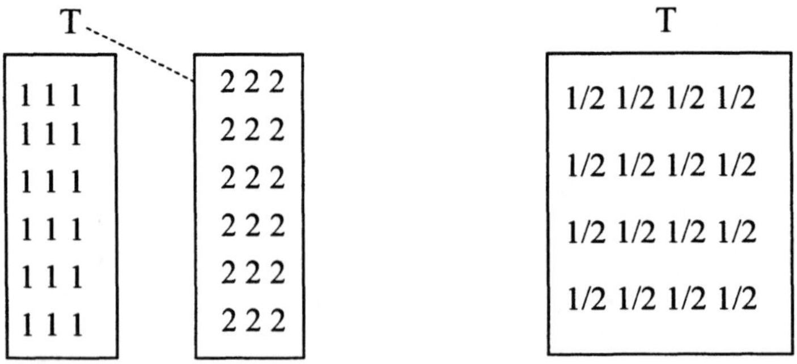

Pattern A: Additional parallel class

Pattern B: Whole class, mixed-grade groups

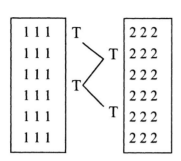

```
1 1 1   T        2 2 2
1 1 1      T     2 2 2
1 1 1            2 2 2
1 1 1   T        2 2 2
1 1 1      T     2 2 2
1 1 1            2 2 2
```

Pattern C: Alternate
teaching

T

```
1 1 1 1 2 2 2
1 1 1 1 2 2 2
1 1 1 1 2 2 2
1 1 1 1 2 2 2
1 1 1 1 2 2 2
1 1 1 1 2 2 2
```

Pattern D: Whole class, separate
grade groups

T

1/2/3/4	1/2/3/4	1/2/3/4
1/2/3/4	1/2/3/4	1/2/3/4
1/2/3/4	1/2/3/4	1/2/3/4
1/2/3/4	1/2/3/4	1/2/3/4
1/2/3/4	1/2/3/4	1/2/3/4
1/2/3/4	1/2/3/4	1/2/3/4

Pattern E: Wide range grade groups

T

```
1/4 1/4 1/4 1/4
1/4 1/4 1/4 1/4
1/4 1/4 1/4 1/4
1/4 1/4 1/4 1/4
1/4 1/4 1/4 1/4
```

Pattern F: Discontinuous range
grade groups

```
1 1 1 1   T        4 4 4 4
1 1 1 1      T     4 4 4 4
1 1 1 1            4 4 4 4
1 1 1 1   T        4 4 4 4
1 1 1 1      T     4 4 4 4
1 1 1 1            4 4 4 4
```

Pattern G: Discontinuous range grade
groups

T

```
3 3 3 3 6 6 6 6
3 3 3 3 6 6 6 6
3 3 3 3 6 6 6 6
3 3 3 3 6 6 6 6
3 3 3 3 6 6 6 6
3 3 3 3 6 6 6 6
```

Pattern H: Discontinuous
range grade groups

Pattern B illustrates a multigrade grouping within the class where Grade 1 and Grade 2 pupils sit in mixed-grade groups. This is a whole-class teaching environment where the teacher is working with all the pupils. This could be in a traditional mode with the teacher at the front of the class. It might also involve groupwork in mixed-grade pupil groups. Grade 2 pupils may be able to support some of the learning of Grade 1 pupils. Teachers may set common learning tasks across the class and differentiate grades by performance.

Pattern C is a more developed strategy than pattern A. In this two single-grade groups are taught on an alternating basis during a single teaching period. The teacher moves between each class group several times. The groups may be in separate classrooms or in different parts of the same classroom. Each grade group is likely to have different learning tasks and different learning outcomes, though these may overlap. Ideally, each grade group has structured learning tasks when unattended.

Pattern D shows pupils in the same classroom grouped by grade level. The class has been split in half and can be treated like two classes part of the time and one class part of the time. In the former case different learning tasks can be set for different grades. In the latter the same task could be set and learning differentiated by outcomes appropriate to different grade levels.

Pattern E illustrates a wide range of grade groups across four contiguous grades. Pupils are in mixed groups in a class with a wide range of ages and grade level performance. This may enhance opportunities for grade hierarchical mentoring, with older, higher grade pupils acting as mentors to younger pupils. Pattern F shows a non-contiguous grouping of Grades 1 and 4 in the same classroom. Pattern E could arise where there are very small enrolments. Pattern F is likely to be the result of a decision to group older and younger pupils for pedagogic reasons.

Pattern G shows alternating teaching between grade groups where there is a wide difference between grades and little likelihood of overlap in learning tasks and outcomes. Pattern H shows two non-contiguous grade groups in the same classroom grouped by grade and is similar to the split class of pattern D where pupils can be taught as a whole or at two different levels.

Multigrade strategies differ from those of double shift schooling (Bray, 2000), with which they are sometimes confused. Multiple shifts can be used to make more intensive use of classroom space by extending the school day and having, for example, morning and afternoon school sessions. Teachers may or may not teach in both. It is possible that multiple shift could be combined with multigrade teaching strategies. Some education systems obviate the need for multigrade organisation by deploying the same teacher to teach one grade in the morning and a second in the afternoon (Little, 1995). The length of the school day for each grade may be as little as two hours.

These patterns of multigrade, and the many others which are possible, may have different implications for costs. Before beginning to explore these it is necessary to consider different types of costs associated with financing education systems.

WHAT KINDS OF COSTS?

A simple map of different types of costs is needed in order to discuss the cost implications of introducing multigrade teaching. The costs of schooling are conventionally separated in national budgets into recurrent and development costs. Recurrent costs are usually divided into salary costs (teaching and non-teaching staff) and non-salary costs (e.g. learning materials, in-service support, transport, maintenance and other operating costs including food if this is supplied). Most costs are usually at the school level, but some will be for common services (inspection, assessment and examinations, curriculum development, in-service support, etc.) and be located at district, provincial, or national level. Primary school systems in poor countries generally allocate 90% or more of their expenditure to salaries, most of which are for teaching staff. At secondary level, especially where boarding is common and is subsidised, 50% of costs or more may be non-teaching salaries and non-salary boarding-related expenditure. Learning materials costs are often a small proportion of total recurrent expenditure. They may be school-level costs or attributable to higher levels if central purchasing and distribution is employed.

Costs can also be divided into those that are fixed (that is, independent of the number of pupils) and those that are variable. The former might include the costs of textbook development and examination writing; the latter would include learning materials distributed per child and subsidies for food or school uniforms. Some costs may be fixed over a range and then increase. Thus the number of teachers in a school may remain the same although the number of pupils increases so teaching salary costs appear fixed. Above a certain level of enrolment a new teacher may be employed, adding to costs.

Costs may also be separated into those that are public and those that are private. Public costs fall on public budgets at national or local level and usually include teachers' salaries in government schools. Private costs are paid by pupils and households and may include expenditure on textbooks, travel, uniforms, food, etc. The largest element in SSA and much of South Asia (SA), especially at secondary level, is likely to be tuition fees.

Development costs, which can include buildings, new equipment and furniture, and the initial investment needed to develop new curriculum materials, are often considered separately from recurrent costs since typically they are incurred to meet specific needs and are regarded as investments over substantial time periods. The largest development costs are usually associated with school and classroom building. The costs can vary across very wide ranges depending on how construction is procured and managed, the quality of design and materials used, and the costs of land. New schools in SSA and SWA typically cost more than the sum of the cost of the individual classrooms they contain, reflecting the costs of infrastructure, staffrooms, boarding facilities, teachers' housing, etc. Simple primary schools may cost only twice as much per classroom as free-standing classrooms; new secondary schools often cost four or more times as much as the sum of the unit cost of classrooms.

There are other kinds of costs that may be more difficult to assess. One example relevant to the adoption of multigrade strategies relates to opportunity costs. Simply expressed, an opportunity cost arises when by doing an activity other activities are foregone. Attending school has an opportunity cost if a student could have gone fishing instead and sold or eaten the fish. The question then is whether the opportunity cost of going to school is balanced by the benefits associated with going to school. Teachers adopting multigrade teaching may have to invest more time and effort in planning than monograde teachers. If so, they have less time for other tasks (marking, pastoral care, etc.) and there is an opportunity cost. If the benefits are not seen to outweigh the costs of adoption by teachers this may discourage the implementation of multigrade strategies.

Common cost indicators include the cost per pupil, otherwise known as the unit cost. This is derived from the total recurrent cost of the system for a year, divided by the number of pupils. Teaching costs per pupil per year are usually derived from school-level costs of salaries and learning materials. Administrative costs (predominantly those of district, provincial, and national infrastructure including inspection and examinations) are generally added to school level costs to arrive at overall unit costs. Costs per graduate are sometimes used to indicate how much each graduate costs after repetition and drop-out is taken into account. Costs per classroom and costs per standard school type are often used in planning development expenditure.

Pupil–teacher ratios (PTRs) are the main determinant of teaching costs per pupil and unit costs in most systems. The PTR is not the average class size, which can be very different and, in monograde schools, is generally always larger than the PTR. The reasons for this include non-teaching teachers, teachers with free periods, and the teaching of large combined classes within grades. The teacher–class ratio (the number of teachers divided by the number of classes), can indicate how much teaching is taking place whereas the PTR alone cannot, since it contains no information about workload.

The multigrade organisation of learning and teaching can affect all the types of costs identified. Depending on the type of multigrade deployed, costs may be greater or less than those for monograde. Where monograde and multigrade co-exist, a likely scenario in many systems, the impact on costs will depend on how they are configured and how they interact. When comparing costs it is important to remember that differences in principle may or may not be translated into practice. Thus rural monograde schools should be staffed with at least a teacher for each grade. In reality they may not be. It is also important to compare like with like so that adequately resourced multigrade is compared with adequately resourced monograde.

AFFORDING EDUCATION FOR ALL

Since the Dakar World Education Forum in 2000 (UNESCO, 2000) many countries in SSA and SA have made progress in expanding access and increasing enrolments at the primary level. Gender differences have also diminished, though not at rates sufficient to meet the EFA target for equity in 2005. Despite this, 14 SSA countries have Gross Enrolment Rates at primary below 80% and another nine below 100% (UNESCO, 2003) – and are a long way from universal access, and even further from universal completion. Sub-Saharan Africa registered the largest relative gains in primary enrolments but remained the region furthest from universalising participation. About 44 million children failed to attend school in SSA, with a further 32 million out of school in South and West Asia (SWA). Girls' enrolments have been increasing faster than boys. However, in South Asia, the Arab States and SSA girls are 66%, 60%, and 53% of those out of school. Sixteen countries were judged to be far from the goal of universalisation in 2015, thirteen of which were in SSA. About 21 countries seemed unlikely to achieve gender parity in primary education by 2015, and 45 countries are likely to miss gender parity at secondary by 2015 (UNESCO, 2002).

Education for All and the Millennium Development Goals (UN, 2000) require the universalisation of primary schooling and achieving the goals will be unlikely without expanded access to secondary (Lewin, 2004). It also assumes quality will not deteriorate and should improve such that basic learning outcomes can be demonstrated. Additional resources will be needed in those countries furthest from EFA. So also will efficiency gains that can mean that more can be enrolled for similar amounts of money.

A simple analysis is informative. Gross Enrolment Rates for primary schools are determined by a simple formula (Lewin and Caillods, 2001). This is:

GER2 = x/ac where:

x = Public expenditure on primary education as a percentage of GNP

c = Public recurrent expenditure on primary schooling per student as a
      percentage of GNP per capita

a = The proportion of the population of primary school age

In the countries with the lowest levels of primary enrolment the value of c, the unit cost per pupil, averages about 20% of GNP per capita. In most poor countries a is generally within the range 10–15% and tends to be closer to 15% in the low enrolment countries with six-year primary systems (Colclough with Lewin, 1993).

On this basis, a Primary Gross Enrolment rate of 100% requires an average allocation of about 3% of GNP to primary schooling. Average overall allocations to education budgets in SSA are currently a little over 4% of GNP, implying that universalising primary schooling will require about 75% of the national education budget. This is more than that found in any of the low primary enrolment countries. Thus external assistance is likely to be needed to help fill the gap; so also are efficiency gains if they are available.

Some inefficiencies in some countries arise from over-staffing small schools using monograde norms for the appointment of staff. If PTRs are very low then costs per pupil will be high. A simple calculation can be used to estimate minimum average pupil–teacher ratios for universal enrolment in primary schools.

PTR = P/T where:

PTR = pupil–teacher ratio
P = number of pupils
T = number of teachers

P = a * N where:

N = national population
T = (x*G*0.9)/dG/N

where G = GNP and d = teachers' salaries as a multiple of GNP per capita.

Teachers' salaries in low enrolment countries account for 90% or more of the recurrent cost per pupil. They appear to average between six to seven times GNP per capita in SSA (Bruns et al., 2003). Thus:

$$PTR = P/T = (a*N)/(x*G/d)$$

which reduces to

$$PTR = (a*d)/x$$

Thus for a hypothetical system with $a = 15\%$, $d = 7$, and $x = 3\%$, the average PTR would need to be at least 35:1.

A system with an average PTR of 35:1 will have class sizes larger than 35:1 since all teachers are unlikely to teach all the time. Some will be spending time on administration (e.g. school principals), others may have some free periods, and others may group classes together to reduce teaching loads. Systems with class sizes of 40 or above are probably approaching the limit of what is consistent with reasonable learning conditions at primary level.

If PTRs average 35–40:1 there will of course be a distribution of schools below and above the average. Those with low PTRs will be proportionately more expensive than those with average PTRs. Most low PTR schools will be rural and in low population density areas. The conclusions are clear. Universalising primary enrolments will need to be achieved with a significant proportion of small schools. The costs of these schools must be contained so that they do not depart far from average levels if universalisation is to be affordable. Recent studies by the World Bank indicate that target PTRs will need to be in the range of 35–40:1 if EFA is to be achieved, and recognise that there will need to be a dispersion around the mean to account for the small schools needed to reach the most marginalised populations (Mingat *et al.*, 2002, Bruns *et al.*, 2003). What little other work there is on the economics of multigrade (e.g. Thomas and Shaw, 1992), draws attention to possible cost saving benefits but needs extending.

THE POSSIBLE COST SAVINGS OF MULTIGRADE TEACHING FOR EDUCATION FOR ALL

The organisation of learning and teaching using multigrade strategies in the context of national commitments to Education for All is associated with two main kinds of benefits for costs. These are:

- Reduction of costs per pupil in small schools;
- Improved quality of learning and teaching, which can increase efficiency and reduce costs per successful graduate.

The small-school problem arises because most of those children who are not enrolled in primary schools are in SSA and South Asia and are most likely to be found in rural locations with low population density. There is much evidence to suggest that enrolment rates in rural primary schools in low enrolment countries are highly correlated with the distance of the household from the school. When the school is more than 3 km from the home, participation falls off dramatically. Distance from school affects girls especially, because of widespread concerns over safety (Lavy, 1992; Anderson-Levitt et al., 1994; Colclough et al., 2003). Greater access will have to be achieved through the creation of more schools and many of these will be small schools. In these there may be too few pupils to justify the creation of monograde teaching groups.

Multigrade teaching approaches allow primary schools with enrolments of less than 150 to be more cost effective than the monograde alternative, sometimes as much as half the cost per pupil. Where resources are limited, multigrade teaching could mean twice as many children experience school for the same costs. Small schools make up between 20% and 40% of all primary schools in much of SSA and South Asia. Most countries with large-scale EFA programmes are already allocating as much to education (4–5% of GDP), and to primary education (50–65%) as they are likely to be able to sustain. This makes it important that costs per child for new pupils do not depart far from average costs across the rest of the system. Multigrade teaching can make this a reality.

Improved efficiency is important since many systems have high repetition rates arising from low levels of achievement. These can average 20% or more in SSA (Mingat et al., 2002). Where repetition is high, it adds costs and reduces access. School places are occupied by repeaters that might otherwise be occupied by those who are not enrolled. Multigrade teaching offers the potential to enhance the quality of learning, improve learning achievement, and reduce repetition. This is true both for small schools and more generally. The possibilities are extensive and include peer and grade hierarchical older-mentor learning, where pupils learn from others (and those who mentor learn from their experience); better structuring of learning tasks related to the age and readiness to learn of children of different ages and capabilities; more time on task, especially where curriculum materials include multigrade strategies and opportunities to modularise learning to allow some level of irregular attendance without loss of coherence. Curricula and learning activities can be organised around discrete units of work that are complete in themselves and that may not have to be followed in a fixed order. Modules that can be used in a self-instructional way allow catching up on missed material. This is important where pupil and teacher attendance is irregular and where seasonality (e.g. attendance linked to the demands of the agricultural cycle) is important. Opportunities can be taken to design learning modules that fit with 'zones of proximal development' and provide 'scaffolding' for further learning linked to the learner's readiness. If these pedagogic changes result in improved learning outcomes, costs per primary school graduate may fall as fewer repeat and fail before completion.

If repetition rates are to fall more flexible patterns of progression through the school curriculum need to be devised. A common practice in mono-grade schools – whereby poorly achieving pupils repeat a whole year in all subjects – may be replaced by more selective repetition within grade groups for different subjects. If multigrade learning materials are modularised it may be possible to repeat some but not all of the work of a grade. Figure 12.2 illustrates possible differences between monograde and multigrade repetition.

Figure 12.2 Repetition and monograde and multigrade class organisation

Grade 1	*Grade 2*
Monograde	
Failure at end of year. Repeat whole year.	Full repetition of all Grade 1 material in all subjects for a year as a result of 'failing' promotion tests in some subjects. No remedial support may lead to failure again second time around, demoralisation as a result of being placed with younger pupils, and development of sinking classes with a majority of repeaters.
Multigrade	
Failure in some subjects at end of grade test, which may not be at end of academic year. Repetition only of that which is failed.	Partial repetition of some subjects to increase attainment to appropriate level for progression, testing based on readiness not necessarily end of chronological year.

In many systems boys outnumber girls because they persist longer in schools and remain enrolled at older ages, partly because of repetition. Figure 12.3 shows that in Tanzania there are more girls than boys enrolled below the age of 16.5 years. Above this there are many more boys, explaining their overall preponderance in secondary schools. If girls repeated less, and graduated from school close to the age they should with no repetition, enrolment rates for girls should increase. Drop-out might well reduce for boys and girls with faster progression through schooling. Overall costs would fall since fewer places would be needed for the same level of net enrolment.

An additional benefit of multigrade teaching is that it can respond to the realities of mixed-age enrolment, where classes contain children who may vary in age by five or more years. In these cases monograde approaches assume that children are at similar levels of cognitive development even though this is manifestly untrue. Data from Tanzania illustrate the point. Figure 12.4 shows the age distribution of students in Grade 1 and Grade 7, the last year of primary school. In both grades enrolments are spread over children with an age range of five years or more. Monograde learning and teaching place together 7-year-olds and 12-year-olds in Grade 1 with the same learning tasks and anticipated learning outcomes. Multigrade organisation could allow more differentiation

Figure 12.3 Male–female enrolment as a percentage of total enrolment by age in Tanzanian secondary schools

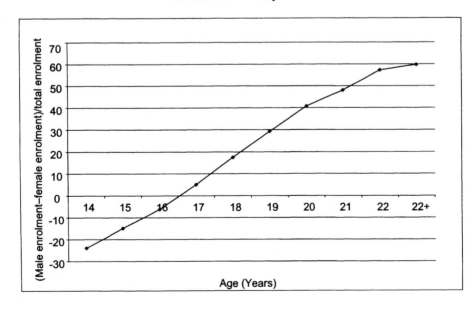

of learning tasks within a class with a wide age range; it could also allow multigrade classes with a narrower overall age range.

Even if it were true that pupils of such widely differing ages were mostly at a particular grade level in their learning capability, substantial overlaps would remain between grades. Figure 12.4 illustrates this possibility. If an indicator of learning achievement or learning readiness is distributed normally within a grade group, as is often the case, then there are likely to be overlaps between adjacent grades. In Figure 12.5 the hypothetical curve for learning achievement (e.g. reading level, or mathematics score) for Grade 1 overlaps by about 50% with Grade 2. Multigrade classs organisation is attractive because it is almost certain that some pupils in Grade 2 will be operating at Grade 1 levels and vice versa. Monograde does not recognise this reality.

Most of these potential quality advantages of multigrade apply independently of school size. In small schools the comparative advantage of multigrade organisation is most compelling. Multigrade allows schools to operate at average PTRs and offer a full curriculum and fully timetable pupils (which monograde cannot do except at much greater costs). It also responds to another widespread difficulty associated with small rural schools. Teacher supply and retention can be extremely problematic and often it is rural schools that are the most understaffed by monograde standards, i.e. one teacher per grade even if the class size is very small.

Figure 12.4 Primary pupils in Tanzania by sex and age in Grades 1 and 7

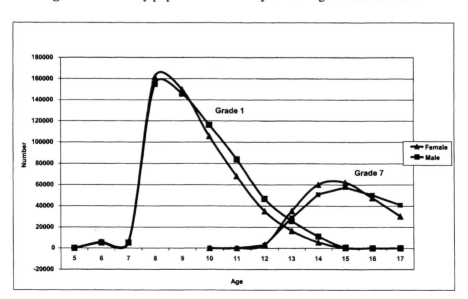

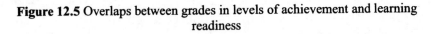

Figure 12.5 Overlaps between grades in levels of achievement and learning readiness

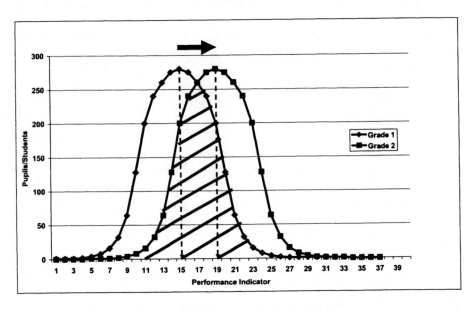

Unless multigrade organisation is adopted, pupils' time on task may be very limited as teachers teach several monograde classes alternatively, leaving class periods where the teacher is not present. A multigrade curriculum can be designed to provide a full complement of learning experiences for all pupils in small schools staffed at average PTRs. Monograde cannot do this. In larger schools choice of multigrade is more often an option rather than a necessity. If the learning gains it promises are real, and the costs no greater than multigrade once it is established, then it is potentially attractive.

SMALL SCHOOLS, MULTIGRADE, AND SOME EFFECTS ON COSTS

The possible advantages of multigrade teaching for staffing small schools can be illustrated by considering schools with enrolments of 60, 120 and 180, in a system that has six grades of primary schooling. Table 12.1 shows this. In a monograde school a minimum of six teachers would be required, one for each grade. In the smallest school this would result in a pupil–teacher ratio of 10:1 and class size of 10 assuming all teachers taught all periods. The teaching cost per child would be three times that in a school with 180 pupils.

If the school had a multigrade pattern of organisation with a pupil–teacher ratio of 30:1 (the same as in schools with 180 pupils), the equivalent school with only 60 pupils would require two teachers teaching all periods to mixed-grade groups. Simply put, teachers' salaries in three schools of this kind could be supported for the same cost as one of the monograde type.

This picture can be refined. Enrolments in many primary schools, where overall enrolments have been growing and repetition and drop-out remain significant, are often uneven. Table 12.2 models this for a school with 180 pupils. Here 50 are in Grade 1, declining to 15 in Grade 6. Those in Grade 6 have more than three times as much spent on teachers' salaries per pupil than those in Grade 1; if one teacher is allocated to each grade group in a monograde pattern Grade 1 has a PTR of 50:1 and Grade 6 of 15:1.

Table 12.1 Teachers needed for schools, by school size and monograde and multigrade class organisation

	Monograde				Multigrade			
School size	Number of classes	Average class size	Number of teachers	PTR	Number of classes	Average class size	Number of teachers	PTR
60	6	10	6	10	2	30	2	30
120	6	20	6	20	4	30	4	30
180	6	30	6	30	6	30	6	30

Table 12.2 Monograde, multigrade and uneven enrolment patterns between grades

	Monograde				Multigrade			
	Pupils	Class size	Teachers	PTR		Class size	Teachers	PTR
Grade 1	50	50	1	50	3 multigrade classes covering Grades 1 + 2	30	3	30
Grade 2	40	40	1	40				
Grade 3	35	35	1	35	2 multigrade classes covering Grades 3 + 4	30	2	30
Grade 4	25	25	1	25				
Grade 5	15	15	1	15	1 multigrade class covering Grades 5 + 6	30	1	30
Grade 6	15	15	1	15				
Total	180		6	30			6	30

A multigrade school with the same number of teachers and pupils at different grade levels might operate differently. Three teachers could teach Grades 1 and 2, two teachers Grades 3 and 4, and one teacher Grades 5 and 6. This would even up the teaching group sizes so that all pupils would be in classes of 30. Arguably this would be more equitable and more efficient.

In practice the differences between the cases may be larger. If a maximum class size policy is operated such that teachers are posted wherever class size exceeds 30 pupils, then the monograde school would appear to qualify for nine teachers, not six. If this is so, then it would be 50% more expensive per pupil on teaching costs, though teaching groups would fall in size in the first three grades (Table 12.3).

If primary schooling curricula are subject-based, and some subjects are taught by specialised teachers who teach only their subject, more inefficiencies can appear in small schools. Most primary school curricula in SSA and SA are subject-based, as are those in lower secondary schools. In higher grades of primary and in lower secondary teacher specialisation is common. Thus, a school of 180 pupils where monograde organisation was used would need at least nine specialist teachers for language, mathematics and science if each subject accounted for 20% of curriculum time. The overall pupil–teacher ratio would be at a low level of 20:1 (Table 12.4). If a class-size maximum were imposed as many as 14 teachers might be needed. If the school were smaller, with only 90 pupils, then specialist teachers would begin to have lighter and lighter teaching loads unless they taught across the curriculum. The PTR would fall to only 10:1 (Table 12.5).

Table 12.3 Monograde and multigrade with a limit on class size

	Monograde					Multigrade		
	Pupils	Class size	Teachers	PTR		Class size	Teachers	PTR
Grade 1	50	25	2	25	3 multigrade classes covering Grades 1 + 2	30	3	30
Grade 2	40	20	2	20				
Grade 3	35	18	2	17.5	2 multigrade classes covering Grades 3 + 4	30	2	30
Grade 4	25	25	1	25				
Grade 5	15	15	1	15	1 multigrade class covering Grades 5 + 6	30	1	30
Grade 6	15	15	1	15				
Total	180		9	20	6		6	30

Table 12.4 Monograde school with teacher specialisation: 180 pupils

	Mono-grade class size	Language periods (20% time)	Maths periods (20% time)	Science periods (20% time)	Other subjects (40% time)	Teachers
Grade 1	50	8	8	8	16	
Grade 2	40	8	8	8	16	
Grade 3	35	8	8	8	16	
Grade 4	25	8	8	8	16	
Grade 5	15	8	8	8	16	
Grade 6	15	8	8	8	16	
Total	**180**	48	48	48	96	
Teachers needed at 35/40 period workload		1.4	1.4	1.4	2.7	
Rounded		2	2	2	3	9
PTR						20

Table 12.5 Monograde school with teacher specialisation: 90 pupils

	Mono-grade class size	Language periods (20% time)	Maths periods (20% time)	Science periods (20% time)	Other subjects (40% time)	Teachers
Grade 1	25	8	8	8	16	
Grade 2	20	8	8	8	16	
Grade 3	17	8	8	8	16	
Grade 4	13	8	8	8	16	
Grade 5	8	8	8	8	16	
Grade 6	7	8	8	8	16	
Total	**90**	48	48	48	96	
Teachers needed at 35/40 period workload		1.4	1.4	1.4	2.7	
Rounded		2	2	2	3	9
PTR						10

Table 12.6 Multigrade with teacher specialisation: pattern one

Combined grades	Multigrade class size	Language periods (20% time)	Maths periods (20% time)	Science periods (20% time)	Other subjects (40% time)	Teachers
1 and 2	45	8	8	8	16	
3 and 4	30	8	8	8	16	
5 and 6	15	8	8	8	16	
Total	90	24	24	24	48	
Teachers needed at 35/40 period workload		0.7	0.7	0.7	1.4	
Rounded		1	1	1	2	5
PTR						18

Table 12.7 Multigrade with teacher specialisation: pattern two

Combined grades	Multigrade class size	Language periods (20% time)	Maths periods (20% time)	Science periods (20% time)	Other subjects (20% time)	Teachers
1, 2 and 3 (two groups)	31	16	16	16	32	
4, 5 and 6	28	8	8	8	16	
Total	90	24	24	24	48	
Teachers needed at 35/40 period workload		0.7	0.7	0.7	1.4	3.5
PTR						25

A multigrade organisational alternative for a 90-pupil school could have several forms. Two are illustrated in Tables 12.6 and 12.7. In the first pattern specialist subject teachers are retained (Table 12.6). Each multigrade class would have two grades contained within it. If teachers taught only within the double grade groups they would be short of a full timetable (average load about 24/40 periods). In this case five teachers would be needed and the PTR would be 18:1, significantly better than the 10:1 for the equivalent monograde case. If teachers taught across the double grade groups the PTR could be increased to as much as 25:1 and teaching loads would rise.

In the second pattern it is assumed that grades could be grouped into two Grades 1–3 classes, and one Grades 4–6 class. Mathematics and science would be covered by 1.4 teachers who would contribute 0.6 teaching to other subjects, and 0.7 language teachers who would cover 0.3 teaching of other subjects. Staffing with three such teachers would leave a shortfall of 0.5 general teaching, which could be covered by an additional teacher (allowing all to have some free periods) or by a part-time teacher or part-teaching principal. The PTR would then be about 25:1.

HOW DO THE BOOKS BALANCE?

It is clear that there is no simple answer to the question of whether multigrade approaches to learning are more or less costly than monograde. In the case of small schools some patterns of multigrade teaching can be very cost-effective. More generally for larger schools multigrade teaching is probably cost-neutral once development costs have been paid and it is established across a school system. The case for medium and large schools then depends on whether or not the potential for more effective learning, and less repetition, can be turned into a reality in particular systems. The complexity of alternative multigrade strategies makes it daunting to identify simple general conclusions. Table 12.8 attempts to capture some of the possible differences in costs that may arise with common types of multigrade.

Table 12.8 Probable effects of multigrade on costs

School costs	Probable effect of multigrade on costs
Teaching salary costs	Teachers' salaries per pupil should fall in multigrade schools when compared to fully staffed monograde schools where enrolments are small. In large schools the effect may disappear and teachers' salaries per pupil for multigrade and monograde may become similar.
Non-teaching salary costs	Multigrade should not be more expensive than monograde in relation to non-teaching salaries; if it is, it is more likely to be a small-school effect than a consequence of multigrade.
Teaching materials purchase costs	Multigrade may benefit from additional teaching aids but the costs of these are unlikely to be much more than those for adequately resourced monograde.

(continued)

Table 12.8 continued

School costs	Probable effect of multigrade on costs
Learning materials purchase costs	Multigrade may require more learning materials (e.g. if multigrade practice involves more periods of self-study); however, multigrade is not necessarily more expensive than adequately resourced monograde. Learning materials are in any case usually a very small proportion of cost per pupil.
Training costs	The costs of training teachers to use multigrade approaches fall on pre-service and on in-service training. There may be some initial costs in setting up new programmes, but the recurrent costs are likely to be similar to those for supported monograde (see below).
Assessment costs	Multigrade school-based assessment may need more time and resources than conventional monograde if learning progress is monitored at the individual level; once systems are established there is no reason why assessment should be more than marginally more expensive.
Teachers' time and application	Multigrade may be more demanding on teachers' time in terms of preparation, and in terms of managing classroom activity when compared to monograde whole-class teaching of standard content; if more and better learning takes place there is a productivity gain.
System level costs	
Training of inspectors/ advisers	Inspector and advisers may need training to evaluate multigrade; this is a once-only development cost after which it should be integrated into training of all new inspectors.
Assessment costs	Multigrade may have no significant cost implications for external national examinations if these are only held at the end of primary school as a summative assessment of competences judged against stated criteria. If educational outcomes are intended to be different for multigrade schools than for monograde, then parallel assessments may be needed.
Revised initial teacher education	Including multigrade competences in initial teachers training should be a once-only development cost after which it would have few additional costs over current practice.
In-service training and support	Offering in-service training to support multigrade may be an additional cost if it is in addition to normal INSET programmes. INSET costs would depend on the proportion of teachers who receive it, the length and intensity of what they receive, and the extent to which it continues over time.

(continued)

Table 12.8 continued

Development of curriculum materials	The development of multigrade materials may be an additional cost, especially if multigrade materials are produced alongside monograde curriculum materials. If curriculum revision produces new materials which can be used in both multigrade and monograde schools and classes the additional costs may be marginal.
Development of learning aids	These costs are unlikely to be significant when compared to teaching costs unless expensive technologies are introduced.

ISSUES ARISING

This paper has considered some cost-related aspects of multigrade approaches to learning and teaching. A number of broad issues emerge which can help shape debate over methods, and their costs and benefits.

First, multigrade teaching has to be understood as a strategy for improving quality and access that will succeed only if there is commitment to its introduction and support. In much of SSA and SWA multigrade teaching is seen as an option of last resort. It is associated with poor quality, remote schools which are under-staffed and unpopular. This image is prevalent and powerful. It is unjustified. Multigrade teaching is a pedagogic innovation which has many potential advantages. It could be the method of choice (as in the *Escuela Nueva* programme) if enough teachers and Ministry staff were convinced of its benefits. It is neither old-fashioned nor necessarily a last resort. These issues of perception are important if hearts and minds are to be converted into commitment and application. Multigrade class organisation is consistent with much progressive pedagogy and curriculum analysis. Paradoxically multigrade is also consistent with many traditional learning systems in civil society and elsewhere. It is clear that in some circumstances multigrade is the best option, and the most cost-effective.

Second, it is important not to see multigrade simply as a way of increasing PTRs in rural schools. It is a strategy to increase access at lower costs than monograde can provide. If PTRs are low because of small school size and monograde assumptions, then more could be enrolled at affordable costs if multigrade was introduced. If PTRs are high because there are too few teachers to staff small rural schools, then multigrade is desirable since it will offer more structured learning time than monograde is likely to do (if there are not enough teachers to cover all grades in a monograde school some will be untaught, unlike in a multigrade school).

Sophisticated multigrade teaching may be more expensive than poor quality monograde. Multigrade organisation is virtually a necessity with small primary schools if learning time is to be maximised and costs kept within reasonable limits; otherwise it is a choice with probable pedagogic gains (Little, 2001). With multigrade more can be enrolled at similar or better quality for the same costs and teacher supply constraints can be eased. It is often forgotten that multigrade can be mixed strategically with monograde.

Third, multigrade will be difficult to implement without appropriate curriculum reforms. At the first level organisational changes and pedgagogic reform can make a multigrade reality out of a monograde curriculum base. Some patterns of multigrade learning and teaching can and do use monograde learning materials. This is necessary and it would be counter-productive and impractical to insist that multigrade could not be introduced without replacing the existing stock of learning materials which are themselves in short supply. The invitation is that subsequent curriculum reform related to EFA should always have multigrade patterns of use as one of its terms of reference. There are no good reasons why learning and teaching materials cannot be designed to support both mono- and multigrade. If there are additional costs they are marginal.

Fourth, teachers do need support and training to adopt new practices. Where multigrade organisation is adopted school level support is essential from principals who understand multigrade. In-service training is desirable, and appropriate teacher manuals are essential. Pre-service training rarely devotes much time to the acquisition of multigrade skills. There is no good reason for this and it would cost little to address this deficiency.

Fifth, for many teachers and parents the most convincing demonstration of the value of multigrade lies in its practice. The role of properly conceived and managed pilot programmes designed with the possibility of going to scale cannot be over-emphasised. If they offer quality learning, are manageable by ordinary teachers, and popular with pupils and parents they will spread. If they are imposed without demonstrating that they work, and without advocates with real experience of their advantages, they may well fail. Successful innovations are generally driven by demand, not pushed by advocacy lacking concrete demonstration of success. The cost of implementation of reforms that are welcomed by teachers is much less than that of those which are resisted.

Sixth, the gains available from adopting multigrade teaching as a complementary strategy for EFA depend on all the above observations. They also require persistence and consistency in approach, and an adequate resource base. To deliver benefits new practices require time to mature and be refined to suit different local circumstances. Innovations of scale need medium-term commitment to embed themselves and deliver gains greater than initial costs. There is a challenge to leadership to follow through multigrade strategies for a sufficient length of time to realise the benefits.

Finally, if the commitment by development partners to support EFA is real, and the pledge to provide resources to any country with a plausible plan to achieve universal enrolment and gender equity is made, then action should follow ambition. Resource questions are critical. Multigrade teaching does offer methods of reaching those currently excluded from primary schooling at affordable costs with reasonable quality. Monograde does not in many of the poorest countries. Achievement of EFA is a problem of the margin. It does involve deciding whether the last 20–30% to be enrolled can be enrolled at sustainable costs in conventional monograde schools within 3 km of households, and if they are enrolled considering how best to organise their learning. Multigrade looks a better option. It also looks to have potential in meeting the learning needs of nomadic communities, refugees and displaced people, migrants, and other groups with characteristics that may militate against monograde solutions to their schooling needs.

In conclusion, multigrade appears to have a range of attractions which includes opportunities to:

- improve quality for those enrolled in different types of school settings
- enhance access for those out of school in areas where schools are small, remote, uncongenial, and under-resourced
- restructure learning tasks to reflect learners' capabilities and capacities which vary widely and are often largely ignored in monograde teaching groups
- reduce age ranges within classes through more effective management of class groups
- manage learning progression more effectively, make greater use of readiness to learn and successful mastery as criteria for progression, and reduce repetition rates where these are high
- make more use of peer learning where pupils learn from each other and from older children
- deploy teachers more efficiently, reduce the range of class sizes, and improve the quality of learning in both small and larger schools
- create possibilities for greater community involvement in primary schooling
- control and in some cases reduce costs of delivering effective learning to marginalised populations.

Realistic appraisals of costs and benefits and comparative advantages of different kinds of multigrade approaches are needed and are widely lacking. Multigrade teaching may offer higher quality at lower cost in some circumstances (especially in small schools). It is not of itself a solution to oversize classes. The development costs may be significant, but probably little more than those for quality learning and teaching in monograde classes.

Multigrade approaches to reorganising primary provision are not a panacea which can resolve all the obstacles that surround achieving EFA. They do open up a range of options that can complement monograde approaches and which promise real gains if selectively applied. Multigrade challenges orthodoxies of how pupils learn, how curricula are designed, how learning materials are presented, how teachers teach, and how schools are organised. Multigrade is best seen as part of a package of interventions that could improve access, efficiency and quality across all schools. It will develop alongside monograde. It has real potential which is under-utilised, under-promoted and under-developed. It is a way forward that cannot be neglected and needs systematic development and application with due attention to its costs and benefits.

REFERENCES

Anderson-Levitt, K., Block, M. and Soumare, A. (1994) *Inside Classrooms in Guinea: Girls' experiences.* Washington, DC: World Bank.

Bray, M. (2000) *Double Shift Schooling: Design, operation and cost effectiveness.* Paris and London: International Institute for Educational Planning and Commonwealth Secretariat.

Bruns, B., Mingat, A. and Raktomalala, R. (2003) *A Chance for Every Child: Achieving universal primary education by 2015.* Washington, DC: World Bank.

Colclough, C., Al Samarrai, S., Rose, P. and Tembon, M. (2003) *Achieving Schooling for All in Africa: Cost, commitment and gender.* Aldershot: Ashgate.

Colclough, C. with Lewin, K.M. (1993) *Educating All the Children: Strategies for primary education in developing countries.* Oxford: Oxford University Press..

Lavy, C. (1992) *Investment in Human Capital: Schooling supply constraints in rural Ghana.* Working Paper 93. Washington, DC: World Bank.

Lewin, K.M. (2004) *Mapping the Missing Link. Financing secondary schooling in Sub Saharan Africa: An overview of key issues for secondary education in Africa and their implications for resource allocation and finance.* Secondary Education in Africa Programme (SEIA). Washington, DC: World Bank. Online. Available HTTP: http://www.worldbank.org/afr/seia/docs_conf_0604.htm (24 January 2005).

Lewin, K.M. and Caillods, F. (2001) *Financing Secondary Education in Developing Countries: Strategies for sustainable growth.* Paris: International Institute for Educational Planning.

Little, A. (1995) *Multigrade Teaching: A review of research practice.* London: ODA Research Serial 12.

Little, A.W. (2001) Multigrade teaching: towards an international research and policy agenda. *International Journal of Education and Development*, 21:6, 481–498.

Mingat, A., Rakotomalala, R. and Tan, J.P. (2002) *Financing Education for All by 2015: Simulations for 33 African countries.* Africa Region Human Development Working Paper Series. Washington, DC: World Bank.

Thomas, C. and Shaw, C. (1992) *Issues in the Development of Multigrade Schools.* World Bank Technical Paper 172. Washington, DC: World Bank.

United Nations (2000), *United Nations Millenium Declaration.* New York: UN.

UNESCO (2000) *A Framework for Action.* Dakar: World Education Forum, and Paris: UNESCO.

UNESCO (2002) *Education for All: Is the world on track?* Global Monitoring Report, 2002. Paris: UNESCO.

UNESCO (2003) *Gender and Education for All: The leap to equality.* Global Monitoring Report 2003/4. Paris: UNESCO.

CHAPTER THIRTEEN

ESCUELA NUEVA'S IMPACT ON THE PEACEFUL SOCIAL INTERACTION OF CHILDREN IN COLOMBIA

CLEMENTE FORERO-PINEDA, DANIEL ESCOBAR-RODRÍGUEZ AND DANIELKEN MOLINA[1]

This chapter presents the results of research on the impact of *Escuela Nueva* methodologies on the peaceful social interaction of children. Three main research questions are addressed. First, does the *Escuela Nueva* schooling methodology have an impact on the peaceful social interaction of children? Second, do the perceptions and behaviour of families and the community change as a result of the influence of schooling methodologies? Third, what long-term impact does *Escuela Nueva* have on selected aspects of democratic and peaceful social interaction behaviours? The chapter will address these questions in three stages. First, it briefly describes *Escuela Nueva* methodologies and reviews previous evaluations of cognitive and behavioural achievements. Second, it describes methods, data bases and statistical procedures used to address the research questions. Third, it presents the results of the analyses in relation to the three main questions.

As part of the analysis of the first question, the impact of external levels of violence on the peaceful social interaction of children was evaluated. The relevance of this research for a country like Colombia, where it was applied, stems from the fact that it has one of the highest rates of homicide in the world. The analysis of the second question goes beyond the debate about the relative importance of family and school in the formation of the social behaviour of children, into showing that these are not independent causal entities. For that, it develops in some detail various relationships between schooling models and family behaviour. The third question is a first approximation to a comparative evaluation of the long-term effects of primary school methodologies on young adults.

A.W. Little (ed.), *Education for All and Multigrade Teaching: challenges and opportunities*, 265–300.

ESCUELA NUEVA

The methodology

Escuela Nueva is an educational innovation applied since 1976 in Colombia and other countries of the world. It is intended to promote 'active, participatory and cooperative learning'[2] among primary school students. The model combines a classroom pedagogy (centred on self-paced and self-directed learning guides, and multigrade schooling) with student government, and with spaces for par-ent and community involvement. It has been mainly applied in the rural areas,but in recent years it has reached urban schools, where it is known as*escuela activa*.

Participation of children and teachers in all components of the schooling system is a central characteristic of *Escuela Nueva*. Each procedure and each agent is part of a participatory process.[3] Individual learning guides, student government, parent and community workshops, and teacher training are intended to build social knowledge and practice democracy. The education process is defined as a project that is shared by students, teachers, administrative agents and the community.[4]

In Colombia, approximately 20,000 of the 29,896[5] rural public schools claim to follow the methodology of *Escuela Nueva*. In Guatemala and Nicaragua, school reform programmes based on *Escuela Nueva* have reached 2,000 schools.[6] Other countries have implemented projects that take some of the features of this model. More than 100 Chilean teachers have been trained in Colombia; 3,800 *escolas ativas*, based on the same principles, are operating in Brazil; in Paraguay they have been called *mitairu*, a Guarani word; and in the Dominican Republic they are known as *escuelas multigrado innovadas*. The methodology has also been influential in all Central American and Andean countries, and in some countries in Africa and the Philippines. In Egypt, individual guides and manuals were published in Arabic. Mexico, Panama, Honduras, Salvador and Guyana are carrying out pilot programmes.[7]

Escuela Nueva was created in 1976, when Colombian rural schools did not offer complete primary education. One of its stated purposes was to 'provide complete primary education and improve the efficiency of rural schools, especially multigrade schools'.[8] The project was created based on UNESCO's *unitary school* and was complemented with pedagogic strategies used in multigrade schools that appeared to be effective in rural schools.[9]

As a system, *Escuela Nueva* integrates curricular, administrative, community-involvement and teacher-training strategies. It develops a curriculum centred in daily life, so that contents are relevant both to children and the rest of the community. Evaluation and levelling are flexible, in the sense that children may meet their learning goals according to their own learning rhythm and time available.

This methodology implements several characteristics borrowed from multigrade schooling:[10]

- Children of different ages and grades may share classroom and tutor.
- Tutors stay with each child during sufficiently large time spans to support individualised learning by students.
- Teachers are trained in group management and the simultaneous use of curricula for children of different ages.
- Classroom spaces are organised to facilitate multigrade schooling.
- A sequence of workshops ensures the training and follow-up of teachers.[11]
- A workshop led by a national team trains regional teams. The objective is to have regional training teams promoting and organising the system.
- Initiation workshops, where teachers learn to implement the system in the school and the community, take place. When the teacher has been able to mobilise the community in favour of the new model, she attends other levels of workshops.
- Teachers are trained in the use and adaptation of individual study guides. The teacher learns to apply the guides in the specific context of her school.
- Teachers are trained to organise and use the school and classroom libraries.
- Teachers attend local follow-up workshops. As the model evolved, they became 'micro-centres' where teachers learn through the evaluation process, analyse individual problems and construct solutions in a participatory learning process.
- Model schools have been organised. These are schools where the model has been fully and successfully implemented. Teachers from the whole region attend special workshops at these schools.

Evaluations of Escuela Nueva

Several evaluations of *Escuela Nueva* have been made concerning the impact of this methodology on both cognitive competences and civic and democratic behaviour.

Cognitive achievements

The evaluations of Rojas and Castillo (1988), Psacharopoulos (1993) and McEwan (1998) have found the same results: '*Escuela Nueva* schools have better levels of Spanish and mathematics in tests to third and fifth graders. On the other hand, it was found that *Escuela Nueva* children have higher degrees of self-esteem'.

Rojas and Castillo (1988) and Psacharopoulos (1993) used the results obtained in the Ministry of Education test of 1987 in Spanish, mathematics, creativity, self-esteem and social and civic behaviour in 168 *Escuela Nueva* rural schools and 60 conventional rural schools, in the regions of Boyaca, Caldas, Cauca, Córdoba, Cundinamarca, Huila, Nariño, Norte de Santander, Santander, Sucre, Valle del Cauca and Tolima. In these regions, *Escuela Nueva* was already well established and developed as a system. Besides, schools in the sample of each region were selected so as to ensure that the system had been implanted at least three years earlier.

Rojas and Castillo (1988) analysed the differences in the achievements reached by students of conventional and *Escuela Nueva* programmes. Their research uses a set of qualitative variables to show that *Escuela Nueva* schools are more involved in the life of the community, and their teachers are better trained and reach higher levels of fulfilment. Although 42% of the *Escuela Nueva* schools in the sample had not established a student government, these schools achieved the highest levels of participation in activities related with the community. These authors conclude that '*Escuela Nueva* shows significantly higher test scores than traditional schools in civic behaviour, social self-concept, third grade mathematics and third and fifth grade language' (Rojas and Castillo 1988: 189).

Psacharopoulos (1993) estimated a production function for the students of third and fifth grade in each type of schooling system: *Escuela Nueva* and conventional. Applying ordinary least squares, he found that third-graders attending *Escuela Nueva* exhibit higher and statistically different achievements in mathematics, Spanish, creativity and self-esteem tests. Further, the achievements of the fifth-graders of *Escuela Nueva* were higher and statistically different in Spanish tests, but were not significant in other tests. Through the estimation of a logit model, he demonstrated that fifth-graders of *Escuela Nueva* have a lower probability of drop-out than students of conventional schools, and found that the labour experience of children – very common in Colombia's rural areas – has the higher explanatory power for the probability of drop-out.

McEwan (1998) criticised the estimation of Psacharopoulos (1993). He argued that although Psacharopoulos' model is parsimonious, its results are biased by the omission of important input variables. Psacharopoulos' study does not take into account variables reflecting the inputs of *Escuela Nueva* associated to the school and the classroom. This omission introduces a bias. The performance of the average school of each type is compared, but this ignores different degrees of implementation of *Escuela Nueva* methodologies, and the observation that some conventional schools apply certain features of *Escuela Nueva*.

Accordingly, McEwan (1998) used data from a 1992 survey of 52 randomly chosen schools (24 *Escuela Nueva* and 26 conventional), in the regions of Cauca, Nariño and Valle. He did not establish an additional criterion to select the schools (like the number of years of operation with the new methodology), so his results might be biased by the number of years that *Escuela Nueva* schools have been working with this methodology: students reported in *Escuela Nueva* might have studied until the fourth grade with the traditional system. Consequently, the results may have underestimated the effects of *Escuela Nueva* methodologies on students' achievements.

Nonetheless, McEwan measured the occurrence of certain inputs that are specific to the *Escuela Nueva* methodology. The proportion of classroom libraries of *Escuela Nueva* doubles that of conventional schools (66% and 33%). Group learning in Spanish and mathematics is significantly more frequent in *Escuela Nueva*. Individual learning predominates in conventional schools.

As in previous studies, McEwan measured the achievements of third and fifth graders in Spanish and mathematics tests.[12] In both tests, third- and fifth-graders of the *Escuela Nueva* system reached a statistically higher score than students of the conventional system. The difference in the results obtained for fifth-graders is not as high as for third-graders. The impact of the *Escuela Nueva* system on mathematics results is not as large as that observed for Spanish. The author suggests that this might be related to a lower quality of the fifth-grade mathematics study guide.

In addition, McEwan observed that although less than 50% of *Escuela Nueva* schools were fully equipped with basic inputs required by the system to function, their impact on the community is consistently larger than that of other educational systems.[13] He concluded that future research should be done to clarify which of the elements of the *Escuela Nueva* system may be eliminated to reduce administrative costs, without affecting the positive effects of the system on student achievements. Also he suggested further research on what happens in the classroom.

The studies by Psacharopoulos, Rojas and Castillo and McEwan are perhaps the most comprehensive comparative evaluations of *Escuela Nueva* and conventional methodologies made before 2001, but there are other important evaluations of *Escuela Nueva*.

Misión Social and DNP (1997) used the results of the SABER tests to study the achievements of *Escuela Nueva*. Controlling for the socio-economic level of the households and for the type of area (urban or rural), they found that students of the *Escuela Nueva* system show a better performance. *Escuela Nueva* students with a socio-economic level lower than average achieve higher test scores than high-income students of rural households attending conventional schools. Their main conclusion is that *Escuela Nueva* methodologies are able 'to compensate for limitations in initial endowments related to the low socio-economic level' of students. This was the first study that applied multilevel analysis to measure academic differences among students. Ordinary least squares had been applied by all previous statistical evaluations, thereby ignoring the hierarchical structure of educational data.

In 1998, the Latin American Laboratory for the Evaluation of the Quality of Education (LLECE) published a study comparing the level attained in mathematics and language by rural and urban elementary schools in all Latin American countries.[14] It found that Colombia, where the majority of rural schools practise *Escuela Nueva* methodologies, had the second highest level in fourth-grade mathematics, after Cuba. Also, contrary to what was expected, rural schools outperformed urban centres and large cities in fourth-grade mathematics. In third grade, Colombian rural schools also were ahead of their urban counterparts in language, and ahead of both urban centres and megalopolis in mathematics. This country was actually the only case in Latin America where rural schools had some advantages over urban centres and large cities.

Beyond Colombia, a study from Nicaragua is reported in the *Estudio Anual 2003*, and studies of Nicaragua, Guatemala and the Philippines are reported in *The Effects of Active Learning Programs in Multi-grade on Girl's Persistence in a Completion of Primary School in Developing Countries* (Juárez and Associates 2003). Methodologically these studies do not go beyond the comparison of average values, but conclude that students in *Escuela Nueva* schools exhibit higher academic test scores, deeper involvement of the community, higher absorption rates and lower drop-out and repeating rates than conventional schools.

Some of the studies reported in this section address the issue of explaining the cognitive achievements of *Escuela Nueva*. Perhaps the most comprehensive explanation is found in Rojas and Castillo (1988), who attribute the success in cognitive achievements of *Escuela Nueva* to the following reasons:

- The *Escuela Nueva* system provides complete primary education; at the time of their research, conventional education did not in 60% of these schools.
- The programme provides children with free study guides.
- *Escuelas nuevas* have a better endowment of textbooks and libraries than conventional schools.
- The objectives of the curricula and their content are relevant for children and their families.
- Children practise group learning.
- Teachers are facilitators: they guide, supervise and evaluate children.
- Promotion to the following level is flexible and students progress at their own rate.
- The flexibility of the system may be related to lower drop-out rates, and these to higher cognitive achievements.
- Students participate in school organisation through student governments.
- The classroom is a lively place with activity centres, thematic corners and learning materials.
- The school has become an information centre for the community, containing information about families and their activities.

Civic and democratic behaviour

While many of the evaluations have focused on academic achievement, some appraisals in Guatemala and Colombia have focused on the democratic behaviour of children. Based on direct observation of behaviour, Chesterfield (1994) compared the impacts of *Escuela Nueva* and conventional systems on the democratic behaviour of students in the first and second grades, in twenty rural schools of Guatemala, ten applying *Escuela Nueva* and ten applying conventional methodologies. The study assumes that schools can generate democratic behaviours and attitudes if they enable students to: (a) demonstrate or express rational, empirical, and egalitarian beliefs about how things should work in different social situations; (b) practise interaction with peers and adults; (c) become involved in the political and social life of the school.

Each of these indicators was evaluated through the observation of specific behaviours: (a) was measured through taking turns and assisting others in different activities; (b) was measured by expressions of opinions and attitudes, and by the ability to choose among a set of viable options; (c) was measured by student participation in school organisations, such as student government, and leading fellow students when carrying out different activities.

Chesterfield (1994) found that 80% of the occurrences of turn-taking involved *Escuela Nueva* students. This result remained unchanged when the sample was separated by gender. Perhaps the most interesting observation concerned the practice of taking turns; taking turns in conventional school is always related to waiting in line to have the teacher review one's work, while in *Escuela Nueva* taking turns was a spontaneous reaction.[15] However there was no difference between the two types of school on the proxy for rational, empirical and egalitarian beliefs, i.e. assisting others in their academic work, a result that the author relates to the young age of the children.[16] Nonetheless, the few cases observed occurred in the case of *Escuela Nueva* students. As for inter-personal effectiveness, it was measured through the child's response to positive and negative feedback when completing a task, and the involvement of the student in the political and social life of the school. Results obtained for the involvement of the student in the political and social life of the school were not statistically different between the two types of school. This is explained by Chesterfield as the result of young age, when they are perhaps more attracted by other activities. Nonetheless, *Escuela Nueva* students are more interested in leading others when accomplishing group tasks.[17]

The analysis of Chesterfield assumes that the school environment and methodology are the only factors affecting civic and democratic behaviour. The study does not consider family and community environment. On the other hand it is the first evaluation of *Escuela Nueva* based on direct observation of behaviour, and this allows the construction of a detailed story of what happens in the school and the classroom.

Pitt (1999) extends Chesterfield's study substantively, in scope and methodology. Following Chesterfield's assumption that the school is the main setting where citizens form their attitudes towards democracy and political participation, Pitt (1999) asks three fundamental questions that guide her study of Colombian *escuelas nuevas*: how do *Escuela Nueva* methodologies function in the schools, how does the formation of civic knowledge differ in the two types of school, and what is the effect of civic education on *Escuela Nueva* alumni?

Pitt (1999) understands civic education as self-government, and this is determined by the knowledge of the ideals of democracy. Civic education is composed of three elements: civic knowledge, civic skills and civic dispositions. Civic knowledge is the background that a person must know before she may talk about a political event. Civic abilities refer to the intellectual abilities used to exert rights and duties. Finally, civic dispositions are understood as motivations and behaviours that must be developed in each individual for democracy to be maintained and diffused. Its main results are: (a) classroom climate is significantly better in *Escuela Nueva* schools than in the control group of *colegios agropecuarios*; (b) the level of democratic indicators is higher in *Escuela Nueva*; and (c) civic participation does not show significant differences in the two types of schools.

Methodologically, this research is very successful in combining diverse instruments to reach consistent conclusions about democratic behaviour of primary and post-primary school children. The evaluation of behaviours is based on interviews, discussion panels, surveys and direct observation of all agents concurring at the school. But the relationship between school, family and community in forming these behaviours is not explored.

RESEARCH QUESTIONS AND METHODS

Research questions and their relevance

The focus of the new research reported in this chapter is a comparison of *Escuela Nueva* and conventional schooling in terms of their impact on the peaceful social interaction of children, in six municipalities of the Eje Cafetero region of Colombia. *Escuela Nueva* has been implemented for many years in this region, ensuring that implementation indexes are high enough to make comparisons possible.

The importance of this issue stems from the fact that Colombia has one of the highest homicide rates in the world. Additionally, the levels of violence of the Eje Cafetero region have been much higher than the average of the whole country, as shown in Figure 13.1.

Figure 13.1 Homicide rates, Eje Cafetero region and Colombia, 1980–2001

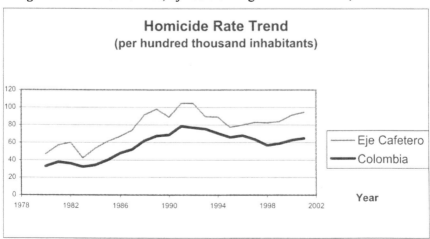

Source: Forero-Pineda and Escobar-Rodríguez (2004) based on statistics provided by DANE and DIJIN

This is of interest because the levels of violence in the communities could be related to the peaceful social interaction of children in schools. Though the results of this study are limited by the fact that only six municipalities are observed, the model controls for the impact of the level of violence in the municipality, measured by the rate of homicides, on the peaceful social interaction of children.

The first question dealt with in the research, the impact of schooling methodologies on the peaceful social interaction of children, needs to be complemented with other questions and analyses, since the behaviour of children in schools is a component of an intricate network of relationships between these children, their schools, their families, and the community. For this reason, an understanding of the determinants of this behaviour requires exploring other closely connected relations. Focusing on the impact of schooling methods and other school-related variables, on the families and the communities, and exploring the traces left by the schooling experience on alumni, a set of subsidiary relevant results is obtained. The hypothesis is that there are significant differences in the perceptions of parents and the behaviour of alumni of the two types of schools.

The research reported in this chapter differs from previous work on *Escuela Nueva* in three respects. First, it goes beyond the debate about the relative importance of school and family in the formation of democratic and peaceful social interaction behaviour, into analysing relations *between* schools and families, and measuring the impact of schooling systems *on* families and communities. Second, it explores the relationships among community, school, family and student variables, and their impact on communicative action, democratic behaviour and the peaceful social interaction of children. Third, it measures the traces of schooling methods on the behaviour of alumni.

These measurements and observations are done using different statistical methods, some of which are also new in the evaluations of *Escuela Nueva*. In the case of the behaviour of children, the methodology used is based on hierarchical multilevel models. This statistical technique allows minimising biases when estimating the impact of variables that belong to different nested contexts. Individual, school and community variables intervene as determinants of the behaviour of children, but large groups of children share the same values of school variables, and this lower variance introduces a bias against the variables of the higher level (school variables).

Until now, the academic literature has not used multilevel analysis to understand the impact of the educational system upon the democratic behaviour and the peaceful social interactions of children. The conclusions of previous behavioural studies on *Escuela Nueva* rely on direct observation and average value comparisons. In addition, this study controls for the different levels of implementation of the *Escuela Nueva* system. Some previous studies recognise the limitation of their comparisons, for not taking into account that inputs of *Escuela Nueva* are not equally provided in all schools and classrooms, and that *Escuela Nueva* methodologies have substantially permeated conventional schools. In this research, the use of the variable 'level of implementation of *Escuela Nueva* methodologies' permits a consideration of the effects of these two phenomena.

Statistical methods

All measurements and evaluations in this study are made comparing *Escuela Nueva* and conventional schools. The analysis of the impact of community, school and individual variables on peaceful social interaction uses hierarchical multilevel models. For the analysis of the relationship between schools and the family, and of the long-term traces left by the school on the behaviour of alumni, the research uses logit, probit and ordered-probit probabilistic models.

The main dependent variable in the first part of the analysis is the peaceful social interaction of children (*convivencia*). The rest of the analysis, which explores the above-mentioned complementary relationships, evaluates the impact of the main explanatory variable, the level of implementation of *Escuela Nueva* methodologies, on different variables describing the behaviour of the family, the community and alumni.

The following two sub-sections respectively describe the methodologies and present the results of the statistical exploration.

Peaceful social interaction and its determinants

Convivencia, or peaceful social interaction, is a concept of common use in Colombia to identify the conditions associated with non-violent human relations. Theoretically, it is composed of (i) active respect for others, (ii) universal solidarity, (iii) fair play and (iv) equity.[18]

Active respect was measured through questions and situations asking students about the difficulties they experience when studying or playing with children of the opposite gender, or of a different race or geographical origin. Universal solidarity was measured through questions and situations asking students about their behaviour when they relate to a stranger who is facing social problems. Fair play was measured by questions related to situations where they could take advantage of breaking rules. Equity was measured through situations where distributional issues were at stake.

Peaceful social interaction of children is assumed to be affected by different contexts. Four levels of determinants are defined accordingly: the student, the classroom, the school and the municipality. Appendix A contains the questions that were used to build this variable.

At the individual (student level) it is assumed that peaceful social interaction is affected by individual cognitive and behavioural variables: the development of communicative skills (communicative action) and democratic behaviours. Higher levels of communicative skills and democratic behaviours are expected to be related to higher levels of the students' peaceful social interaction. The results are also controlled by several variables associated with this level: age, grade, gender, moral development and household socio-economic level. The socio-economic level of the family is very hard to obtain for all children. Besides, the variance of income among the 343 parents who participated in the survey is very low. For this reason, though it is certainly a variable that may change some results in a wider context, it was not included.

For parsimony in multilevel modelling, school and classroom variables, were included in the same hierarchical level. In this level, the main independent variable is the degree or level of implementation of *Escuela Nueva* methodologies. The study controls for the impact of school and classroom climate, school management, level of education of teachers, and quality of the school infrastructure (defined in a scale from 1 to 3). We have called those variables "school variables", but we are actually referring to classroom variables, as they may take quite different values in the same school. Even the index of implementation of *Escuela Nueva* may vary between two classrooms in the same school. Other variables take the same value for all classrooms in one school.

The municipality level was explored to take into account the possible effects of the external levels of violence on the behaviour of children, the influence of a rural–urban environment and a dummy variable for the subregion where the municipality was located. The third level includes variables related to the municipality: the urban or rural environment of the school, the size of the municipality, the current rate of homicide of the municipality and the sub-region (*departamento*). The third level was not statistically significant. At the risk of introducing a bias, an additional exploration was made putting these variables at the second level, but again none of them was significant at this level, reinforcing the conclusion that only school and individual variables are significant determinants of the peaceful social interaction of children, as is shown in the following sections.

Appendix B describes in more detail the variables of the different hierarchical levels just listed. Nonetheless, additional comments are necessary concerning the 'level of implementation of *Escuela Nueva* methodologies', and the three indicators that were used to measure it.

Table 13.1 Classroom rankings and *Escuela Nueva* implementation indexes

Classroom ranking	Classroom index		Teacher index		Global index	
	New	Conventional	New	Conventional	New	Conventional
1–10	10	0	10	0	8	2
11–20	10	0	9	1	8	2
21–30	9	1	8	2	7	3
31–40	1	9	3	7	7	3
41–49	0	9	0	9	0	9
Total	30	19	30	19	30	19

The index of implementation of Escuela Nueva methodologies
Although the system of *Escuela Nueva* is not established in all primary rural schools of Colombia, its influence has been pervasive and most rural conventional schools have adapted some aspects of its methodologies. Though many schools practise the whole combination of methodologies of *Escuela Nueva,* some schools that claim to follow these methodologies actually do so in a limited manner, or each classroom implements these methodologies to varying degrees within the same school. At the same time, some conventional schools use the methods of *Escuela Nueva* variously.

Accordingly, an index is built for the purpose of measuring the degree to which these methodologies have been implemented in each school and classroom. This allows going beyond the formal classification of schools as *Escuela Nueva* or conventional, and overcoming the limitations of a binary classification.

The level of implementation of *Escuela Nueva* has two components: the organisation of the classroom and the training of teachers are the most important. Accordingly, two different implementation indexes are built, measuring the degrees of classroom implementation and teacher implementation. A composite index, called global implementation combines the two measures.

The classroom implementation index is an aggregate measure of the existence and practice of certain physical and organisational features of *Escuela Nueva*: desk or table organisation (individual, couple, group), the way subjects are presented and developed, the use and number of personal study guides available, the frequency of group activities, the existence and use of classroom libraries and learning corners, and curricular flexibility. The teacher implementation index measures the level of pedagogical training received by the teacher to apply this methodology. Its two main components are the number and level of training workshops they have attended, and level of micro-centre activities. The global implementation index aggregates the variables of the other two indexes. The indexes range from 0, describing the purely conventional school, to 100, for a school reporting the full implementation of *Escuela Nueva* methodologies.

The use of continuous-value indexes like these to describe the degree to which an educational innovation has been implemented is of great importance for the research about innovations that are not fully applied or those that have a pervasive influence on other systems.

Table 13.1 shows that despite spillovers of *Escuela Nueva* methodologies across all types of schools, those formally classified as *Escuela Nueva* have a higher index of implementation. In general these indexes show a good discriminatory power between self-declared *Escuela Nueva* and conventional schools, and this validates the choice of a continuous index rather than a dichotomous or dummy variable.

The mobility of teachers, from one type of school to the other, explains the lower discriminatory power of the teacher implementation index when applied to predict the methodology declared by the administration of each school. In general, it was observed in the field that these teachers bring the *Escuela Nueva* training with them, when they are appointed to conventional schools, though they face material limitations. On the other hand, classroom implementation is an almost perfect predictor of the declared type of school. Only one *Escuela Nueva* classroom appears to be below one conventional school classroom. As the global index aggregates these two indexes, its power to differentiate between the two types of schools is intermediate.

Appendix C describes the methods used to build composite indicators for the different variables (both dependent and explanatory) using principal component procedures.

The database

The database was constructed with information obtained from a survey applied in 2001 to third- and fifth-grade students of 25 schools in six municipalities of the Eje Cafetero region in Colombia.[19] The total number of observations is 989. The survey was applied in 15 *Escuela Nueva* schools, and in ten conventional schools. Additionally, the study gathered information from 49 teachers, 24 school principals, 343 parents, and 179 alumni. These surveys were used to estimate the effects of the educational system on the families, the community and the alumni.

SCHOOL IMPACT ON PEACEFUL SOCIAL INTERACTION

Mean values of peaceful social interaction

Table 13.2 shows the mean value of peaceful social interaction, the dependent variable. These differences do not attain statistical significance and the more powerful tools of hierarchical models are required to compare the two types of schools, so as to analyse and compare the effects of the implementation of *Escuela Nueva* and other variables on the index of peaceful social interaction.

Table 13.2 Mean values of peaceful social interaction, by school type

School type	Grade	Peaceful social interaction
Conventional	3	**70.02** *16.07*
	5	**79.28** *14.12*
	Total	**75.33** *15.66*
Escuela Nueva	3	**74.22** *17.20*
	5	**78.99** *13.86*
	Total	**76.66** *15.75*

Mean values in bold *Standard deviations in italic*

Determinants of children's behaviour

Results of hierarchical models
Table 13.3 shows the results of running the empty model and four alternative full models. Each column presents the results of one regression model. These models differ in the indicators that were chosen to measure key independent variables. Specifically, only one index of democratic behaviour and only one index of implementation of *Escuela Nueva*

methodologies were included. Also, in one of the regressions, grade was not included to observe the sensitivity of the results to this change.

The following variables that were explored in the model were not included in Table 13.3, because they were not significant in any of these regressions: school climate, political management of the school, level of formal education of the teacher, infrastructure of the school (quality and state of the building), habitat (urban, semi-urban, rural), homicide rate of the municipality, and sub-region *(departamento)* where the municipality is located (see Appendix B).

The statistical exploration with hierarchical models summarised in Table 13.3 shows positive significant relationships among communicative action, democratic behaviour of three types (those related with the institutions of direct, participatory and representative democracies) and peaceful social interaction. This validates a general hypothesis of the study in the sense that communicative action is directly related to democratic behaviours, and these are related to peaceful social interaction.

Table 13.3 Determinants of peaceful social interaction *(convivencia)*

Variables	Empty model	Model 1	Model 2	Model 3	Model 4
Constant	**75.94** *1.05*	**64.5** *2.61*	**64.58** *2.62*	**65.13** *2.62*	**64.28** *2.62*
Age		**0.55** *0.25*	**0.53** *0.25*	**0.53** *0.25*	**0.54** *0.25*
Grade		**4.78** *0.82*	**4.89** *0.82*	**4.63** *0.83*	**4.6** *0.82*
Sex		**4.78** *0.7*	**4.74** *0.7*	**4.66** *0.7*	**5.14** *0.71*
Moral development		**0.09** *0.02*	**0.09** *0.02*	**0.09** *0.02*	**0.08** *0.02*
Democratic behaviour (direct democracy)		**0.08** *0.02*	**0.08** *0.02*	*	*

Table 13.3 continued

Variables	Empty model	Model 1	Model 2	Model 2	Model 4
Democratic behaviour (participatory democracy)		*	*	**0.07** *0.02*	*
Democratic behaviour (representative democracy)		*	*	*	**0.11** *0.03*
Communicative action		**0.06** *0.02*	**0.06** *0.02*	**0.07** *0.02*	**0.08** *0.02*
Global index of implementation of *Escuela Nueva*		**0.08** *0.03*	*	*	*
Classroom index of implementation of *Escuela Nueva*		*	*	*	*
Teacher index of implementation of *Escuela Nueva*		*	**0.05** *0.01*	**0.06** *0.01*	**0.06** *0.01*
Classroom climate		**0.09** *0.03*		**0.1** *0.03*	**0.1** *0.03*
School variance	**23.32** *7.71*	**21.6** *7.07*	**21.54** *7.06*	**21.59** *7.07*	**21.53** *7.05*
Student variance	**195.74** *6.78*	**170.88** *5.92*	**171.54** *5.94*	**171.5** *5.94*	**170.28** *5.9*
School-level explanation	**10.64%**	**11.22%**	**11.16%**	**11.18%**	**11.22%**
$R^2_{students}$		0.12	0.12	0.12	0.12
R^2_{school}		0.09	0.09	0.09	0.10

Coefficients in bold
Standard deviation in italic
* Variables not included in the regression shown in that column

All statistically significant variables in the peaceful social interaction models (both school- and children-level variables) have a positive impact on the peaceful social interaction of children. It is interesting to note that both the level of teacher and classroom implementation of *Escuela Nueva* methodologies have positive effects on the peaceful social interaction of children. Nonetheless, classroom implementation is not significant. The training of teachers and their participation in 'micro-centre' activities, the two main variables in defining the level of implementation of *Escuela Nueva*, show a greater impact on peaceful social interaction than the way the classroom is arranged, the use of libraries, and other physical and organisational components of the *Escuela Nueva* system.

Age, grade and moral development of children are children-level variables that improve the conditions for peaceful social interaction. Gender comparisons show that boys have slightly higher levels of peaceful social interaction behaviour. Besides the level of implementation of *Escuela Nueva* methodologies, the only variable of the school level that has a significant impact on peaceful social interaction is the classroom climate.

Violence in the environment and the behaviour of children
The most important variable of those considered at the municipality (third) level of the model was the rate of homicides. This variable should allow testing of the hypothesis that the behaviour of children is related to the levels of violence in the social environment where the school is located. If this hypothesis could be verified, there should be significant differences between the behaviours of children of municipalities with low and high rates of homicides.

Running the model with three levels showed that the third-level group of variables was not significant. To check the validity of this result, these variables were then introduced as second-level variables, and the model was run with only two levels. As expected,[20] none, including the homicide rate, appeared to be significant. These results suggest that the differences of behaviour between municipalities with high and low rates of homicides are not significant.

The municipalities chosen for the study exhibit a wide range of values in their homicide rates, going from values close to the average of the whole country to almost four times that average value. The variance of the six municipalities is actually larger than the variance of the 24 regions of Colombia, and it is also above the variance of the 40 municipalities in the two sub-regions (Caldas and Quindío) where the six municipalities chosen are located.[21] The bias introduced by the larger variance of the group of six should favour the appearance of a statistically significant influence of the rate of homicide on peaceful social interaction. Still, this variable does not show to be significant in the model, either when it is part of a three-level model, or when it is included with the variables of the second level. Though the municipality sample is small (six out of 40 in the two subregions), these results are indicative that this is not a significant variable in the determination of peaceful social interaction of children in the schools. The result is certainly valid for the schools and grades observed in the study, where the peaceful social coexistence of children from different municipalities cannot be expected to be significantly different, despite the very large differences in the surrounding levels of violence.

Figure 13.2 Homicide rates, 2001 by six municipalities, Eje Cafetero and Colombia

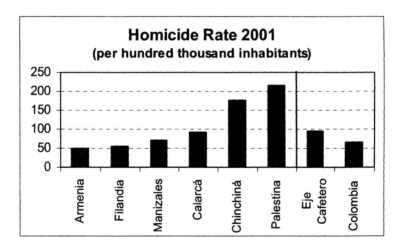

Source: Forero-Pineda and Escobar-Rodríguez (2004) based on statistics provided by DANE and DIJIN

THE IMPACT OF SCHOOLING METHODOLOGIES ON THE FAMILY, THE COMMUNITY AND ALUMNI

In the following sections, the complementary results concerning parents, alumni and community are presented. The main research questions addressed in this section are: (i) do the perceptions and behaviour of families and the community change as a result of the influence of schooling methodologies? (ii) What long-term impact does *Escuela Nueva* have on selected aspects of democratic and peaceful social interaction behaviours? The first question is addressed in the next two sections, and the second question is dealt with in the last subsection before the conclusion.

Differences in perceptions and behavioural changes acknowledged by parents and alumni were the basis for the analysis of the impact of the school type on the family and the community and alumni. The first hypothesis was that *Escuela Nueva* and conventional schools would show significant differences both in perceptions and behaviour of parents. The second was that it is possible to detect significant traces on alumni of the schooling received in the two types of schools.

The analysis of impact of school methodologies on parents and alumni was made through probabilistic logit and probit models. These models show the progression of the probability of a certain answer when the value of the independent variable changes. The independent variable chosen for most models was the index of implementation of *Escuela Nueva* methodologies in each school. The value of this index for each school was calculated as the average of the implementation indexes of the different grades surveyed. Other independent variables whose effect on these answers were explored, and which sometimes exhibited a significant impact, include the age of the child, the socio-economic level of the family, the experience of the teacher and the frequency of each parent's participation in school activities.

The impact of the school on parent behaviour and perceptions

A total of 343 parents answered complete questionnaires. In order to balance the sample so as to have approximately the same number of observations among *Escuela Nueva* and conventional school parents, the base was expanded to 746 observations. The general result of these explorations is that parents of children attending *Escuela Nueva* show a higher propensity to change their behaviour, and a higher probability that they would consider that the school has an influence on the community. This could be explained by the closer involvement of these parents in the activities of the school, and also, as one of the questions they answered confirmed, that this influence was mainly exerted through the children at home. Table 13.4 below shows the results having a statistical significance higher than 95%.

When asked whether there is an influence of the school on the way they reprimand or punish their children, 73% of all parents give an affirmative answer. The probability that a parent gives a positive answer to this question significantly increases with the global implementation of *Escuela Nueva* methodologies. Other variables having a favourable influence on positive answers to this question are the age of the child and the family's socio-economic level.

When asked whether the assignment of domestic activities has changed as a result of what children have learned in school, 70% of parents answer affirmatively. The number of years of the child in that school is the first variable associated with a positive answer to this question, and the level of global and teacher implementation are also associated with a positive answer.

Parents were asked if they stimulate their children to become school ombudswomen or ombudsmen: 79% of them gave a positive answer. The probability of a positive answer increases with the global implementation index of *Escuela Nueva* methodologies, socio-economic level and the experience of the teacher in *Escuela Nueva*.

Though, on average, parent participation in school activities is higher in *Escuela Nueva,* it is interesting to consider the frequency of this participation in the case of each parent as an independent variable. It was found that when parent participation in school activities is higher, it is more likely that they perceive that their children accept different opinions among their peers, and that what children have learned at school has had an influence on changes in permission rules at home and the way family decisions are made.

Table 13.4 Estimation of the influence of the global level of implementation of *Escuela Nueva* on perceptions and behavioural changes of parents

Question	Probability of a positive answer	Coefficient	Standard deviation	Other significant determinants
Was there an influence of the school on changes in the way you reprimand or punish your children?	73.12	0.1661	0.075	Age of child, socioeconomic level
Has the assignment of domestic activities changed as a result of what children learn at school?	71.52	0.5854	0.0113	Years at same school, teacher implementation
Do you stimulate your children to become school ombudsmen or women?	79.54	0.192	0.057	Socioeconomic level, teacher experience in

Also, with a higher participation in school activities it is more likely that the family collectively solves home problems rather than putting this responsibility on the shoulders of one of its members. Other results show that when a child is forbidden to do something the probability that she asks for an explanation increases with the socio-economic level of the family. As the level of global implementation increases, children tend to help their parents more in their labour. Appendix D shows other questions for which no significant relationships with independent variables were obtained.

The impact of the school on the community (as indicated by parent perceptions)

In this sub-section, the impact of the level of implementation of *Escuela Nueva*, and other secondary variables, on community-related decisions of parents is explored.

The level of teacher implementation of *Escuela Nueva* is significantly related to a positive answer when parents are asked whether what children learn at school has influenced family decisions relating to the community. A variable showing the same positive influence on these decisions is the frequency of parent participation in school activities.

Sixty per cent of parents gave a positive answer when asked whether the work done by the school has had an influence on the community electing their leaders with a criterion of quality in their expected performance. The probability of a positive answer increases with the level of classroom implementation of *Escuela Nueva*. The coefficient of this (positive) relationship is 0.5038 and the standard deviation is 0.113.

The classroom level of implementation of *Escuela Nueva* is also strongly related to the probability that parents participate in monitoring community projects and resources and acknowledge that this is related to school activities. When the index of implementation is low, the probability of a positive answer is 33%, and almost doubles as the level of implementation approaches 100%. The coefficient of this relationship is 0.7776 and the standard deviation is 0.134.

The analysis shows that the level of teacher implementation is highly related to parents claiming that trust and respect among families has increased as a result of school activities. While the probability of a positive answer for the whole sample is 0.7951, the coefficient of the relationship between teacher implementation and this probability is 0.1237 and the standard deviation is 0.038.

Seventy-two per cent of parents claim that school activities have helped them to organise and solve community problems. The probability of a negative answer diminishes with the socio-economic level of parents.

Sixty-three per cent of parents answered that school activities have encouraged them to learn about the problems of other families and help solve them. A higher socio-economic level is related to lower probabilities of a positive answer.

Thirty-nine per cent of parents believe that school activities have encouraged them to participate in the sessions where the Municipal Education Plan is drafted. The regression shows that the number of years that the child has attended an *Escuela Nueva* school has a positive relationship with an affirmative answer to this question.

No significant results were obtained for whether parents believed that the activities of the school developed with the parents have helped the community to participate in the process of making the Municipal Education Plan or in monitoring it.

Long-term impact of the school on alumni perceptions and behaviour

The long-term effects of schooling methods are analysed through questionnaires applied to 179 alumni from both types of school. The average age of alumni in the sample is 15.9 and standard deviation is 4.9. Most are in secondary school, but some have finished or dropped out of school. Alumni from conventional schools have an average age of 16.3 years, with standard deviation of 5.4; the average age of alumni from *Escuela Nueva* is 15.5 and the standard deviation is 4.4. Schools were responsible for identifying alumni and inviting them to the meetings. All those who came to the meetings filled in the questionnaire.

Table 13.5 Structure of the alumni sample

Schooling system	Interviews	%
Conventional	80	44.7
Escuela Nueva	99	55.3
Total	**179**	**100.0**

The questionnaire for alumni shared some questions with that of students, though with some adaptation. Some questions, such as one related to their participation in voluntary organisations, were added. The size of the sample and the smaller number of questions did not allow researchers to apply multi-level hierarchical analysis, but probit, ordered probit and multinomial logit probabilistic models were used for the analysis of the different items in the questionnaire.

Participation of alumni in voluntary social organisations
The research explored the propensity of alumni to join voluntary organisations. The affiliation of citizens to voluntary organisations has been identified with social capital, an asset explaining differences in the success of adults having accumulated the same levels of physical and human capital,[22] and also facilitating the accumulation of human capital. The central issue here was whether there is a relationship between the type of school and the propensityto join various types of voluntary organisation. The questionnaire asks about membership in different types of organisation in the past two years. The number of organisations where the alumni has been a member in the past two years is set as the dependent variable, and the type of school is the independent variable.

The regression obtained through a simple probit model, though significant only to 80%, shows that alumni participating in a larger number of voluntary organisations have a higher probability of being alumni from *Escuela Nueva*.

When using an ordered probit model, which allows multiple values, the dependent variable is defined as the number of organisations the alumni has been affiliated to in the past two years. This number is larger for *Escuela Nueva* than for conventional schools, at 90% significance.

Other significant results about alumni
The probability that *Escuela Nueva* alumni vote to decide what to do for Labour Day is higher than that for conventional school alumni. In contrast, it is more probable that conventional school alumni vote to change the president of the community grass-root organisation board.[23] This shows a relative preference on the part of *Escuela Nueva* alumni for participatory democracy, while conventional school alumni seem to be more oriented towards representative democracy.

Comparing it with other results reinforces this conclusion. While conventional school alumni have a higher probability of acknowledging that the mayor of the town has asked them to vote for a certain initiative, *Escuela Nueva* alumni are more likely to present an initiative of their own to the mayor of the town. Furthermore, *Escuela Nueva* alumni collaborate more with local authorities, as shown by a regression with 90% significance.

Escuela Nueva alumni also show more respect for ideas proposed by women. With 90% significance, they are more open to deal with persons from other races, though the question was asked in negative terms, and this limits its validity. Another regression shows that *Escuela Nueva* alumni are more disposed to expect discussions to end with an agreement.

The second part of Appendix D shows the questions that did not show significant results.

CONCLUSIONS

The comparison between *Escuela Nueva* and conventional schools was made for children, their parents and alumni. It was shown that the use of *Escuela Nueva* methodologies has a significant positive impact on the peaceful social interaction of children. Other variables positively related to peaceful social interaction in the five full models that were run are the following:

- *Child level*: age, grade, sex, moral development, the three types of democratic behaviour defined, and communicative action.
- *School level*: global index of implementation, teacher index of implementation, and classroom climate.

Variables such as school climate, political management of the school, level of formal education of the teacher, infrastructure of the school (quality and state of the building), habitat (urban, semi-urban, rural), homicide rate of the municipality, and sub-region *(departamento)* where the municipality is located did not show a significant influence on peaceful social interaction.

An unexpected result was that the level of violence of the municipality was not a significant determinant of peaceful social interaction of children. This means that, when considering the set of municipalities where the study was carried out, the behaviour to be expected from children in municipalities with relatively low homicide rates does not differ from that of children living in municipalities with homicide rates almost four times higher. This is extremely important for a country like Colombia, which has one of the highest rates of homicide in the world. Despite the fact that the variance of homicide rates in the municipalities chosen for the study is larger than the regional and national variances, a word of caution should be said concerning the present state of this result, since the size of the municipalities' sample is not sufficient to make a country-wide generalisation.

Notwithstanding, the system of education where children form their peaceful social interaction behaviour extends beyond the school. To obtain a more complete picture of this behaviour formation, the study also explored some relationships between the school methodology, the home and the community. We found significant positive effects of *Escuela Nueva* on some family behaviour related to home educational practices and to the influence of the school on parent participation in community life. The final question of the research was whether these behavioural differences remained after children had left primary school. We explored the traces left by schooling methodologies through questionnaires to alumni from conventional and *Escuela Nueva* schools. Some significant differences were found. The inclination of *Escuela Nueva* alumni towards participatory democracy contrasts with the inclination of conventional school alumni towards representative democracy. The propensity of *Escuela Nueva* alumni to join voluntary organisations, thereby forming social capital, was shown to be higher, though the level of significance of the relationship was only 90%. In this and other aspects, an extension of the research to other regions would considerably increase its validity.

REFERENCES

Bobbio, N. (1992) *El futuro de la democracia*. Bogotá: Fondo de Cultura Económica.

Bosker, J. (1997) *The Foundations of Educational Effectiveness*. Oxford: Pergamon.

Chesterfield, R. (1994) *Indicators of Democratic Behaviour in Nueva Escuela Unitaria (NEU) Schools*. Research Report. Guatemala: Academy for Educational Development, Juárez and Associates, Inc., and IDEAS Ltd USAID.

Colbert, V. (1999) *Mejorando el acceso y la calidad de la educación para el sector real pobre. El caso de la Escuela Nueva en Colombia*. Available at http://www.campus-oei.org/revista/rie20a04.htm (accessed 25 February 2005).

Colbert, V. (2000) Mejorando la Calidad de la Educación para el Sector Rural Pobre. El caso de la *Escuela Nueva* en Colombia: Fundación *Escuela Nueva* Volvamos a la Gente. Páginas 13 y 14.

Coleman J.S. (1990) 'Social Capital'. In *Foundations of Social Theory*. Cambridge, MA: Harvard University Press (Belknap Press).

Dewey, J. (1997) *Democracia y educación: Una introducción a la filosofía de la educación*. Madrid: Ediciones Morata S. L. 2ª edición (1ª reimpresión).

EDIHR (World Bank), Tacro (UNICEF) and Fundación *Escuela Nueva* Volvamos a la Gente (1999) *Hacia una nueva escuela para el siglo XXI*. Bogotá, Colombia: World Bank and UNICEF.

Fernández, M. and González, J. y A. (1997) *'Desarrollo y situación actual de los estudios de eficacia escolar'*, Revista electrónica de investigación y evaluación, 3: 1–3.

Forero-Pineda, C. (2001) 'Participatory democracy in Latin America: A comparative analysis'. International Society for New Institutional Economics Conference, Berkeley, Septiembre de 2001. Available online at http://www.isnie.org/ISNIE01/Papers01/forero-pineda.pdf (accessed 25 February 2005).

Forero-Pineda, C., Cortés, D., Riaga, S., Escobar, D., Molina, D., Jaramillo, H., Colbert, V., Gutierrez, M., Castillo, Z., Bernal, M., Contreras, M., Hernandez, G., Franky, J., Matiz, J.P. and Gamboa, L.F. (2002) *Escuela Nueva, Comportamiento Democrático y Convivencia.* Informe Final, Universidad del Rosario y Fundación Volvamos a la Gente, Bogotá, Julio de 2002.

Forero-Pineda, C. and Escobar-Rodríguez, D. (2004) 'School rules, democratic behaviour and peaceful social interaction of Colombian children'. In R. Ruzicka, J.H. Ballantine and J.A. Ruiz San Román (eds) *Key Contexts for Education and Democracy in Globalising Societies,* Proceedings, Education, Participation and Globalisation, Prague 2004 Conference.

Goldstein, H. (1995) *Multilevel Statistical Models.* Kendall's Library of Statistics 3. London: Arnold.

Hart, R. (1993) *La participación de los niños: De la participación simbólica a la participación auténtica,* Bogotá: UNICEF, Oficina Regional para América Latina y el Caribe.

Henao, M.L. and Acosta, O.L. 'Mejorando la Calidad de la Educación para el Sector Rural Pobre. El caso de la *Escuela nueva* en Colombia'. *Coyuntura Social,* No. 22, May.

Habermas, J. (1981) *The Theory of Communicative Action.* Two volumes. Boston, MA: Beacon Press.

Habermas, J. (1990) *Moral Conscience and Communicative Action.* Cambridge, MA: MIT Press.

Hoyos, G. (1998) 'Ética comunicativa y educación para la democracia'. In *Educación, Valores y Democracia.* Bogotá: Instituto Ser.

Instituto SER de Investigación (1980) *Seminario nacional de investigación educativa: informe final.* Bogotá: Instituto SER.

Instituto SER de Investigaciones (1982) 'El logro en matemáticas y lenguaje en la educación primaria colombiana. Una contribución a su determinación'. Bogotá: Instituto SER.

Instituto SER de Investigación (1993) *Propuesta para el diseño y desarrollo de un modelo de gestión educativa para municipios pequeños: presentada a consideración del Plan Pacífico.* Bogotá: Instituto SER.

Juárez and Associates (2003) *The Effects of Active Learning Programs in Multigrade on Girl's Persistence in a Completion of Primary School in Developing Countries.* Guatemala: Agencia para el Desarrollo Internacional USAID.

Junn, J. and Norman, H. (1999) *Education and Democratic Citizenship in America.* Washington, DC: NIE.

McEwan, P.J. (1998) 'The effectiveness of multigrade schools in Colombia'. *International Journal of Educational Development,* 18(6), 435–452.

Misión Social y DNP (1997). La calidad de la educación y el logro de los planteles educativos. *Planeación y Desarrollo,* 28(1), 47.

Nino, S. (1996) *La Constitución de la Democracia Deliberativa.* Editorial Gedisa. New Haven: Yale University Press.

Pitt, J. (1999) 'Civic Education and Citizenship in *Escuela Nueva* Schools in Colombia'. Unpublished thesis, University of Toronto, Canada.

Psacharopoulos (1993) 'Achievement evaluation of Colombia's *Escuela Nueva*: is multigrade the answer? *Comparative Education Review*, 37, 3.

Rojas, C. and Castillo, Z. (1988) *Evaluación del Programa Escuela Nueva en Colombia*. Bogotá: Instituto SER de Investigaciones.

Scheerens, J. (1998) *School Effectiveness in Developed and Developing Countries: A review of the research evidence*. Washington, DC: University of Twente/The World Bank.

Scheerens, J. and Boxer, R.J. (1997) *The Foundations of Educational Effectiveness*. Oxford: Elsevier Science.

Schiefelbein, E. (1993) *En Busca de la Escuela del Siglo XXI: ¿Puede Darnos la Pista la Escuela Nueva de Colombia?*, UNESCO-UNICEF, Orealc, Santiago de Chile. Junio.

Snijders, T.A.B. and Roel, J. (1999) *Multilevel Analysis and Introduction to Basic and Advanced Multilevel Modelling*. London: Sage.

APPENDIX A

An instrument to measure the peaceful social interaction of children ('convivencia')

Peaceful social interaction (*convivencia*) is related (Hoyos, 1998) to four behaviours: active respect for others, universal solidarity, fair play and equity. In order to measure each of these components, the following questions were asked:

Active respect

1   I help my classmates with their homework, independently of who they are.
2   I only play with a student of my own gender.
3   I do my homework with students of my own gender because they are more intelligent than the students of the opposite gender.
4   I don't care if the person with whom I work is male or female.
5   When I choose a classmate to work with, I don't care if he is older or younger than me.
6   If I have to elect a classmate to work with, the choice is not affected by his/her ethnicity.
7   If there is a new child in the school and I am asked to choose the members of a team, I start by choosing children that I already know.

Universal solidarity

1   I don't throw garbage into the river because other people might use this water.
2   What would you do if a person in your class could not afford to buy pencils?
      a   I lend my pencils.
      b   I do not lend my pencils.
      c   I talk to the teacher, so she takes care of the problem.

3   What would you do if, when you are walking out of the school, it is raining strongly:
      a   I ask a classmate if he/she wants to share my umbrella.
      b   I run away with my umbrella so I do not have to share it.
      c   I lend a small part of my umbrella, making sure I do not get wet.

4   What would you do if you are the only one to notice that your teacher
    takes two more oranges than she is supposed to, from a parent's gift.
    a   I agree with my teacher. She is older than me and she knows
        what is correct.
    b   I do not agree with her attitude because some children are
        not going to receive their orange.
    c   I propose that all children share their oranges so that
        everyone can eat fruit, and the teacher can keep the extra
        oranges.

Fair play

1   Do you agree with the following statement: Poor people can steal from
    rich people, because they do not share what they have.
2   If I am the only one to notice that one of my team-mates made a fault,
    I demand the referee to sanction the fault against my team.
3   If my best friend asks me to let her copy my answers during a test, I let
    her copy.
4   What would you do if you are the only person to notice that there are
    some leftovers from the cake we bought to celebrate the teacher's
    birthday:
    a   I eat the cake.
    b   I share it with my friends.
    c   I give it to the teacher.

Equity

1   If you have two pieces of bread, and you eat one of them, what would
    you do with the second one?
    a   I give the other to a friend.
    b   I give the other to a poor child who does not have anything
        to eat for lunch.
    c   I save the other bread for later.

2   Several days ago, some new families arrived in my town. They were
    running away from violence in their home town. Now, they are asking us
    to lend them our school for five days, but we must replace these days
    with five days of our vacation. My teacher is doing a poll to see if we
    accept this proposal:
    a   I agree because these families do not have anywhere to go.
    b   I withdraw from the decision and let other children decide.
    c   I am against it because I do not want to lose part of my
        vacation.

3   In the school 'Little Mountain', students have organised an excursion to
     Parque del Café. Francisco is in charge of collecting the money to pay
     for the bus and lunch. When he asks Marcela for her money, she says
     she cannot come because her mother does not have the money. What do
     you do?
          a   I let Marcela's mother solve the problem.
          b   Marcela should not go on the trip because she does not have
               the money to pay for it.
          c   We organise a raffle to collect the money, so Marcela can go
               with us.

APPENDIX B

Variables determining the peaceful social interaction of children

Independent variables

The independent variables of the model are directly associated to the first
and second levels of the hierarchical analysis.

First level

Age, grade, gender, moral development, democratic behaviour, communicative action and households' socioeconomic[24] level are variables directly
linked to the student. The socioeconomic level of the family is a family
variable, but as only a few children in a school share the same family, it may
be considered as an individual variable.

Communicative action is a concept developed by the German
philosopher Jurgen Habermas, related to the ethics of rational communication. To make it operational, the variable was defined as measuring the
abilities to comprehend others, to argument, to build consensus, and to
accept dissent.[25] The results of these four measurements were used to construct a composite index of communicative skills using principal components or factor analysis.

Another index was constructed for moral development. It is based on the
methodology used by Pitt (1999), which was previously explained, and
derives from the theory of moral development of Lawrence Kohlberg.[26]

The study assumes that different democratic behaviours are related to different types of democratic institutions. Accordingly, indexes were constructed for three democratic behaviours, each related to one form of democratic institution:[27] direct democracy, representative democracy, and participatory democracy.

Direct democracy is associated to groups making collective decisions. Representative democracy is associated to the process of selecting representatives who are in charge of making decisions. Participatory democracy refers to mechanisms whereby citizens and authorities act in conjunction to seek the welfare of society.[28]

Empirically, the survey measured the children's democratic behaviours with questions related to their possible reactions in specific situations related to their school, family and community. Statistical factor analysis showed that it is not appropriate to estimate a global democratic behaviour index. This implies that an improvement in direct democratic behaviour is not necessarily related to improvements of representative democratic or participatory democratic behaviours.

Second level

The second-level group variables related to the classroom and school. The level of implementation of the new school system, school and classroom climate, the quality of school management, the educational level of teachers, the quality of school infrastructure belong to this level.

School climate measures certain organisational aspects and the school's orientation towards achievement. Organisational aspects include the existence and common knowledge of rules, forms of the reward and penalty system, absenteeism, morality, and general behaviour of students. The orientation towards achievement includes aspects such as the motivation and commitment of teachers, communication among them, relations among students, and trust between the principal and teachers. Questions like the presence of alcoholism, drug dependence and other problems in the school and among parents, vandalism, occurrence of violence at school and in the families, lack of interest in learning on the part of students or parents, general attitude of teachers are included in the questionnaire that serves to measure school climate.

Classroom climate is an index that captures aspects related to organisation, good relations between the teacher and the students and satisfaction in the classroom. Organisational aspects include expectations of teachers, opinions about justice in the classroom, consistency in class management, order in the classroom, and clear rules. Good relations are related to empathy and warmness in the attitudes of teacher and students. It captures the priorities, the conflicts and the reasons for the teacher to have certain attitudes with the students.

As opposed to the variable defined as peaceful social interaction, school and classroom climates are not individually measurable behaviours but refer to general social conditions.

The index of school governance contains information about the functioning of the academic and discipline councils. Additionally, it captures whether the school follows the Institutional Education Plan[29] that schools are required to construct with the community.

Third level

The third-level variables, which include the municipality population, a dummy variable for the *department,* and the homicide rate of the municipality, were obtained from national and regional sources.[30]

APPENDIX C

The construction of indexes

The principal components procedure allows obtaining aggregation coefficients that are independent from the bias or values of the researchers. The method consists of finding an aggregate indicator of the valued response to different positively related questions. Questions that are negatively related to the indicator are successively discarded. This methodology enables the researcher to identify the variables that are positively related and statistically significant.

The procedure maximises the variance of the variables associated with the index, applying a monotonic transformation to the initial values of the variables, which guarantees that the weights assigned to answers are unchanged. Because of the ordinal nature of the answers, the procedure transforms this qualitative information into quantitative data that keeps the implicit subjective ordering of the answers. In this case, the study selected the (as good as) preference transformation rule.[31] In addition, this tool allows the wiping of the non-significant information, and assigns a weighted value to each of the final variables selected to construct the index. All the indexes are standardised and re-scaled into the 0–100 interval.

APPENDIX D

Questions to parents and alumni where no independent variables appeared to be significant

Parents

No significant results were obtained for the following questions:

24   Who establishes family rules?
- a   Each member of the family establishes his/her own rules.
- b   The family as a whole.
- c   All adults together.
- d   The father.
- e   The mother.

25   How do you help solve the problems of your children?
- a   The father helps the child to solve the problem.
- b   The mother helps the child to solve the problem.
- c   The child solves his/her problem on its own.
- d   Friends help to solve the problem.
- e   The teacher helps to solve the problem.

26   If the family has to decide what the child needs,
- a   The child receives what she wants.
- b   The child receives what she really needs.
- c   Somebody explains to the child what the family needs.

42   Which of the following home rules have been changed, influenced by what your child has learned at school:
- a   How decisions are made.

Alumni

In six questions to alumni, no significant results were obtained.

5   I have demanded that the decisions made by the grassroots' organisation board (*Junta de Acción Comunal*) be respected.

6   I participate in the activities organised by the *Junta de Acción Comunal*.

7 When we select a leader to develop a project in the community, I follow his leadership.

8 I have asked to the president of the *Junta de Acción Comunal* to explain what he has done for the community.

9 I want to be elected as a member of the *Junta de Acción Comunal*.

10 In the organisations with which I have been affiliated, I have demanded that women's opinions be respected.

NOTES

[1] Clemente Forero-Pineda is professor at Universidad de los Andes in Bogotá (Colombia). He may be contacted at cfp@adm.uniandes.edu.co. Part of the research for this chapter was carried out while he had a part-time appointment with Universidad del Rosario. Daniel Escobar Rodríguez is professional economist at Fundación Social and graduate student in Economics at Universidad del Rosario. He may be contacted at descoba@claustro.urosario.edu.co. Danielken Molina is research assistant at the Inter-American Development Bank, where his contact details are DANIELKENM@ Contractual.iadb.org, and graduate student at Universidad del Rosario. This paper reports some of the results of a research project carried out at Universidad del Rosario with the academic and logistic support of Fundación *Escuela Nueva* Volvamos a la Gente and its director, Vicky Colbert. The financial support of Colciencias is acknowledged. The authors of this paper are grateful to Darwin Cortés, Sergio Riaga, the psychologists Marybel Gutiérrez and Zoraida Castillo, all the other members of the research team, and acknowledge their participation in obtaining the results reported here. The comments and technical advice of Manuel Ramírez, Luis Piñeros, Alfredo Sarmiento, Hernán Jaramillo, Ian Plewis and of attendants to workshops and lectures at ISNIE, Stanford University, International Institute of Education and the Symposium *Prague 2004: Education, Participation, Globalisation*, were very valuable.

[2] EDIHR (World Bank), Taro (UNICEF) and Fundación *Escuela Nueva* Volvamos a la Gente (1999) Hacia una nueva escuela para el siglo XXI, pp. 20–22.

[3] Colbert, V. (1999) Mejorando el acceso y la calidad de la educación para el sector real pobre. El caso de la *Escuela nueva* en Colombia. Section 4.3. Available at http://www.campus-oei.org/revista/rie20a04.htm.

[4] EDIHR (World Bank), Taro (UNICEF) and Fundación *Escuela Nueva* Volvamos a la Gente (1999), p 5.

[5] Figures of Ministerio de Educación, Colombia.

[6] Juárez and Associates (2003).

[7] Agencia para el Desarrollo Internacional USAID y Juárez and Associates (2003), and EDIHR World Bank, Taro UNICEF and Fundación *Escuela Nueva* Volvamos a la Gente (1999).

[8] Colbert, V. (1999) Section 4.
[9] EDIHR World Bank, Taro UNICEF and Fundación *Escuela Nueva* Volvamos a la Gente (1999) p. 19.
[10] McEwan, P. (1998) The Effectiveness of Multigrade Schools in Colombia. *International Journal of Educational Development.* 18(6) pp. 435–452.
[11] SER Institute Evaluation (1987) p. 9.
[12] Institute SER designed the tests in 1992.
[13] The number of activities that were organised jointly by the school and the community measured the impact on the community.
[14] UNESCO Santiago de Chile 1998.
[15] Chesterfield (1994), *Indicators of Democratic Behaviour in Nueva Escuela Unitaria (NEU) Schools*, p. 5.
[16] Idem, p. 8.
[17] Idem, p. 12.
[18] The last two components are defined as components of justice (Hoyos, 1998).
[19] The survey was conducted in the municipalities of Manizales, Chinchiná and Palestina in the *departamento* of Caldas, and Armenia, Filandia and Calarcá, in the *departamento* of Quindío.
[20] The expectation is based on the fact that introducing a third level gives more chances to the variables included in it to be significant.
[21] The values for the standard deviation of these observations of the rate of homicides are: for the six municipalities in the sample, 0.70; for the forty municipalities of Caldas and Quindío, 0.53; for twenty-four subregions and four metropolitan areas of Colombia, 0.44.
[22] See James S. Coleman (1990) *Foundations of Social Theory.* Harvard (Belknap), chapter 12, 'Social Capital', p. 300.
[23] 'Juntas de acción comunal'.
[24] This variable was used to control for possible differences in the economic levels. It was useful in some logit and probit analyses, but due to its low variance (most households had incomes between one and two minimum wages) it was not significant in the multilevel model.
[25] See Habermas (1981) and Hoyos (1998).
[26] See Kohlberg.
[27] See Forero (2001) for a taxonomy of forms of democracy based on the theoretical work of Bobbio and Sartori and the recent practice of some Latin American countries.
[28] Forero (2001).
[29] Every school in the country is required to draft and follow an Institutional Education Plan.
[30] Population figures were obtained from www.dane.gov.co and homicide rates from National Police DIJIN statistics.
[31] Mas-Colell (1995) chapter 1 explains the implications of maintaining a specific preference ordering.

CHAPTER FOURTEEN

MULTIGRADE LESSONS FOR EFA

A Synthesis

ANGELA W. LITTLE

Chapter 1 of this book and previous reviews of research on multigrade teaching highlighted an educational paradox (Little 1995, 2001; Pridmore, 2004). If children are to learn effectively in multigrade settings teachers need to be well trained, well resourced and to hold positive attitudes to multigrade teaching. The realities of the multigrade teacher stand in stark contrast. Many teachers such as Maheswari (Chapter 1) who find themselves in settings that require multigrade teaching are either untrained or are trained in monograde pedagogy. Many teachers in multigrade settings have few if any teaching/learning resources. And, as we saw in Chapter 1, many teachers in multigrade settings regard the multigrade classroom as inferior to the better resourced monograde classroom found in large, urban schools, staffed by trained teachers.

During the nineteenth and twentieth centuries a monograded structure of mass schooling emerged as a universal ideal (Chapter 1). This ideal is reflected in the dominant construction of academic and professional knowledge that continues to surround teaching and learning worldwide. National curriculum frameworks are graded for cohorts of learners who entered school within the same calendar year. National Curriculum Authorities generate syllabi and guides for teaching based on single year grades. Teachers like Maheswari in Chapter 1, Olga in Chapter 3 and the teacher in the Tomorro mobile multigrade school in Chapter 10 struggle to meet the expectations of national education authorities using syllabi and teaching guides that have not been designed with their types of school in mind, or, in many settings, with no teaching materials at all. To meet this challenge education officials frequently express the view that multigrade teachers should adapt curriculum materials to suit their circumstances. While this view may be consistent with the rhetoric of the 'professional autonomy' of teachers it belies the fact that monograde teachers, working in the same system and in often far more advantaged settings, are not expected to do likewise. It also belies the fact that in order to meet this curriculum challenge in settings where resources are few, life is extremely hard and teachers

A.W. Little (ed.), Education for All and Multigrade Teaching: challenges and opportunities, 301–348.
© 2007 *Springer.*

isolated, effective curriculum adaptation is unlikely to occur and certainly not on a large scale.

Few teacher education systems in developing countries acknowledge the fact that many of their trainees will find themselves posted to multigrade rather than monograde schools on initial appointment. Few educational planning and financing systems embrace the fact that millions of children still live in sparsely populated rural areas requiring multigraded models of schooling (Chapters 10, 11 and 12). As we saw in Chapter 1, monograded schooling is a relatively recent historical development and educational form and arose in urbanising areas with dense populations and large student enrolments. Neither then nor now is it a form of school organisation that corresponds well with the demography of rural areas. Yet, the monograded model of schooling continues to dominate the thoughts and actions of national education policymakers, planners and the majority of local practitioners. Its dominance in the mindset obscures the fact that millions of children worldwide, both in industrialised and developing countries, are *de facto*, if not *de jure*, learning in multigrade settings. This poses a major challenge for the achievement of EFA worldwide.

This final chapter revisits the challenges posed by EFA and the potential of multigrade schooling to meet them through a synthesis of the research presented in this book and elsewhere. The synthesis is structured around three dimensions of the most recent EFA policy framework – the learner, the processes of learning and teaching and the enabling environment. The chapter concludes with '40 policy questions for proponents of EFA'.

THE CHALLENGE FOR EFA

The challenges that face multigrade teachers carry added significance in the context of the worldwide movement for Education for All (EFA), especially in relation to EFA Goals 2 and 6: viz:

> The expansion and completion of Primary Education that is free, compulsory and of good quality (Goal 2).

> The improvement of all aspects of the quality of education and ensuring excellence so that recognised and measurable learning outcomes are achieved by all, especially in literacy, numeracy and essential life skills (Goal 6).

For millions of children worldwide the *only* type of schooling to which they will gain access, *if they gain access at all*, will be multigraded. Economically and socially disadvantaged areas support disproportionate numbers of multigraded schools. Areas experiencing conflict and civil strife offer limited learning opportunities for children and, where opportunities do exist, the arrangements are often multigraded. In many disadvantaged areas the fundamental educational issue is *not* whether a school is multigraded or monograded. Rather, it is whether there is a school at all. In Chapter 10 Aikman and El Haj suggested that 15–25 million nomadic and pastoralist children are 'out of school' worldwide. To the extent that these children have a chance of any schooling at all it is likely to mobile and multigraded. Chapter 1 underlined the scale of the quantitative challenge if UPE is to be achieved. With an estimated 219 million children likely to be learning in multigraded settings in developing countries in any one year in the foreseeable future the scale of the EFA challenge is immense. This 219 million represents 33% of all primary school-age children in the developing world. And these 33% are among those for whom the EFA challenge is greatest. EFA is not a major challenge for large urban and rural schools catering to the middle classes. It is not, in most developing countries, a huge challenge for medium-sized schools organised on age-graded lines with reasonable class sizes, regularly attending teachers and learning resources. Children in these schools are supported by the system of education, by households and by communities. Improvements in the quality of education can and must be made in these and all schools. But the greater challenge for EFA is posed by those children and communities the system does not reach. These include communities where children are out of school or communities served by multigraded schools and a curriculum structure and teacher training system designed for monograded schooling.

Despite these challenges and realities it is the thesis of this chapter – and indeed of the book more generally – that multigraded schooling can make a significant contribution to the EFA goals of access and quality.

Our research has not addressed the challenges posed by EFA for adult and youth learners and adult and youth learning pedagogies. Suffice it to say that EFA Goal 6 addresses the quality of all learning and teaching settings and all learners whether child, youth or adult. How many youth and adults worldwide find themselves learning, *de facto*, in multigraded settings is completely unknown.

The most recent EFA Global Monitoring Report (UNESCO, 2004: 36, 143) sets out a policy framework for improving the quality of teaching and learning that locates learners at the centre of analysis and policy. Policies and practices for learning should start from the recognition of diversity of learners' prior knowledge, learning styles and home and social backgrounds.

> Education should be inclusive, responding to the diverse needs and circumstances of learners and giving appropriate weight to the abilities, skills and knowledge they bring to the teaching and learning process.
>
> (UNESCO, 2004: 143)

Teaching and learning are the dual, integrated processes through which learners acquire literacy and numeracy and a range of knowledge, skills, values and beliefs that constitute a good education. The Global Monitoring Report (GMR) stresses that policy priority be given to where teaching and learning takes place. It supports reforms that focus on teaching and learning outcomes: appropriate goals and relevant content; values as well as skills; sufficient and effective instructional time; structured teaching in child-centred classrooms; and assessment for learning improvement.

The GMR speaks of 'getting the enabling environment right' with good learning materials used well by teachers; a safe, healthy infrastructure; motivated teachers; and well-organised, well-led schools, strong professional support systems and knowledge infrastructures. Surrounding this enabling environment are long-term education sector policies and a nationally owned, financially realistic framework for quality related reforms (UNESCO, 2004: 185).

The first three layers of the EFA Policy Framework – (i) the learner, (ii) the learning and teaching process and (iii) the enabling environment will be used to synthesise the original research reported in this book and related research on multigraded schooling. In the final section of this chapter the outer layer – the policy framework – will be addressed through the generation of policy questions for all proponents of EFA.

THE LEARNER

We start here with the learner. We began our book with a teacher, Maheswari, and the challenges she faced. As our exploration of those challenges progressed we began to focus more and more on the learner.[1] In Maheswari's class we observed, with some concern, the amount of time learners spent awaiting her attention, awaiting instruction, as Maheswari struggled to work across six grades.

We took a step back in time and wondered how learners and teachers in Roman, Medieval, Renaissance and industrialising Europe spent their time. We noted how, in the Roman literacy class, learners arrived and left school at times of their choosing; and how they interacted individually with the teacher. Over time we found learners in groups – large and small, and of all ages – receiving instruction from a single teacher. Gradually these groups came to be graded and the printed materials on which they worked similarly so. Later still, in early nineteenth-century England we found the beginnings of organised mass education and found learners sitting and standing in large halls in groups or 'rows' directed by monitors who in turn were directed in their teaching task by a single master. The groups/rows and the materials on which learners worked were graduated by achievement and difficulty respectively. And by the twentieth century learners were sitting in groups or classes of learners of a similar age in separate classrooms with separate teachers. Large 'systems' of education began to emerge in the late nineteenth and twentieth centuries and the organisation of schools that divided and graded learners by age and learning achievement became the norm. The organisation of mass learning in schools bore resemblances to the organisation of mass production in factories in nineteenth- and early twentieth-century Europe.

While monograded schooling became the ideal that system planners strove to put in place, multigraded schooling persisted and took new forms. The several reasons for its persistence were explored in Chapter 1. By the beginning of the twenty-first century millions of learners worldwide find themselves learning in multigraded classes.

In the Turks and Caicos (Chapter 2) we observed learners in monograde and multigrade classes in teacher-dependent, learner-independent and learner-interdependent learning. In monograde classes learners spent their time in teacher-dependent whole-class work followed by silent and independent seat work. We also observed this in multigrade classes. But there were two important contrasts. Learners in multigrade classes spent more time than their monograde peers working in pairs or in small groups. And when they undertook work alone learners in multigrade classes were less likely to await direction from the teacher and more likely to take initiative in its organisation. In the monograde classes the learners' independent work remained strongly directed by the teacher (exercises corrected by the teacher followed by more exercises). A further contrast was that learners in monograde classes were exposed only to work deemed appropriate to their grade. Learners in multigrade classes, by contrast, were exposed to work of two or more grade levels. This exposure provided opportunities to both reinforce and extend learning processes.

In England (Chapter 3) we were informed by teachers that learners in multigrade classes had more opportunities than learners in monograde classes for cognitive and behavioural 'stretching and modelling' and peer tutoring. Although peer tutoring occurs in monograde classes and is thoroughly consistent with a monograde teaching and learning strategy, it seems to be encouraged more as a learning strategy by teachers in multigrade classes. In Nepal (Chapter 5) we observed how some learners were abandoned for part of the school day as their teachers divided the available time by the number of single grade classes they had to teach. In other multigraded classes we observed how learners received instruction for half the timetabled lesson and were then abandoned as the teacher moved to teach the other grade. In still others we saw how learners were provided with self-learning materials and sometimes a monitor to supervise their work when the teacher attended to another class.

But it was in the Malawian case (Chapter 6) that the issue of learner diversity – the starting point of the GMR policy framework – was addressed directly. Diversity is a feature of all classes, monograde and multigrade (Little, 2001). Learner diversity in the Malawian lower primary class manifested itself along many dimensions, including age, regularity of attendance, hunger, warm clothes in winter and possession of pen and paper. Teachers attempted to respond to learner diversity through the informal grouping of children within whole-class teaching (through, for example, different questions for different achievement levels and questions directed at specific individuals), through some individual help, and through the adjustment of task levels. Croft's account illustrates well how diversity is a characteristic of all classes, monograde and multigrade. The challenge of diversity in the multigraded class is compounded because not only are learners diverse, but the teacher is expected to 'deliver' a diverse curriculum: a different one for each grade.

LEARNING AND TEACHING

In this section on the dual and integrated processes of learning and teaching we address several dimensions. These include considerations of time, of curriculum, of assessment, of social organisation and of learning outcomes.

Learning time

One of the most crucial aspects of the teaching and learning process concerns learning time and the ways in which teachers manage time for teaching and students' time for learning. This is true for learners in multigrade and monograde settings. 'Learning Time' features at the heart of several frameworks for assessing educational quality (UNESCO, 2002, 2004/5). Most official estimates focus on *intended* learning time rather than *actual* learning time spent on learning. In Grade 1 primary the highest income countries allocate, on average 752 hours and the lowest income countries 667 hours of time for learning in school. At Grade 4 primary the averages are 818 and 751 hours respectively (UNESCO, 2002). Even in the highest-income countries this means that less than three hours per *calendar day* is, on average, available for formal learning; and in the lowest-income countries just over two hours per calendar day.

If we were to examine *actual* time spent learning we would probably find that discrepancies between intended and actual time were large and larger in poorer than in richer countries. The following two examples illustrate the discrepancy between intended and actual time. Ames (2003) examined the number of official or intended school days available in the months of June and July 2001 in one of her case study schools in the Peruvian Amazon.

> There were 20 official school days in June, but the school remained closed for 12 of these days for various reasons. On only three days were all three teachers in their classrooms, and during five days one or two of the teachers were absent. The situation improved in July, when all teachers were at school at least three days each week.
>
> (Ames, 2003: 213)

The Ministry of Education in Peru prescribes a school year of around 1,000 hours. It has estimated that children in urban schools spend approximately 500–600 hours in school each year compared with just 250 hours in rural schools (MED, 2002: 11, quoted in Ames 2003). One reason for the disparity is the time lost by teachers travelling to and from isolated communities by public transport whose schedules do not coincide with the start and finish of the school day. From Chapter 1 the reader will recall that Maheswari's colleague, Siva, faced a similar obstacle. Other reasons in Peru included the closure of schools at the end of the month to enable teachers to collect pay cheques, public holidays and climatic conditions. Teachers are sometimes posted to schools after the start of the school year, are required to attend training courses on school days and headteachers in particular are often called to administrative offices to attend to school matters (Ames, 2003). In other settings both short and prolonged periods of sick leave on the part of both teachers and students can reduce and disrupt time for learning.

The second illustration of discrepancy between intended and actual time for learning is drawn from an example in rural Sri Lanka by the author and a small group of teachers in the late 1990s (Little, 1999). Officially there were 189 days in the school year, each with eight periods of 40 minutes each, yielding an official total of 1,008 classroom instruction hours. In order to estimate time available for formal learning we deducted time spent on sports, health days, parents' days, in-service training for teachers, tests and examinations, and teacher marking of tests, plus an estimate of combined teacher and student absence (the average student and teacher absenteeism, separately, were 15% and 32% respectively). We deducted time spent by teachers moving between classes at the end of each period, and by students in eating their midday snack, tidying up and winding down at the end of the day. Teachers were keen that we also deduct their estimates of 'student day dreaming'. We were left with just 469 hours per year of actual learning time, a little under half the official/intended time – but also, we note almost twice the official estimates of actual time available for learning in Peruvian rural schools. Another way of expressing this is to say that just 1.3 hours per calendar day was available to students in rural schools in Sri Lanka for formal learning. We did not deduct students' estimates of teachers' day dreaming!

In our research we have not examined differences in learning time between rich and poor communities, rich and poor households. However we do know that many households in many countries invest in private tuition of various kinds for their children, shadow systems of teaching and learning that run in parallel with the formal institution of the school. Richer families buy into this non-formal system of schooling more than poorer. Hence any differences between actual learning time in the formal school between learners from rich and poor households are likely to be magnified when all opportunities for learning and teaching are taken into account.

Distribution of teacher time and curriculum organisation

In both estimates of learning time (above) we assumed that if the teacher was in the class then children were presented with opportunities to learn. But this assumption may be invalid. In multigrade classes *how* teachers distribute their time between learners is also critical in assessing real opportunities to learn. Some have argued that if a teacher divides her time between two grades equally the time available for learning is halved (Hargreaves *et al.*, 2001). This will be true only in classes where learning opportunities for some are abandoned when the teacher attends to others. As we shall see below, this condition obtains in some multigrade classes, but not all. In many, learners engage in independent or interdependent learning and are guided minimally by the teacher and more intensively by structured learning materials, tasks, activities and by each other. Notwithstanding the beliefs of many teachers learners are not always completely dependent on them for learning.

Earlier reviews identified approaches to curriculum organisation and timetabling in multigrade classes (Little, 1995, 2001). Drawing from teacher training work in Zambia three approaches to timetabling and curriculum organisation were identified (Lungwangwa, 1989). In the common timetable, all children learn the same subject in a given timetable period but each group follows its own work according to grade level. In the subject stagger strategy, subjects are staggered on the timetable. Subjects requiring high teacher–pupil contact are matched with those requiring little. In the subject grouping strategy, subjects are presented to all grade groups together at the same time: music, art, religious knowledge and social studies lend themselves well to this option. Laukkanen and Selventoinen (1978) illustrate the common timetable approach by describing how, in Finnish multigrade schools the same general topic in the same subject may be covered at the same time in up to four combined year groups, with each group studying the topic at its own level. Mason and Burns (1996) suggested that the pattern of curriculum organisation depended on the subjects in question. Some teachers taught the whole class for all subjects. Others used a 'mixed approach' in which maths and reading were taught separately to different grade groups and social science and science were taught in whole classes. Miguel and Barsaga (1997) identified three strategies in their observations of multigrade teachers in the Philippines. In the first, the 'skill' subjects were taught separately in each grade level (subject stagger or common timetable with different levels of work), with art and music taught to the whole class (subject grouping). In the second, skill subjects are taught by ability group, irrespective of grade level. In the third, basic skills are taught to the whole class, with students splitting into ability groups for extension skills (subject grouping plus differentiated group work).

Most recently Kalaoja (2004, drawing on Kalaoja 1982) has identified four ways in which, historically, Finnish teachers organised the curriculum and distributed their time. At the end of the eighteenth century teaching was teacher-centred. Independent learning consisted mainly of rote memorisation, copying, drawing and listening to the teacher's teaching of other grades. The curriculum was identical to that followed in a monograded school. During any given timetabled period all pupils were taught the same subject but different themes or topics were taught to different grades. In a second phase, from 1881, the same theme of the same subject was addressed by each grade at the same time. The grades were differentiated in terms of the depth and breadth of material covered by the teacher. Kalaoja terms this the parallel curriculum system or 'expanding circles'. By 1904 the system changed again to an 'alternating' curriculum. Grade groups were combined and the combined group followed the prescribed curriculum for one grade during their first year and the other grade during the next. This system was adopted for the teaching of most subjects, with the exception of maths and language where the teaching of separate grade groups continued. In the final stage of curriculum innovation there was a return to the main principle of 'expanding circles' but with a difference. Known as the 'spiral curriculum system' learners in different grades studied the same subject and same topic simultaneously, even across combinations of four grades. The main difference was that this approach to the curriculum was promoted in both multi- and monograded schools in recognition of the diversity of learners in both settings and of the need to differentiate material to the individual level of the learner.

These various approaches to curriculum organisation for multigrade classes were re-organised into four (Little, 2004).

(i)   *Multi-year curriculum spans.* Units of curriculum content are spread across two or more grades rather than one. All learners work through common topics and activities.
(ii) *Differentiated curricula.* The same general topic/theme in the same subject is covered with all learners. Learners in each grade group engage in learning tasks appropriate to his/her level of learning.
(iii) *Quasi monograde.* The teacher teaches grade groups, in turn, as if they were monograded. Learners follow the same or a different subject at the same time. Teachers may divide · their time equally between grade groups. Or they may deliberately divide their time unequally, choosing subjects or tasks within subjects that require different levels of teacher contact.
(iv) *Learner and materials-centred.* This strategy depends more on the learner and learning materials than on teacher input. The curriculum is translated into self-study graded learning guides. Learners work through these at their own speed with support from the teacher and structured assessment tasks. Learning is constructed as involving a relationship between learner, learning materials and teacher.

Evidence in this book confirms each of these approaches but also extends them in important ways.

In Chapter 2, Chris Berry reports that teachers in the Turks and Caicos Islands used a 'grade-by-grade' approach, especially in mathematics and language arts and a whole-class approach to social studies and science. In the grade-by-grade approach teachers review curriculum material for, say, Grades 1, 2 and 3 and plan two or three different lessons at different levels on the same subject. Their strategies were consistent with what we have termed above differentiated curricula and multi-year curriculum spans respectively. But Berry's account is also consistent with (iv) above, the learner and materials-centred strategy. In the multigrade classes students spent substantial amounts of time in independent and interdependent learning and were supported in this by their learning materials. Significantly,

Berry reports that these strategies were created by the teachers themselves and were not the result of specific training.

In Chapter 4 we identified three main approaches to organising the curriculum for a single subject adopted by London teachers. The first, 'integrating frameworks' involved teachers reconstructing the national curriculum framework for each of two or more years (grades) into one by identifying learning objectives and/or topics in common. The teacher focused her attention on the common elements and taught the whole group as one, with some differentiated tasks and activities. In the second, teachers developed a 'two-year span' for a curriculum subject. This was commonly found in science, history, geography, art, information and communications technology, design and technology, music and physical education. In the third – common curriculum and differentiation – teachers worked to the curriculum framework for one year in terms of its learning objectives but adapted the related specific learning tasks to the ability/achievement levels of the pupils. The second is an example of a 'multi-year span' approach; the first and third are differentiated curricula. The difference between the first and third is the way in which the learning objectives for different grades are handled. In the first the teacher combines objectives from the curriculum frameworks for two or more grades with some differentiation in the tasks and activities for learners at different levels. In the third the teacher focuses on objectives/topics from one grade only and differentiates tasks and activities in relation to them. In all cases teachers were actively involved in the reconstruction of the curriculum and exerted some control over its re-organisation.

The observations of approaches to multigrade teaching practices in Peru (Chapter 3) suggest an additional way of thinking about curriculum differentiation. In the teaching of literacy in the Peruvian Amazon teachers adopted three patterns of organisation. In Pattern 1 the grade groups were taught the same subject but separately with different teacher inputs, different activities and different expected outcomes for the different grade groups. In Pattern 2 teachers did not differentiate the students and taught them as one. Pattern 3 integrated Patterns 1 and 2 over time. Students were grouped and taught as one from the start of the lesson and differentiated subsequently. These observations help us to distinguish two sub-approaches within the differentiated curriculum. In the first (Ames's Pattern 1) the timetabled subject was common but the grade groups were clearly differentiated in terms of teacher input, task and expected outcomes. In the second (Ames's Pattern 3) the timetabled subject was common, the *initial* teacher inputs were common but the subsequent tasks and expected learning outcomes were differentiated. Like Berry's teachers in the Turks and Caicos Islands the Peruvian teachers had received no training in the organisation of their time.

Suzuki's observations of teachers in Nepal (Chapter 5) advances our thinking about the organisation of time and curriculum in multigraded schools, though not necessarily in a positive direction. The reader will recall the five patterns of teacher distribution of time. In Pattern 1 teachers divided the time available for a school day by the number of grades they were timetabled to cover. This generated the time the teachers allocated to each graded class. These classes were then taught as a monograde class. The implication was that some students were ignored for some part of each day. They were not guided towards self-study because no teacher felt responsible for them. Although this may seem an extreme way of organising the distribution of teacher time it needs to be acknowledged as a coping strategy adopted by teachers in some schools. It might be described as a strategy of avoidance. We may not be impressed by it nor would we wish to recommend it as an effective strategy. But it happens, it is a reality and should not be ignored either by those who are interested in EFA or by those interested in supporting teachers in their work. A basic consideration in the discussion of the learning and teaching process is whether at any given time a teacher perceives him/herself to be responsible for organising the learning time of a class of children.

Patterns 2, 3 and 4 are variants on the quasi-monograde strategy (above). In Pattern 2, the teacher divides his/her time during a single period into two equal time sections and teaches each grade separately, as if they were two monograde classes. When attending to the second grade group the teacher ignored the initial group and did not guide them to self-study activities. In Pattern 3 the teacher distributed her time differentially between the two groups, treating one grade as the 'main' group and the other as the 'additional' group. Students in the additional group worked on self-learning activities. Included in this strategy were settings where a pupil 'monitor' was sometimes appointed to supervise a group; and some where no monitor had been appointed. In Pattern 4 the teacher divided his/her time more equally between the groups. Not only did he/she ensure that students were engaged in self-learning activity when he/she attended to the other group but he/she also monitored the work undertaken on the self-learning activities. In Pattern 5 the teacher merged the separate grades and treated the class as one large group, with similar inputs, similar processes followed and similar learning outcomes expected. This approach was most often observed in sports, music and arts and conforms to the 'subject grouping' approach. Suzuki's categories (Chapter 5) underline the point, made earlier in relation to noting how *both* teachers and students are spending their time. The teacher may be very active throughout a lesson period. But are all students similarly active? Suzuki's list also draws attention to the role of pre-prepared self-learning activities in the guiding of student's learning time (though it is not clear whether the teacher prepared these activities or whether they were prepared for her by educationalists working beyond the classroom).

The underlying principle uniting almost all the patterns of class organisation above is curriculum differentiation. Differentiation is the corollary of learner diversity. It refers variously to teacher decisions and actions in differentiating the subject taught, the content introduced, the activities undertaken by learners and/or the outcomes expected of learners. It is the teacher's way of responding to the principle of learner diversity on the one hand and curriculum diversity on the other.

Curriculum goals and organisation in multigrade classes

What teachers and learners talk about in class and what they write and otherwise do is determined to a very large extent by curriculum decisions taken far beyond the classroom walls. Teaching and learning tasks and teaching and learning materials are but one link in a chain of curriculum decisions and manifestations. Warwick (1975) refers to the 'geology' of the formal curriculum comprised of interdependent layers. At the school level these include, *inter alia*, (i) teaching and learning activities observable in classrooms, supported by teaching and learning materials, (ii) the lesson of which these activities are a part, (iii) the theme of which the lesson is a part, (iv) the syllabus of which the theme is a part, (v) the subject to which this syllabus pertains, and (vi) the timetable in which the subject will appear for one or more periods on one or more days.

The number and descriptions of these interdependent layers will vary from education system to education system. In Vietnam, the subject of health has a syllabus constructed by theme, topic, learning objective and content and grade (Chapter 9). In Sri Lanka, the subject of mathematics is organised by theme and by topic in the syllabus and by grade, theme and topic in the teachers' guides (Chapter 7). In the national curriculum for literacy in England (Chapter 4) the layers are severally described as framework, range, strand (word, sentence, text), year group, learning objective (e.g. phonological awareness) and task (organised by whole class, guided group, independent group and plenary) (www. standards.dfes.gov.uk).

Each of these layers is linked in turn to philosophical notions of curriculum and knowledge. *Inter alia* these concern the direction, purpose, divisions, balance and sequence of curriculum on the one hand and the philosophical and psychological theories of how learning occurs in education on the other.

While the shape and content of many of these curriculum layers will be determined by teachers (e.g. charts, lesson plans) many fall beyond their control. For example, National Education Commissions potentially exert a strong influence on the purpose and direction of the curriculum. Curriculum developers in curriculum development centres exert a strong influence on curriculum divisions, syllabi, themes and even lesson plans; teacher trainers potentially exert a strong influence on teaching methods; and public examinations certainly exert a strong influence on both teaching method and content and learners' motivations and orientations to learning.

Notions about what constitutes quality in learning and teaching and how it should be conducted are embedded in the society and culture at large (Alexander, 2000; McLaughlin, 2004). Their depth and strength and the potential for the quality of learning and teaching in the classroom to change in an enduring way and in spite of them is unknown. What is evident is the variety of pedagogy observable in classrooms in the same country. In India, for example, the pedagogy of the primary class can vary widely depending on the nature of local teacher training, local control and funding and local philosophies (see for example Alexander, 2000; Shotton, 1998; Little *et al.*, 1994; Lok Jumbish 1993; Rishi Valley Education Centre, 2000).

The division and control of knowledge

When we are concerned with reform and change – as we are in this book – we need to consider the various sets of people (actors and agencies) who make decisions about those layers. Who has the power to act and change? What can be changed and what cannot? What decisions and actions can be taken by actors in homes, classrooms, schools, local authorities, national authorities and, in some cases, international or extra-national authorities? The locus of power and change – refers to the relative degrees of power held by different agencies over curriculum – all of whom contribute to the realisation of what does and does not happen in the classroom.

For Bernstein (1971) the notion of power and control was central to his two-dimensional framework for describing curricula. The first dimension – classification – describes the construction and maintenance of boundaries between the content of curricula. Where classification is weak contents blur into each other, boundaries are indistinct, and the hierarchy of content is unclear. Where classification is strong subjects are insulated from each other and subjects are arranged in a well-accepted value hierarchy. The second dimension – frame – refers to the degree of control possessed by the teacher and students over the selection, organisation, pace and timing of the knowledge transmitted. Where frame is weak, what is and what is not appropriate subject matter for learning is unclear, the pace of learning is negotiated between teacher and pupil and the relationship is one of discovery. Where frame is strong the teacher or the education system determines the appropriateness of content to be transmitted, the pace is determined by the teacher or the curriculum and the teacher possesses all knowledge needed to be learned by the student. While these two dimensions generate, in principle, four possible combinations – or educational codes – Bernstein maintained that only two obtain in general practice. The collection code – in which both classification and framing are strong – refers to teachers as subject specialists and transmitters of knowledge defined outside the classroom. Subjects are clearly distinguished and the pace and direction of learning are fixed by the teacher. In the integration code teachers co-operate with colleagues and pupils, authority is personalised, the power of teachers is concealed; projects/topics are used to organise content. The direction of learning is less focused and more open to negotiation (Ross, 2000: 99).

The concepts of classification and frame have value for the analysis of the pedagogy of the multigrade class in several ways. The classifications of national curricula within which our multigrade teachers work are strong. Curricula are organised by subject but also by grade. With their subject *and* grade boundaries their classification is strong indeed. In his analyses of curricula in the English school curriculum Bernstein explored the classification of knowledge by subject but he took its classification by grade for granted.

The notion of 'frame' is also useful but deserves extension in two ways. First, in Bernstein's scheme, the learner either negotiates content and pace with the teacher (weak frame) or is directed by the teacher (strong frame). In many of our multigraded classes, the teacher either ignored the learners completely or failed to guide them towards meaningful activity for much of the school day. This suggests an absence of frame. The absence of frame arises because of the extremely strong classification of the curriculum by subject and grade, the mismatch between this type of curriculum construction and the organisation of the school, and the lack of professional autonomy of the teachers and resources (time, academic, financial) to reconstruct the curriculum. One could say that the curriculum frame within which the teacher worked is so strongly controlled by the system that both the teacher and the learner lose control over learning. One might even label this as a 'disintegrated curriculum code' – a code in which the teacher strives to deliver a strongly classified curriculum within a pedagogic environment (in this case one teacher and two or more curriculum grades) that differs radically from that embedded within a particular classification.

The second extension of 'frame' concerns the control that teachers and learners have over the different elements of a formal curriculum. We saw earlier how the material curriculum might be thought of as consisting of interdependent layers. These include teaching and learning activities obser-vable in classrooms, the lesson of which these activities are a part, the theme of which the lesson is a part, the syllabus of which the theme is a part, the subject to which this syllabus pertains and the timetable in which the sub-ject will appear for one or more periods on one or more days. Each of these curricular layers relates to that immediately below it. The question is how much control can and does the teacher exert over each layer and with what implications for learner control.

Curricula can also be described in terms of their orientation and focus. Most recently Ross (2000) distinguishes content-driven curricula from objectives-driven and process-driven curricula. One might then ask how much control teachers and learners have over determining the content within an objectives-based curriculum; or the process within a content-based curriculum; or the process within an objectives-based curriculum. Aspects of control and change are explored in the following sections.

Changing national curricula
Our research has demonstrated how actors operating at different locations in the education system can exert power over the material curriculum. The developmental work on curriculum re-organisation undertaken by Pat Pridmore with Vu Son (Chapter 9) in Vietnam engaged national-level curriculum developers in active support for teachers. The curriculum content of the subject of 'health' was re-organised to enable teachers to address the same subject, same theme and same topic across grades, using some whole-class teaching followed by differentiated tasks and differentiated expected learning outcomes for each grade. This was done by identifying the themes and topics related to health from within the subjects of Natural and Social Sciences (Grades 1–3) and Science (Grades 4–5) that were repeated across two or more grades and re-sequencing the order of themes and topics within grades. The pedagogy adopted for each theme was also changed towards a stepped enquiry and activity-based approach. The national-level curriculum developers provided detailed step-by-step advice to teachers in multigrade

schools (Son *et al.*, 2002). The potential advantages of this approach for the multigrade teacher are several. First, children from different grades can be grouped together and taught the same curriculum subject at the same time. Second, children of all ages, abilities and grades learn together. By structuring the stages of the lesson through a mix of whole-class teaching, same and mixed-grade discussion groups, individual enquiry and activity the teacher can appreciate the unity of the lesson planning task – one topic across several lessons, albeit with differentiation within. Most importantly she has been supported in the planning task by professional support from a national authority. She has not been expected to carry the burden of planning for two or more grades alone.

Multigrade teachers should not be expected by external authorities to adapt curriculum to their multigrade circumstance alone. In most monograde systems teachers are not expected to exercise such levels of adaptive professional autonomy (and indeed are often discouraged from so doing). Why should so much more be expected from the multigrade teacher? The involvement of national level curriculum developers in the adaptation, re-organisation, re-alignment or reform of the curriculum framework legitimises the work of the multigrade teacher. It dispels the message that she is a second-class teacher trying her best to teach in the monograde style. It indicates that there is another way which meets with the approval of higher authorities.

During our research we looked at a number of similar, independently conducted, curriculum re-organisation or re-alignment exercises. In Bhutan the primary curriculum is currently being 'realigned' to meet the needs of the multigrade classroom and similar work is under way in several countries in Africa (Chapter 10). In Sri Lanka and Nepal developmental work is being undertaken by small groups of curriculum development and university staff on the national primary education curriculum to meet the needs of multigrade teachers. In Nepal the subjects of Environmental Education, Health Science and Mathematics are being reviewed; and in Sri Lanka, Mathematics, Sinhala and Tamil (LATIMS, 2003, 2004). These current examples are demonstrating how national curriculum developers can re-sequence the content of curricula so that themes and topics that are repeated across grades are brought together for teaching at the same time with space for individual learners to approach learning tasks at different levels.

In England the Department for Education and Skills has issued 'additional guidance' for small schools and schools with mixed-year classes on the implementation of the National Literacy Strategy (www.standards.dfes.gov.uk/literacy). This advises teachers to re-organise the graded curriculum framework into a two-year rolling programme. Some local education authorities and private trusts offer supplementary curriculum schemes (for example www.norfolkesinet.org.uk, www.hamilton-trust. org. uk).

Changing learning materials and the relative power of the learner
A different approach to curriculum change starts with materials for the learner rather than the teacher (category (iv) above). Here the curriculum does not necessarily need to be re-sequenced. Rather learning materials designed to help the learner progress through the curriculum sequence need to be available in plentiful supply. We note that learning materials are located within the GMR framework as part of 'the enabling environment' rather than being central to teaching and learning. We locate them more centrally since we believe that deliberate change at this level alters the two-way dynamic between teacher and learner, creating instead a three-way dynamic between learner, teacher and materials. Moreover, in this approach the sequence of the curriculum overall need not change in order to align topics and themes to assist the teacher to teach across grades. With the focus on the learner the materials can follow the sequence of the current curriculum. But the materials need to engage the learner and be usable by him or her without too much intervention by the teacher.

Perhaps the most thoroughgoing re-organisations of the primary school curriculum along these lines that we have come across in recent years are to be found in Colombia and India. In both examples the multigraded organisation of classes may be considered as an asset rather than an impediment (Rowley and Nielsen 1997).

The *Escuela Nueva* programme, originating in rural Colombia in the 1980s and adapted for use in many other countries, was described in Chapters 1 and 13. The development of the curriculum focused on the learning needs of students. Self-learning guides were developed for each of the subjects of the national curriculum reflecting its objectives. Regional and local adaptations were made to the content where appropriate. Guides were organised by sequences of learning tasks and presumed levels of difficulty. Series of sequences equate broadly with grades but, because learners work through the material at their own pace, children who in a monograded system would be working on the same material at the same time may in the *Escuela Nueva* system be working at different levels within the same grade or even at different grades. Guides direct learners to learning activity centres and class libraries. Assessment of learning is built into the study guides and flexible promotion systems allow students to progress at their own pace.

Learners working at several curriculum grades are grouped together in the same classroom.

Learners, teachers and learning materials appear to form a three-way relationship. Learners as well as teachers appear to take active decisions about learning tasks on a daily basis. Curriculum embodies the social and moral as well as cognitive and is promoted via a structure of school governance that encourages students to participate in democratic decision-making processes. Teacher training is conducted through in-service workshops and involves demonstration schools and centres of best practice. The pedagogy employed in the teachers' training reflects that intended to be used in the classroom. Teachers new to the programme are trained via three workshops in the first year and follow-up workshops thereafter. The school–community component brings families into school activities and schools into communities. And local management systems are designed to encourage municipality and community ownership of the schools and the programme.

The second example is from the Rishi Valley in the state of Andhra Pradesh, India (Rishi Valley Education Centre, 2000; Menon and Rao, 2004; Padmanabha Rao, 2005). The Rishi Valley elementary school programme has developed over the past 15 years and is premised on both multigraded and multi-levelled learning, both of which are consistent with the idea of differentiated learning implicit in the GMR framework.

> The programme scales down the learning outputs of each class into a meaningful sequence of concrete and manageable units. Each unit is taught through a sequence of five types of activities: introductory, reinforcement, evaluation, remedial and enrichment. Work cards supported by learning aids are designed to require the child's serious involvement. Every child has to participate in each of the five types of activities. These multiple activities are gathered into units called 'milestones'. Milestones are organised into an ascending order, beginning with the first rung of the learning ladder and ending with the topmost rung, which denotes the end of a class. This whole learning continuum – an ascending series of milestones, with activities leading up to each milestone – is visually represented in a 'Ladder of Learning' a classroom tool used by teachers and children to track their progress on the learning continuum. Four such ladders cover the entire curriculum from Class 1 to Class 4 in the areas on language, mathematics and environmental studies … examples for curriculum activities are drawn from the local environment and children's daily-life experiences.
>
> (Menon and Rao, 2004: 43)

The Rishi Valley programme is a good example of an outcomes-, outputs- or competencies-driven curriculum (Ross, 2000). The learning outputs are derived from the nationally mandated minimum levels of learning, followed by all states. The Rishi Valley curriculum designers divided each of the competencies into smaller units and used these as the basis for the five types of activity detailed above: instruction, practice, review, remediation and enrichment (Menon, personal communication, 2004).

With their emphasis on supporting the learner as much as (if not more than) the teacher, neither the *Escuela Nueva* nor the Rishi Valley programmes have need to realign the curriculum in the way described above in the experimental work in Bhutan, Nepal, Vietnam and Sri Lanka. Themes and topics are repeated but the repetition is embedded in the work cards through which pupils progress. In principle, pupils could be working on the same theme at the same or at different times. Because they focus on a progression through activities the materials can be used flexibly – by the whole class or a group as well as for individual level learning. Children who miss school for a few days need not miss out on lessons; they pick up their learning activities where they left off. In principle, children work through the ladders at their own pace. Both programmes are comprehensive examples of what is termed above a 'learner and materials-centred' approach to curriculum organisation for multigrade classes (category (iv) above).

Most researchers and practitioners agree that successful strategies for multigrade teaching depend on adequate supplies of learning materials, including the ubiquitous textbook, designed for use in individual and group-based learning. This enables teachers to spend time with some groups of learners while other learners work alone, in pairs or in small groups. But the mere existence of materials does not guarantee quality of learning. Self-study materials must be of the highest quality and relevance, and must be used by teachers as part of an *integrated* teaching strategy, in which teachers continue to play a vital part. The availability of self-study materials must not be viewed by the teacher as a substitute for his/her teaching. Our research suggests that successful strategies for multigrade teaching also depend on teacher beliefs about how learning occurs. The three-way nature of the relationship between learner, teacher (whether adult or peer) and materials needs to be at the forefront of teachers' minds as well as curriculum developers'.

Curriculum redevelopment by teachers
Some might argue that the amount of curriculum realignment and materials development undertaken by curriculum developers in the above programmes emasculates teachers and limits their opportunities for professional development. But this critique has to be seen in the context of those education systems in which curriculum design traditions are highly centralised, in which teachers enjoy limited professional autonomy and in which teachers, especially multigrade teachers, are often working alone in

difficult circumstances. As we saw in Chapter 4, even in the more decentralised systems of curriculum control in England inexperienced teachers of multigrade classes are crying out for some level of support in the planning and reorganisation of curricula.

Chapters 7 and 8 demonstrated how teachers in Vietnam and Sri Lanka, working within an action-research framework, improved not only the organisation of their teaching time but also the cognitive achievement levels of their students. The curriculum redevelopment undertaken by these teachers was supervised and sanctioned by researchers working at the national level. The curriculum work was neither wholly nationally nor wholly locally determined. A professional bridge was built from the national to the local.

Assessment of learning

The regular assessment of learning is key to quality learning and teaching. Assessment is used for many purposes, ranging from selection of individuals for further education and jobs, the monitoring of performance of teachers, schools and systems usually for 'accountability' to the promotion of learning (Little and Wolf, 1996). From the perspective of EFA (in particular Goals 2 and 6) this third purpose of assessment, assessment for learning, is the most important. Assessment *for* learning is 'formative' and distinguishable from assessment *of* learning which is 'summative'. The purpose of formative assessment is to diagnose how a learner is learning and is intended to improve teaching and learning. It is usually criterion-referenced and/or pupil-referenced and is undertaken in a variety of ways including a review of assessment tasks at the end of short learning sequences, observation of learning activities, learner self-assessment and peer assessment. The purpose of summative assessment is to evaluate and record learning achievement. It may be either criterion- or norm-referenced and the assessment tasks and tools used are often externally devised tasks (UNESCO, 2004; Black and Wiliam, 1998). Formative assessment fits the purpose of promoting learning in the classroom. Summative assessment fits the purpose of system monitoring and accountability. It also fits the all-important purpose of selection. In the context of EFA in many developing country education systems with still limited access to secondary education rationed by selection hurdles, the importance of assessment for selection and its backwash on classroom practices should never be under-estimated (Dore, 1997).

Hargreaves (2001) has suggested that multigraded learning settings lend themselves to formative assessment designed to promote learning because they encourage teachers to recognise individual differences in learning. Although multigraded settings lend themselves to, or are consistent with, regular and frequent formative assessment designed to improve differentiated paces of learning they do not guarantee that formative assessment will be undertaken. From its inception the curriculum designers of the *Escuela Nueva* programme worked hard to build assessment tasks into learning guides and to design levels of mastery required before the learner can move on. Learners are guided by their learning texts, not by their teacher, towards assessment tasks. Learners take the initiative in approaching the teacher to mark the assessment tasks, to record achievements and determine progression to the next learning unit. Should the learner not achieve mastery the teacher decides on the remedial work to be undertaken. In the Rishi Valley programme the programme designers built evaluation and remedial activities very deliberately into the range of learning activities at each and every milestone of learning achievement. And in the adaptation of the curriculum for teaching health in Vietnam (Chapter 9) curriculum developers built frequent and regular formative assessment tasks into the series of steps that underpinned the enquiry-based pedagogy. In none of these cases was the decision to use formative assessment tasks left to the discretion of the multigrade teacher. Assessment activity is built into the design of the learning materials. And in none of these programmes was the teacher the sole arbiter of formative assessment. Self-assessment and peer assessment could be observed, alongside assessment by the teacher.

Formative assessment is most valuable when it assists the teacher and the learner in the diagnosis of learning difficulties. Where the organisation of learning is focused on the individual (as in *Escuela Nueva* and Rishi Valley) the likelihood that a teacher will guide a learner to remedial work may increase. Where learners remain dependent on the teacher in the definition of the pace of learning within whole classes and groups (as in the Vietnam case) then the likelihood of individual learners being guided to remedial learning activity may be less. Neither proposition has been explored in our research and both remain hypothetical.

Formative assessment also has the potential to alter the way in which learners repeat lessons and grades. In Chapter 12 Lewin presented a hypothetical model of how both summative and formative assessment could be used to shorten the period learners spend repeating a grade. Typically, in monograded systems, learners who fail a summative promotion test are required to repeat all subjects for a complete year. In multigrade settings that adopt a learner-centred approach to curriculum progression, learners who 'fail' a promotion or progression test might repeat some subjects and not all and some parts of the curriculum material and not all.

The social organisation of learning

Classrooms are social spaces in which particular forms of social organisation emerge. These are determined in part by the ways in which learners are grouped for teaching and learning. There are many ways of describing how learners are grouped for teaching. We have already used the terms teacher-dependent, learner-dependent and learner-interdependent (above).

Alexander (2000) uses three basic 'organisational frames' to describe how learners are organised for teaching and learning in primary schools – whole-class, group and individual. Groups are subdivided further into three – learners work as individuals within a group setting, learners work together collaboratively as a team, and as groups attended to by the teacher. These five frames – whole-class, individuals within groups, collaborative groups, teacher-led groups and individual – allow for several modes of social interaction. These include interactions between the teacher and whole class, the teacher and individual, the individual and class, the teacher and group, the individual and group, and the individual and individual. This last is sometimes termed 'peer learning'. As we saw earlier each of these organisational frames could be observed in the multigrade classes in our research. The dominant frames were individuals working alone or in teacher-led groups, where the group was contiguous with the class grade.

Groups may be differentiated in several ways – by grade, age, gender, ability, learner interests, friendship, etc. When asked about how they group students for teaching and learning activity in multigrade classes, the majority of the London teachers reported using ability, just as they would in a single-grade class (Chapter 4). High ability students from a lower grade would often work alongside similar ability students from a higher grade. Lower ability students from a higher grade would often work alongside similar ability students from a lower grade. In Vietnam (Chapter 8), by contrast, teachers are trained to work with two or more grades simultaneously in the same classroom space. Within that space, groups remained sharply differentiated by grade. Each grade group had its own space in the classroom, its own furniture and own blackboard. In Nepal (Chapter 5), students in different grades are sometimes seated in separated classrooms, with the single teacher moving between the two spaces, even when they are some distance apart. There is little mixing of students by criteria that cut across grade boundaries. In Sri Lanka grade groups are taught separately by a teacher moving between the groups, or by ignoring one group altogether (Vithanapathirana, 2005). In Peru, grade is also the main criterion for grouping. Teachers either teach each grade separately or mix two grades and teach the same lesson with or without some differentiation (Chapter 3). In the Turks and Caicos Islands, teachers tend to deliver separate material to each grade level in maths and science and to teach the class as a group for other subjects with limited differentiation. Even within so-called multigraded classrooms, graded-ness remains deeply embedded within the social organisation of the class.

The Rishi Valley multigrade programme adopts a rather different way of describing the social organisation of learning, based on the learner rather than the teacher (Menon and Rao, 2004). While there are interactions between teacher and whole classes of learners, there is a greater focus on learners in groups. Groups are differentiated by the level of learner autonomy and the role of the teacher and the peer in relation to the learner. Classes usually comprise five types of group:

1   Partially teacher-supported. The teacher initiates activity followed by learner activity (e.g. making pictures, sorting letters, words, sentences, etc.).
2   Completely teacher-supported. The teacher introduces new concepts, evaluates work or when the learner needs special attention.
3   Partially peer-supported. Learners work largely alone but support each other.
4   Completely peer-supported. Learners teach and learn from each other.
5   Self-learning. Learners read and write and test their own abilities using evaluation cards.

The composition of groups is reported to be dynamic and activity-dependent and

> Based on the strong belief that real and meaningful learning takes place through the dynamic interaction between teacher and children and among children themselves.
>
> (Menon and Rao 2004: 44)

We will return to questions of social organisation and its impact on social skills in the next section.

Learning outcomes

Learning outcomes lie at the heart of EFA Goal 6 and the teaching and learning process. The GMR (UNESCO, 2004) distinguishes outcomes in terms of (i) literacy, numeracy and life skills, (ii) creative and emotional skills, (iii) values, and (iv) social benefits.

Many of those interested in our work on multigrade schooling want to know how learning outcomes compared with those in monograded schooling. This is a natural concern and the research synthesised below will explore those comparisons. But a more fundamental point about multigrade schooling is that in many settings the key learning achievement comparison is not between learners in multigrade and monograde schools but between learners in multigrade schools and potential learners who attend *no* school (Little, 1995).

Cognitive achievement outcomes
A number of meta-analyses have been conducted of the effects of multigrade and monograde organisation on cognitive achievement. Pratt (1986) reviewed 30 studies undertaken in the USA and Canada between 1948 and 1983. The multigrade classes studied spanned 2–3 years. There was no general pattern in the achievement results. Learners in multigrade classes showed higher achievement in maths and reading in 10 studies, worse in five and no difference in 13. Miller's (1991) review of 21 studies in the USA confirmed that learners in multigrade classes performed no better and no worse than students in monograde classes. Veenman's (1995) review of studies, mainly from OECD countries, distinguished (i) multigrade classes, formed of necessity from imbalanced or inadequate enrolments; (ii) single-grade classes, and (iii) multi-age, non-graded classes, formed for pedagogical or philosophical reasons. Learning in multigrade or multi-age classes was neither inferior nor superior to that in monograde classes. Mason and Burns (1997) confirmed the general picture of no consistent cognitive achievement differences. Most recently, Hattie (2002) has suggested that there is no consistent evidence to argue that multigrade or single-grade teaching is more effective. Relatedly, Ireson and Hallam (2001) report no consistent effects of ability-grouped single-grade classes on achievement compared with heterogeneous (mixed-ability) groups within single-grade classes. Classroom effects are much more likely to be attributable to the quality of teaching and the expectations of principals, parents and pupils rather than to the composition of classes.

Studies of cognitive achievement in multigrade and monograde classes in developing countries are few in number. In Burkina Faso and Togo, Jarousse and Mingat (1991) found that learners in multigrade classes performed better than those in monograde classes. In Colombia, within the *Escuela Nueva* programme, Grade 3 learners in the multigrade schools performed better in Spanish and maths and Grade 5 learners better in Spanish (Rojas and Castillo, 1988; Psacharopoulos *et al.,* 1993; McEwan, 1998). In Pakistan, Rowley (1992) showed cognitive differences in favour of monograde schools. In the Turks and Caicos Islands, Miller *et al.* (1994, cited in Berry, 2001) found that learners in multigrade schools consistently outperformed those in monograde schools in the terminal grade of primary school. Berry (2001) found that learners in multigrade schools performed better on a test of reading than those in monograde schools but that the advantage was greatest for the lowest achieving learners.

Cognitive achievement gains in multigrade classes were also demonstrated in the action research work undertaken by our researchers with teachers in Sri Lanka and Vietnam. These two pieces of action research demonstrated how changes in lesson plans and small adaptations to the sequence of curriculum material changed the way that teachers used their time in class and raised the level of cognitive achievement of learners in multigrade classes in comparison with learners in monograde classes (Chapters 7 and 8).

Social and personal esteem outcomes
Pratt (1986) identified 15 studies that addressed, variously, children's friendships, self-concepts, altruism and attitude to school. Overall, he claimed that the socio-emotional development of learners in multigrade groups is either accelerated or showed no difference, when compared with learners in monograde groups. This conclusion was confirmed in Miller's (1991) review of 21 studies. And in her review of studies from the US and UK, Ford (1977) reports both positive and negative findings on the reduction of anxiety levels, the maturity of friendship patterns and on personal and social adjustment and positive findings on self-concept, self-esteem and attitudes to school.

Studies of the social effects of learning in multigrade settings in developing countries are very few indeed. In the *Escuela Nueva* programme in Colombia an early evaluation credited the programme with positive effects on self-esteem and civic behaviour (Colbert *et al.,* 1993). A subsequent study confirmed the positive effect for civic behaviour but not for self-esteem (Psacharopoulos *et al.,* 1993)

The two chapters in this book that explore further the cognitive and social effects of multigrade teaching are therefore most welcome. Chapter 2 extends earlier work (Berry, 2001) on achievement effects in monograde and multigrade classes in the Turks and Caicos Islands by exploring the practices inside the classroom that might explain why low achieving students in multi-grade classes performed better than low achieving students in monograde classes. He suggests a range of possible reasons. Low achievers have opportunities to revisit material. When teachers interact with pupils it tends to be in the context of a small rather than large group. Learners engaged in more independent work in the multigrade class and as a result they learned how to learn. There seemed to be more opportunities for peer instruction.

Chapter 13 explores in some detail the social effects of participation in a multigrade teaching programme – the *Escuela Nueva* programme in Colombia – through the concept of peaceful social interaction. Peaceful social interaction is operationalised through questions designed to measure its four dimensions – active respect, universal solidarity, fair play and equity. Children in *Escuela Nueva* schools demonstrated higher levels of peaceful social interaction than children in conventional schools. And comparisons between alumni of *Escuela Nueva* and conventional schools demonstrated differences in their attitudes to democracy. *Escuela Nueva* alumni were more inclined to be members of voluntary organisations and more inclined towards participatory democracy. Alumni from conventional schools were more inclined towards representative democracy. These findings are of considerable interest and are most likely to be attributable to the active promotion of democratic behaviour in *Escuela Nueva* classes rather than the multigraded composition of classes.

Teachers' perceptions of learning outcomes
Several studies focus on teachers' *perceptions* of the benefits for students of learning in multigrade settings. A UNESCO/APEID study (1989: 5) collated perceptions about the benefits of multigrade teaching from educators in twelve countries in the Asia and Pacific Region. These included: learners develop self-study skills; learners learn to co-operate across age groups, resulting in collective ethics, concern and responsibility; learners learn to help each other.

Our study of 47 multigrade teachers and headteachers in an inner-city area of London, England (Chapter 4) reported a number of positive learning opportunities presented by the multigrade classroom. The most commonly mentioned (24/47) was the opportunity for 'cognitive stretching' of the younger, less able and lower achieving learners. This was expressed variously by teachers as 'stretching', 'modelling', 'moving on and developing', 'extending', 'looking up and emulating'. The second most commonly mentioned (13/47) was the opportunity for the use of peer tutoring learning strategies. While such strategies are not unique to multigrade classes, the strategy appears to work particularly well in the multigrade class. Unlike cognitive stretching, which was considered a benefit mainly for the less able, the lower achieving and the younger learner, peer tutoring was perceived to benefit *all* pupils, cognitively, socially and personally. More able, higher achieving and older learners 'cement' their learning through teaching and helping others. The less able, lower achieving and younger learners look up to and learn from others. A third commonly mentioned opportunity (12/47) was 'behaviour stretching', or the opportunity for younger learners to learn appropriate social behaviours from the role models offered by older learners. In short, teachers perceived that the multigraded class presented learning benefits for both older and younger and higher achieving and lower achieving learners. Whether these perceptions are all borne out in practice is a matter for future research.

ENABLING TEACHING AND LEARNING

In this section we address four main dimensions of the enabling of teaching and learning: teacher development, the conditions of teachers' work, physical spaces for learning and finance.

Teacher development

While learners and learning lie at the heart of EFA, teachers are a key human resource in motivating learners and enabling learning. Our research has explored how teachers themselves may be prepared and motivated to support learning in multigraded settings.

Pre-service teacher preparation
Very few of the teachers encountered in our research had received any formal preparation for teaching in multigraded classes.

In our London study (Chapter 4) only five out of 37 teachers and none of the 10 headteachers reported having received any pre-service training in multigrade teaching. None of the rural teachers in Peru, Sri Lanka and the Turks and Caicos had received pre-service training in multigrade teaching. Croft's survey of teacher education programmes in South Africa, Ghana, Lesotho and Malawi (Chapter 6) found scant mention of multigrade teaching in teacher education curriculum materials even in those countries where such classes were very common.

But absence of training in a practice named multigrade teaching, or mixed-year teaching, does not necessarily leave teachers totally unprepared for the pedagogic challenge of the multigrade classes. Many of our London teachers alluded to differentiation (of task, materials, expected learning outcomes) within class grouping of students by ability and other criteria, and peer learning as sound pedagogic principles. These are principles that work well in both monograde *and* multigrade classrooms and are usually addressed in teacher preparation programmes. In most industrialised countries with substantial proportions of multigrade classes (see Chapter 1) teachers are familiar with whole-class, group-based and individual learning strategies and with the principle of differentiation. They adhere to a philosophy that views learning as a dynamic process between learner and teacher in which learners' previous learning styles and experiences play an important determining role in current learning. Even when national reforms urge a return to whole-class teaching as a dominant pedagogic tool, as in England in the late 1990s with the introduction of the national literacy and numeracy strategies, teachers continue to employ a wide range of pedagogical approaches including task differentiation (Jones, 2004). A teacher versed in the value of a range of methods (whole-class, group and individual learning), a supply of learning materials and a reasonable class size is more likely to be able to manage the challenges of a multigraded class than one who has been trained in a teacher-led pedagogy, with a paucity of materials to support independent work and a large class size.

Where pedagogy remains teacher- rather than learner-centred teachers are less inclined to address learner diversity and to offer differentiated learning opportunities.

In-service training
In-service training for multigrade teachers was available for teachers in some of our research sites but not in others.

In Peru no in-service training on multigrade teaching was available. In recent years (1996–2001) in-service teacher training focused on the intro-duction of the new curriculum and new teaching strategies. But the orientation of this training was towards the monograde classroom. The impact of even this training on teachers was limited because of the isolation of schools, the difficulties teachers faced in attending training and the lack of visits from local educational authorities. The absence of a culture of team work among teachers in the same school left the multigrade teacher thrown back on his/her own resources.

In Sri Lanka no in-service training in multigrade teaching had been made available to teachers. Indeed, most of the recent in-service training to which all teachers had been invited was linked to the successive year-on-year implementation of the revised primary curriculum, starting with Grade 1 in 1999 and ending with Grade 5 in 2003. This approach to an already graded curriculum reinforced the 'gradedness' of the primary school and hindered rather than helped the work of teachers responsible for two, three and sometimes four or five grades simultaneously.

In the Turks and Caicos Islands the only specific training that multigrade teachers had received in their entire career was a two-day course based on the work of Collingwood (1991). This was included as one part of a series of in-service training inputs for primary teachers in a project run by the British government between 1993 and 1996.

Three countries where in-service training has been made available on a systematic basis have been Vietnam, Nepal and Colombia. In Vietnam multigrade training was made available throughout the 1990s through the MOET/UNICEF Multigrade Teaching Project, which developed a system of master teachers and demonstration schools. In-service training has been developed alongside pre-service. In Nepal in-service training on multigrade teaching is conducted in all of the 75 districts by the Primary Teacher Training Unit of the central government as one of the components in the Basic and Primary Education Project. As noted above, there is no pre-service teacher preparation programme in Nepal, and training in all aspects of pedagogy, including multigrade, is addressed through the in-service system. In Colombia, and also in other parts of Latin America, in-service training has been the means by which teachers have been oriented to the *Escuela Nueva* programme.

Worldwide, there are many examples of *ad hoc* in-service teaching training programmes to meet the needs of the multigrade teacher. Many of these programmes have been supported by multilateral organisations (www.ioe.ac.uk/multigrade/teachertraining materials.htm) and have been designed to fill a pressing need and gap in system provision. A recent example from Sri Lanka is provided by Sibli and Cash (2003).

Cascade training
In-service training programmes in multigrade teaching are frequently characterised by a cascade model of dissemination. As such they encounter the issues of effectiveness that pervade cascade training programmes more generally.

Our research in Nepal demonstrated the issues well. Suzuki traced the effectiveness of an in-service training programme from content design at the national level to the training process at local level and implementation of strategies in the classroom (Suzuki, 2004; Chapter 5 this volume). Although teachers made gains in their knowledge of useful strategies for multigrade teaching (especially in the provision and use of self-learning activities and classroom monitors), evidence on the implementation of the training 'messages' at the classroom level was modest. Suzuki (2004) identifies a number of areas where improvements could be made in the future, but also identifies 'hearts and minds' obstacles that would endure even if training were to improve. These include the lack of awareness on the part of policymakers of the existence and needs of multigrade classes, the absence of teacher trainers expert in the practices of multigrade teaching, and the overwhelmingly negative attitudes towards it held by teachers, their trainers and supervisors.

School-based teacher development
An alternative or additional approach to the training of teachers is offered by the action research undertaken within our research project in Vietnam and Sri Lanka. Both offer models for working with small groups of teachers at school level which could be simplified for the purpose of replication. In both cases the teachers, facilitated by the action researcher, focused on the development of lesson plans within existing curriculum frameworks to facilitate the curriculum organisation of the multigraded class.

In the Vietnam case the work with teachers pre-dated and complemented the national-level curriculum adaptation described earlier in this chapter and elsewhere in this book (Chapter 9). The researcher, as facilitator, worked with five teachers and three headteachers to adopt an enquiry-based approach to the teaching and learning of topics in health. The work was undertaken over a period of time and enabled the teachers to try out their ideas and plans, to review and to modify their actions in the classroom (Chapter 8).

Similar school-level developmental work was undertaken in Sri Lanka with a small group of rural teachers (Chapter 7). The subject chosen was mathematics, often considered to be the subject least amenable to be taught in a multigraded class. Working with teachers and with support from a curriculum developer from the national level, teachers identified common themes and topics in the mathematics syllabi and identified the differential outcomes expected by grade. Lesson plans were developed. Lessons commenced with whole-class teaching, continued with differentiated tasks for different grade groups and were concluded by whole-class revision and consolidation. Initially, teachers worked within a group setting to develop plans for their individual classes. Subsequently, teachers developed plans for implementation by every teacher-member of the group. The mutual collaboration spurred the implementation of plans in the classroom. Once teachers were supported in their awareness of the structure and the contents of subject curricula from Grade 1 to Grade 5 they re-planned a series of lessons for different combinations of grade levels. Some reported transferring the principles of common themes and differentiated tasks to other subject areas (Vithanapathirana, 2005). Teachers' attitudes to multigrade teaching changed as they realised that there are strategies that can be used to improve student achievement outcomes and lighten the burden of intensive planning for several grades. While many of these teachers still prefer monograde teaching, they recognise the necessity for multigrade and are keen to 'do a service' for the rural schools.

These two modest developments were part of action research with the well trained researcher also acting as facilitator, critical friend and evaluator of outcomes. But aspects of the approach adopted are potentially transferable to teacher development more generally. The 'trainer' works to support or facilitate teachers in identifying problem areas, in identifying strategies to overcome the problem, in trying them out, reviewing and modifying. The facilitator implements the trial strategies alongside the teacher in the classroom as time permits. The key lies in support rather than direction and in practical support over time rather than in a one-off day, week or month of training.

Conditions of teachers' work

The conditions of service under which our teachers worked varied enormously. Our London teachers enjoy reasonable and regularly paid salaries and pensions, paid on nationally agreed pay scales. Teachers generally reside no further than one hour away from the school using public transport. They work regular hours. School closures for holidays are known well in advance and adhered to. Teacher and student attendance is, with a few exceptions, high. Absent teachers can usually be replaced on a daily basis through a system known as 'supply teaching'. Primary school teaching is considered to be a middle-class occupation.

The contrasts with the teachers in other contexts are great. In many developing countries while primary school teaching may be considered a middle- or lower-middle-class occupation, the financial rewards are low. Teachers may reside in the communities they serve. They are more likely to reside elsewhere and commute long distances by various means of transport, or live locally for a few days each week, travelling 'home' at weekends. Transportation constraints may mean that the days and hours in which the teacher is physically in school are less than those prescribed by the national authorities. School closures are likely to be more frequent and teacher and student attendance lower. In none of our other local contexts studied is there a system of cover for teacher absenteeism. Pastoralist teachers in Darfur (Chapter 10), by contrast move and live with the communities they serve. Cash rewards are not high but are supplemented with livestock.

Vietnamese teachers provide an interesting contrast. Teachers in Vietnamese multigrade schools receive additional salary in recognition of their increased workloads. The Government's policy is to place only the best educated and trained teachers in multigrade classrooms. Despite official state recognition teachers do not always view their position favourably. Teachers are generally deployed to remote rural areas away from their family and friends where they do not own land to farm. Communities in remote areas live by subsistence farming and do not have resources to pay teachers for the additional tutoring, often a major source of additional income for teachers in urban settings. And because of their remote location education officers visit the teachers' schools infrequently.

Physical spaces for learning

The contrasts between the physical space within which learners and teachers work could not be much greater than those described in Aikman and El Haj's account (Chapter 10) of mobile multigrade schooling in Darfur and those described below for teachers in London. The Darfur schools in which mobile multigrade teachers work are not permanent. The 'school' moves with the pastoralist community. It comprises the teacher, the students, a blackboard, one collapsible chair, textbooks and chalk. Once the community 'settles' for a short period of time temporary thorn bush shelters may or may not be built to house the class or the school. If temporary structures are not constructed then tree shade determines the space within which the students learn, seated on the ground. In the larger of the two schools temporary shelters were built for each of the four grades. The teacher attended to two of these in the morning and two in the afternoon. Whether in the morning or the afternoon the teacher moved between two grades in the two shelters and treated the groups separately, as if they were monograded classes.

The physical spaces within which our London multigrade teachers worked (Chapter 4) could not have been more different – nor more permanent. All the school buildings and classrooms in which the teachers included in our research worked were a century or more old. Usually two-storied solid buildings, each classroom was spacious and high-ceilinged. Notwithstanding heating facilities, north-facing classrooms were often cold, especially in the winter months. Each classroom housed approximately 30 students and one teacher. For certain periods of the day a classroom assistant joined the teacher in the classroom. Every student had a chair and workspace at a movable table shared with other students. In one corner there was a carpeted area where students congregated for whole-class teaching or for reading alone or in pairs. Students' work was displayed on the walls alongside wall charts and other displays. Students had access to a range of textbooks, computers and workbooks. The teacher had access to national curriculum guidelines, schemes of work, sample lessons and teaching materials that could be downloaded from the worldwide web..

In Vietnam, Peru and Turks and Caicos we encountered a few teaching and learning spaces approximating those we saw in London. But the volume and quality of teaching and learning resources (e.g. computers, books) were vastly inferior. In Vietnam and Peru there was also great variation between schools, with some teachers and students working in extremely cramped conditions with large, immovable furniture, or no furniture, and no classroom partitions.

Finance

Financial inputs are necessary enabling conditions for learning in all types of school. Multigraded schools pose particular issues, not generally addressed by education planners (Chapters 11 and 12).

Very little research has been undertaken on cost efficiency and effectiveness connected with multigrade schools. Hence, much of Chapter 12 is based on theoretical principles and models. At a policy level the perceived and actual high costs of small (*de facto* multigrade) schools in rural areas in developed countries has, periodically, been the main rationale used by policy makers for their closure and consolidation. In part these have arisen because of the fixed costs that deployment norms of ancillary staff for schools (e.g. caretakers and cooks) imply and the high costs per student attributed to maintenance of land and buildings. Communities have argued that to close the village school is to close down the community. Such externalities are rarely valued in cost analyses. Savings through the amalgamation and closure of small schools may be offset by the added costs of transportation of learners and, in some cases, the costs of boarding facilities. Communities and teachers have also argued that there are learning gains associated with smallness and localness, especially for young learners.

The policy and costs issues in many developing countries are often very different from those faced in developed countries. In many settings, as noted above, the options of transport amalgamation do not exist. If the cost of maintaining small monograde schools is too high, the next policy choice is between a multigrade school or no school at all, a point that is reinforced in Chapter 11.

The main cost element in all primary schools is teacher salary or salaries plus supervisory support (Chapters 11 and 12). In some systems (e.g. Bangladesh) there are few multigrade schools. Instead many schools operate a double shift with teachers teaching one grade in the first shift, another in the second. While this obviates the need for multigrade teaching, a key question for EFA is the amount of effective instructional time such systems deliver, at what cost and what benefit. In many schools that operate a double shift system, learners attend schools for as little as 2 hours per official school day. Combine this with teacher absenteeism and inefficient use of the timetabled school day and opportunities for learning diminishes further. Teachers may teach more, but learners may experience less. Costs per learner may appear acceptable but learning costs per hour may look different.

Cost-effectiveness is the ratio of learning gains to the costs of inputs. Some costs are borne by the system as a whole; some at school level. While the main school-level cost is the teacher salary, system costs include the development and delivery costs of reorganised curricula, assessment systems, learning and teaching materials and teacher training. The opportunity costs of learners depend on the time they spend in school (as distinct from time spent learning in school). The costs of learners 'teaching' others while teachers work intensively with other groups of learners are low and may in fact be negative as learners learn themselves by teaching. The comparative costs of multi- and monograde classes depend partly on whether national policymakers view multigrade teaching as a separate subsystem of education or as a strategy that needs to be understood and practised by teachers throughout the system.

If the latter approach were adopted and if all teachers were exposed to multigrade teaching as part of mainstream teacher preparation, if curricula were revised to meet the needs of the multigrade class, and if assessment formats and instructional materials were geared towards the learner, these costs would be similar to those in monograde classes, especially where overall pupil–teacher ratios and student learning hours were the same.

Because of the association with school size, multigrade teaching strategies may, on average, yield higher costs than monograde schools. But the issue here is size, not multigrade *per se*. Every system has small schools located in low density populated areas and unpopular schools in areas of high population density. And every system that has achieved EFA maintains schools in these areas, albeit, sometimes, at a higher unit cost per learner.

While this does not mean that all small schools have to be kept open at all cost it does mean that the location and characteristics of learners are paramount. It also means that where multigrade does result in cost savings and learning gains it is very attractive.

The potential learning gains within multigrade settings have been alluded to earlier in this chapter. There is some evidence that learners in multigrade settings may be at an advantage, in terms of social and personal learning, over those in monograde settings, and at no disadvantage cognitively. Precisely why this should be so is unclear but it would appear to be a function, variously, of self-study, of learning and teaching to learn, of collaborative learning with peers, of mastery-oriented assessment formats and of contact with teachers in small, rather than large, group settings. Since, with a few exceptions, several of these elements are almost cost-free once established, then if the multigrade pedagogy is effective, the overall impact on cost-effectiveness is likely to be great.

CULTURES OF LEARNING

Finally, a note on cultures of learning and teaching that cross-cuts each of the previous sections on the learner, processes of learning and teaching and the enabling environment. The notions of diversity and differentiation referred to in much of the above discussion challenge some deep-seated cultures of teaching and learning in which the teacher is the main arbiter of knowledge, most classroom activity is teacher-directed, whole-class teaching is dominant and in which all students are expected to progress through the curriculum at the same pace (notwithstanding high levels of student absenteeism in many countries). More broadly, ideas about human nature, about the purpose of education, about the role of the teacher, about how learning occurs, about what constitutes quality in education and about the nature of knowledge (epistemology) also lie at the heart of cultures of teaching and learning. The GMR (2005), for example, refers to four broad, contemporary approaches to primary education – humanist, behaviourist, critical and indigenous. These approaches are embedded more or less consciously, more or less systematically, and more or less exclusively in curriculum design and teaching methods – both in principle and in practice. Simultaneously the GMR asserted that educational methods should be responsive to the diversity of learners in terms of needs, circumstances, prior abilities, skills and knowledge. *Inter alia* this implies an approach to teaching focused on the learner. But how does this universal advocacy square with pedagogic cultures focused on the transmission of knowledge by the teacher? And how does it square with the swing away from 'child-centred' education and individualised methods and the return to whole-class teaching apparent in some countries in the West over the past two decades?

In short, do deep-seated cultures of teaching and learning pose a major obstacle to enduring reforms designed to meet the needs of learners and teachers in multigrade classes? Do they pose a major greatest obstacle to the realisation of all the goals of EFA more generally?

Fifteen years ago, in the run-up to the First World Conference on EFA held in Jomtien, Thailand in 1990, I argued for an approach to EFA that implied a *reversal* of the dominant flow of educational ideas and practices. I suggested that if effective learning by all is to occur:

> The imperative for the educator is one of learning from the learner, an imperative which must ripple through the education system from its base to its apex.... A reversal of the conventional education and learning relation – teachers educate while students learn – is called for... Teachers need to learn to apprehend the learning needs of their students, teacher educators the learning needs of their trainee teachers, the university lecturers the needs of their teacher educators, the international theorists, policymakers and gurus the needs of all.
>
> (Little, 1990: 65–66)

This call for 'reversals of thinking' is consistent with the recent GMR call for the recognition of learner diversity and locating the learner at the heart of EFA policy. It is also evident in the conclusion of a recent review of teacher education curricula in five developing countries that called for a transformation of teacher education: a redrawing of the map of learning and knowledge.

> Many of the (teacher) education curricula we analysed seemed premised on the idea that if (teacher trainees) are given enough knowledge and skills at college these can be applied unproblematically, like 'recipes', to any classroom. A more useful model is one that sees teaching as interactive problem-solving, requiring a thoughtful and reflective approach to one's own practice. Thus learning to teach means acquiring not only knowledge and skills, but also a situated understanding of pupils and how they learn, along with repertoires of skills and strategies for dealing with unique and ever-changing circumstances. The aim of the training should be the development of professional reasoning ability, rather than the acquisition of pre-defined behaviours (Akyeampong 2001). Such a model requires an epistemological shift towards a view of knowledge that recognises the value of teachers' personal, experiential and craft knowledge as well as the public propositional knowledge offered in college.
>
> (Lewin and Stuart, 2003: 203)

The call for transformation, reversals of thinking and recognising and valuing the view of the learner (whether the learner is the pupil in school or the trainee in a teacher education college) does *not* imply that the learner's view and the learner's construction of knowledge are or should be the *only* determinants of learning or teaching. Such a position is tantamount to solipsism – the universe and knowledge is nothing but myself, my mind and its ideas, however random or organised. Adherents might wish to reflect on its implausibility when flying through the air at 500 mph at 39,000 feet. The knowledge of aero-dynamic principles, mathematics and engineering necessary for effective aircraft design is not generated simply from the meaning-making of an individual learner.

Rather, the call is for a shift of thinking about how teaching influences learning from one that is premised mainly on what the teacher does or says – to one in which the teacher looks and listens to what the learner does and says and modifies subsequent action. Elsewhere I have spoken of learning *arenas* in which the process of learning is akin to the bridging of cultural gaps between teachers and learners. Learners bring to a learning arena customary ways of learning, values of learning, and customary cognitions. Teachers or educators also bring customary fare to the arena: customary knowledge and customary pedagogy. Within the arena there is a gap between the customs of the learner and teacher. The educator offers what may appear to him or her customary, well-established and familiar fare. To the learner the fare appears new and unfamiliar – new content, or a new motivator, a new teacher behaviour, a new type of assessment task. There is a gap between what the learner brings to the arena and what the educator offers. Learning is achieved when the teacher apprehends the learner's starting point, learns from that understanding and modifies what he/she does and says; and when the learner strives to make the unfamiliar familiar. Learning is achieved when this gap has been bridged. Both learner and teacher need to work hard to build that bridge and meet at some point on it. Equilibrium is achieved, is temporary and contains its own dynamic for change. The meeting is temporary and the educator and learner are motivated to learn and teach more. The gap widens and the search for a meeting of minds – of achieving another temporary equilibrium – begins again (Little, 1990).

That is a personal view informed partly by experiential and private knowledge of learning and teaching and partly by a reading of a range of propositional and professional knowledge. Alexander (2000: 556–557) offers a more considered view of learning and teaching through reflection on Bruner's (1996) dominant models of children's minds. Bruner's first model – children as imitative learners – is consistent with apprenticeship and the process of leading novices towards the skills of the expert. The second – children learn from didactic exposure – is consistent with the transmission model of teaching geared to the acquisition of facts, principles and rules. The third – learners as thinkers – is premised on the idea that children think for themselves. The teacher's task is to apprehend that thinking and help the learner to move from private to shared knowledge. The fourth – children as knowledgeable – recognises that in no culture is knowledge exclusively personal. The teacher's task is to guide the learner to being able to distinguish personal from shared knowledge. These four models of learning and teaching are powerful reminders of the variety of ways in which learners and their teachers, individually and severally, glide or stumble towards the EFA learning targets.

Perhaps the most important message that emerges from this consideration of cultures of learning is that there is, currently, no single, universal and effective pedagogy that embraces all types of learning and knowledge in all types of setting. We have seen how teachers schooled and trained in monograde practice experience difficulties in applying this practice to a multigrade setting. We have also seen a wide range of approaches to the multigrade setting embracing the notions of diversity and differentiation, of grouping, of curriculum reorganisation and of designing materials for independent and interdependent learning. Just as there is no single, universal and effective pedagogy for all types of learning, so there is no single best pedagogy for either mono- or multigrade teaching. But there is a range of approaches and strategies.

These different approaches allow for differences between cultures in the relative values attached to the whole class, groups and individuals as social contexts for learning and for change over time within the same culture. While Alexander (2000: 546) has questioned the compatibility of individualistic orientations to learning with the collective orientation of Indian primary teaching, we see in Rishi Valley in India a pedagogy that employs and reinforces both. And while Croft reminds us (Chapter 7) that the collective orientation of Malawian society, together with large class sizes and lack of material resources, reinforces a teacher-intensive pedagogy, we see attempts made by some teachers to cater to individual needs. And while current multigrade teacher-training models in Vietnam encourage quasi-monograde teaching of graded groups, developmental work on the realignment of the curriculum shows how teachers might move to a differentiated curriculum approach (Chapters 8 and 9).

Meeting the challenge of learner diversity does not require a tight embrace of the learner-centred approach in order to meet learner diversity, just as one cannot assume that whole-class teaching implies a standardised approach to all learners. But teachers do need to develop the ability to *reverse* their thinking about pedagogy – and to be able to view curriculum and pedagogy from the perspective of the learner and to build bridges to that view in order to meet half way. Teachers also need to be supported in their quest to develop a repertoire of teaching approaches and increase their capacity for choice and flexibility. In a similar vein teacher educators need to reverse their thinking about curriculum and pedagogy, to apprehend the learning needs of teacher trainees and to understand that many will be teaching in classrooms that differ from the monograded norm. Common curricula will meet the general principles of effective teaching that all teachers need to know; differentiated curricula will meet more specific teacher needs. As the reversals ripple through the system university staff will listen more to the teacher educators and their students, the curriculum developers to the teachers and the policymakers and planners to local communities (Chapter 11). One size does not fit all even for mobile multigrade schools in Darfur (Chapter 10). Support systems (whether for teacher education, curriculum, assessment and materials supply) need to be flexible and differentiated as well as rigid and standard.

LESSONS FOR EDUCATION SECTOR POLICY

The policy lessons of multigrade schooling for EFA should be becoming clear by now.

The most basic lesson concerns *invisibility* and *awareness*. In none of the countries included in our research was it easy to find information about the numbers of multigrade schools, or classes, or teachers or learners. The evidence presented in Chapter 1 was difficult to locate and took time to assemble. International databases do not exist and the UNESCO Institute of Statistics does not, currently, invite National Ministries of Education to collect or submit such data. This absence of information reinforces the general invisibility of multigrade schools and the challenges posed for teaching and learning in these settings. Many educational policymakers, planners, professional support staff and the public at large, are unaware of the extent and the nature of the needs of multigrade classes. Since curriculum, educational materials, teacher preparation and assessment systems are predicated on monograded schools and classes, it is hardly surprising that many teachers hold negative attitudes towards their role in the multigrade class.

It should also be clear from our research that curriculum, learning materials, teacher education and assessment are necessary components of an integrated strategy to support learning and teaching in multigrade settings.

The implementation of a single strategy component is unlikely to lead to significant improvements in the effectiveness of teaching in multigrade settings.

Movement towards an integrated strategy in the classroom may be managed in at least four ways. The first is the gradual strategy of diffusion and managed evolution – piloting and trialling of innovations in curriculum, teacher education, learning materials and assessment and their gradual introduction over time in multigrade schools. The second is wholesale reform of curriculum, teacher education, learning materials and assessment focused on multigrade schools only. The third is the gradual reform of curriculum, teacher education, learning materials and assessment for learners in all types of school, whether monograde or multigrade. The fourth is the wholesale reform of curriculum, teacher education, learning materials and assessment for learners in all types of school. The last is the most radical of all and implies a view of teaching and school organisation that treats multigraded teaching as the more general form of peda-gogic organisation and monograded teaching as a specific form of it. Teachers trained in multigraded teaching can transfer their skills readily to either a multi- or a monograded setting. Teachers trained only in teacher-directed mono-graded teaching experience difficulty transferring their skill to multigraded settings.

Paradoxically a multigrade pedagogy is viewed by many as a second-best and/or old-fashioned education and by many others as 'progressive'. With its stress on the learner, on differentiation, on mastery and learning readiness, on formative assessment, on learning how to learn and on the development of social and behavioural skills and values as well the cognitive, it resonates with much current thinking about what constitutes 'good education'. But whatever labels one wishes to attach, the fact remains that many learners find themselves *de facto* in settings that call for multigraded pedagogies that work.

And so to conclude. In the spirit of a philosophy of learning based on continuous enquiry our 'policy lessons' are summarised and posed as policy questions. They derive from the synthesis of research presented above and from previous chapters in this book. They are presented as a checklist of questions for all those with a responsibility for Education for All – teachers, communities, policymakers, planners, financiers, curriculum developers, teacher educators, teacher unions, assessment professionals, government organisations and non-government organisations.

FORTY QUESTIONS FOR PROPONENTS FOR EFA

Awareness

1   How many learners are learning in multigraded classes?
2   How many teachers are teaching in multigraded classes?
3   How many support staff are supporting learning and teaching in multigraded classes?
4   How many learners are there in monograded schools who, because of teacher absenteeism, find themselves in settings which de facto call for multigrade teaching strategies?

Learning time

5   How much time in a school year do learners in a multigrade class have for learning?
6   How much time do learners spend waiting in a multigrade class for teacher input?
7   How much time do learners spend learning alone?
8   How much time do learners spend learning in groups?

Teacher time and method

9   Does the teacher employ the concept of differentiation in the multigraded class? If so does she/he differentiate by grade, by subject, by content within subject, by level of teaching input, by learning tasks, by learning outcomes?
10 How does the teacher manage the curriculum in a multigraded class? Does he/she merge two or more curriculum frameworks and teach them as one, i.e. the multi-year curriculum spans? Does he/she teach common topics/themes and differentiate individual or group tasks? Does he/she treat the class as if they were two or more single (mono) grades? Does he/she focus on the learner and the provision of graded learning materials?
11 Does the teacher use a repertoire of organisational methods in his/her class, or is he/she dependent on one or two only?

Curriculum

12 How many layers/elements does the curriculum have (goals, aims, frameworks, syllabi, teacher guides, texts for teachers, texts for learners, lesson plans, tasks, etc.)?

13 How 'graded' are each of these layers/elements?

14 Are curricula content-, process- or outcomes-based?

15 Who is responsible for designing which layers/elements of curriculum? Over which layers does the teacher exert some control? Over which layers does the expert curriculum developer exert control?

16 To what extent can curricula be re-sequenced or otherwise re-organised in order to support the teacher of multiple grades?

Learning materials

17 With what types of curriculum material do learners work?

18 In what quantities are they available in the classroom?

19 Do teachers encourage the use of materials by learners?

20 What is the quality of the material? (Is the material attractive? Is it easy to use? Is the use of the material dependent on language? If so, is it of a level that learners can understand?)

21 Are materials available for learning remediation and extension?

Assessment

22 What types of assessment tasks does the teacher use to assess learning?

23 Does the teacher use assessment information to adjust her method with individual children and/or groups?

24 Are assessment tasks built into sequences of learning materials?

25 Is assessment always directed by the teacher? Do learners self- and peer-assess?

Social organisation

26 Are learners completely dependent on the teacher for all learning activity?

27 Do learners support each other in their learning?

28 Do learners take responsibilities for the general organisation of school and its activities?

29 Is the teacher able to attract volunteers and community members to support him/her in the classroom?

Teacher training

30 Are teachers trained in the principles and practice of multigrade teaching?
31 Do teachers demonstrate their understanding of principles in the classroom?
32 Are teachers trained in the concepts of diversity and differentiation and in their application?
33 Are teachers exposed to a range of teaching methods and do they understand their respective purposes?
34 Are teacher educators able to demonstrate to teacher trainees good practices in multigrade teaching?

Conditions of service for teachers

35 What incentives could be put in place to support the deployment of teachers to work in disadvantaged areas in general and in disadvantaged areas with multigrade schools in particular?
36 What incentives could be put in place for teachers and schools to reach out to and enrol out-of-school learners?
37 What is the number of small schools (<50 enrolled) which could benefit from multigrade teaching strategies that generate more learning time for learners?
38 How can repetition be reduced through managed progression that does not involve the repetition of complete years in all subjects?
39 Are affordable strategies available to support multigrade learning and teaching that do not involve system level reforms of all learning materials?
40 Can resource allocation practices (teacher deployment, learning materials supply) and professional support systems be changed to promote a multigraded pedagogy rather than hinder its use?

REFERENCES

Alexander, R. (2000) *Culture and Pedagogy: International comparisons in primary education.* Oxford: Blackwell.

Ames Ramello, P.P. (2004) Multigrade schools in context: literacy in the community, the home and the school in the Peruvian Amazon. Unpublished PhD thesis. Institute of Education, University of London.

Berry, C. (2001) Achievement effects of multigrade and monograde primary schools in the Turks and Caicos Islands. *International Journal of Education Development*, 21 (6), 537–552.

Bernstein, B. (1971) *Class, Codes and Control, Vol. 1: Theoretical studies towards a sociology of language*. London: Routledge and Kegan Paul.

Black, P. and Wiliam, D. (1998) Assessment and classroom learning. *Assessment in Education*, 5 (1), 7–74.

Bruner, J.S. (1996) *The Culture of Education*. Cambridge, MA: Harvard University Press.

Colbert, V., Chiappe, C. and Arboleda, J. (1993) The New School Program: more and better primary education for children in rural areas in Colombia. In H.M. Levin and M.E. Lockheed (eds), *Effective Schools in Developing Countries*. London: Falmer Press.

Collingwood, I. (1991) *Multiclass Teaching in Primary Schools: A handbook for teachers in the Pacific*. Apia, Western Samoa: UNESCO Office for the Pacific States.

Dore, R.P. (1997) *The Diploma Disease: Education, qualification and development*, 2nd edition. London: Institute of Education, University of London.

Ford, B.E (1977) Multiage grouping in the elementary school and children's affective development: a review of recent research. *The Elementary School Journal*, November, 149–159.

Hargreaves, E. (2001) Assessment for learning in the multigrade classroom. *International Journal of Educational Development*, 21 (6), 553–560.

Hargreaves, E., Montero, C., Chau, N., Sibli, M. and Thanh, T. (2001) Multigrade teaching in Peru, Sri Lanka and Vietnam: an overview. *International Journal of Educational Development*, 21 (6), 499–520.

Hattie, J.C. (2002) Classroom composition and peer effects. *International Journal of Educational Research*, 37, 449–481.

Ireson, J. and Hallam, S. (2001) *Ability Grouping in Education*. London: Paul Chapman Publishing.

Jarousse, J.-P. and Mingat, A. (1991) *Efficacité pédagogique de l'enseignment à cours multiples dans le contexte africain*. IREDU-CNRS: University of Dijon.

Jones, D.V. (2004) National numeracy initiatives in England and Wales: parallel attempts at achieving large-scale reform. *Compare*, 34 (4), 463–486.

Kalaoja, E. (2004) Multi-grade teaching and its innovation in Finland. Paper delivered at Second International Multigrade Teaching Conference: Turning biases into benefits. Armidale Centre for Research on Education in Context, University of New England.

LATIMS (2003, 2004) unpublished reports of the work of the Learning and Teaching in Multigrade Settings Research Group, London.

Laukkanen, R. and Selventoinen, P. (1978) *Small Schools and Combined Grades in Finland*. Paris: Centre for Educational Research and Innovation, OECD.

Lewin, K.M. and Stuart, J. (2003) *Researching Teacher Education: New perspectives on practice, performance and policy*, London: Department for International Development.

Little, A.W. (1990) *Understanding Culture: A pre-condition for effective learning.* A special study for the World Conference on Education for All. Jomtien, Thailand.

Little, A.W. (1995) *Multigrade Teaching: A review of research and practice.* Serial no. 12, London: Overseas Development Administration.

Little, A. W. (1999) *Labouring to Learn: Towards a political economy of plantations, people and education in Sri Lanka.* London and New York: Macmillan and St Martin's Press.

Little, A. W. (2001) Multigrade teaching: towards an international research and policy agenda. *International Journal of Educational Development*, 21 (6), 481–498.

Little, A.W. (2004) Learning and teaching in multigrade settings, Background Paper for the Global Monitoring Report. Available online: http://portal.unesco.org/ education/en/file_download.php/548cfe4ac0864fcea666900c2144e4d1Little.doc (Accessed 10 March 2005).

Little, A.W. and Wolf, A. (1996) *Assessment in Transition: Learning, monitoring and selection in international perspective.* Oxford: Pergamon.

Little, A.W., Hoppers, W. and Gardner, R. (eds) (1994) *Beyond Jomtien: Implementing Primary Education for All.* London: Macmillan.

Lok Jumbish, (1993) *Learning Together.* Stockholm: Swedish International Development Authority.

Lungwangwa, G. (1989) *Multigrade Schools in Zambian Primary Education.* SIDA Education Division Documents no. 47. Stockholm: Swedish International Development Authority.

McEwan, P. (1998) The effectiveness of multigrade schools in Colombia. *International Journal of Educational Development*, 18 (6), 435–452.

McLaughlin, T. (2004) Education, philosophy and the comparative perspective. *Comparative Education*, 40 (4), 471–484.

Mason, D.A. and Burns, R.B. (1996) Teachers' views of combination classes. *Journal of Educational Research,* 89 (1), 36–45.

Mason, D.A. and Burns, R.B. (1997) Reassessing the effects of combination classes, *Educational Research and Evaluation*, 3 (1), 1–53.

Miguel, M.M. and Basaga, E.B. (1997) Multi-grade schooling in the Philippines: a strategy for improving access to and quality of primary education. In D.W. Chapman, L.O. Mahlck and A.E.M. Smulders (eds) *From Planning to Action: Government initiatives for improving school-level practice.* Paris: Pergamon/UNESCO.

Menon, L. and Rao, P. (2004) Multigrade for remote and disadvantaged schools. Paper delivered at Second International Multigrade Teaching Conference: Turning biases into benefits. Armidale Centre for Research on Education in Context, University of New England.

Miller, B.A. (1991) A Review of the Qualitative Research on Multigrade Education. *Journal of Research in Rural Education*, 7 (2), 3–12.

Padmanabha Rao, Y.A. (2005) Quality Schooling: enriching the commons. Paper delivered at the 8th UKFIET *International Conferences on Education and Development*, Oxford, 13–15 September, 2005.

Pratt, D. (1986) On the merits of multiage classrooms. *Research in Rural Education*, 3 (3), 111–115.

Psacharopoulos, G., Rojas, C. and Velez, E. (1993) Achievement evaluation of Colombia's *Escuela Nueva*: is multigrade the answer? *Comparative Education Review*, 37 (3), 263–276.

Pridmore, P. (2004) Education for All: the paradox of multigrade teaching. Paper delivered at Second international multigrade teaching conference: Turning biases into benefits. Armidale: Centre for Research on Education in Context, University of New England.

Rishi Valley Education Centre (2000) *Report of Second National Workshop on Planning and Implementation of Multigrade Programmes*. Rishi Valley, Andhra Pradesh: Rishi Valley Education Centre, Krishnamurti Foundation India.

Rojas, C. and Castillo, Z. (1988) Evaluación del programa Escuela Nueva en Colombia. Bogotá: Instituto ser de investigaciones.

Rowley, S.D. (1992) Multigrade classrooms in Pakistan: how teacher conditions and practices affect student achievement. Unpublished PhD thesis: Harvard University.

Rowley, S.D. and Nielsen, H.D. (1997) School and classroom organisation in the periphery: the assets of multigrade teaching'. In H.D. Nielsen and WK. Cummings (eds), *Quality Education for All: Community oriented approaches*. New York and London: Garland.

Ross, A. (2000) *Curriculum, Construction and Critique*. London: Falmer.

Shotton, J. (1998). *Learning and Freedom: Policy, pedagogy and paradigms in Indian education and schooling*. New Delhi: Sage.

Sibli, M.P.M.M. and Cash, T. (2003) Multigrade Teacher Training Manual for ISAs. Colombo: National Institute of Education, Primary Mathematics Unit.

Suzuki, T. (2004) 'Multigrade teachers and their training in rural Nepal: practice and training'. Unpublished PhD thesis. Institute of Education, University of London.

UNESCO/APEID (1989) *Multigrade Teaching in Single-Teacher Primary Schools*. Bangkok: Asia and the Pacific Programme of Educational Innovation for Development.

UNESCO (2002) *Education for All: Is the world on track?* Paris: UNESCO.

UNESCO (2003) *Gender and Education for All: The leap to equality*. Paris: UNESCO.

UNESCO (2004) *Education for All: The quality imperative*. Paris: UNESCO.

Veenman, S. (1995) Cognitive and noncognitive effects of multigrade and multi-age classes: a best-evidence synthesis. *Review of Educational Research*, 65 (4), 319–381.

Vithanapathirana, M. (2005) 'Improving multigrade teaching: action research with teachers in rural Sri Lanka'. Unpublished PhD thesis. Institute of Education University of London.

348   Angela W. Little

Vu, T.S., Pridmore, P., Nga, B.M.D. and Kick, P. (2002) *Renovating the Teaching of Health in Multigrade Primary Schools: A teacher's guide to health in natural and social sciences (Grades 1, 2 and 3) and Science (Grade 5)*. Hanoi: British Council and National Institute of Educational Sciences.
Warwick, D. (1975) *Curriculum Structure and Design*. London: University of London Press.

Internet sites

www.hamilton-trust.org.uk (Accessed 11 October 2004).
www.ioe.ac.uk/multigrade/teacher training materials.htm (Accessed 20 November 2004).
www.norfolkesinet.org.uk (Accessed 7 June 2004).
www.standards.dfes.gov.uk/literacy/publications/framework 'additional guidance' (Accessed 11 January 2004).
www.standards.dfes.gov.uk/literacy (Accessed 6 June 2004).
http://portal.unesco.org/education/en/file_download.php/548cfe4ac0864fcea666900 c2144e4d1Little.doc (Accessed 10 March 2005).

NOTE

[1] Over the period of our research the name of the research programme changed from *Multigrade Teaching* to *Learning and Teaching in Multigrade Settings*.

PLATES

1. Colombia: self-learning guides encourage learners to use books from the class library, *Escuela Nueva* programme

2. Colombia: students learn together using self-learning guides, *Escuela Nueva* programme

3. England: in the monitorial system in 19th Century England students, grouped by achievement level, were taught by young monitors. A single adult teacher taught and supervised the monitors.

4. Nepal: a student receives personal support from a teacher in a small multigrade school

5. Malawi: students enrolled in Standard 1 (Grade 1) class: same class, same grade but clearly not same age

6. Malawi: where resources are scarce, what you bring from home makes a significant contribution to pupil diversity. Here, students without pencil and paper are encouraged by their teacher to learn to write in the sand.

7. Peru: children learn after school

8. Peru: girls learn together to become literate

9. Sri Lanka: one teacher is responsible for three grade groups, working in a temporary classroom in rural Sri Lanka

10. Sri Lanka: grade 1 students work together in a multigraded class

11. Turks and Caicos Islands: the teacher divides the blackboard space between two grades: students work individually on individual grade-level work

12. Turks and Caicos Islands: students work collaboratively

13. Vietnam: a grade-group monitor takes charge of her peers while the teacher works with another grade-group

14. Vietnam: a typical multigrade school in the Northern Highlands

15. Sudan: the El Shiekh teacher with his sheep, Darfur

16. Sudan: Large class of learners in temporary classroom, Darfur

INDEX